D1261329

PARAGON
ISSUES IN
PHILOSOPHY

PARAGON ISSUES IN PHILOSOPHY

THE PARAGON ISSUES
IN PHILOSOPHY SERIES

At colleges and universities, interest in the traditional areas of philosophy remains strong. Many new currents flow within them, too, but until recently many of these—the rise of cognitive science, for example, or feminist philosophy—often went largely unnoticed in undergraduate philosophy courses. The Paragon Issues in Philosophy Series responds to both perennial and newly influential concerns by bringing together a team of able philosophers to address the fundamental issues in philosophy today and to outline the state of contemporary discussion about them.

More than twenty volumes are scheduled; they are organized into three major categories. The first covers the standard topics—metaphysics, theory of knowledge, ethics, and political philosophy—stressing innovative developments in those disciplines. The second focuses on more specialized but still vital concerns in the philosophies of science, religion, history, sport, and other areas. The third category explores new work that relates philosophy and fields such as feminist criticism, medicine, economics, technology, and literature.

The level of writing is aimed at undergraduate students who have little previous experience studying philosophy. The books provide brief but accurate introductions that appraise the state of the art in their fields and show how the history of thought about their topics has developed. Each volume is complete in itself but also aims to complement others in the series.

Traumatic change characterized the twentieth century, and the twenty-first will be no different in that regard. All of its pivotal issues will involve philosophical questions. As the editors at Paragon House continue to work with us, we hope that this series will help encourage the understanding needed in a new millennium whose times will be as complicated and problematic as they are promising.

John K. Roth   Frederick Sontag
Claremont McKenna College   Pomona College

POSTMODERN RATIONALITY, SOCIAL CRITICISM, AND RELIGION

HENRY L. RUF

POSTMODERN RATIONALITY, SOCIAL CRITICISM, AND RELIGION

PARAGON HOUSE ◆ ST. PAUL

PARAGON
ISSUES IN
PHILOSOPHY

First Edition 2005

Published in the United States by
Paragon House
2285 University Avenue West
St. Paul, MN 55114

Library of Congress Cataloging-in-Publication Data

Ruf, Henry L.
Postmodern rationality, social criticism, and religion / by Henry L.
Ruf.--1st ed.
   p. cm.— (Paragon issues in philosophy)
Includes bibliographical references and index.
ISBN 1-55778-839-1 (pbk. : alk. paper) 1. Postmodernism. 2. Pragmatism.
3. Religion and sociology. 4. Religion and science. I. Title.

B944.P67R84 2005
190--dc22
                          2004026992

The paper used in this publication meets the minimum requirements of
American National Standard for Information Sciences—Permanence of Paper
for Printed Library Materials, ANSIZ39.48-1984.

Manufactured in the United States of America
10 9 8 7 6 5 4 3 2 1

For current information about all releases from Paragon House,
   visit the web site at http://www.paragonhouse.com

57043472

To my wife,
Wenying Xu
Dialogue and Tennis Partner

To my son,
Alan Xu Ruf
Master of Enjoyment

━┼━ CONTENTS

⊹ ACKNOWLEDGMENTS

I want to thank my undergraduate students at West Virginia University who pleaded with me to help them find a way to interpret and understand texts written in the traditions of existentialism, social and cultural criticism, pragmatism, and postmodernism. I want to thank my graduate students and faculty colleagues in Literary Theory, American Studies, and Comparative Philosophy and Religion at Sitzuan University and Xiamen University in China, and Mahidol University in Thailand, who demonstrated the possibility and fruitfulness of cross-cultural dialogue on philosophical and religious matters. I especially want to thank the gentle and wise Buddhist monks who were more my teachers than my students in my graduate seminars at Mahidol University. From them I received living proof that faithfulness to a particular religious tradition is thoroughly compatible with respect for other religious traditions and with the desire and hope to learn and grow through dialogical encounters with them.

I want to thank a number of writers who without knowing it greatly influenced my intellectual orientation and my interpretations and appropriations of the thinkers dealt with in this book: Alastair Hannay on Kierkegaard, Alexander Nehamas on Nietzsche, O. K. Bousma, Gordon Baker, P. M. S. Hacker, and D. Z. Phillips on Wittgenstein, Hubert Dreyfus on Heidegger, David Hoy on Gadamer, Thomas McCarthy on Habermas, Richard Rorty and Cornell West on pragmatism, Adriaan Peperzak on Levinas, Huston Smith on the world religions, and Masao Abe and David Kalipahana on Buddhism. None of these thinkers, of course, are responsible for the ways I have appropriated their teachings, ways about which they probably have many reservations. Although these interpreters never present themselves as substitutes for the texts with which they are in dialogue, for me they have been invaluable aids in my construction of my interpretations.

I want to thank David Hoy, Bill Lawson, Tom Phillips, Rod Stewart, Bill Rottschafer, Iris Marion Young, and the readers at

Paragon House for reading through earlier versions of this book and giving me valuable comments.

I want to thank my philosophy teachers at Macalester College (Thomas E. Hill, Sr., Hugo Thompson, David White) who, though embodying wildly different philosophical traditions, trained me to be a dialogical reader long before I ever read Gadamer. I want to thank Hubert Dreyfus and John Hoagland for organizing the 1982 NEH conference at Berkeley, California, on Intentionality in Continental and Analytic Philsophy. Through the exchanges at that conference between Dryfus, Follestal, Searle, and Rorty, I became convinced of the need for and the promise of dialogue across intellectual traditions. I want to thank the Fulbright Program for giving me four opportunities to teach and learn by engaging in dialogues with students and teachers in universities in Japan, Thailand, and China.

Finally, I want to thank my wife, Wenying, to whom this book is dedicated, for forcing me to think through with her the intellectual positions represented in this book and to carry on this dialogue with an intellectual, who is trained in English and Cultural Studies and not philosophy, whose first language is not English, and who was nurtured in a cultural world free from ontotheological concerns. Her passion to understand forced me to read and reread the texts with which we were wrestling and to write and rewrite what I was trying to communicate.

—⁘— CHAPTER ONE INTRODUCTION

People in all ages and cultures have tried to make sense of their lives and the worlds in which they live. For the past century and a half, people have been having a very difficult time trying to do this. The worlds in which we live are so fractured that we just do not know how to put the pieces together. People have failed to reach any kind of consensus about how to understand the major social practices that are molding their lives: making discoveries in science and technology, practicing religion, pursuing freedom and justice, rationally indicting and criticizing unjustifiable claims and practices, and avoiding unnecessary conflicts between these social and cultural practices. The conflicts are many and deep. As a result, our social/cultural worlds and our individual ways of thinking, perceiving, and valuing ourselves and others suffer from multiple fractures that exacerbate the anxiety in many people who are trying to make sense of things.

Making sense of things is the central goal of this book. Dialogical engagement with many of the major texts written in the last 150 years is the means chosen to reach this goal. The writings of existentialists, social and culture critics, pragmatists, and postmodernists will be analyzed, criticized, selectively appropriated, and reconstructed in an effort to find a coherent interpretation of our current human form of life and its future possibilities. Readers are invited to join in this quest to gain understanding by engaging themselves in a critical dialogue with this book and the texts being discussed in it.

Trying to make sense of things requires trying to find answers to a host of extremely difficult and complex questions. This book is written for those readers deeply concerned about making sense of things in a world that so often seems senseless. It is written out of a conviction that these difficult and complex questions can be addressed in such a way that quite ordinary readers can handle these questions and end up finding a workable understanding of themselves and their social/cultural environment. I will present interpretations of a large number of controversial writers who have wrestled with many of these questions. I have tried to give fresh interpretations and reconstructions so the insights in these texts can be preserved in spite of the many criticisms leveled against them. I have attempted to present my interpretations in a language relatively free of technical jargon. I do not promise an easy read. The issues are too complex and the needed distinctions and extended lines of reasoning are too demanding for that. I do promise that it is not a hopeless undertaking. Serious interest, careful reading, hard thinking, and sensitive reflection are all that is required. That's asking for a lot, but making sense of oneself and one's world is seeking to gain a lot.

Let's begin by thinking about why scientific reasoning, human understanding, existential concern, social justice, and religious faithfulness are problematic in our age and in tension with each other. Consider the following questions. How can science be respected without being transformed into an idol to be worshiped as a new, saving god? What are the limits of scientific rationality? If history, social/cultural interpretation, ethics, and religion lie outside the domain of science, how does one gain understanding in these areas? Can useful dialogue replace the warring polemics that have been taking place for the past 150 between the postmodernists who interpret human norms of meaning, truth, and justice as historical and social ,and those predecessors who insist that such norms can function only if they transcend historical and social contingencies? Does a postmodern interpretation of norms leave room for radical social criticism and for avoiding turning the social itself into a new sacrilegious idol? Can there be a postmodern understanding of what is involved in living well and resisting injustice? Is there still space for religion once science frees people from superstition? Can religion divorce itself from the oppressive social practices with which it often has been allied? Must religion maintain its long-standing alliance with the antagonists of postmodernism in order for purported religious encounters with the infinite not to be explained away as just one more finite, social phenomenon? Can religious pluralism make possible creative spiritual dialogue rather than destructive social and cultural warfare?

In this book I will not only be interpreting other thinkers who have wrestled with these questions. I will be making appropriations from them and criticisms of them as I construct my own interpretation of our world and our place in it. Thus, I too will be attempting to address these questions and anxious concerns. I will attempt to present an interpretation of our contemporary human form of life that suggests ways of eliminating unnecessary disharmonies while also showing the desirability of prizing differences within and between ways of living scientifically, rationally, and religiously, while pursuing the kinds of freedom that living well and resisting injustice requires. I will present an interpretation of human rationality (human conceiving, asserting, experiencing, knowing, desiring, evaluating, explaining, and justifying) that stresses its thoroughly human, social, historical, and pragmatic character. If modernity is often defined as what immediately preceded this accent on rationality's social and historical nature, then this book is postmodern. I will argue that an existential, pragmatic, postmodern interpretation of rationality leaves ample room for criticism of unworkable lives and unjust social/cultural practices and ample room for religious encounters with social rationality's other and for faithfulness to religious traditions grounded on such encounters. Before presenting this interpretation, however, it will be helpful to specify in an introductory way some of the conflicts and fractures that exist in our current world and the kinds of problems that must be dealt with in offering and considering such a social interpretation of rationality, our world and our lives. More detailed analyses will be given in later chapters.

For centuries, science has been seen as both a great benefactor to the quality of human life and as a threat because of its very success. If scientific thinking produces so many wonderful accomplishments, why not proclaim that it is the only kind of rationality worthwhile, the only kind worth passing on to our children? This would turn science into scientism, an ideology that leaves no room for history, literature, art, or religion to add any unique contributions to human understanding.[1] Already in the eighteenth century, fearful that proponents of scientism might try to make human science into such a sacred absolute, defenders of religion criticized such sacrilegious pretentiousness. (For a full description of scientism and other terms, see the glossary at the back of this book.) Likewise, in the name of history, literature, art and music, eighteenth- and nineteenth-century Romanticists resisted scientism's attempts to colonize their domains. These efforts to resist domination by scientism culminate in the work of nineteenth- and twentieth-century existentialists, pragmatists, and postmodernists who would have us believe that science is done by scientists, people functioning in ways that require factors that scientism's conception of rationality cannot explain or explain away. In the next chapter we will take detailed looks at these thinkers who tried to keep science from becoming scientism. Through dialogue with their texts we can try to deal with the challenge of locating science in a world of human social and cultural practices in a way that does justice to its great virtues while still accenting its human, all too human, character.

The importance of religion in people's lives is as widespread in our current world as science. Religion faces two challenges in our current world, fractured as it is by modernists and postmodernists. On the one hand, many people today sense the need to harmonize religion and science, religion and reason. This is no easy thing to do. One has to remain religiously faithful while also opposing superstitions that confusedly mix scientific claims about natural laws and events with religious claims about the creative heart of human living and the sacredness of nature. Since many thinkers about religion believe that they must ally themselves with rejections of postmodernist social interpretations of rationality, they are hard pressed not to turn modernist interpretations of rationality into a philosophical theology above all religious theologies. Aren't modernist religious thinkers putting the faithfulness of their adherents in jeopardy when they trap themselves into trying to give "ultimate" explanations by appealing to a philosophically conceived divine being? If supporters of religion, however, ally themselves with postmodernism, can they prevent religion from being reduced to an all too human social phenomenon? Is there something other than the social, and thus other than what can be socially conceived, which is what religious people encounter? How can words governed by social norms, however, be used to talk about this mystical other to social rationality?

The second challenge to religion stems from the fact that it is fractured into competing traditions. Doesn't this show that these traditions are either irrationally dogmatic or thoroughly social? Can we find something common in all religions that still allows us to prize the faithfulness that people have to different religious traditions? Can one remain religiously faithful to one tradition without being oppressively intolerant of those who do not commit themselves to any religious tradition and of those whose religious faithfulness is to a different tradition? At this very time when people are passionately turning to religion because they find it so difficult otherwise to make sense of their fractured worlds and lives, Christians, Hindus, Jews, and Muslims are under attack for their refusal to critically examine dogmatic elements in their traditions that are being used to justify using social and political power to restrict the freedom of those who are different from them, to justify terrorizing and even killing those who oppose them. Never has religion been so needed and yet so dangerous. Part of the tragedy is the inability of people to enter into dialogue about religious matters or to even believe that dialogue is possible between different religious traditions. How can the faithful commitment of suicide bombers be respected while still ethically and religiously condemning what they are doing? The challenge is to find concepts of rational understanding and religious faithfulness that leave space for each other. The challenge is to find space for dialogue between faithful followers of different religious traditions that does not require abandoning their faithful commitment to what is religious in their traditions. Finding such space, I suggest, will require finding nontraditional ways of thinking about rationality and religious traditions. In chapter 5 I will suggest that an existential, postmodern interpretation of religion can meet this challenge.

Part of the appeal of science and religion is their promise to provide increased freedom. Science has done wonders to free millions of people from hunger and disease and to free them to travel and communicate with each other.. Examples of scientific liberation and empowerment are endless. Yet, hundreds of millions of people similarly claim that their immersion in their religious traditions have liberated them from despair and hopelessness and have empowered them to live rich and contented lives in the midst of the fractured worlds that surround them. It is at the political, social, and cultural levels, however, that in the last half century the desire of people to be free to live enjoyable, significant, and just lives has led them to be passionate freedom fighters. People nationalistically have fought to be free from imperialistic, colonial and conquering domination by foreign governments. When in a minority situation, people have fought against the tyranny of majorities. They have fought for freedom from oppressive discrimination based on race, sex, disability, age, religion, ethnicity, and sexual preference. People have fought for governmental regulation of dominating and oppressive corporate power, and they have fought for government programs to free and empower those who cannot sufficiently aid themselves (the poor, the unemployed, the handicapped, the aged). Many critics of existing social and cultural practices have initiated efforts to free people from portions of what they are (socially inculcated concepts, beliefs, self-images, values, unexamined ways of behaving) that others have trained and nurtured them to be.

Seeking to minimize unjust oppression and domination, seeking to maximize negative freedom from conditions preventing a good life, and seeking positive freedom to be able to lead beautiful and just lives are projects that face many difficulties in our fractured world. Different groups have conflicting nationalist designs on the same pieces of land. Removing barriers to freedom for some people often requires restricting within barriers the freedom of action by other people. Government empowerment of some people often requires coerced taxation on other people. Seeking to free people from restricting customs and conventions always runs the risk of going too far, of removing the kind of rearing and nurturing necessary for any person to be able to reason about anything. Seeking to aid people to free themselves from what they have been nurtured to be may require freeing them from what they have always taken to be the rational and reasonable way of thinking and doing things, and this can easily lead some to aspire to be free of all rational constraints. Trying to aid people to refuse to be what they are may put the rationality of the one offering assistance in conflict with the rationality of the one being assisted. How does one rationally justify preferring one form of rationality over some other form? Your gaining freedom to enjoy yourself in certain ways may conflict with the moral beliefs that other people have about how everyone ought to live. Different people from different cultural or religious traditions may have different ideas about what constitutes unjust coercion or a beautiful way of life. How does one harmonize a desire to be faithful to a religious tradition and a desire to free oneself from confining traditions? The challenge is to find a way to harmonize freedom and justice, freedom and religous faithfulness, freedom from and freedom within traditions. The challenge is to find a way of reasoning about freedom, goodness, justice, and beauty that provides justifications of one's claims, when required, and which does not itself actually contribute to unjust domination and oppression. For the postmodernist, the problem is to do radical social criticism using norms that always remain social and historical.

The problem with reasoning about science, religion, and freedom is that there does not exist any consensus today about what rationality is all about or what constitutes good and justified reasoning. Let me draw together the introductory comments I have already made about the difference between modernist and postmodernist interpretations of rationality. Modernists say that we must stay with the notion of rationality that many philosophers have accepted for hundreds and thousands of years. That tradition claims that all ideas of truth, knowledge, justice, goodness, beauty, and good reasoning have remained and must remain the same throughout human history and must be applicable in every cultural and social setting. For the past 150 years, however, existentialists, pragmatists and so-called "postmodernist" thinkers have denied this claim and instead have claimed that all standards and norms, even those of rationality itself, are not sacred gods to be worshiped, but social products of human constitution at certain historical moments in the development of human forms of life. The interpretation of rationality that I am offering in this book is such a pragmatic, existential, postmodern interpretation. The challenge to postmodernists is to find interpretations of conceiving, knowing, reasoning, and justifying that give the generality and temporal character needed for norms to function as norms while still avoiding deification of these human activities and norms. The challenge is to do so in a way that leaves science as a model of a certain kind of important rationality, without reducing historical, literary, artistic, and religious understanding to the requirements of such a scientific model. The challenge is to find a social form of rationality that permits radical social/cultural criticism (so that the social does not become a new god immune to criticism). The challenge is to find a form of rationality that leaves space for religious encounters and faithfulness to religious traditions grounded in such encounters.

These are the challenges that I take up in the remaining chapters of this book. Prior to attempting that undertaking, however, there are a number of methodological issues that it would be useful to address in this introduction. These have to do with finding a place to begin writing such a general interpretation of human life as I am offering here, finding a way to respectfully listen to the many different kinds of voices that have addressed these concerns, and then finding a way for appropriating in a coherent way the valued insights that have been given voice. There is also the problem of interpreting, without using technical jargon, texts often filled with such jargon. Finally, there is the need to alert readers to the fact that there exists a powerful academic institutional apparatus aimed at dismissively sneering at postmodern interpretive projects by labeling them as amateurish, unprofessional, anti-intellectual, self-refuting, and irrational. As will become apparent, nothing less than this entire book can deal with these methodological concerns. Method and content cannot be separated when seeking to give a global interpretation of human forms of life. Nonetheless, a few introductory remarks about these methodological problems might make it easier to hear what is being said in later chapters.

I.   LOCATING TEXTS IN HISTORICAL TIME

Where should an interpretive text begin? It should begin by recognizing that no text is an isolated island in time. What is said in any book is inescapably tied to what has been said in other, previously written books. Also, the meaning of what is written in a book is always a function of what it means to those who read the book in the future. Its meaning, therefore, is always growing and changing, often in ways not anticipated by the person listed on the book's cover as its author. The very identity of a text is historical through and through.

Beginnings of texts always come too late to be radically new. What is being written here by me is heavily indebted to the intellectual traditions and practices that make what I am thinking and writing possible. It is those traditions and practices that supply me with the problems, vocabulary, challenges, and therefore the boundaries of conceptual and textual possibilities open to me as I begin to write, boundaries that are difficult although not impossible to cross. Saying something radically new is a very difficult thing to do. Interpretive texts are never created ex nihilo, out of nothing. Even when new concepts are created and new things said, this is achieved only by appropriating and reconstructing old concepts and statements. Every writer must be a respectful and charitable reader, a partner in dialogues with earlier texts who creatively listens and thus finds new meaning in old texts. Before writing any interpretive text, many writers are tempted to try to specify what one has heard that makes one's current writing possible. That, of course, is impossible because such specifications are themselves dependent on the literary inheritance one has appropriated and reconstructed. One can only begin where one is, indebted to one's heritage and with one's literary legacy remaining at the mercy of future generations of readers.

The dream of creating a text ex nihilo is the fetishizing nightmare of historically situated authors seeking what is impossible, escaping their inescapable historical dependencies in order to control all relationships of a text to its past and future. We cannot choose the social and cultural inheritance that makes us what we are. We cannot gain complete understanding, much less complete control, of the unlimited number of threads and woven patterns of our social/ cultural inheritance and thus of ourselves as we seek understanding of our world and ourselves. We can only humbly begin our thinking, writing, and reading fully aware that we are latecomers even to our own thinking, writing, and reading. Our beginnings always come too late to be free of a debt to the past. I suggest that this is not something to be lamented because this means that our very identity and life as thinkers and writers is tied to a primordial past that was lived prior to our biological birth. Part of the fabric of our very identity as persons is made up of strings tied to the past.

Just as before the text begins it has already begun, so endings to books never arrive even though there is a final page number in every printed book. Neither the origin nor the final closure on what has been written lies under the control of the writer. Readers help determine what a text means. Texts continually can say new and different things, even incommensurately different things, to the readers who enter into dialogue with them, readers who have different and changing discursive and nondiscursive background conditions. This understanding of dialogue is one of the great contributions to contemporary understanding.[2] Just as writers bring with them to their writing that cultural heritage that makes their writing possible, so readers bring their historical background to their reading, a background that sets the framework of their initial dialogue with the text. In a dialogue in which readers really listen to a text, that background can undergo significant, surprising changes but it never disappears. It remains a constitutive factor in determining what the text means to the reader and thus what it means. The content of what we write will continue to live and develop in unpredictable ways as the identities of future readers become the inheritors of the legacy we have given them. As we shall see in the next chapter, this creative aspect of dialogical reading does not imply that failures to understand texts are impossible. The historically situated character of writing and reading does require that such failures and misunderstandings are themselves situated in a context of historically developing meaning. The historical identities of the meanings of texts are traceable back as far as history extends and can find closure only in that closure of history that produces their annihilation. Final closure on what I am saying in this text does not lie under my control.

Nevertheless, texts begin and end, even if their beginnings have a constitutive prehistory and their endings do not end the ongoing constitution of what the text has to say. Literary customs, conventions, and practices enable us to talk about the beginnings and ends of texts. The problem is that these conventional beginnings and endings seem to come too soon for writers who are aware of the roles played by the heritage and legacy of their texts. Some writers fruitlessly try to maintain control over the meaning of what they have written. They offer preludes in which they try to explain to the reader exactly what they have appropriated from the past, as if such instructions did not have their own extended historical preconditions and contested implications, as if such instructions were not part of the texts themselves, as if such instructions were not open to creative, dialogical reading. As hard as writers might try, they cannot specify all the historical factors influencing their writing and they cannot prevent such specifications from being dialogically interpreted. Similarly, for writers trying to maintain control over what their texts will mean to future readers, endings always come too soon. Writers often would like to write a little more, some postlude, in an effort to block future interpretations of their texts that will be other than their own current interpretations. One, however, cannot in this or any other way control the legacy of one's texts. Authored texts and authorial interpretations of those texts remain subject to creative reading by future generations.

It is very possible that very few readers will enter into dialogue with what I am writing in this book. Some academic professionals probably will interpret it instead in terms of background presumptions to which they dogmatically adhere, refusing to hear anything that rejects those presumptions. Only if I can write so that my readers are willing to give dialogue precedence over polemics dare I hope that what I am writing will be listened to. This is one of the reasons why so much of this text consists of reports of what I have heard through my dialogues with many different texts speaking against many different backgrounds: ancient, modern, and postmodern; European, British, American, and Asian. Dialogue requires respecting the writer so that one can open oneself to listening to what the writer is saying. Listening must always precede answering back. In this book I have tried to do that. To some texts in certain traditions I have answered back more strenuously than to others, but from each and every one of these traditions I have heard important things that I have appropriated into that way of understanding myself and my world that I will be sharing with you in the ensuing chapters. I don't know that anyone will be persuaded by what I write, but I hope that some readers will listen and answer back.

II.   DIALOGUE IN A PLURALISTIC WORLD

Dialogues with texts that have radically different historical and social pretexts need not be interpreted as worse than useless eclecticism. Eclecticism is cutting incompatible pieces from radically different texts and then pasting them together without any concern about contradictions or incoherence. Dialogue involves creative listening and not cutting and pasting. Even a pluralism of incommensurate texts, which cannot be translated into each other or some newly created text, is not a set of contradictory texts. Claims have to be operating in the same conceptual schema in order for them to contradict each other. The pretexts that readers bring to their dialogues will heavily influence what they will hear and what they will say back to the text. Readers are not culturally blank tablets or passive sponges uncritically soaking up everything being said. They will not, however, demand a single reading. Neither are dialogical readers forced by their pretexts to read and respond in one determined way. The pretexts of readers may be altered if they openly listen to what texts with radically different pretexts have to say to them. Altered background pretexts mean changed people. This can occur if people do not insist that different voices be so reduced that what they have to say is the same as what they as readers would have heard prior to their reading. Responsible, non-reductive, dialogical readers will openly and critically listen and then creatively appropriate what helps them understand in a more coherent way themselves and the worlds in which they live. It is one of the goals of this text to show how much coherence can be gained when one dialogically listens to the many different Western and Asian writers thinking about the nature of science, history, social/cultural practices, existential freedom, and religion.

Coherence, however, is only one goal to be sought by the responsible thinker. It must not be purchased at too high a price. Differences must not be disrespectfully reduced to a single schema simply to totalize everything in one coherent way of understanding things. That would be intellectual totalitarianism, a position that too often has served as the ideological cover for other forms of social, economic, and political totalitarianism. Both before and after dialogue with a text, the socially constituted pretexts of the text and the reader still will be as fractured as the world of social practices constituting them and within which they now function as social individuals. Such worlds and individuals will contain aspects in dialectical tension with each other. Seeking to make sense out of things, I will try to show, does not consist in eliminating such dialectical tensions. In fact, learning to live with such tensions may be just what is involved in remaining religiously faithful to our encounters with what is other than our ever-fractured socially constituted selves and worlds.

There can be and are a number of different, more or less coherent ways of living within human social ways of understanding and appraising things. Different vocabularies and language games, integrated sets of linguistic actions, are possible. This can mean that different ontologies (ways of constituting what exists), moralities, and religions are possible. Seeking clarity in my vocabularies and language games and seeking coherence in my way of understanding things are not the same things as seeking to get everyone to think, experience, or understand things as I do. Self-clarity can permit me to make room for different operating vocabularies, sets of norms, and spiritual quests. One can make sense of things only when one admits that there is ontological, moral, and religious pluralism and that in this plurality there are differences that are not unjustified, even when they are not justifiable to those living in other, radically different traditions. Avoiding totalitarianism and respecting the people constituted by and living within these differences requires letting these social differences simply be, something that goes beyond merely tolerating these differences. It requires accepting the responsibility to care about the person speaking out of such worlds, no matter how strange we find what is being said, no matter how much this person remains a stranger to our ways of understanding people.

Caring more for the speaking person than for what is being said, caring for people whose personal identities are not exhausted by their social and psychological identities, I shall try to show, is understanding that there is that which is other than the whole world of the social, with all its pluralisms, discourses, regimes of truth, tensions, clarity, and confusion. It is this otherness to the social that is found in the singular uniqueness of persons that prevents coherence from ever being totalized, since it is a precondition of the social and it is the air that all actors breathe when constituting, reconstituting, and participating in the social practices that make the social world what it is. It is this caring respect for the singularity of the people we encounter that prevents both the intellectual totalizing and the political totalitarianism that would attempt to reduce difference to sameness and other people into merely social individuals who can be dominated and oppressed in order to meet the needs of other social individuals.[3]

Why enter into dialogue with this text, since it is primarily an example of one person's dialogue with texts from many different traditions, a kind of report on what I have dialogically heard, criticized, and appropriated? Different readers, of course, might have many different reasons for reading this text or for not doing so, for choosing to do so or choosing not to do so. I likewise undoubtedly have many different reasons for writing this offering. Any reasons I could give for reading this text, however, are themselves part of the text. Anticipating what I will say later, let me simply say that none of the texts that have become part of one or more of the world's philosophical or religious traditions have had nothing to say to me. Although I too will have much to say back to most of these texts, I have found too many intellectuals either not reading anything outside their own tradition or speaking back to straw men they have created by reducing other traditions to their own. This makes me doubly sad because many of these intellectuals are some of the most brilliant and skillful minds in the world. Probably few of these intellectuals will ever read this text or enter into dialogue with it or with many of the texts that have had much to say to me. Nevertheless, I write in the hope that some academic and some nonacademic readers will read, listen, and speak back to me and the texts I have read. Since the Buddhist text, "If you see the Buddha, kill the Buddha," has said volumes to me, I do not write to secure agreement on a thesis, although I will present many theses in this text. I write to be part of a dialogical intellectual community, dreaming of more and more sensitive spirits and brilliant minds becoming dialogically engaged.

III.   ORDINARY PEOPLE IN DIALOGUE WITH TEXTS BY INTELLECTUAL "EXPERTS"

Three problems confront writers and readers who want to think reflectively about what has been written in many different traditions.

First, there is the problem of thinking only in English about what has been written in many languages other than English. Second, there is the problem of thinking in nontechnical language about what has been written by professional academicians using many technical expressions whose use is familiar to only a select set of specialists. Third, there is the problem of dialogically listening to writers from many different academic disciplines (philosophers, literary theorists, social/cultural interpreters and critics, religious writers), not reducing what they have to say to the particular vocabulary and project of one particular tradition in one particular discipline. I suggest that one can do serious and deep reflection even if one is only or primarily reading texts and translations of texts written in English. One can learn a great deal when thinking in nontechnical, ordinary English about what one hears when engaging in dialogue with texts written using specialized, technical language. One can hear radical critiques of long-standing intellectual traditions. The proof that one can do this, of course, can only be found in the pudding. A few optimistic, preparatory comments, however, might be helpful in maintaining hope as we write and read.

This text is an instance of the thinking and reflecting that I am doing in English as a response to what I hear when reading English language texts and translations of texts written by many different European and Asian thinkers. In my dialogues with these texts, I will write what I hear them saying to me and what I think I must say back to them. I realize that I may not be able to hear in English much of what was originally said in German, French, Danish, Sanskrit, Chinese, or Japanese. Even reading English translations, however, will permit me to hear much that would be totally lost if translations were treated as totally useless. Important reflections appear in translations and that they differ from authorial meanings or meanings of originals does not make them not worth listening to. Translations, of course, are interpretations, but so are "originals." Although one wants to hear as much as possible that will aid one's reflections, one also must not get caught up in thinking that a return to origins can legitimate one's reflections. Scholars, capable of researching and thinking in many different technical and natural languages, can play extremely important roles in aiding readers to hear texts to which they otherwise would be deaf. Scholarship and technical and linguistic virtuosity, however, is no guarantee of insight or wisdom. Neither must they be permitted to become an elitist barrier to widespread participation in thinking about how to make sense of ourselves and our world. The intellectual populism supported in this text need not be interpreted as being antiintellectual, but it is an effort to resist intellectual elitism.

It is also an effort to resist the excessive, reductionist, self-destructive isolationism of so much of current professional philosophizing. The different kinds of thinkers to whom I have attempted to listen have been labeled by different groups in different ways: philosophers, literary theorists, social/cultural critics, poets, novelists, religious writers, mystics, sociologists. I suggest that the labels be ignored. I will attempt to show that every effort should be made to avoid disciplinary exclusions and marginalizations or a scholarly elitism that prohibits any interested reader from engaging in dialogue with these texts. For example, many philosophers want to reduce intellectual differences between themselves and thinkers in the fields of religion or literary and culture studies to fields within their same old traditions (philosophy of religion, philosophy of language, logic, philosophy of the social sciences, political philosophy, aesthetics, ethics). These reductionist philosophers want to tell others what is the "real" foundation or significance of intellectual and reflective efforts in all other areas. In this text an effort will be made to show the fruitfulness of listening to those who say things that sound strange to many philosophical ears, listening to those who locate many philosophical projects within a general interpretation and critique of social/cultural practices, to those who call for adding textual logic and a logic of desire to mathematical and dialogical logic, those who see no need for grounding general normative principles in some theory of philosophical ethics and who see theories of reality or knowledge presupposing ethical responsibilities and spiritual quests. I will attempt to show that the idea of rationality endorsed by philosophical reductionists is not exhaustive of human rationality and that rationality in all its forms is not exhaustive of responsible human life.

Is it possible, however, for postmodernists to avoid creating their own extraordinary uses of language in order to talk about a textual logic in which words get related to words by tonal, inscriptional similarities or historical, etymological, and literary associations? What makes the texts of postmodern writers such as Jacques Derrida[4] and Mark Taylor[5] so difficult for most readers to interpret is the way they seem to be playing with such material similarities and literary associations. We will look in detail at their texts later. At this introductory moment, let me simply make two suggestive responses to this question. First, what Derrida and Taylor are trying to do cannot be done without them being linguistically creative in the brilliant manner in which they write. Second, it may be possible to understand what they are doing without writing in the same style. Unless such is possible, very few persons, including this writer, have the skills needed to write, read, or think with them. Their rhetorical style, however, may be dictated by their target audiences: professional philosophers and theologians who are working with philosophical taken-for-granteds that Derrida and Taylor want to show are self-defeating or simply unnecessary. It may also result from their conviction that ordinary language is too contaminated by such philosophical taken-for-granteds to be useful in interpreting ourselves and our world. I shall try to show that a great deal can be learned from these two writers without trying to imitate their writing style. As we shall see, the Austrian thinker, Ludwig Wittgenstein, tried to carry out a project very similar to that of Derrida, and he utilized a very different, nontechnical style of writing.[6] Wittgenstein, however, never believed that ordinary language was so saturated with philosophical confusion or corruption that it could not be used to present an interpretation of human thinking and writing. Neither does this writer.

IV. DEFENDING A POSTMODERN INTERPRETATION OF RATIONALITY ITSELF

I will be making claims about the social and historical nature of all the intellectual tools we use trying to make sense of things in general. These tools include our concepts, thoughts, experiential reports, truth claims, knowledge claims, arguments. The umbrella term I use to cover all these tools is "rationality." These are the very tools, of course, that I must use in writing about rationality. I also will be claiming that there is more to human life than rationality, that social rationality has an ethical and religious other that makes rationality possible. These two claims raise three kinds of questions: (1) How is it possible to make general statements about all concepts, thoughts, statements, and texts while being situated in a specific, contingent social space and historical moment? (2) How is it possible to justify general statements about all conceiving, thinking, asserting, and writing without stepping outside one's own particular social setting and historical location? (3) How is it possible to conceive of encountering that which is other than the conceivable? These three questions will be addressed again and again in the following chapters. In anticipation of what will be said, let me sketch what I hope to show in those chapters.

[1] Interpretations of human concepts, statements, and texts are not prevented from containing general statements simply because they are socially and historically situated interpretations. Asserting that all interpretations are socially and historically situated is such a general statement. All interpretations and general claims use socially and historically situated vocabularies. Self-reflective thinkers, making such an interpretation of statements and interpretations, admit that other vocabularies, claims, and interpretations are possible. Using a specific vocabulary in order to claim in the abstract that vocabularies other than one's own are possible is not proceeding in a pragmatically self-refuting manner, in which one's act of saying something is an example proving the falsehood of what one is saying. Were one in a concrete situation to encounter people using radically different

vocabulary items, then responsible listeners would face the need of entering into dialogue with these people, listening, reconstructing, reconstituting, and speaking back. When dialogue breaks down, creative reconstruction of backgrounds is needed for dialogue to resume. Having in the past engaged in such creative dialogue, one can project that it is possible that one will have to do so again in the future. One is not pragmatically refuting oneself when one makes such a projection.

Similarly, that all general claims and interpretations are historically situated does not turn them into biased, relativistic viewpoints serving unjustly the interests of the holders of those viewpoints. Socially constituted forms of social and cultural criticism are possible, as I will show in chapters 3 and 4. Social/cultural critiques are not merely expressions of relativistic perspectives on what concepts, claims, and thoughts really are like independent of any particular perspective on them. The claim that postmodern critiques are relativistic and perspectival assumes that there is a reality characterizable with nonsocial, nonhistorical concepts and statements that could be viewed from different perspectives. It is just this assumption that is rejected by those who claim that all concepts and statements are socially and historically situated. The language of perspectives is also social and historical. What different people can have different perspectives on is also something always specifiable only with social and historical concepts. Postmodernists simply are making some general assertions that they are willing to defend as correct against those who deny them. They and their concepts may be situated, but they are not asserting that what they are asserting is true merely relative to their position.

Rejecting the charge of relativism while affirming the social and historical character of assertions does require not interpreting the correctness or truth of assertions in terms of correspondence to facts supposedly free of all ties to the social and historical. I will attempt to show that a correspondence theory of truth can be avoided if one attends to the pragmatics of "true," "false," and "real." Much more will be said about this in the next chapter, but for now let me merely illustrate one feature of the way these words are used. Just as the British philosopher John Austin claimed that the expression "real" is a substantive hungry, context dependent double negative,[7] so I will claim that "true" is a substantive hungry, context dependent double negative. Real diamonds are nothing but diamonds. The word "real" has work to do in the statement, "That's a real diamond," because there are occasions when one wants to reject someone's supposition that it is in some specific way unreal (only glass, only a picture or mirror image of a diamond, only an illusion). Similarly, saying that it is true that all concepts are social and historical is in one sense saying no more than that all concepts are social and historical. The word "true" has work to do in the first statement because there are occasions when we want to reject someone's rejection of our claim that all concepts are social and historical. First there are statements or supposals; then there are rejections of them or claims or supposals of falsity; then there are rejections of rejections, reaffirmations, or claims of truth. Examining how the word "true" works in questions and requests lends further support to this interpretation of the pragmatics of the use of "true." We ask "Is it true that Cal touched Ann?" when it has been suggested that Cal didn't. Otherwise we ask "Did Cal touch Ann?" Similarly, we might request someone to find out if Cal touched Ann, but we would request someone to find out the truth of the alleged affair only if conflicting claims had been made.[8]

[2] Universal claims about all possible claims have a very special status. This is because claims have existence conditions as well as truth conditions. Some claims can exist only if they are false and other claims necessitate that they be true. The claims that there are no claims or no people making claims can't be true. The claim that language does not exist must be false because without language there could not be any claims. Claims have presupposed conditions that are undeniable. In a general interpretation of human rationality, certain claims about all claims or about the conditions necessary for the existence of any claims would turn out to be undeniable and in that sense necessary.

Interpretive undeniables bear interesting similarities to what were called synthetic a priori judgments by the eighteenth-century philosopher Immanuel Kant. He claimed that such judgments specified the necessities that are undeniably required by all thoughts which can possibly be true, false, or knowable. My interpretation of undeniable claims, though similar, is also significantly different from Kant's. First, the interpretive approach advocated in this text rejects any Kantian division between analytic claims true by definition and synthetic claims true by virtue of the way things contingently happen to be.[9] The difference between definitional dictionary entries and informative encyclopedia entries is strictly pragmatic. Second, given the self-reflective acknowledgment of the social and historical situatedness of all concepts and claims, general interpretive undeniables are never interpreted in a Kantian fashion as necessarily necessary. They are only undeniable by those who endorse a general, corrigible interpretation of the social and historical conditions that are seen to be preconditions of all concepts and claims. Even my claim that in all general interpretations there will be some undeniable claims is only a part of my interpretation of the social, pragmatic character of all rationality and the conditions required for any and all claims. Also, my interpretations of the normative concepts of truth, knowledge, and justice, which are framed by interpretive undeniables, only produce claims about the pragmatic, context dependent character of norms; they are not Kantian claims about categorical demands binding on all practical reasoners.[10] Making undeniable, general claims about anything that might be true or false has a different character from making deniable claims, but both kinds of claims remain social and historical through and through.

[3] Finally, let's consider whether it is possible to conceive of a way of understanding that which is other than the conceivable? Is it possible to understand that something (which is not an object falling under a concept) lies radically beyond our ways of understanding such objects? I will attempt to show that it is, if understanding is interpreted as a certain kind of skillful "know-how."[11] One understands the meaning

of a word in a language if one knows how to use it in accordance with current social practices of use and normative appraisal. One understands life in a certain social/cultural world when one knows how to act and respond to others' actions in accordance with the socially sanctioned practices which constitute that world. Linguistic know-how is an instance of knowing how to use tools and how to participate with people in social practices.[12] Although many thinkers who accent this kind of practical know-how restrict it to knowing how to act in a socially constituted world, I will suggest that people also can come to understand how to deal with that which is other than a tool, that which is other than socially constituted, conceptualizable beings in such a world.

One might come to know how not to absolutize or deify social and cultural practices and their constituted beings and norms. Certainly one of the major motivations for negative theologies, which say that God is not this, not that, not any conceivable being or characteristic of a being, is to express the understanding that the human world is only human, often all too human. One additionally might come to understand life as not being restricted to conceiving, knowing, and having conceptualized cognitive experiences. One might come to understand and appreciate the significance of not thinking or conceptually categorizing things at all and thus come to simply enjoy breathing, walking, feeling a cooling breeze or a warm summer rain hitting one in the face.[13] One might come to understand that the general conditions that make understanding possible (the laws of nature, the human social practices of constituting objects and social and psychological identities for people) are themselves not capable of being made understandable by being placed in a larger context. One might come to understand that no one existing set of socially constituted objects and no past, present, or future set of such sets can exhaust the possibilities of such constitutions; the indeterminateness made determinate through social constitution always exceeds all determinateness.[14]

One can in one's attitudes and actions show one's understanding that "ultimately" everything rests on nothing and simply has to be allowed to be what it will be whether one seeks to control it or not.[15] Similarly, one can show one's understanding of life as filled with inexplicable chanciness and precariousness. One can show in one's way of living one's understanding of one's own death as something that cannot be conceived as a specific possibility. One can, in assuming responsibility to let other people, whom one encounters face to face, simply be in the otherness of their singularity, show one's understanding of people as unique not because of the conceivable differences in their social and psychological identities but as being different from each other because of their uniqueness. I can show such understanding by responsibly listening to the one calling to me and speaking to me, no matter how incomprehensibly strange I find them or what they are saying. In assuming such responsibility, one can show that an ethical understanding of what can be interpreted is necessarily presupposed by socially constituted moralities of rules and principles, moralities which may have to be suspended when demanded by one's responsibilities to people in their unclassifiable singularity.

These modes of understanding, as I will attempt to show in chapter 5, are what is at the heart of what have been historically present in the religious lives of people in many times and places. One can do a great deal of living which is other than classifying, judging, explaining. One can encounter and respond to that other than a conceivable being. One can hear a call from that which is other than the social and, although what is heard obviously is conceptualized, this does not require that the one calling is describable by any set of socially constituted concepts, the only kind of concepts there are. Although one can conceive of and interpret such living, encountering, and responding, this does not require that what one encounters be a being falling under a concept.

I will attempt to show that an interpretation of religious life in terms of such living, encountering, and responding will require that it not be an ontotheological interpretation. Since the time of Aristotle in the fourth century B.C., thinkers have bound themselves to such ontotheological interpretations. In ancient Greek, *ontos* meant being, *theos* meant the highest cause and value, and *logos* meant the principle in terms of which everything is to be explained. Ontotheologies claim that ontos, theos, and logos are timeless, locationless, eternal, and invariable. There have been many different ontotheologies, but all of them claim that some timeless and spaceless, necessarily existent being is the ultimate explanation why anything exists and why everything is as it is and not otherwise and that it is to be seen as the ultimate justification for all values, norms, and ideals.

The interpretation of religious encounters and faithfulness that I will offer rejects all such ontotheologies and all desires for them. I suggest that this rejection is simply an insistence that religion not be subjected to philosophical imperialism and totalitarianism. Religious discourse and linguistic activities using the word "god" must be allowed to be what they are, different from talk about socially constituted objects in natural or supernatural worlds. Religious talk is to be seen as different from ontotheological or superstitious talk about causes of events in the world or about a cause of the world itself, when such talk about causes is modeled on science's use of talk of causes in giving explanations of events in terms of laws of nature or when it is modeled on talk about people causing a person's death by shooting them.[16]

In order to avoid efforts to maintain human control over that which is other than the social by reducing such otherness to the sameness of everything that is a conceivable, socially constituted being, it is helpful to remember that religious language is not primarily thematic but rather a language of devotion, prayer, and the proclamation of what one has heard when responding to the call from such otherness, what one has heard when responding to the other revealing itself as radically other in such calling. Such religious discourse, speech, and texts are socially constituted and their variety reflects the different social/cultural worlds in which they, their speakers, and writers are situated. The encounters and responses that give birth to such discourse, however, remain encounters with and responses to that which is other than the social. Religious discourse, when freed from ontotheological or superstitious interpretations, shows that people need not respond to radical otherness only with silence or with paradoxical, poetic efforts to textually give voice to silence. There can be linguistic responses to the radically other and linguistic expression of what is heard when responding to the call of the other.

These religious utterances or writings can be folded back into the historically developing world of social/cultural practices. Actually, it will not be so much a matter of folding back into the social something radically other than the social as it will be a matter of making explicit in the social that otherness to itself upon which the social itself is thoroughly dependent. The whole world of the social has as one of its preconditions its own otherness. It is not autonomous. It is constituted ("created") in response to the call of the singularity of other people, the indeterminate possibilities of determinateness, the unsurpassable bruteness of natural law and the chanciness of human life, the impossibility of conceiving the possibility of no more possibilities for oneself, the impossibility of conceiving one's own death. We need to interpret only the social to find the social's otherness. The religious is not merely other to social rationality, but it is a response to the precondition of such rationality.

The tasks undertaken in this text, therefore, are fourfold: (1) Present an interpretation of the social nature of all human rationality, of all conceiving, understanding, perceiving, inferring, interpreting, doubting, explaining, judging, criticizing, indicting, and justifying. (2) Present examples that show that such an interpretation of social rationality leaves ample resources for critiquing current social/cultural practices if they are personally unworkable or socially unjust. (3) Present a critical interpretation of certain ways of understanding an otherness to social rationality and of encounters with and responses to such otherness. (4) Present an interpretation of religious and ethical discourse expressive of encounters with and responses to such otherness that understands such discourse as folded into social life even if not governed by the norms of social rationality.

V. INSTITUTIONALIZED OBSTACLES TO READING POSTMODERN TEXTS DIALOGICALLY

Many academic philosophers would say that people should not waste their time with many of the texts I am dealing with in my postmodern attempt to make sense of things. The philosophical community is fractured into different traditions that sometimes are hostile and sometimes barely tolerant of each other. As a bridge from this introduction to the main body of this text, it will be helpful to locate in a social and historical setting these traditions not interested in dialogue with each other. These efforts to save readers from wasting time illustrate much of what I will be criticizing in this book. It is important for writers and readers of global interpretations to remain cognizant of the powerful institutional forces discouraging crosstradition dialogue.

Philosophical reflection in many traditions has done a great disservice by institutionalized exclusions or marginalizations of philosophical texts whose voices they branded as worthless for current reflection. Since the nineteenth century, when the history of Western philosophy became an identifiable academic field of its own and university courses in this field were offered, a canon of great texts was formed, a canon that omitted many texts which were not of apparent service to philosophers then who were dominated by interests in theories of knowledge, ethics, politics, ontotheologies, or the Kantian synthetic a priori. For many of these philosophers, especially those in the English-speaking world, it seemed incredulous that any serious contemporary philosopher would think that philosophy might be anything other than what they were doing. Philosophy was codified as excluding or marginalizing writers who affirmed or presumed a social and pragmatic character to thinking, who wrote in any style other than argumentative prose, who saw philosophy itself as a historically situated practice, who treated human rationality as not exhaustive of human life.

The constitution of a philosophical canon was a practice reinforced by a set of other social practices. Not wishing to be left behind in the wake of the success of mathematical sciences and technology in Western universities and economies, many philosophers sought to go scientific and technical themselves. For many, philosophy became the scientific study of unchanging meanings. Closely related to this practice of maintaining status by scientizing philosophy was the professionalizing of philosophy, the establishment of a microphysics of power (practices governing philosophy curricula, admission, and graduation of graduate students in philosophy, use of reference letters in hiring and promoting teachers of philosophy, selection of articles and books for publishing). Philosophy became a professional academic discipline with students being disciplined into line and college administrators and thinkers outside the profession being excluded from meddling with what had to remain the business of professional philosophers. In this self-defined, self-serving world of professional philosophy, a lively intellectual industry was created and maintained, one that provided space for brilliant, creative entrepreneurs who could produce new intellectual puzzles, creating new polemical work for graduate students and new professors. Many philosophers deeply involved in this world of professional philosophy find it impossible to believe that these practices (producing for them some degree of social status, job security, and independent space to pursue their disciplinary interests) might be excluding significant philosophical possibilities and producing an insulated independence that makes their work appear to outsiders as irrelevant to the main currents of contemporary social and cultural life.[17]

Several important consequences of this scientizing and professionalizing of philosophy deserve highlighting. First, in building professional philosophy departments, especially in the United States where single philosophy/religion departments had been common in the early twentieth century, a split between those teaching religion and those teaching philosophy was demanded by the philosophers and also by some teachers of religion who were likewise often caught up in efforts to scientize and professionalize an academic discipline of their own. The result was an exclusion from philosophy of any concern for religious and spiritual quests. Philosophy of religion courses became restricted to analyses of philosophers' ideas, claims, and arguments about knowledge of an onthotheological god. The actual wrestling with questions concerning the quality of the human spirit was excluded from "serious" philosophizing, and texts dealing with such questions, when taught at all, were marginalized (and often mutilated) in historical courses on existentialism or Asian philosophy.

There is a second undesirable consequence of current practices that reinforces the power of professional, academic philosophical scholars. On the one hand, everyone is declared to be a philosopher or to operate on the basis of unexamined philosophical assumptions. On the other hand, it is made clear that only professional academics are capable of seriously examining philosophical issues and judging the worth of nonprofessional philosophizing. Everyone, therefore, is seen as indebted to professional philosophers and must become consumers of their academic labor or defer to the authority of their clearer and deeper understanding. When outside critics criticize or ignore what they perceive as academic philosophy's presumptuous, arrogant, blind, self-serving pretentiousness, this is interpreted by academic philosophers as verification of the confused amateurism of these critics. Likewise, thinkers are branded by philosophical scholars as incompetent anti-intellectuals if they refuse to give up their quest to make sense of things because they cannot think in the technical jargon of the professionals, refusing to believe that their efforts are in vain because they are not keeping up with the intramural polemics appearing in professional journals. Among these professionsals one can find some of the most brilliant intellects in the world. Unfortunately, many of them became masters of a rhetoric of ridicule, dismissing their challengers with some form of *argumentum ad sneerum.* Their ridicule and sneers is the price one must pay when one tries to make sense of things in a postmodern way.

Unfortunately, these cultural diseases of professionally protecting intellectual elites and of canonizing a restricted set of texts while excluding all others from serious consideration are global, contaminating intellectual traditions in all parts of the world. Many British and American philosophers exclude Hegel and his legacy from the canon, and many European philosophers do the same to Bertrand Russell and the analytic philosophy tradition he authored. Both generally ignore texts by Asian philosophers, although a number of European thinkers have tried to engage in dialogue with Taoist and Buddhist texts.[18] Striving for institutional legitimization by imitating science has infected many in academic disciplines in universities: analytic philosophy and phenomenology in philosophy, new criticism in literary theory, number-crunching in communication studies and political science. Postmodern thinkers such as Heidegger and Derrida, with their own technical vocabularies and their doctrines of metaphysical contamination of ordinary understanding and language, also seem to be engaged in elitist projects of guaranteeing status and security for professional academics by establishing the continuous need for technical specialists providing interpretations of interpretations of interpretations. Asian philosophers also have been infected with the viruses of exclusivism and elitist professionalism. Many Hindu philosophers have perfected the art of either reducing Western philosophical differences to Hindu sameness or of excluding them as being hopelessly fallen into spiritual blindness. Also, as the Indian philosopher Nagarjuna pointed out, many Buddhist philosophers abandoned the Buddha's injunction to maintain a "noble silence" on metaphysical issues, creating instead competing schools of professional thinkers developing technical vocabularies and highly complex theories.[19]

The difficulty that intellectuals have in listening to voices in other traditions is only matched by the need to do so. This book is written with the conviction that ordinary people can make sense of their lives and world without always deferring to an elitist group of intellectual priests. The book aims at helping people make sense of things by sharing with them the products of years of critical dialogue and creative appropriation. This book is a record of one person's fifty-year effort to understand things. I encourage its readers to engage it dialogically so that it can gain meaning in ways I never could have imagined. I encourage readers to always keep in mind the Zen saying, "If you see the Buddha, kill the Buddha." Being a follower is no substitute for being a creative thinker. This book is offered to readers who want to try to make sense of things while thinking in English. Experts are invited to join in dialogue but this book is aimed at people who do no have much or any expertise, but who are willing to do some difficult and complex thinking.

─╾─ CHAPTER TWO THE DEBATE BETWEEN MODERNISM AND POSTMODERNISM

Talking about social rationality is being redundant. There is no other kind of rationality. Exercising rationality in any and all of its forms is always a matter of participating in social practices. Conceiving, perceiving, remembering, asserting, inferring, explaining, justifying, acting, understanding, interpreting, wanting, wishing, hoping, fearing: all are forms of exercising human rationality and they all involve participating in social practices. The products of all these rational activities are also socially and historically situated: concepts, perceptions, what one says or thinks, the intentional objects of one's experiences. People and their acts and experiences are social through and through. This is one of the primary themes of postmodernism and of this book. Individual persons are not born. Homo sapiens are born and become individual persons through interpersonal encounters, socialization, acculturation, nurturing, and training.

It is a sign of the great divide existing in contemporary intellectual life in the North Atlantic world that many postmodernist thinkers find a book insulting if it repeats once again the thesis that people are inescapably social or if it rehearses once again the reflections that led to this conviction. They find it incredulous that any serious student of the human condition would think otherwise. On the other hand, many modernists think that it is the postmodernist position that is incredulous. Modernism gets born responding to the seventeenth-century revolution in physics while also trying to preserve many aspects of medieval and ancient intellectual traditions. Modernists believe that asocial (nonsocial) and ahistorical (nonhistorical) concepts, propositions, and meanings do exist. Furthermore, they argue that the socially invariable and the timeless must be postulated in order to account for socially different people at different times being able to say the same thing, for one person's ability to deny what another person says, for misinterpretations of what has been said or written to be possible. They also believe that an asocial, ahistorical foundation must exist in order for there to be any human knowledge because, they think, there must exist asocial and ahistorical truth conditions and justification requirements. Finally, many modernists believe that there are asocial and ahistorical moral principles and that these are necessary if the moral appraisal of social practices is to be possible. Postmodernism comes to life in the middle of the nineteenth century with its assertion that human thinking and living is thoroughly social and historical. After having attempted to make their case again and again during the past century and a half, many postmodernists want to move ahead. They wish to leave the issue of whether rationality is social behind them so that they can get on with the business of critically interpreting the social/cultural worlds that exist and of reflecting on the possibility of an "other" to such social worlds. They don't want to waste time listening to those whom they see as still lost in the backwaters of intellectual history or to those reactionaries trying to preserve old myths in an effort to hold on to fading power.

I would suggest that it is irresponsible arrogance for postmodernists to refuse to listen to the advocates of the asocial and ahistorical, to mimic the very arrogance of many modernists who will not listen to postmodernists who challenge the basic presuppositions of the modernist effort to find a rationality that transcends the social and historical. In this chapter I will try to listen to both groups, although it is with a form of postmodernism that I will finally side. Listening to those who argue for the necessity of eternal meanings, foundations, and standards will help us remember what must be accounted for in any postmodernist interpretation of rationality as thoroughly social. Listening to the voices of the early-nineteenth-century thinkers who criticized the modernist advocates of the asocial will help us see possible ways for us to talk back to those who in the twentieth century attacked these early defenders of the social and historical character of rationality. It also will help us recognize the problems that still remain in the way that thinkers such as Kierkegaard, Nietzsche, Dewey, Wittgenstein, Heidegger, Derrida, Gadamer, and Rorty present their affirmation of the social character of rationality and human beings.

There is, I believe, a need to listen to and talk back to those in both traditions.

One important reason for continuing to enter into dialogue with the modernist advocates of ahistorical and asocial foundations, facts, norms, and meanings is that they have had and still do have great influence on contemporary social and cultural practices. Hundreds of thousands of college students every year have asocial theories preached at them by modernist professors who often are masters at the rhetoric of ridiculing their opposition. Millions of worshippers in churches, temples, and synagogues hear sermons colored by the same modernist themes and aimed at branding postmodernism as irrational, dogmatic, and antireligious. Also, because of the current imperialistic globalization of North Atlantic social and cultural practices, often the texts available in places like China (where this text is now being written) are those written by modernist advocates of the asocial and ahistorical. All of these people need to know that the interpreters of the rational as social have listened to opposing modernist and religious voices and are engaged in a continuing dialogue on a global scale with a wide variety of such voices. All of these people need to be enabled and invited to join in this dialogue.

Dialogue will not come easily. On the one hand, many modernists think that the whole postmodern project is so infected with irrationalism and social relativism that reasoned discussion is impossible. They believe that widespread social evils cannot be justifiably condemned or combated by postmodernists. In this and the next two chapters I hope to show that there are good reasons for rejecting these charges. On the other hand, some postmodernist thinkers have claimed that ancient, medieval and modern efforts to transcend the social have so contaminated the whole of our language and Western culture that radically new ways of speaking are necessary, ways that will be labeled as meaningless and irrational by modernists. I shall try to show that our ordinary language is not fatally infected, even though there is some truth in this postmodernist claim. Democratic liberalism, capitalism and neocapitalism, humanism, phallocentrism, religious fundamentalism, and "moral majoritism" do have an ideological aspect in their mosaic that is heavily influenced by modernist asocial and ahistorical theories of knowledge, metaphysics, and ethics. Nevertheless, the postmodernist claim of total contamination really is an intellectualistic overstatement of the influence on Western society and culture of traditional philosophical ideas and arguments. I shall try to show that dialogue between modernism and postmodernism is possible and that out of such dialogue we can develop an interpretation of our human form of life that makes sense of things.

Exasperation with opponents who will not join in such a dialogue is no excuse for doing the same. As we shall see, Nietzsche and Foucault shared that exasperation and still continued to write genealogies of their present so as to show that its many asocial and ahistorical taken-for-granted meanings, norms, standards, discourses, and philosophical theorizing need not be simply accepted as sacred truth. Wittgenstein probably was too intellectualistic and too generous when he blamed such modernist taken-for-granteds simply on philosophical confusion about the nature of language. He did write, however, so that his readers could develop a sense of the need to question these taken-for-granteds and so that they could develop the skills needed for identifying and unraveling the snarls into which they confusedly had tied up their thoughts. He did not show disrespect for modernists. He recognized how deep were the reflections that led defenders of the asocial to their positions. They believed they had to say what they were saying. He wanted to aid them, and those tempted to agree with them, to see for themselves that there really are no nonquestion begging reasons that require one to try to transcend the social. Such aid can be supplied only by entering into dialogue with the modernists, taking seriously all their reasons for thinking they had to say what they were saying. The reflections of many thinkers may be so deeply seated within their personal makeup that they never will sense a need or develop an ability to radically critique their own asocial, ahistorical taken-for-granteds, but this often is not true of those whom they have influenced or might influence in the future. On that hope I write this report of what I have heard when entering into dialogue with modernist and postmodernist texts debating the pros and cons on the issue of the social character of rationality.

This report in this chapter will consist of four parts. First, I will present my critical interpretation of the texts of the modern metaphysicians and epistemologists (theorists of knowledge) from Descartes to Hegel. This will be followed by an examination of the postmodernist critiques of Hegelianism written by Kierkegaard and Nietzsche, and of the postmodernist critiques presented by the American pragmatists, Peirce, James and Dewey, of the whole epistemological project. Then I will report what I hear and have to say in reply when reading the texts of the twentieth century, modernist Neoplatonists who have attempted to leapfrog Hegel and his critics by establishing sciences of asocial and ahistorical meanings (Frege, Husserl, Saussure, Chomsky). Finally, I will present my critical interpretations of the writings of those postmodernist thinkers who have challenged these Neoplatonists by presenting interpretations of meaning and understanding as being thoroughly social and historical (Wittgenstein, Heidegger, Derrida, Foucault, and the neopragmatists Rorty and Bernstein).

I. WHAT IS THE MODERNISM THAT POSTMODERNISM OPPOSES?

Postmodernist defenders of the thesis that rationality is social through and through often see only Hegelianism or positivism as alternatives to their own position. Hegel (1770–1831) is seen by most postmodernists as the last great philosopher to defend a metaphysical theory that seeks to explain everything, including human history, in terms of something that transcends all social variations and historical changes. Positivism is the philosophy of scientism, which sees the scientific knowledge gained in physics as the model of all human knowledge. Most defenders of the asocial, ahistorical character of rationality, however, do not believe that they must limit their choices to Hegel, positivism, and postmodernism. Why this difference? Postmodernist social interpreters of rationality see modern Western thinking from Descartes to Kant as leading to either Hegel or positivism. They claim that only when one has reflectively passed beyond Hegelianism and positivism can one focus on the implications of affirming the social character of human rationality. However, the twentieth-century defenders of the asocial and ahistorical character of propositions, concepts and meanings, especially the meanings of "true," "valid," "justified," "good," and "just" almost always also reject Hegelianism and often reject positivism. Why don't their readings of the texts of Descartes and Kant lead them to the either/or choice of Hegel or the positivism of Comte,[1] Mach,[2] and the logical positivists?[3] A critical interpretation of modern European thinking from Descartes to Hegel is needed to account for this difference. I suggest that the crucial difference between the two positions lies in their respective responses to Cartesian doubt and the supposed significance of the issue of the origin of human ideas or concepts.

Seventeenth-century Cartesian doubting really begins in the sixteenth century with the Copernican revolution. Copernicus had taught modern Western thinkers that we cannot naively trust our eyes. Although it seems as though the sun moves through the sky from east to west, treating this appearance as the way things really are is based on the assumption that we are totally passive in perceiving things. This assumption is false. We are rotating on the surface of the earth, and because of our motion we actively contribute to the appearance of things. Galileo expanded on the position of Copernicus when he recognized that we must be actively contributing the colors, smells, tastes, sounds, and tactual feels of the sensory objects we perceive because, he believed, these objects are nothing but atoms without any of the qualities of color, smell, taste, sound, or feel that we attribute to the objects that are collections of such atoms.

Descartes (1596–1650) recognized the intellectual revolution that was taking place in his age. In addition to the scientific revolution occurring around him, his French countryman, Michel de Montaigne

(1533–1592),[4] had further convinced him of the unreliability of our senses and of the need to put under question the basic assumptions of medieval thinking. Philosophy during the Aristotelian era of the Middle Ages, had sided with the naive realism that Copernicus and Galileo had undercut. Medieval Aristotelians had assumed that the perceiver is first of all passive in the perceptual situation, merely receiving presentations of sensible particulars that are other than the perceiver. Knowledge of these particulars is gained when the perceivers actively use their intellects to explain why these particulars are as they are presented to be: what stuff were they made up of, how was the stuff organized into a specific form so as to fulfill a specific purpose or attain a certain goal, and who did the organizing. The idea of the relevant form for the perceived object was acquired by abstracting it from the sensory presentations passively received.

Descartes turned back to Augustine (354–430) to strengthen the challenges of Copernicus, Galileo, and Montaigne. Augustine had argued that the reason we are trapped in Plato's cave, naively seeing sensory appearances as ultimate realities rather than as the mere shadows of the unseen realities causing the shadows, is that our fallen wills are causing us to see things this way. As Augustine interprets the human situation, we believe as we do, we think as we do, we reason as we do, because we do not want to acknowledge the God who created these shadows, because we do not want to obey the will of this God, desiring instead to be gods ourselves. People actively are rebelling against the truth. People are not passive in the knowing situation. The mere possibility that we are actively distorting all sensory input was enough to convince Descartes to endorse Montaigne's recommendation to join with the ancient Greek skeptics in suspending (at least until all doubts could be removed) all metaphysical judgments about ultimate reality. Descartes, therefore, prioritized doubting over believing and placed the burden of proof on the believer. Thus was born the modern philosophical industry of epistemology, theory of knowledge.

Descartes turns back to Plato (428–347 B.C.) to challenge the theory of Aristotle (384-321 B.C.) that ideas originate by abstraction from sensory presentations. Long before Kant (1724-1804) provided the famous slogan that sensations without conceptions are blind, Plato had claimed that sensory presentations always already are representations, conceptually structured perceptions. To perceive anything is to perceive it as something. Without the idea of a circle one cannot perceive circles and then begin inquiring why they are as they are. Ideas are necessary to have perceptual experiences and can't be resultant products produced by such experiences. For Descartes, since experience can't be the origin of ideas needed in cognition, the only possible explanation of their existence is their innateness to knowing minds.[5] Not until Hegel (1770-1831) is the alternative explanation provided that we acquire the ideas with which we perceive things when we are socially trained to see things as we do, to conceive of things as we do. For Hegel, it is not our individual sensory states that are the origin of our ideas. The origins of our ideas are lost in the historical antecedents of the habits, dispositions, and social practices of speaking, conceiving, perceiving, and remembering by those who have nurtured and trained us in an effort to reproduce in us their social and cultural world.

The British empiricists in the seventeenth and eighteenth centuries saw difficulties in Descartes" theory of innate ideas, but they too were unable to anticipate Hegel's insight into the social and historical character of all concepts. Whereas Descartes accented individual doubts and rational answers to those doubts, the British empiricists accented the sensory experiences of individuals. They bought into the widespread modernist appeal to atomistic individualism. Borrowed from the new physics, this idea was used to challenge the medieval Church's claims to authority over cognition and culture and the claims of the kings of the new nation-states to political authority over its citizens. It was used to legitimate the emerging economic forms of private property ownership and capitalist relations of production. Empiricists used it in their theories of knowledge. Ideas, they claimed, must originate from the sensory states of individual persons, separate atomic substances. Thus, Locke (1632-1704) introduced his epistemological question begging claims that such sensory states are incorrigible impressions caused by collections of atoms and that ideas originate out of such impressions. (Later we will want to acknowledge that the realm of the sensory is other than the realm of ideas and concepts, but this is because it is other than the cognitive and social and not because it is the origin of ideas or an ultimate, incorrigible foundation for human knowledge.)[6]

Descartes's rejection of the Aristotelianism of the medieval world in the area of epistemology was not extended by him to a rejection of the Aristotelian project of seeking to supply ultimate metaphysical explanations of why everything is as it is and not otherwise. The primacy of doubting over believing replaced the Aristotelian doctrine of the presentation of the forms of sensible substances to passive minds, but the Aristotelian principle of sufficient reason was not doubted. This principle says that there is a reason why everything is as it is and not otherwise. Thus, the Aristotelian project of explanatory metaphysics was continued as modern metaphysical rationalists sought to give explanations, in terms of unquestionable necessities, for the physical necessities that the laws of the new physics represented, physical laws and necessities that we can conceive of as being different and that therefore, according to the rationalists, need a superscientific explanation, a metaphysical explanation. The principle of sufficient reason requires that there be a reason why any contingent matter of fact is as it is and not otherwise. Spinoza (1632-1677) even demands that ultimate possibilities, claimed by him to be free of all contingent social and historical preconditions,[7] require a reason why, if they are mere possibilities, they are merely possible and not actual. Since it is not possible to supply a reason why the reason for all possibilities and actualities does not or even might not exist, this reason's existence is necessarily necessary. Thus, Spinoza returns this form of the ontological argument for the existence of an ultimate being (Substance, God, the ultimate Idea and Logos of Being) to the modernist project of explanatory metaphysics.[8] When Newton had declared that in the world of physical necessities motion is as natural as rest (the Law of Inertia), the project of Aristotle and his medieval followers of using a cosmological argument to prove the need for an unchanging cause of motion seemed to become outdated. (Just as rest for Aristotle needed no explanation, so now motion needs no explanation. Only acceleration and deacceleration need explanations, and the laws of physics give these.) Modern metaphysicians such as Descartes, Spinoza, Leibniz (1646–1716), Hegel, Whitehead[9] (1861–1947), and Hartshorne[10] offer the ontological argument and the principle of sufficient reason as the primary justifications for their ultimate explanations.

Kant attempted to separate Descartes" epistemological project of giving ultimate justifications for beliefs from the metaphysical project of giving ultimate explanations for possibilities and actualities being as they are. He brands as dogmatically unknowable Spinoza's initial metaphysical assumption that possibilities are the potentialities of Substance (God) which are actual unless there is a cause (reason) in God for their nonactualization.[11] In Kant's interpretation of things, only three kinds of modalities (necessities and possibilities) exist:[12] (1) Physical necessities and possibilities as identified by the laws of nature discoverable by science. (2) Necessarily false and necessarily true analytic judgments (contradictory judgments and judgments whose negations are contradictory) whose truth conditions are internal to the judgment and do not depend, as do synthetic judgments, upon any external contingent matters of fact. Because their truth conditions are internal, knowledge of the truth of analytic judgments can be a priori, that is, they need not be justified by any appeal to perceptual judgments.[13] (3) Synthetic a priori judgments that are either necessarily (undeniably) true, because the conditions necessary for their existence as judgments include their own truth conditions, or necessarily (undeniably) false because their existence conditions exclude their truth conditions. Reflection and argumentation about what must be the case if such judgments are to exist provides the justification needed for them to constitute knowledge. Not needed for synthetic a priori judgments are sensory perceptions of how things are; such perceptions are useless here because they could not show the necessity, the undeniableness, of synthetic a priori judgments. To do that one must show that any attempt to deny such judgments would be pragmatically self-defeating because such denials can exist only if they are false; their existence conditions exclude their truth conditions.[14]

Since synthetic a priori judgments about how things are, Kant claims, only specify the undeniable preconditions of our judgments, they only specify how the world generally must appear to us in order to be able to make such judgments. It is possible that things really are as they must be in order to appear to us, but it is also possible that they only appear that way to us because of the demands made by any and all acts of judging. We can never know. We only know that this is how they appear to us.[15] Making claims about how things are or must be, independent of how they must be for us, is, according to Kant, making unjustifiable dogmatic claims.

All the ultimate claims in any explanatory metaphysical system seeking to satisfy the requirements of the metaphysical principle of sufficient reason are dogmatic in this manner. The metaphysician cannot be satisfied with any explanation that utilizes only contingent laws of nature because one can always ask why such laws are as they are. Even the undeniable character of nature and morality, how they must be in order for us to think of them, cannot meet the explanatory needs of the principle of sufficient reason because we and the formal demands we place upon a knowable nature and morality are contingent. Explanatory metaphysics requires first principles that are so necessary that they could not be otherwise and yet which, unlike analytic a priori judgments, are material descriptions or prescriptions that allow contingent judgments to be deduced from them so that contingent matters of fact can be explained or justified. Different metaphysicians keep offering different first principles because their choice of first principles has to remain unjustifiably dogmatic.

Kant attempts to limit the ideas present in cognition that do not originate out of historical conditions to the few which he believed represented the synthetically a priori undeniable preconditions categorically required if it is to be possible to distinguish true and justifiable judgments from false and unjustified judgments about how things are or about what we categorically are mandated to do.[16] He also attempts to give an account of the origination of these categorical ideas that could both meet the objections of the British empiricists to innate ideas and silence the doubts of Descartes and Hume about the reliability of perception, memory, and science's purported knowledge of causal relations between physical objects. Categorical ideas, Kant claims, originate with thinking, knowing, and reasoning themselves. They undeniably represent the form of all the conceiving involved in all possible human knowledge of what is the case or ought to be the case. Perception and memory, according to Kant, must be reliable (although not incorrigible) because knowledge of perceptual and memory errors presupposes such reliability.[17] Universal causality between physical events, he asserts, is necessary if perception of the motion of physical objects continuing to exist through time is to be distinguished from fleeting impressions of possibly different objects and distinguished from mere figments of one's imagination.[18]

Kant's claim, that the synthetic a priori categorical requirements represented by these few categorical ideas are universally and timelessly necessary, depends upon his assumption that the thinking, knowing, and reasoning he is talking about are themselves universal and unchanging. This is the first key Kantian assumption that Hegel rejects. For Hegel, most ways of conceiving of things, thinking about things, reasoning about things are practices specific to a particular social/cultural world as it is constituted during a specific historical epoch. Likewise, our ways of reasoning about what we ought to do are historically situated. We reason as parents, husbands, wives, neighbors, and citizens whose very identities and duties are a matter of our locations in historical communities. No purported categorical requirements of a supposedly pure (asocial, ahistorical) practical reason would give us the concrete duties constitutive of our social identities in historically changing social/cultural worlds. From Hegel's point of view, Kant's second Copernican revolution had been aborted too soon. Kant had agreed with the Romanticists that knowing is not passive reception of presentations but did involve active conceptualization in addition to undergoing the sensory causal effects of what is conceptualized.[19] Kant rejected the Romanticists" claim, however, that all such conceptualization is a matter of participating in social practices that are not globally uniform and which do historically change. For Kant, keeping the categories of empirical knowledge and the categorical imperative of morality free from social variation or historical change is necessary to preserve the distinctions between the true and the false, the justified and the unjustified, the morally mandated and the prudentially preferred. In Hegel's interpretation of things, however, no such necessity exists. The social and historical can provide all the truth, justification, and morality needed.

In addition to socially and historically situating Kant's categories, Hegel argues for the need to make two other major changes in the Kantian position. First, he rejects the Kantian project inherited from Descartes of making the search for a foundation for human knowledge the first order of business for philosophers. Kant thought it a scandal that philosophers had not yet established such a foundational silencing of the philosophical skeptic.[20] Hegel problematizes the skepticism motivating this prioritizing of the problem of knowledge by questioning whether Descartes" and Kant's fear of error isn't the error itself.[21] Why should we ever assume that it is easier to have knowledge about our knowledge, knowledge about the nature of judgments, truth, and justification, than it is to have knowledge about physical objects right in front of us or about things we saw a few moments ago? Human practices of conceiving, judging, justifying, and explaining, Hegel claims, must be located in a whole set of interdependent, historically changing social, linguistic, cultural, political, and economic practices that need to be interpreted in order to be understood. The same is true of the identities and natures of all knowable particulars. They all are socially constituted and possess only functional identities in such social and historical worlds.

Second, Hegel rejects as unintelligible Kant's claim that it is possible that we could have complete understanding of how things must and do appear to us and yet that these things really might be very different from this appearance. There is no room in Kant's set of possibilities (physical, analytic, and synthetic a priori) for such a possibility and no room within the limits drawn by Kant around possible human knowledge for Kant's purported knowledge of such a possibility.[22] Once all of our questions are asked and answered, Hegel charges, there is no space left for us to wonder whether there is something else that has been left out—things as they are independent of how they appear to us.[23] Rather than Kant's project of rejecting explanatory metaphysics in favor of theory of knowledge, Hegel locates our understanding of our knowledge in a metaphysical system that incorporates an understanding of why everything ultimately is as it is and not otherwise. Although Hegel accents the social character of our ordinary rationality, he still is a modernist seeking ultimate explanations in terms of something asocial and ahistorical. For Hegel, metaphysics, not epistemology, takes priority. Human cognitive efforts must be socially and historically located and an explanation must be given why they are as they are and not otherwise. Previous metaphysicians, Hegel claims, have failed to provide explanatory understanding of the most crucial aspects of human thinking, knowing, living, and self-identity, the social and historical character of what we are and what we do. Hegel acknowledges the thoroughly social and historical character of human life and yet still attempts to carry out the classical project of explanatory metaphysics. This is why many postmodern thinkers, who also emphasize the social and historical, see Hegel's philosophical system as the final culmination of the whole Western ancient, medieval, and modern intellectual tradition, a tradition they reject.[24] Recent modernist thinkers, however, who still believe in asocial and ahistorical meanings, representations, truth, justification conditions, and moral principles find nothing in

Hegel because they reject his social account of reasoning and his metaphysical explanatory system. For them, thinkers are to jump from the rationalists, empiricists, and Kant to twentieth-century efforts to analyze asocial and ahistorical meanings.

For Hegel, however, to understand human life one must understand its social character and its historical development. To gain a metaphysical understanding of why everything is as it is and not otherwise, one must recognize that there is a law governing the evolution of social history which guarantees that such understanding will be attained. Human history, as interpreted by Hegel, is primarily intellectual history with all historical processes being driven by the human passion to understand why everything is as it is and not otherwise. All social, cultural, political, and economic practices are as they are at any historical moment because of the way people understand things at that moment. This passion to understand is at the same time a passion to be free *from* any and all alienation from the social and historical world, of which we are functional parts, and *from* the world of nature as socially constituted by us. In all historical periods prior to the gaining of complete understanding and freedom from alienation, our attempts to live with understanding and free from alienation fail. Our interpretation and understanding of our world and ourselves as people located within it at a given historical moment (the thesis of our lived understanding of things at that moment) is in conflict with the necessary preconditions of such lived understanding (the antithesis of that mode of interpretation and understanding which shows it to be a flawed form of misunderstanding). This conflict is experienced as alienation from aspects of ourselves, from aspects of our social world. The passion to understand and end alienation drives us to overcome this conflict, this alienation, by finding a synthesis (a new thesis, a new form of living understanding) that does not presuppose any conflicting antithesis and that enables us to understand why everything is as it is and not otherwise. Final and total living understanding is possible, Hegel claims, only if human life is thoroughly social and historical and if history is driven toward the gaining of such understanding.

Much of European thinking since Hegel and much of American pragmatism consists of various interpretations of the human social and historical world once Hegel's metaphysically necessary law of historical evolution is dropped. Twentieth-century modernist thinkers reject both Hegel's metaphysical explanations and his accent on the social and historical character of rationality. They excommunicated him from the philosophical canon of texts worth reading. Since postmodernists endorse Hegel's accent on the social and historical, many modernists would like to excommunicate them also.

Positivism, in the nineteenth-century form given it by Comte and Mach and in the twentieth-century form of logical positivism given it by Moritz Schlick and Rudolf Carnap,[25] shares Hegel's questioning of Kant's approach to the problem of knowledge. For all of them there is no doubt that modern science, especially modern physics, consists in knowledge. That was more assured than anything that philosophical arguments could ever prove. Anything that ever was to be called "knowledge" had to bear an essential resemblance to the scientific knowledge contained in physics. Physics" language and statements had to be grounded in sensory observations and empirical testing and verification. Some positivists (Mach, Schlick) still spoke the language of the British empiricists and talked about meaningful language and knowledge in physics being grounded in "direct," noninferential awareness of "sense data," but it was clear that philosophical failure to work out such a grounding was no reason for doubting that physics consisted in knowledge and was the paradigm of all knowing. Thus, logical positivists in the mid-twentieth century constructed ever new formulations of the verification principle of cognitive meaning, whenever philosophical objections to previous formulations seemed unanswerable, without finding such needs to shift any reason for doubting physics. Carnap seems to reveal best the ultimate commitments of the positivists when he drops all the sense data talk of the phenomenalists and utilizes the physical descriptions of physics as the protocol sentences to be used in asserting the evidence claims backing up physical theories. Most positivists accept without question a correspondence theory of truth, with truth being a semantical relation holding between sentences and "empirical" facts, although some phenomenalists offer operational definitions of theoretical terms in physical theories. All positivists accept Kant's category of the analytic–a priori (contradictions and negations of contradictions). They locate logic and mathematics there. They reject, however, Kant's category of the synthetic–a priori (seeing even the most general principles of physics as not being undeniable).

Physics, however, for Hegel and for those postmodernists developing nonmetaphysical interpretations of the social and historical, is just one more human enterprise that needs to be situated in a social and historical context. This is why postmodernists have so much sympathy with the project of Thomas Kuhn[26] and his reminder that science is done by scientists and that its theoretical products cannot be divorced from the human social and historical practices that have produced them. Therefore, postmodernists claim that it is not the positivist's sentences in physics texts, abstracted as they are from the historically changing social worlds of their production and use, that are to serve as the models of human knowledge. Knowledge is always a matter of socially constituted understanding, an understanding that can be understood only when it is interpretively located in a specific historical and social world. Locating mathematics and logic there will be one of the most challenging tasks facing the postmodernists who interpret rationality as social all the way down.

Hegel's metaphysics and positivism's interpretation of physics and human knowledge therefore are seen by many postmodern thinkers as the only two major alternatives to their interpretation of the social and historical character of all human speaking, thinking, and reasoning. Many modernists see this as a very forced set of choices. They see Hegel as an "absolute idealist" who can be ignored once his metaphysically determined law of history is rejected. Many modernists see positivism trapped in its shifting versions of the verification principle, in its failure to provide a foundation for physics, and its attempt to reduce all cognitive claims (especially moral claims) to the descriptions or theoretical claims in physics. The commitment by modernists to asocial, ahistorical meanings and modalities provides them with their projects of analyzing meanings and their rationale for rejecting what they see as the relativism and irrationality of those claiming that all human rationality is socially and historically situated. In order to do a better job of critically interpreting the basis of such charges of relativism and irrationality, it will be helpful to examine existentialist challenges to Hegel's metaphysics and pragmatist challenges to the Cartesian and Kantian epistemological projects. Existentialists and pragmatists reject Hegel's metaphysical system, but they also attempt to take most seriously Hegel's interpretation of the social and historical character of rationality. As a result, they in particular have been branded as relativistic and irrational.

II. EARLY POSTMODERN CRITICISMS OF MODERNISM

A. KIERKEGAARD'S AND NIETZSCHE'S EXISTENTIAL REJECTIONS OF METAPHYSICAL EXPLANATIONS

Kierkegaard and Nietzsche charge that Hegel's project is uncompleted and uncompletable.[27] What supposedly takes Hegel beyond the modern rationalists is his attempt to include the historical and social in an explanatory metaphysical system. This, Kierkegaard claims, is what Hegel has not done and cannot do. His system cannot provide understanding either of historical agency, the social character of human thought and rationality, or this system's effort to seek such understanding. It can only reductively attempt to explain them away. Nietzsche points out similarly that this is all that Hegel can do with the inexplicable necessities and chanciness so much at the center of human living that it drives people into nihilism and nihilistic attempts like Hegel's to deny such life itself. Furthermore, both Kierkegaard and Nietzsche charge that by failing to understand the historical agency involved in interpersonal relationships, Hegel is unable to understand that social rationality is not autonomous but that it rests on such historical agency. By challenging Hegel's ability to include the historical, the social, and the human character of life in his system, Kierkegaard and Nietzsche, like Kant and the positivists, challenge the whole project of explanatory metaphysics.[28]

As Kierkegaard interprets Hegel's system, in Hegel's final understanding of things, historical agents become mere social functionaries. Furthermore, social practices and institutions are not constituted, sustained and reconstituted by agents but are just metaphysically necessary momentary developments of an evolutionary process of changes in human contemplative understanding and thus in human subjectivity and life. People are not even mere social functionaries; they really are social robots, metaphysical robots behaving, like everything else, in accordance with one master metaphysically necessary program.

Hegel claims that history's driving force is our passion to understand and be free from alienation, but in his final interpretation of things this passion is only an epiphenomenon of the necessary underlying development of things, and alienation is never present or possible. In Hegel's system, a sense of alienation is always an effect of failing to understand that we always already are perfectly integrated functionaries in an evolutionary process governed by the iron hand of metaphysical necessity, with even failures to understand being nothing but necessary moments in this evolutionary process moving on to a full understanding of the nature, necessity, and final result of this process.

As Kierkegaard interprets the human situation, passion has to be at the heart of the human effort to become an individual person who is more than a mere social conformist, but it is the passion of a historical agent's commitments and not just a passion to *gain,* as a spectator of all times and places, a total understanding of things. The social and cultural practices into which we are initiated through nurturing and training are not sufficient to finalize what any social individual will be like. They are too general and they are conflictual. The great insight present in Hegel's thesis-antithesis characterization of social and cultural life is the affirmation of the conflictual character of our social inheritance. Only a personal existential commitment to one or another of the possible ways of life left open by our inheritance will give us an individual identity. Furthermore, constitutive social practices continue to present historical options only if they are continuously re-endorsed by historical agents participating in them even though they might refuse to do so.

Kierkegaard charges that not only does Hegel's reduction of historical agency to metaphysically preprogramed behavior fail to take him beyond the metaphysics of the modern rationalists, supposedly by finding a place for history in metaphysics, but his metaphysical interpretation of things makes it impossible to do justice to Hegel's own claims about the social and historical character of all interpreting and understanding. In Hegel's system, only interpretations containing conflicting elements, only partial misunderstandings, remain socially and historically located. Only people who have inadequate interpretations and alienating ways of trying to understand things are social and historical. Hegel's own interpretation, were it a thesis without a presupposed antithesis, would be an asocial and ahistorical one that was adequate for understanding things in all social situations and at all historical moments. The person holding such an interpretation and "living" with such understanding would have escaped the finite limitations on the subjectivity (concepts, beliefs, desires, feelings) of people in any and all social situations and historical moments. Such a person would live as an infinite and eternal contemplator of the necessary evolutionary movement toward people's liberation from all social and historical limitations. This, for Kierkegaard, is not a matter of including the historical in the metaphysical but rather it is a matter of reducing the social and historical playing field of life to merely partial and temporary appearances of the asocial and ahistorical which is, according to Hegel's system, what things really and ultimately are like. Hegel has not really overcome Kant's dualism of appearances and things in themselves because it is not socially and historically situated human understanding that overcomes this dualism by being completed. Hegel's complete metaphysical understanding is no longer social and historical, no longer human. It has become universal, timeless, and necessarily necessary. It has become the divine understanding of a God understanding itself. Hegel's project is one more explanatory metaphysical effort by finite men to deny their finitude and affirm that they are God.

Hegel has not escaped Kant's charge that all explanatory metaphysical systems are dogmatic, the presentation of an explanatory hypothesis that is not contingent like the widest laws of the physical sciences but which supposedly is undeniable and therefore necessary. Kant uses arguments in an effort to prove the undeniable character of the categorical form of nature and moral imperatives. Hegel charges that Kant's categories are contingent and not undeniable because they presuppose their own social and historical character, a presupposition not accounted for by Kant's categories. Hegel attempts to transform Kant's project of using arguments to prove the formal character of nature and morality into his own project of using a dialectical logic to prove that only one thesis of understanding every actuality and possibility does not presuppose conflicting antithetical precon-ditions. Kierkegaard charges that Hegel, and every other explanatory metaphysical system, make a deniable and unjustifiable assumption that makes them dogmatic. They assume that the metaphysician is at one with the truth.[29]

This assumption really consists of two unjustified and unjustifiable assumptions. The first assumption is that there is something called "the truth," one and only one way of explaining and understanding things and one vocabulary to use in giving such explanations. The second assumption is that there is a neutral, independent, autonomous, and interest-free human way of conceiving and understanding things, and that loyalty to this mode of rationality and its requirements will yield understanding of "the truth." Kierkegaard challenges both assumptions. He points out that Plato in *The Meno* had already recognized the need for the metaphysician to assume that people have within themselves the capacity to know "the truth,"[30] if they remain loyal to their own rationality rather than getting lost in the cave of irrational, desire-driven sensory shadows. If people on their own are to be able to know "the truth," then, when it comes to the final and ultimate tests of adequate conception and understanding, the ability to recognize "the truth" must always already lie within them.

Kierkegaard points out that it is possible to challenge this assumption. The Christian understands everything in terms of the saving incarnation of the infinite in the finite. Affirming such an incarnation makes sense only if rebellion against the truth has rendered people incapable of knowing the truth on their own. If people can gain saving knowledge all by themselves, there is no need for any incarnation. The truth of the infinite, Kierkegaard claims, must come to them and call them to abandon notions of self-sufficiency, to stand faithfully loyal to this call no matter how irrational this might seem when viewed through conceptions and ways of understanding that assume self-sufficiency and autonomy for human reason. Kierkegaard presents this challenge to Hegel and all explanatory metaphysicians through the voice of John the Climber, a non-Christian, in order to make clear that it is the mere possibility of a Christian understanding of things that shows the dogmatic character of the whole project of explanatory metaphysics. Just like Christianity's use of its conceptions and way of understanding things, so the metaphysician's system is affirmed only as an act of faith. Metaphysicians, however, have blinded themselves to the contingent character of their own mode of subjectivity (concepts, beliefs, desires, and lines of reasoning) and to their unexamined loyalties.

Explanatory metaphysics and positivistic scientism, Kierkegaard claims, share an objectivistic mode of subjectivity that focuses on objects and seeks for "objective" beliefs about such objects, objective in the sense of having erased all influence from variable social and cultural practices and personal commitments. In an objectivistic way of living, all attention is focused on the objects of one's thoughts and beliefs, what they are like independent of their relation to socially constituted individuals and their variable contributions to such thoughts and beliefs. Kierkegaard writes, "Objectively we consider only the matter at issue."[31] "If only the object to which he is related is truth, the subject is accounted to be in the truth."[32] "The objective accent falls on what is said…"[33] Objectively the interest is focussed merely on the thought content…"[34] Trying to focus only on the "objective" character of objects, however, Kierkegaard claims, is itself not an interest-free, impartial, neutral way of approaching things, a neutral mode of subjectivity. All ways of focusing are specific modes of subjectivity to which there are alternatives. Johannes Climacus interprets the effort to be primarily an objective observer erased of all variable subjectivity, particularly the metaphysical effort to be an observer from an eternal point of view, as a matter of striving to abandon one's inescapable finiteness, a tactic for fleeing from our mere finiteness, a tactic that always fails. He charges that we can leap like a dancer but we cannot fly emancipated from our finite, social, historical conditions.[35]

Even though it seems so to metaphysicians and positivists, all alternatives to the objectivistic mode of subjectivity are not unjustified. Rather than focusing on objects, one might live in a mode of subjectivity that focuses on various ways of focusing, that focuses on alternative modes of subjectivity. Kierkegaard calls this a subjective mode of subjectivity, a subjectivistic mode of life focused on finding a way of living, conceiving, believing, desiring, hoping, feeling that works. Kierkegaard endorses the stance that only in such a subjectivistic mode of subjectivity will one find a truth to which one can be faithfully loyal and committed even after reflecting continuously on its implications for life. In the subjectivistic mode of subjectivity all attention is focused on the quality of one's mode of subjectivity, one's social rationality, one's way of living. "…subjectively we have regard to the subject and his subjectivity, and behold, precisely this subjectivity is the matter at issue…the subjective problem is not something about an objective issue, but is the subjectivity itself.[36] "When the question of truth is raised subjectively, reflection is directed to the nature of the individual's relationship; if only the mode of this relationship is in the truth, the individual is in truth…[37] Every person's most basic ethical task is to live in a mode of subjectivity in which one is able to give a living endorsement to one mode of subjectivity rather than another. In the objectivistic mode of subjectivity, one lives as though no choice between an objectivistic and a subjectivistic mode of life is necessary or possible. In the objectivistic way of living, one looks away from one's way of looking and focuses only on the objects of one's thoughts and perceptions. One dogmatically recognizes no alternative to the assumption that people are at one with the truth, and thus one has the ability all on one's own to know the truth about objects and about oneself, now viewed as just one more such object. One dogmatically makes a fetish of one contingent set of historically constituted social practices of conception, perception, interpretation, and understanding. One recognizes no alternatives and one turns oneself into a god.

In Hegel's system, faithfulness to the passion to understand things will automatically determine that an objectivistic mode of subjectivity will be endorsed because it is this passion that drives one to find a final thesis that will synthesize the partial understanding in earlier modes of subjectivity, earlier theses, and their conflicting antitheses. Kierkegaard charges that loyalty to the passion defining Hegel's objectivistic mode of subjectivity is only one possible loyalty of this type. An objectivistic synthesizing of inadequate earlier forms of objectivistic modes of subjectivity can be contrasted with a subjectivistic exploration of the living implications of "choosing" either an objectivistic mode of subjectivity (metaphysics or positivism) or a subjectivistic mode (the aesthetic, the moral, or the religious ways of life). The objectivistic mode of subjectivity cannot constitute total and complete understanding because it blinds itself to its own nature as only one among contending modes of subjectivity. Apart from considerations about the correctness or incorrectness of any claims made by any people in any particular mode of subjectivity is the need to understand the place of subjectivity itself in all understanding. "Subjectivity is truth, subjectivity is reality."[38] A contingent mode of social subjectivity, a historical way of life, is a necessary precondition for the existence of all true or false claims, for the conceptual differentiation of all characteristics, for the criteria of all objectivity, and for the socially constituted identity of all subjects and objects.[39] Every metaphysical system that attempts to give an explanatory reason why everything is as it is and not otherwise presupposes social and historical rationality and reasoners, and these sound the death knell for such metaphysical systems.

It is important to note that in giving his interpretation of the subjectivistic mode of subjectivity, Johannes Climacus is not treating modes of subjectivity as objects about which it is possible to have interest-free objectivistic knowledge. He is making from within a subjectivistic mode of subjectivity a set of general interpretive claims about modes of subjectivity. These claims are parts of a way of understanding the character of such ways of life. They are interest-driven. The general claims being made presuppose an agent pointing out these characteristics. The historical act of pointing can no more be included in what is pointed out than a point of vision can be included in its field of vision.[40] These general claims also presuppose a background of practices and skills that cannot be completely delimited and thus which are not totally representable.[41] For the same reason, what these claims are about cannot be delimited objects about which one can have "objective" knowledge. Finally, it is vital to note that making this general claim that all claims, including one's own, are part of a non-interest-free understanding or interpretation of things is not claiming that the truth of a claim is relative to the mode of subjectivity of the one making the claim. That would be to give an objectivistic interpretation of them. To claim that a claim is true is to endorse the claim, something Johannes Climacus would not do with the totalizing or scientistic claims of objectivistic metaphysicians or positivists.

It is Nietzsche who points out that Hegel's project of seeking total understanding falls victim to its inability to account for, and thus its need to reductively eliminate, its most fundamental precondition—human life as humans inescapably find it. Hegel's passion for total understanding, all too common among humans, runs head on into the human passionate need to live with conditions and events that are uncontrollable, that are found to be inexplicable, beyond all possible human understanding. A mother's son is discovered to have leukemia and she cries out in despair, "Why my son?" even as he cries out "Why me?" Scientific explanations in terms of biochemical necessities only intensify their anguish and in no way respond to their cry. Such explanations tell us only "how things are." Why, however, has this mother and this son been caught in the sights of nature's deadly crossfire? Why does the apparently unanswerable character of this question make it seem as though questioning is the wrong sort of response to make to such encounters with natural necessities? A father is walking down the street with his son who is delighted with his new balloon. The balloon breaks loose. The boy chases it out between parked cars and is crushed by an oncoming truck. The father cries out, "Why?" Why this stupid accident? Again, explanations in terms of strengths of strings, wind drafts, momentum of trucks, and resistance potential of children's bodies offers no understanding to those whose lives are filled with pain by the chanciness of life.

As Nietzsche interprets human life, it is a cruel joke to attempt to make sense of such losses by supposedly showing, in a Hegelian manner, how they are necessary moments in the rational evolutionary development of some ultimate reality. Only by leaving such losses inexplicable, beyond understanding, only by ceasing to try to explain away these most important events in their lives can one avoid insulting the people involved. When Nietzsche rejects all ultimate metaphysical explanations by affirming that there is no reason behind the stars,[42] no ultimate purpose to things in the universe, no spiderweb of reason, but over everything there is the heaven of chance,[43] he is not denying that there is the kind of physical necessity characterized by general claims in science about how things regularly occur. It is just the uncontrollable explosion of such necessities into human lives of planning, hoping, and wanting that makes life so chancy. Nietzsche may have rejected metaphysical accounts of causality as one of the four "great errors"[44] and he may have rejected talk of "natural laws" as outdated metaphysical theology,[45] but he did not reject natural regularities. These he called recurring tunes that never should be anthropomorphized as melodies.[46] When Nietzsche denies that there is ultimate metaphysical meaning and significance to the natural necessities and chanciness of human life, he is not denying that human life has significance. He was simply affirming that this significance consists only in human beings socially and personally finding things significant; he was inviting people to see as beautiful, to make beautiful, even the necessities and chanciness of life,[47] beautiful enough so that you would be willing to will their eternal return.[48]

If we endorse Nietzsche's interpretation of the efforts of metaphysicians, we shouldn't be surprised that he has become labeled by modernists as a nihilist even though he interprets his project as a matter of resisting what he saw as the nihilistic efforts of metaphysicians (including metaphysical theologians and moralists) to find in the eternal the significance that they found lacking in human life, given its uncontrollable chanciness. Again and again Nietzsche proclaimed that he is a life-affirmer and not a life-denier. It is life with all its uncontrollable necessities and chances, with all its inexplicabilities that he wishes to affirm. For Nietzsche it is the metaphysicians, like Hegel, who are the life-deniers. Labeling Nietzsche as a nihilist is just one more instance of life-denying metaphysicians attempting to maintain dominating control over all life-affirming resistors to such domination.

As Nietzsche interprets things, Hegel fails at two different levels to see that, for us human beings, life is more than gaining complete and total knowledge and understanding. First, there is our encounter with nature, our confrontation with natural necessities and the chanciness they throw in our efforts to control our lives, our confrontation with the contingent way things just are, a way that passes beyond human understanding. Seeking a metaphysically total understanding is simply refusing to let life be as it is. It is a willful effort to tell a lie supposedly to provide comfort to those too weak to affirm a life filled with inexplicable suffering and with failures at matching socially traditional virtues and vices with personal happiness and misery. As Nietzsche diagnoses his current age, Hegel's proclamation, that at last mankind has available in Hegel's metaphysical system the total understanding and comfort people seek, is belied by the fact that thinking people are falling into a madness of nihilistic despair, crying out that God and all the ultimates of explanatory metaphysics are dead.[49] The metaphysician's willful effort, when successful in acquiring believers in the lie, gives dominating power over others to the life-denying high priests of total understanding who also are fearful of life. It sometimes even gives them power over some potential life-affirmers who get duped by the big lie. It is especially the courageous people who can affirm life, with their eyes wide open to its chanciness, who are resented by the fearful life-deniers who in turn react with renewed efforts to get them to buy the big lie or, failing that, to minimize their power by marginalizing them as irrational and dangerous deviants. The power of the priests of ultimate explanations and justifications is threatened by those who can affirm life while accepting its inexplicables and the merely human, merely social and historical character, of all human understanding and interpretation.

This leads us to Nietzsche's interpretation of Hegel's second failure to understand human life. Hegel fails to see that social practices, conventions, customs, and institutions are historically established and continued because of people's efforts to exercise power over each other. In interpreting human understanding as the key to the evolutionary development of everything that exists, Hegel fails to see that locating the passion to seek total understanding at the center of human living covers up the primary relationship between people, which is the exercise of power, people getting other people to do things. History, Nietzsche tells us, is not primarily social intellectual history, as Hegel would have us believe. History is primarily a power struggle between historical agents. The metaphysical passion to gain total understanding, and the epistemologist's and moral theorist's passion to find ultimate justifications for beliefs, actions, and social institutions, are not just the result of innocent philosophical curiosity. They are part of an effort to control people. The will to metaphysical truth and knowledge is part of a power move.[50] Only by blinding themselves and others to their own efforts to secure power, by presenting a metaphysical interpretation that feeds off of people's fears and hatred of life and their resentment of life-affirmers, can Hegel and other metaphysicians, epistemologists, and moral theorists believe that their ultimate systems give a total account of things that is free of all contingent historical and social preconditions.

Neither Kierkegaard nor Nietzsche deny Hegel's great insight into the historical and social character of all human rationality. Both, however, believe that Hegel the metaphysician is unable to appreciate the character of his own insight. Loyalty to the metaphysical use of the principle of sufficient reason prevents Hegel from applying his insight to his own conceptions, explanations, and justifications. Kierkegaard and Nietzsche see all human conception, perception, explanation, and justification, including their own, as elements in a historically and socially situated way of interpreting and understanding things. As we shall examine in detail in chapter 3, both Kierkegaard and Nietzsche want to present a critique so radical that it would make social rationality itself problematic. Kierkegaard does this by responding to a call from something totally other than social rationality and socially constituted finite beings. Nietzsche does it by affirming life and historical exercises of power. This, however, is not interpreted by them as requiring any abandonment of their interpretation that rationality is thoroughly historical and social. Their interpretations, they claim, can be contested by alternative interpretations similarly situated. Attempts, however, to judge their interpretations from some ultimate and absolute representation of things are attempts to make a power move that would take the modernist out of the contest so that control over all other contestants would be guaranteed. The great delusion of the modernist is that such control is possible and desirable.

B.   CLASSICAL PRAGMATISM'S REJECTION OF MODERNIST
       THEORIES OF KNOWLEDGE

Hegel challenges the prioritization of epistemological issues that had dominated philosophical concerns from Descartes to Kant. He points out that knowing could be understood only if it were placed in a wider context of understanding the historical and social character of human cognition. In the nineteenth century, however, the thrust of Hegel's challenge to epistemology temporarily dropped out of sight as attention focused on criticizing his metaphysical system in which human knowing is located in the necessary evolutionary development of the history of Being. The positivists also challenged the prioritization of the epistemological project by giving priority to actual scientific knowledge (especially in physics) over any philosophical theory of knowledge, although many positivists still continued the practice of seeking a "firm foundation" for their unquestioned faith in science. The force of the positivist's challenge was greatly diminished by two factors. First, there is their failure (with the exception of Pierre Duhem, who retained much of Hegel's theoretical holism) to consider the historical and social status of science itself.[51] Second, there is in positivism a kind of "physics-imperialism" that requires all knowledge claims to be of the same general type as the claims they see in physics at the pain of being marginalized as mere expressions of emotion and feeling. The imperial demand that claims in biology, the social sciences, history, law, ethics, aesthetics, and religion fall into line with one particular interpretation of physics led to the marginalization of positivism itself. It remained therefore for the American pragmatists to make the most radical challenge to the modern epistemological project.

Charles Sanders Peirce and John Dewey challenge Descartes's initial beginning point, the prioritization of doubt over belief. They claim that doubting is parasitic on believing.[52] In his essay, "The Fixation of Belief,"[53] Peirce, influenced by Darwin, points out that in order to survive as animal organisms, we form habitual ways of behaving. On the basis of our sensory encounters with our environment, we conceptualize the world in a certain way and form a set of beliefs about the world, a set of dispositions to behave in certain ways when having sensory encounters and to expect things to behave in certain ways if we act in certain ways. When our behavioral dispositions, our beliefs, conflict, then doubt arises and we confront a need to resolve the conflict and fix on a revised set of beliefs in order to continue to act. Inquiring about what to believe begins in actual situations of conflicting beliefs; inquiry achieves its goal when the conflict is ended and action again is possible.

Dewey socializes Peirce's individualistic narrative about doubt and inquiry.[54] For Dewey's Hegelianism without Hegel's explanatory metaphysics, individual doubts become originating points for inquiry only when the general social and cultural setting contains conflicting elements that render the situation problematic. Dewey maintains that individuals may have doubts due to any number of idiosyncratic causes even though there really is no reason to have such doubts because nothing is problematic in the situation. Not understanding their own beliefs, they may sense a conflict among their beliefs when there really isn't any. (For example, some people, being pathological, may think that no one cares about them even though many people may care deeply.) Furthermore, being unaware of conflicting elements in one's social and cultural situation, one may unquestioningly believe something even though reasons exist for doubting. For Dewey, a situation is problematic when there are believed-in reasons existing in the social setting at that historical moment that conflict with each other. Inquiry is an effort to make unproblematic such problematic situations.

The thrust of the pragmatic positions of Peirce and Dewey, as opposed to the positions of Descartes and the users of a decontextualized epistemological version of the principle of sufficient reason, is that we need corrigible reasons (beliefs) for our doubts and not some indubitable foundation reason for our corrigible beliefs. For the pragmatist, all of our beliefs are corrigible. For each of our beliefs, there might come a time when we will believe that what we had believed needs to be doubted, revised, or dropped. Until we have specific reasons (corrigible beliefs) for doubting them, however, we have no reason for not doing what we will do, continuing to believe them, and acting upon them. The later Wittgenstein shows his kinship to the social pragmatism of John Dewey when he asks, "Doesn't one need grounds for doubt?" and then points out that "...giving grounds... (comes) to an end sometimes. But the end is not an ungrounded presupposition: it is an ungrounded way of acting."[55] "We could doubt every single one of these facts, but we could not doubt them all.... Our not doubting them all is simply our manner of judging, and therefore of acting."[56] "Doubting and non-doubting behavior. There is the first only if there is the second."[57]

Even Descartes's attempt to engage in a program of universal doubt[58] shows the primacy of believing over doubting. Descartes recommends his program because he believes that it is better not to believe any sort of belief (such as our sensory perceptual beliefs) about which it had been shown that we have been in error. Not only is this belief about preferable beliefs a belief needed to get the doubting project going, but some of Descartes" perceptual beliefs could have been shown to him to be in error only if he were relying upon other perceptual beliefs. As Kant claims, only if we take our perceptual and memory beliefs as reliable is it possible for us to come to believe with reason that some of our beliefs in these two areas are incorrect. When our beliefs in these areas conflict, we try to get more beliefs to settle the conflict (look again, look more closely, get better light, get glasses, touch it, try to remember what else was happening, ask others what they saw or remember).

Only beliefs, for which there are reasons to doubt, need to be justified. Adequate justification is supplied when one finds better reasons for continuing to believe than for continuing to doubt or for changing the belief. *Beliefs can be not unjustified without having been justified.* This is why one need never begin the pursuit of the impossible goal of seeking ultimate justifications for all corrigible beliefs. Only in certain circumstances do the questions arise of whether or how we know what we believe. As Wittgenstein put it, "If someone believes something, we needn't always be able to answer the question "why he believes it'; but if he knows something, then the question "how does he know?" must be capable of being answered."[59] Claiming that one knows that something is so and so is appraising one's beliefs; such appraisals have as contextual preconditions a problematic situation, a conflict of specific beliefs or supposals.

Justification and knowledge claims always have to be pragmatically indexed to the person making the claim, the social and cultural world in which the claim is made, and the time when the claim is made. I can justifiably claim that people once were justified or not unjustified in believing something that now we are not justified in believing. Unproblematic beliefs can become problematic when reasons for doubting them become available. Justification talk, therefore, applies primarily to people and actions and gets extended to what people believe only because beliefs are the products of processes of coming to believe or continuing to believe for which, to some extent, people can be held responsible. Attempts to apply justification talk to the contents of beliefs as such are attempts to erase the dynamic pragmatic preconditions of the practice of requesting and offering justifications. That knowledge claims also have to be indexed is a consequence of claims to know being more than mere guesses about what to believe in problematic situations. They need to be backed up with justifications.

Knowledge claims also involve claiming, in the face of counter-claims or supposals, that what one justifiably believes is correct, is true. Although using "is true" also needs contextual indexing, it does not function, as we shall see, just like "is justified." I can claim that we are unjustified in believing that which people once were justified in believing; I cannot claim, however, that what they believed was true or known by them because then I would be giving a positive appraisal or commendation for what they believed, something I would not do if I now believed we are unjustified in believing this. However, since "is true" and "is justified" have work to do only in certain conflictual or problematic situations, many of our beliefs and claims need not be subjected to appraisal, need not be claimed to be true, justified, or known. Cartesian universal skepticism is the necessary precondition for the whole epistemic project of attempting to divide any and all beliefs into binary oppositions (true and false, justified and unjustified, known and not known). It is just this project that Pragmatism rejects by rejecting the primacy of doubting.

The pragmatic contextualization of doubting and using the principle of sufficient reason in justifying believing is part of a larger project of contextualizing the use of all of our epistemic words ("justify," "explain," "understand," "interpret," "true'". Requests for explanations also have a point only when certain contextual preconditions are satisfied. When things are or happen as they are expected to be or happen, we don't ask "Why are they so?" It is when our belief about how things are is in conflict with our general background expectations that the request for an explanation is in order. An adequate explanation has been given when the conflict between beliefs has been reconciled. This can be done in many ways. We stick with our general beliefs about how things are and explain away apparent discrepancies as perceptual or memory errors. We make massive changes in our general background beliefs. (Copernican astronomy replaces Ptolemaic astronomy.) We restrict the range of applicability of background beliefs. (Newtonian mechanics applies only to relatively big and slow objects; it is located within a larger, more extensive relativistic and field theory in physics.)

In this pragmatic interpretation of the practice of explaining, adequate physical explanations eventually end up with corrigible claims about how things contingently are and not with metaphysical claims about how things necessarily are. There are conditions that need no explanation, but they are not metaphysical necessities that could not be otherwise. They are the conditions of things and the events occurring that are unproblematic and not unexpected, given our background beliefs; they are the widest conditions and generalizations about how things are that are asserted in our currently accepted explanatory theories. Today's adequate explanations, of course, may have to be replaced tomorrow when we experience new surprises that we conclude it is best not to explain away. Science, in other words, needs no superscientific metaphysical explanations. Explanations of why things are as they are, when needed, end with corrigible, workable claims about how things generally, but contingently, are.

What holds for explanations in the physical sciences also holds for explanations of historical events and social phenomena, only now a whole new set of issues arises because of what is involved in understanding and interpreting human actions, practices, and texts. These issues will be discussed in greater detail in later chapters, but let me sketch out here how a pragmatic interpretation of understanding and interpretation can proceed.[60] Understanding is a matter of knowing how to do something; it is a matter of knowing how to use a word, ride a bike, play skillfully and unselfconsciously with children, read a text or see a play in a certain way (read it as such and such, see it as such and such), live with people in one's own social, cultural world (read their behavior, their faces, act with them, respond to their actions), live in another social, cultural world. Understanding is often pre-theoretical, a matter of possessing an ability to handle situations or respond in consensually shared, sanctioned, and inculcated ways which, although relatively stable, are still open to change. Understanding, of course, is not an all-or-nothing matter. It can be shallow or deep, narrow or broad. One can be very skillful in some areas and barely competent in others.

It is when understanding breaks down that interpreting has a point. One might be totally unable to understand how to use a word, read a text, interact with certain sorts of people, be totally unable to respond appropriately or inappropriately. Although texts, people, and actions may be understood in many different ways (read as this or that, seen as this or that), one also can misunderstand a text or an action if one ignores whole portions of the contexts in which they are located. It is in such failures to understand that our pretheoretical know-how breaks down and interpretations are needed. Such interpretations in turn can modify our understanding by enabling us to take things differently and to interact differently.

An interpretation that repairs the breakdown is one that achieves the task of enabling people to go on. Interpreting begins with a pretheoretical, problematic situation of knowing how to do something, and its goal is to make this problematic situation unproblematic. There can be many different ways of repairing the breakdown and going on, given the different ways that people with different social and cultural backgrounds and different interests can read, see, and take things and given the different strategies of interpreting that will be needed at different times, depending upon what is being interpreted (a poem, the daily newspaper, a constitution, Chinese students playing basketball, a Chinese husband and wife negotiating living space with their parents). In spite of the multiplicity of interpretations possible, however, misinterpretations also are still possible. We misinterpret when we misunderstand the meaning of a word in a text, when we take sentences out of context and ignore the rest of the text, when we ignore large portions of the way of life of the people whose actions we are seeking to interpret.

Furthermore, since reading a text or understanding what people are doing always takes place in a context of many other actions, the know-how involved in reading, understanding, and interpreting depends upon how it fits into these other actions and the goals being sought in such actions. Understanding and interpreting always are active, motivated and thus not "neutrally" free of interests and purposes. Neither understanding nor interpreting consist of passive mirroring of meanings, events, actions, or situations. They are inescapably tied to the norms, ideals and desired goals inculcated in us when we were socialized and acculturated to understand things in a certain way and are reconstructed by us during our lifetimes. Knowing how to read the United State Constitution or a treaty, in service to a reactionary or imperialistic political agenda, is very different from knowing how to read it in service to a political agenda calling for radical resistance to oppression at home and domination abroad. Interpretations of texts and people, therefore, always are rhetorical efforts to get people to read and understand things in a certain way.[61]

The pragmatists, in their interpretations of justification, explanation, and interpretation, reject the epistemological project by pointing out that only in certain sorts of human interactions do epistemic words or their negative counterparts have work to do. Beyond pragmatic interpretations of the practices of justifying, explaining, and interpreting, the central expression that needs a pragmatic interpretation if one is to undermine modernist theories of knowledge is the expression "is true" when applied to what people say, think, or believe. Again, pragmatists contextualize the use of the expression. William James identifies the situations in which work for "is true" takes place as the ones in which doubts arise. "The individual has a stock of old opinions already, but he meets a new experience that puts them to a strain. Somebody contradicts them; or in a reflective moment he discovers that they contradict each other; or he hears of facts with which they are incompatible...he seeks to escape by modifying his previous mass of opinions. He saves as much as he can... New truth... marries old opinion to new fact so as ever to show a minimum of jolt, a maximum of continuity. We hold a theory true just in proportion to its success in solving this problem of maxima and minima."[62] John Dewey endorses James's treatment of the issues of truth and reality as incidental to the consideration of methods of inquiry to be used in problematic situations, although he is concerned about the individualistic and voluntaristic element in James's accent on truth as what is true for me rather than what is true for the community of inquirers.[63]

The thrust of this pragmatic position is that we affirm that our opinions or claims are true only when we are confronted with a charge that they are or might be false. Otherwise we just make our claims and do not talk about their truth. Asserting that a claim is true is asserting that it is not false; it is reasserting an opinion or claim in a context in which a conflicting claim has been made; it does so in order to reject the rejection of the original claim. The human dynamics of holding opinions and encountering conflicting opinions, of making claims and counterclaims, is all that is needed to explain the use of "is true." There is no need to get trapped within the unusable epistemological language of a correspondence theory of truth in which truth is said to be a relation holding between beliefs or things said and the things or events in the world that are being talked about. The belief or supposal that the sky is cloudy this morning certainly is different from the sky's being cloudy but, in addition to talking about the spatial, temporal, and causal relations between the former and the latter, there is no work for the expression "the correspondence of the first to the second" to do.

We can talk about people believing or supposing things; we can talk about the weather; we can have beliefs about the weather that contradict other people's beliefs; we can reject each other's beliefs, calling them false; we can reject each other's rejections by claiming that our beliefs are not false, they are true. Nothing further gets explained by saying that what makes beliefs true is that they correspond to reality.[64] "Is real" also is a substance hungry, context dependent double negative. There is a point to claiming "This is a diamond" is "true" only when one is rejecting the charge that "This is a diamond" is "false." There is a point to claiming "This is a real diamond" rather than "This is a diamond" only when one wants to reject the claim or suggestion "This is a fake diamond." Talk about truth and reality cannot be divorced from the pragmatic dynamics of conflicting human claims. "Truth" and "reality" are not linguistic expressions that can be used to talk about metaphysical realms of which one supposedly can give final or ultimate descriptions.

Epistemologists have tended to attribute to pragmatists an epistemological "theory of truth" in which it is supposedly claimed by pragmatists that statements are true if they work. These epistemologists then try to show that such an instrumental theory of truth presupposes an epistemologically traditional correspondence theory of truth. They charge that the pragmatist's claim "This statement works" can be true only if it is a claim that objectively (noninstrumentally) corresponds to the fact that it works.[65] This claim by epistemologists fails to take seriously the claims by pragmatists such as James and Dewey that they are not giving one more epistemological theory but that they are rejecting the whole epistemological project. When people use the word "true" they need not be meeting the requirements of a correspondence, coherence, redundancy, or pragmatic theory of truth that supposedly explains the supposed truth component in accounts of propositional knowledge (beliefs that are true and properly justified). When James interprets talk about claims being true as talk about claims that work, what he says can be interpreted as a reminder that such claims work as rejections of rejections in a context of contested claims and thus in a context of competing justifications and explanations.

In order to get clearer on the pragmatic contextual conditions that give "is true" its use, we need to remind ourselves of several aspects of this use:

(1) Since my saying that "P is true" is rejecting a charge of falsity applied to my belief that P, I can't say "P is true but I don't believe it."[66]

(2) When I reaffirm that one of my beliefs is true, I am not just saying that I now have no reason to doubt it or that I have better reasons to believe it than to doubt it, and thus that I am justified in believing it. I also am saying that, were I to find good reasons to change my mind, then I would say that what I had previously believed was incorrect, false, not true. In this sense, the "is" in "is true" is a tenseless "is," and truth itself is timeless.[67] Thus, although "is true" has work to do only in certain situations of conflict, and although all claims including truth claims are corrigible and all beliefs are subject to revision, still we cannot say that something "was true" or "is presently true" or "will be true."[68]

(3) Although this interpretation of the pragmatics of "is true" treats this predicate as a double negative, a rejection of a rejection of a claim, it is not presenting a redundancy theory of truth in which "'P' is true" is taken to say the same thing as "P," only with emphasis.[69] As John Austin pointed out, "It's foggy almost every morning here"

is about the weather, while " "It's foggy almost every morning here" is true" is about a claim about the weather.[70] In addition, redundancy theories seem unable to explain our use of "is false" or our talk about the possible truth of supposals, disjuncts, or antecedents and consequents in hypothetical statements in which something is said but nothing is asserted.

(4) Since this interpretation of our use of "is true," when predicated on what has been said, rejects a correspondence theory of truth, it does not get caught up in the dilemma of either restricting truth to singular descriptive sentences said to represent or picture the contingent conditions of things (facts)[71] or of trying to find some ontological status for "facts" corresponding to claims about necessary logical entailments and mathematical equivalencies, to counterfactual or subjective conditional claims (legal punishment rules, causal claims) about what would happen if such and such were to be done, to claims about social institutions, to ethical claims about what ought to be done, and to claims about aesthetic significance or religious responses to what lies beyond human understanding. One can reject claims made in any of these areas as false and one can reject such rejections and assert the truth of one's original claims. The claims in each of these areas, of course, are quite different from each other and so are our ways of justifying them when they are problematic. In order for truth to exist in these areas one only needs people who have been socially trained so as to know how to make such claims and justify them when challenged, people who know how to participate in these social practices that the later Wittgenstein called "language games."[72]

(5) This interpretation of truth helps one understand better Nietzsche's claims about the will to Truth being an exercise of a will to power. People who claim to possess "the Truth" about a matter claim that all opposition to their opinions is inappropriate. This gives them tremendous power over others, especially if their opinions can become socially institutionalized (in educational, political, moral, mass media practices) as generally unquestioned taken-for-granteds. Crucial to such power is the ability to control taken-for-granteds about

the way to understand knowledge, truth, justification, explanation, understanding, and interpretation. This, postmodernists point out, is the driving power behind the epistemological project.

There is a huge academic industry dependent upon keeping operational the epistemological project. There is much heated opposition by workers in this industry to the interpretations of epistemic terms given by thinkers such as Dewey, Nietzsche, and Rorty. Major economic, political, and religious groups have vested interests in the continuation of the epistemological project, seeking legitimization from it. This helps explain the passion involved in current clashes over interpretations of human knowledge, the texts to be used in training new generations of people, and who is to be silenced or marginalized as irrational and dangerous. It also helps explain why many thinkers believe that resisting the oppressive and dominating powers operating in our world requires resisting the epistemological project. Pragmatists, like Dewey, are not focusing on the pragmatics of epistemic terms in order to gain intellectual one-upmanship over epistemologists. They interpreted their own interpretations as part of a practical project of resisting oppression and domination.

III. MODERNIST COUNTERATTACKS WITH "SCIENCES OF MEANING"

Even while the pragmatists were challenging the epistemological project by focusing on the social practices that were the preconditions of our talk about doubts and beliefs, justifications and explanations, understanding and interpretation, truth and falsity, new intellectual projects had begun that purported to show that language or experience requires the existence of asocial, ahistorical meanings and structural relationships. Engaged in these projects were the analytical philosophical followers of Gottlob Frege and Bertrand Russell, the phenomenologists developing the work of Edmund Husserl, and the linguistic, sociological, cultural, and psychoanalytic structuralists building on the work of the linguist Ferdinand de Saussure. Common to the participants in all these intellectual projects was the conviction that human rationality is not social through and through but that it is possible and necessary for there to be a science of meanings and structures that remains unaffected by social variations and historical changes.

The motivations for the development, growth, and continued life of these intellectual projects are both intellectual and social. Intellectually, there are a number of considerations in the areas of language, logic, and mathematics that lead these thinkers to reject social interpretations of human rationality. Socially, one can view these projects as defensive efforts by intellectuals in the humanities and social sciences to "scientize" and professionalize themselves so as to not allow the natural sciences to monopolize power and prestige in the rapidly expanding academic world of universities, research centers, and professional associations, and to enable them to be participants in the ever-increasing use and management of intellectuals by economic, governmental, and mass media power constellations.

Let me focus my critique here on the intellectual motivations, leaving the investigation of the social motivations until the next two chapters. Beginning this way is not without risks. There is danger in taking a "history of ideas" approach to these movements. I might get caught up in assuming the very contextless meanings and structures postulated in the projects I want to criticize. That something here is dangerous, however, is only a reason for being cautious and autocritical, not a reason for abandoning the effort to show that it is not really necessary to postulate asocial and ahistorical meanings and structures in order to account for language and mathematics. Only by examining the modernists reasons for thinking that transcending the social and historical is necessary can we go beyond merely sneering at them.

Frege (1846–1925) writes that in order for it to be possible to use language to communicate and talk about things, it is necessary to provide a semantic interpretation of assertions such that what we say, think, or believe, and the signs we use in saying things, always have sense and sometimes have reference.[73] His arguments for this position are derived from his reflections about identity statements. The statement that the morning star is the evening star is about Venus, but it can't just be the claim that the object being designated or referred to by the expression "the morning star" is identical to the object designated by "the evening star." Were one to claim that, one would not be able to separate this cognitively informative claim (which not everyone might believe) from the uninformative identity claim that the morning star is the morning star. Similarly, the informative claim can't just be the claim that the mere marks produced in writing one expression are identical to the marks produced in writing the other. Not only is this false, but this again would reduce a=b assertions to a=a assertions. To avoid these reductions, Frege claims, we must see these marks as signs with different senses, different ways of designating Venus. Although the same object is being designated, we might not know that what is being designated in one way is identical with what is being designated in the other way.

Frege claims that these ways of designating objects, these senses that signs possess, cannot be the mental images arising from memories of sense impressions as some British empiricists had held. Communication between people is possible only if the sense of an expression can be the common property of many people. The sense of "the morning star," when I use the expression as a sign to designate Venus, is identical to the sense of the expression when you use it to designate the same object. For the same reason, what is said when someone asserts that the morning star is the evening star (the thought expressed, the proposition asserted, the content of what is believed) must have an identical sense, regardless of who says it, when it is said, or what language is used in saying it. The sense of thoughts, like the sense of designating expressions, must transcend individual, social, and historical variations.[74]

Since the sense of thoughts is determined by the sense of the designative and predicative signs making it up, the sense of signs used in predicating properties of designated objects also must remain constant regardless of which language is used in making the predications. Frege imagines a "logically perfect" language in which every different expression usable for designating objects or predicating properties would be a different sign with a different sense. He acknowledges, however, that with actual, natural languages, different expressions in the same language or different languages can have identical senses, and the same expression used in different contexts can have different senses. The first phenomenon reinforced his conviction that senses must be asocial and ahistorical; the second strengthened his conviction that the necessities involved in logic and mathematics require interpreting them as dealing with the senses of signs and thoughts and with the truth or falsity of such thoughts.

In Frege's semantical interpretation of signs, the pragmatics of people using words to refer to objects in order to describe them was marginalized as "imperfect." Instead, he writes of signs and "thoughts" themselves having sense and reference, even though such a semantical interpretation of signs and thoughts continually creates problems for him. It turns out to be very difficult for him to separate linguistic expressions or linguistic signs, treated as independent objects, from the use of such expressions or signs as designating or predicating terms in thoughts, terms which only have a functional identity within such thoughts. Similarly, Frege finds it difficult to match designating expressions to signs. When I say that I don't believe that the morning star is the evening star, I am not using "the morning star" and "the evening star" to designate the same object. When I say that someone doesn't understand the sense of the expression "the morning star," I seem to be using the expression to designate some sense and not Venus.

Additional problems arise when dealing with "thoughts." The word "thought" is used by Frege only to designate what is said when what is said can be claimed to be true or false. Many modernist philosophers substituted the word "proposition" for Frege's word "thought." For Frege, each "thought" is interpreted as designating either the circumstance that it is true or the circumstance that it is false, what Frege calls "the two truth values." Truth and falsity for Frege are semantical relations holding between "thoughts" and the two truth values, being true and being false. Not all declarative sentences, however, express thoughts and this generates new problems. On Frege's interpretation, the truth of a "thought" is determined by the correctness of predicating certain properties of the designated objects. No such correctness or incorrectness is possible, however, when the object one is attempting to designate does not exist. For Frege, the sentence "The present king of France is bald" cannot be a sign used to express a thought because there is no present king of France. For Frege, what is said when this sentence now is uttered is not a proposition, even though it seems as though someone might incorrectly think and believe what is said.[75]

Specifying the identity criteria for thoughts, propositions and the contents of beliefs becomes even more problematic when one considers that the truth of a thought is determined only by the correctness of one's attribution of properties to presupposed objects. If in two utterances or thoughts the same properties are attributed to the same object, then it seems one and the same thought is being expressed. However, Mary might use the expression "the tallest man in the room" to refer to a person she knows to be John in order to express her belief that he alone is wearing a red coat. Not knowing that John also is the oldest person in the room, however (he looks so much younger than others), Mary might deny that this oldest person is wearing a red coat. Were thought or propositional identity only a matter of same predications of same objects, then Mary would both believe and not believe the same thought.[76]

The problems multiply even when one considers the status of expressions used to predicate properties of presupposed objects. What is the status of "is a planet" when one says that Venus is a planet? It has a sense, the same sense as certain expressions in other languages. Frege calls the predicative use of expressions "concepts" and declares that concepts are incomplete and thus different from designating expressions that can have reference as well as sense. Frege interprets concepts ("is a planet," "is green") as functions. Just as the square root function needs an argument (9, 16) in order to have a value (3, 4), so concepts are incomplete because they are functions needing an argument to complete them so that they can have a truth value as their value. Frege is well aware, however, of the difficulties involved in trying to make clear what a function is.[77] When one talks about such a way of functioning, such a concept, one ends up designating an object and not engaging in an act of actually functioning with the concept.

Most analytic philosophers have spent the whole twentieth century trying to resolve these difficulties in Frege's writings about sense and reference, concepts and objects, while still operating with a purely semantical interpretation of reference and truth and while still postulating asocial and ahistorical meanings for expressions, signs, propositions, and their constituent terms. Language is taken to have a semantical relation to something other than language, and timeless meanings are seen as necessary for this relationship to hold. Are they, however, really necessary?

If one focused on the pragmatics of saying things about things, on the relationships holding between people, the words they use, and the claims they make with these words, a very different interpretation is possible, one that bypasses this whole nest of problems and postulations of asocial and ahistorical meanings. I will expand on this claim when investigating the accent on such pragmatics by Wittgenstein and Heidegger. Let me say some things here, however, about how such an accent on pragmatics would modify Frege's problems.

Instead of talking about expressions or signs designating objects, one would be talking about people designating objects. People refer, not expressions.[78] (Frege's dream of an ideal language freed from contamination by personal, social, historical, and contextual considerations is fortunately an unrealizable intellectual nightmare.) Instead of talking about radically distinguishing what we are talking about (reference) from our manner of designating such objects (sense), one would be talking about specific writers or speakers using certain specific socially constituted words in certain specific contexts to talk about certain socially constituted objects, some of which are linguistic and some of which are not. One would drop the notion of being able to talk about objects (referents) without designating them in some manner or other. Talk about "ideal," nonsocially constituted objects that can be designated in this manner or that manner would be dropped as one attended to the pragmatics governing the use of the expression "object" when one says things like, "There are lots of objects which we still know nothing about and which we have not yet characterized in any way." Such "not-yet-characterized" objects certainly could not be that to which any speaker is referring. Instead of saying that the statement "The morning star is the morning star" is a trivial analytic truth, while the statement "The morning star is the evening star" is an informative, synthetic statement, one would point out that there is only a pragmatic difference between what we claim is true due to socially trained forms of linguistic usage and what we claim is true due to socially inculcated beliefs.[79] Instead of talking about concepts and functions that always turn out to be objects when one tries to talk about them, one would talk about people actually functioning referringly and predicatively with words and about social, relatively stable ways of functioning with words. What one still can't do is function with an expression predicatively (The ball is round) while also using the expression to designate a socially constituted way of functioning with it (Use "round" to describe a shape). One can linguistically point at anything except that very act of pointing.[80] Finally, instead of talking about propositions referring to truth values, one would be talking about how people challenge claims and reject challenges to their claims.

Frege's and Husserl's marginalization of pragmatic considerations probably was due to their concern about the nature of mathematical claims. It is their concerns about mathematics that lead Frege and Husserl into philosophical reflections about meaning. They are convinced that mathematical claims need a form of objectivity that could be gained only if timeless meanings were postulated.

Frege rejects the idea that mathematical axioms could have merely the objectivity of empirical generalizations about actual objects. Mathematical axioms and theorems must be interpreted as covering all possibilities and there must be a necessity to them not present with contingent empirical claims. This necessity, he claims, also must be more than Kant's synthetic a priori characterization of mathematics because then mathematical claims would cover only possible appearances to humans, given, as Kant put it, their undeniable but contingent way of knowing things. Frege still clings to the modern rationalist's dream of talking about possible objects that are not just objects that people would characterize in some particular way. Finally, Frege writes, mathematical axioms must not be interpreted as mere conventional stipulations about how a mathematical symbolism is to be used. This never could explain how mathematical calculations remain reliable in predictions in physics of motions or in the construction of buildings and bridges.[81]

Frege was all too aware of the crisis created in mathematics by the discoveries of alternative geometries and algebras.[82] Frege believes arithmetic could be saved from the subjectivity of Kantianism and conventionalism only if its claims could be reduced to claims in the logic of an ideal language that dealt with the necessary relations between the truth values of thoughts (propositions) and between universal and existential quantification of variables whose values were pure objects not yet characterized in any way.[83] Frege's logically perfect language of signs and thoughts, with their senses and references, is supposed to provide the foundation that he believes arithmetic needs.

The postmodernists, Wittgenstein and Heidegger, have attempted to show how focusing on the social pragmatics of a Kantian type construction of mathematical objects through an idealization of perceptual objects can provide all the objectivity that mathematics needs. Husserl (1859–1938) charges that this is not sufficient. To show this, however, he claims that it is necessary to generalize Frege's notion of sense so that it applied not only to linguistic signs, and what is said or thought with them, but to all human experiences and acts. Kantian constructive idealizations are possible, he believes, only because human experiences already contain ideal forms that can be isolated by a methodology which he calls "phenomenological."

Husserl begins his analysis of experience by starting with the notion of intentionality.[84] All experience, he claims, possesses intentionality, pointing beyond itself to some object that might or might not exist. We fear something; we hope for something; we have a visual experience of something; we believe something. Our fear may be unfounded. What we hope for does not yet exist. Our visual experience might be illusory. Our belief might be false. For Husserl, it is intentionality that separates human beings from rocks. We can say all it is possible to say about rocks by talking about their actual qualities and spatial, temporal, causal relations to other actual objects. Talking about humans, however, requires talking about their relations to what might be merely possible. It is the sense present in our experiences that makes it possible to be related to what might be the mere intentional object of our experience. Husserl uses the old Greek word *noema* instead of Frege's word "sense" to designate what experiences mean to the persons having them. He acknowledges the significance of social, cultural, and personal differences in determining such experiential meanings, but he holds that these variations in one's lived world are possible only because of the presence of different sets of asocial and ahistorical meanings in these experiences. Husserl endorses the claim of Plato that we can experience an object only if we experience it as something, only if we already possess the idea of it. Thus, Husserl sides with Plato's rejection of the claims of Aristotelians and British empiricists that ideas are derived from experience. Husserl rejects the notion of the post-Hegelians that training to participate in social practices could originate an individual's ideas and meanings. He does so because he believes that such a "historicist" approach could provide neither mathematics with the necessities it needs nor epistemologists and ethical theorists with the socially transcendent norms they need to escape relativism.

Husserl claims that whenever we consciously experience anything we are consciously aware of what that experience means to us. The meaning present in the experience is present in such a way that it can be isolated for analysis if we will reflectively focus our attention on it in the right way. The phenomenological method provides a way of reducing the focus of our attention so that accidental and thus irrelevant factors, possibly present in our conscious experiences, are removed and only the noematic sense of the conscious experience remains present for our description. This phenomenological method consists of two reductions.

The transcendental reduction calls for us to "bracket out" from our focus all considerations of factors transcending what we are experiencing the object as (a house or a movie set of house fronts) or our ways of experiencing it (see it, remember it, hope for it). Bracket out consideration of whether the intentional object is actual or not. Bracket out all efforts to give psychological or metaphysical explanations of the experience. Focus only on what the experience means to us and then describe that meaning.

Since social, cultural, and personal idiosyncracies have an impact on that meaning, a second reduction is necessary to isolate the asocial and ahistorical meanings present. An "eidetic reduction" is needed to focus on the Platonic *eidos* or idea present in the experience. Trusting that these ideas are present to reflective consciousness, we perform thought experiments to isolate the essential meaning of the object experienced and our ways of experiencing it, to separate them from other accidental features of the object or ways of experiencing it. Concentrate on separating being a house from being a movie set by describing the expectations of additional experiences that one would have in each case. (We would expect to see sides and backs if we walked around a house; we would not expect all houses to be the color of the one we are experiencing.) Separate seeing a house from touching a house or hoping to see a house. (Different sensations are involved in seeing and touching and none need be involved in hoping to see one; also, seeing would still be seeing even if one saw the house under different lighting conditions.)

For Frege, asocial and ahistorical meanings (concepts and

propositions) have to be postulated in order to account for the fact that one person can say the same thing at different times and that different people can say the same things. For Husserl such meanings have to be postulated in order to account for the fact that one person could experience the same thing in different ways or at different times and that different people could experience in different ways the same object. Husserl augmented Frege's position by setting forth a methodology that supposedly could be used to give us knowledge of such asocial and ahistorical meanings.

Husserl's phenomenological method bears remarkable similarities to the method used by "ordinary language" analysts seeking to discover the supposedly necessary and sufficient conditions for the correct use of words, conditions they believed had to exist if logical relations between "propositions" containing these words are to be possible. Assuming that people intuitively know what they mean when they use words, these analysts carried out thought experiments to see whether we would call something an F if it did not have characteristics G and H and whether having G and H was enough for us to call it an F. These necessary and sufficient conditions were specifiable in terms of rules whose implicit presence supposedly is required by our ability to separate correct from incorrect usage and in order for there to exist necessary, timeless logical relations between what is meant when we say things with these words, timeless propositional meanings dependent upon timeless word meanings.[85] According to such analysts, the meaning of the words we use remains timeless even though different words at different times have to be used due to the fact that words over time change their meanings. Meanings themselves have no history, only the linking of meanings to words has such a history. It is just such an assumption of ahistorical meanings or ideas that historians of ideas reject. Such historians think they are studying the history of the changes taking place in ideas such as space, causality, or democracy.

Whereas ordinary language analysts postulate timeless semantical relationships, linguistic structuralists such as Saussure[86] and Chomsky[87] argue that timeless syntactical relationships had to be postulated in any adequate systematic interpretation or explanatory theory of language. Although both of them are still modernists, their arguments for the primacy in language of syntactical rules (governing relations of linguistic elements to linguistic elements) undercut Frege's accent on semantical relations and Husserl's reliance on intuitions of meaning. Although Saussure's characterization of the words we use in our speaking and writing places a heavy accent on social conventions and customs, he is not a postmodernist because he still postulates timeless linguistic values that are determined by systems of differentiation.

In interpreting Saussure it is helpful to begin by distinguishing language words (words seen as items in our vocabulary that can be used again and again by different people) from utterance words (words as seen as items in the sentences actually uttered in speech or writing by some person at some specific time). In the utterance "The cat is on the mat," six words are uttered but only five language words are used since "the" is used twice.[88] Saussure focused on the systematic, functional relationships existing between language words *(Langue)* as these relationships exist at a particular historical moment in the life of a language community. He does not focus upon utterance words as they are functionally related in a particular act of speech or writing or upon historically shifting linkages between the sound or inscription types of words and their meanings *(Parole)*.

Saussure claims that every word has two aspects, as signifier and as signified. This implies that every word has a meaning. Although Saussure prioritizes sound types as signifiers over written mark types (a prioritization that the postmodernist Derrida will severely criticize), it is his distinction between material signifiers and signified concepts or meanings that requires initial attention. For him, neither signifiers nor signifieds are substances that simply can be present to the mind, as Husserl and the ordinary language analysts presume. They are idealized functional values in systems of differentiation. First of all, the signifier aspect of the word "cat" can be sounds or written marks; it can be spoken with different accents, pitches, and volumes, and it can be printed or written cursively, small or large, in capitals or lowercase letters, in great varieties of penmanship or printing. Furthermore, a socially acceptable set of sounds or marks is a single signifier only because of the way it is functionally located in a system of signifiers, each individuated by its differences from all the other signifiers in the language. "Cat" is not "mat" or "cut" or "cap" or… It is its functional value in a system of signifiers that gives it its identity. Any set of sounds or marks that had the same functional location would be the same signifier.

Likewise, the signified aspect of a word (a concept, the meaning of a language word) is an idealized functional value. When I and other speakers of my language talk about a chair, we think of many characteristics of the chair that are not socially prescribed as necessary features for something to be called or conceived of as a chair. The signified conceptual value of the word "chair" results from a social process of differentiating unessential thoughts associated with chairs from an essential thought, the concept of a chair, the meaning of the language word "chair." Furthermore, as with signifiers, the conceptual identity of the signified aspect of the word "chair" is a function of this concept's differences from all other concepts. The essential thought or concept of a chair is specified by spelling out all the concepts it is different from. A chair is not a table, not a book, not essentially blue or wooden or…

It follows from Saussure's interpretation of language that only by interpreting a whole system of concepts can we identify any particular signified. Concepts and language word meanings are not substances that can be simply there for intuitive inspection, as Husserl presumes. Nevertheless, for Saussure, relations between values, relations between signifiers, and relations between signifieds are timeless. Signifiers are linked to signifieds only by social conventions, but the relations in the systems of signifiers and signifieds, which give functional identity to each signifier and signified, are timelessly what they are once social customs have established them. We can study language synchronically, taking a time slice out of the historical social development of the language, and discover these timeless relational, functional values.[89] (This notion that the identities of signifiers and signifieds have no ties to the past or the future is one of the crucial parts of Saussure's theory that Derrida attacks, along with the very distinction between material signifiers and conceptual signifieds.)

Chomsky criticizes Saussure for not recognizing that beneath the surface syntactical relationships between signs there lie even more fundamental, deep syntactical structures. The differences in the meaning of some sentences that seem on the surface to have the same syntax ("John is eager to please" and "John is easy to please"; "There is a splinter in my finger" an "There is a pain in my finger") can only be accounted for, he claims, if we postulate the existence of deep structures and transformational rules that can take us from deep syntax to surface syntax. Our ability to generate an indefinitely large number of sentences, he claims, can best be explained by postulating the existence of recursive rules that we use to generate from a limited base this unlimited number of surface sentences. Chomsky criticizes psychological behaviorists such as B. F. Skinner[90] and W. V. O. Quine[91] by arguing that our ability to learn our language so quickly in childhood can only be accounted for if we postulate that there exists in the child an innate knowledge of this deep grammar and these recursive rules, an innate skill present because of the evolutionary development of our genetic code or because of the physical structure of the brain or both. Since any child can learn any language as its first language, we need to postulate one single deep syntactical structure to all languages.

In his arguments against Saussure and Skinner, Chomsky uses again and again one general form of argumentation. (Either they are correct or I am correct; they are incorrect; therefore, I am correct.) No interpretations of language other than those of Saussure, Skinner, and Chomsky are even entertained as possibilities. Totally missing is any consideration of the social pragmatics of language. Totally missing is any consideration of the Hegelian social alternative to both Skinner's individualistic behavioral learning and Chomsky's Platonic innateness. Children are socially trained to participate appropriately in existing social practices. There is no reason for thinking that sufficient time does not exist for children to acquire these skills.[92] The physiology of our brains and our genetic inheritance from evolutionary development only need to be such as to permit us to acquire linguistic skills and they need not consist of possessing biologically those skills themselves. It makes sense to talk about being born with the capacity to learn how to use language correctly, but it is doubtful that it makes any sense to talk about being born knowing how to use language correctly. In a parasitic sense of "knowing how," we can say that dogs are born knowing how to swim and babies are born knowing how to suck (learning was not needed to acquire this ability, although learning is normally required in gaining know-how). Dogs, however, cannot mis-swim and babies cannot mis-suck. Children can misuse the language they are being trained to use correctly. Linguistic know-how does require learning. It requires social training and that is all that it requires. Learning to use the language of pains involves learning that pains are not in a finger in the way that splinters are, and learning to use correctly the words "eager," "easy" and "to please" enables us to know that with "eager" John is doing the pleasing while with "easy" John is being pleased, just as in playing baseball one learns the difference between the catcher throwing the ball back to the pitcher and the umpire throwing a new ball to the pitcher. If the pitcher drops the first, a runner can steal home, but not if he drops the second.

In all the interpretations of linguistic practice and meaningful communication and experience given by Frege, Husserl, Saussure, and Chomsky, one line of argumentation remains constant. Appealing only to the social, with its historically changing character, is seen as not sufficient to account for language, communication, and experience. Frege, Husserl and de jure ordinary language analysts charge that Platonic type meanings must be postulated in order for such an account to be given. Saussure and Chomsky charge that universal and unchanging syntactical relationships and structures must be postulated, with Chomsky turning to biology to provide the universality and stability that social practice supposedly cannot provide. The arguments of these thinkers, however, are persuasive only if an interpretation of meaningfulness and linguistic practice in terms of social practice is not possible. Throughout the twentieth century, in addition to the development of intellectual projects out of the work of Frege, Husserl, Saussure, and Chomsky, there has been a second line of intellectual development striving to present the very social interpretation that they claim to be impossible. It is to the development of this defense of the social character of rationality by Wittgenstein, Heidegger, Foucault, Derrida, and Rorty that I will now turn.

IV.   POSTMODERNIST SOCIAL AND HISTORICAL INTERPRETATIONS OF LANGUAGE

Neither Wittgenstein, Heidegger, Derrida, Foucault, nor Rorty present direct refutations of the claims that universal and timeless meanings and structures must be postulated in order to explain the meaningfulness of our linguistic practices and experiences. Attempting to present such refutations would require attempting to prove that such meanings and structures cannot or do not exist. Either attempt would place these thinkers again on the old modernist playing field, trying to present and defend an alternative metaphysical explanation of such meaningfulness. The "cannot" in the claim that asocial, ahistorical meanings cannot exist would have to be a metaphysical "cannot" requiring its own a priori proof. Alternatively, merely presenting an interpretation of meaningfulness that did not require postulating universal and timeless meanings would be counted by many of these modernist postulators as a disproof of their position only if that interpretation itself could be proved to them to be a correct picture of the meaningfulness of language and experience, an effort that would tie the interpreter back to the very modernist theories of truth as correspondence that all five of these writers want to problematize.

These thinkers have elected instead to attempt to redirect their readers away from such modernist projects, to attempt to radically alter the expectations that have become customary when reading interpretations of meaning and truth. The later Wittgenstein writes about dissolving and not solving metaphysical and epistemological problems. Heidegger calls for the destruction of all the traditional ontotheological forms of Western metaphysics. Derrida works at showing how all logocentric metaphysical texts deconstruct themselves. Foucault draws the reader's attention to the manner in which users of metaphysical and epistemological discourse attempt to polemically muscle their opposition aside rather than enter into dialogue with them. Rorty writes in order to update Dewey's project of showing the uselessness of metaphysical and epistemological theories and the need for thinkers to be useful in helping make the future different from the past. While trying to pull the playing field's carpet out from under the movements of the players in these modernist games, these writers make major contributions to reestablishing, deepening and strengthening the credibility of social interpretations of human rationality. That they do so as part of a set of rhetorical moves aimed at practical, existential, and political goals rather than some ideal theoretical goal of merely representing "objective" facts, only further reveals their distance from merely semantic conceptions of reference and truth and from metaphysical theorizing. It also reveals why many twentieth-century modernist defenders of universal and timeless meanings and structures either seek to transform these social interpretations into just some more metaphysical theories of meaning or they tend to dismiss them as philosophically confused and irrelevant.[93] If we will dialogically listen to the texts of Wittgenstein, Heidegger, Derrida, Foucault, and Rorty, I think we will be able to understand that they are neither irrelevant, confused, nor just more instances of the same old modernist theorizing.

A.   WITTGENSTEIN'S DISSOLUTION OF MODERNIST PROBLEMS WITH MEANING

Wittgenstein's texts have always resisted the efforts of those interpreters who would reduce them to metaphysical or epistemological claims. Bertrand Russell, in his introduction to the *Tractatus Logico-Philosophicus*,[94] could interpret Wittgenstein's text as a slight variant of his theory of logical atomism[95] only by dismissing as irrelevant the whole musical form in which the *Tractatus* is written[96] and the sentences numbered 6.1 through 7 at the end of the book. It is in these sentences that Wittgenstein indicated that, if one works with a merely semantical and syntactical theory of representation, there is much that cannot be representationally pictured but only can be shown. The unpicturable in fact includes all the things philosophers such as Frege and Russell were trying to say: what language, the world, and the semantical relations between them must be like if true or false linguistic representations are to be produced and if the same things are to be said at different times. In a meeting with Russell at which Wittgenstein tried to show how Russell had misunderstood him, Russell came away with the conviction that Wittgenstein, by putting so much into the realm of the unsayable, had become a mystic (hardly a term of praise in Russell's lexicon).[97]

Similarly, the Logical Positivists could take their interpretation of the *Tractatus* as the perfect vehicle for their quasi-epistemological project (claiming that their interpretations of scientific knowledge is the sole form of all possible knowledge) only by once again dropping what Wittgenstein seemed to be indicating in 6.1 through 7. In place of these sentences they attempted to substitute their talk (about what is said in a metalanguage about what is said in an object language) for his talk about what can be shown but not said (represented), about what must be passed over in silence. After attending several sessions of the Vienna Circle of logical positivists, Wittgenstein came away overwhelmed by the ability of professional philosophers to misunderstand him.[98] By not attending to problems involved in their need for an unending series of metalanguages for talking about the relation between a metalanguage and its object language, the logical positivists could not find any sensible interpretation of Wittgenstein's passage in the *Tractatus* where he wrote that those who understood him would see that even the sentences, in which he seems to be talking about what cannot be said but can only be shown, are nonsense.[99] The positivists could not entertain the possibility that this passage showed Wittgenstein's recognition that what he was writing lacked sense in the manner in which Frege claimed that propositions and logically proper names had sense, that what he was writing showed that many very important facets of human life lie beyond what is conceptually and propositionally "sensible," beyond the representable, beyond where one must be silent with a silence filled not merely with an inability to represent or picture but also with an understanding of the importance of living without always trying to picture. In his preface to the *Tractatus*, Wittgenstein wrote, "The book deals with the problems of philosophy... the value of the work consists in that it shows how little is achieved when these problems are solved."[100]

Reductionist tactics also were applied to Wittgenstein's *Philosophical Investigations*[101] by metaphysicians of meaning and by epistemologists. Again the form of his text was dismissed as an irrelevant, personal idiosyncracy, and the supposed content of the text was extracted as a series of theoretical claims. According to these modernist, reductionist interpretations, there were embedded in Wittgenstein's text, although never fully developed, three philosophical theories: (1) a new theory of linguistic meaning (the meaning of a word is the use of the word as determined by social norms of propriety, meanings are Fregean concepts with vague boundaries); (2) a new theoretical solution to the "body-mind" problem (observable behavior serves as the criteria for unobservable pains), and (3) a new epistemological theory about the foundations of human knowledge (unquestioned beliefs serve as standards of knowing). Such modernist interpreters want to keep Wittgenstein's writing safely confined within traditional philosophical projects. In their attempt to do so they have to set to one side such passages in Wittgenstein's texts as "Philosophy simply puts everything before us, and neither explains nor deduces anything... If one tried to advance theses in philosophy, it would never be possible to debate them, because everyone would agree to them."[102] "The philosopher's treatment of a question is like the treatment of an illness."[103] "What is your aim in philosophy? —To shew the fly the way out of the fly-bottle."[104] Dismissed as unimportant was the text's apparent form as a dialogue that a thinker is having with himself, a thinker familiar with a great deal of current philosophical rhetoric, a dialogue that is broken into rather short segments (with segments sometimes connected in series), a dialogue in which it often is not clear when the thinker is recalling what he heard or read and when the writer is thinking about what he has recalled, a dialogue form that at times seems to be abandoned and replaced with direct assertions to the reader.

I suggest that we can strengthen our understanding of the social character of rationality if we work with interpretations of the *Tractatus* and the *Philosophical Investigations,* which (1) do not seek to separate form from content; (2) take seriously passages in the *Tractatus* that indicate what cannot be represented; and (3) take seriously passages in the *Philosophical Investigations* that specify how one is to read what he has written about what many philosophers take as problematic; that these should be taken as writing about an illness, as writing providing rhetorical treatment for an illness, as writing assisting philosophers to understand that they need not be trapped by the assumptions that blind them to the modernist opening in that fly bottle of discourse that they have constructed as their own prison.

When Wittgenstein, after working on the *Tractatus* all during his service in the Austrian army during World War I, finished writing this text, he believed that he had written the text that would end the project of technical philosophy that had reached its penultimate climax in the writings of Frege and Russell. "I therefore believe myself to have found on all essential points the final solution of the problems."[105] Motivated by his continued meditation during his war years on the religious texts of Tolstoy, he went back to Austria to train for service as an elementary school teacher, thereby becoming part of the movement by Austrian intellectuals to build a new Austria as the cultural center of Europe.[106] The inseparable "form" and "content" of the *Tractatus* can be interpreted as a rhetorical effort to get its readers to likewise end dealing with old philosophical problems and to move beyond merely representing how things are in the world, and to begin to do the other sorts of things that silently show one's practical, moral, aesthetic, and religious life in the world and which express in a living way one's attitudes toward things, events, and the world itself.

Wittgenstein interpreted the philosophical texts of Frege and Russell as attempting to account for our ability to say true and false things by making reference only to syntactical and semantical relationships. If (1) saying something true or false (producing a proposition) is picturing a possible fact (that one object is possibly and contingently related to another object), (2) saying something meaningful is syntactically relating "logically proper names," whose meanings are the objects of which they are names, and (3) truth and falsity are semantical relations between propositions and actual facts, then a true proposition is the fact that certain "logically proper names" are related to each other in the same way that the objects they name are actually related in the fact being pictured. If this were to be the case, however, some very drastic consequences would follow, consequences so drastic that this project had best be ended so that attention could be turned elsewhere. In 6.1 through 6.4, we read that if all we can say is how "simple" (qualityless?) objects are related to "simple" objects, then scientific generalizations and theories say nothing, math and logic say nothing, ethics, aesthetics, and religion say nothing, and (the ultimate reductio ad absurdum) even the sentences in the *Tractatus* (supposedly the final version of the Frege-Russell account) "say" nothing. If the Frege-Russell account were sayable and true, then all that thinkers would be able to do would be to present this account and then point out that most of the things we normally think are important to say really say nothing. We would have to confess that we simply are confused when we think that they do say something. If the only choice is between Frege-Russell sayings and silence, then we must choose silence. Only by transcending this choice can we "see the world aright."[107]

Since even the attempt to state the absurd implications of the Frege-Russell account end up saying nothing, carrying out a rhetorical effort to move philosophical readers beyond Frege-Russell type philosophizing needs to be done without "saying" anything; it needs to be done in some other manner, such as singing a musical score, a score written so that its method of representation changes in the middle (after 1.2 1), a score written with instructions for interpretation that do not apply to the whole score, a score which one can read understandingly only if one understands the rhetorical point of the *Tractatus*. "My propositions serve as elucidations in the following way: Only he who understands me, eventually recognizes them as nonsense."[108] Just trying to write and talk about saying things that are true or false while interpreting language only in terms of syntax and semantics shows in the failure of such talk that pragmatics can't be excluded from the interpretation.

After conversations in the 1920s with Frank Ramsey, a young British philosopher, in the village cafes of Austria where he was teaching elementary school, after visiting a meeting of the Vienna Circle of logical positivists, and after listening to lectures on the foundations of mathematics by the Husserl influenced intuitionist Brouwer, Wittgenstein seems to have recognized that his rhetorical effort in the *Tractatus* had failed. These modernist philosophers were still putting forward theories of meaning and knowledge. Modernist theorists, it seems, can't be moved by someone else to end their philosophical projects. They may be confused, but their confusion is "deep." They believe that they must say what they are saying. They have reasons for their reasons for their reasons. Their reasons may be nothing but unexamined pictures that are forcing their reasoning to move along prechanneled lines, but this is something they have to find out for themselves. What someone else tells them or tries to show them will just be interpreted and responded to in terms of their old framing of issues and rationales. Besides, modernists seem to have a virtually unlimited capacity to find new ways to tie their thinking into confused sets of knots. No set of clarifications given by some one therapist could unravel the many different kinds of snarls into which other thinkers could entangle their thinking. Modernists have to discover by themselves their confusion, and they have to learn by themselves how to get out of the fly bottle that they have constructed with their unexamined "this is how things must be." The best a postmodernist can do for modernists, the mission to which Wittgenstein committed himself on his return to philosophy, is to teach them (1) the art of finding "strange" the things they are saying and (2) the art of untangling the twisted set of assumptions, lines of reasoning, and motivations that are trapping them into thinking in a certain way.

Even such instruction has to be done indirectly. Branding a modernist's thinking as confused will only produce defensive resistance. *Philosophical Investigations* is Wittgenstein's rhetorical effort to teach modernists (who think that they must postulate ahistorical and asocial meanings, must find a foundation for human knowledge [especially our knowledge of each other]), the art of recognizing the strange implications of their postulations and the art of removing the "taken-for-granteds" that lead them to think such postulations must be made.[109] He does so by practicing this art on his own thinking, his own consideration of reasons that seem to require metaphysical or epistemological postulations, his own internal dialogues and debates with the reasons given by Frege, Russell, and the logical positivists. The rhetorical effect of indirectness is further enhanced by an almost total absence in the text of any indication of who is the "author" of any particular line of reasoning. Furthermore, sometimes the dialogues are brief and seem to jump from topic to topic, while at other times a rather lengthy, continuous, repetitive dialogue seems to be the case. The dialogical reflections often seem to move through the same areas of thought, although thinking about them from a slightly different angle. In many ways this text is a philosophical stream of consciousness, written not to autobiographically communicate information but to attract philosophers to and to train them in the art of philosophical liberation from self imposed imprisonment in fly bottles.

As a by product of the *Philosophical Investigations*" rhetorical effort, however, the text is filled with a host of reminders about how people use language, especially their language about meaning and understanding, simple reminders about ordinary speech that challenge the claim that asocial and ahistorical meanings must be postulated. Even though doing so is not the rhetorical goal of the text, once these reminders succeed in taking us out of the fly bottle, assembling them together allows us to begin constructing a general but nonmetaphysical interpretation of the social character of human rationality. I have assembled these reminders in the following way.

Words are interpreted as socially constituted tools that we use in doing many different sorts of things with language.[110] They are not primarily names of objects (physical objects or relations, or ideal Platonic forms or universals) that we use in describing things. Nothing gets said by the completely general Saussure-type claim that all words signify something.[111] Writers and speakers use words to communicate knowledge of their beliefs, desires, intentions, and feelings, and they also use them to perform certain sorts of official acts (calling strikes in baseball, and marrying two persons in a church).[112] Words also are tools used by people in one generation to socialize and enculturate children in the next generation, to train them to classify and individuate things in a certain way (including themselves and other people) and thus to train them to think, experience, and understand things in a certain way. Words are used in buffoon spectacles, anecdotes, and parodies of official or elitist language.[113] This accent on words as tools gives to pragmatics priority over syntax and semantics. Words don't have reference; people use words to refer to things and events and to describe them. The fact that words are related to words (in syntactically customary ways) does not picture possible relations among objects that supposedly exist independently of people doing linguistically with words what they have been trained to do, such as describing things and sometimes reasserting the correctness of their descriptions when these are challenged.

Linguistic actions are performed as parts of different groups of linguistic actions. There are legal language games, scientific language games, religious language games. These language games can be played, these different sort of linguistic actions can be performed, only because they are performed in different contexts of nonlinguistic actions and processes, human forms of life.[114] What may look like the same word will end up being used differently in different language games. "Evidence" is used one way in science and another way in a court of law, where considerations about how the purported evidence was gathered or when it is introduced into the trial are relevant to its being counted as evidence. Words that seem to have identical syntactical relations in two different sentences may have very different uses. "In" functions very differently in "I have a beetle in a box" from the way it does in "I have a pain in my finger." It makes sense to ask "When it is 8:00 P.M. in New York, what time is it in London?" but it makes no sense to ask "When it is 8:00 P.M. in New York, what time is it on the Sun?" Special social conventions have to be introduced for telling time in space. One will fail to understand what people are doing with words if one attempts to reduce usage in one language game to usage in another language game, for example, if one tries to reduce religious language to primitive scientific language.[115]

If one focuses on people using words in the ways they have been trained to use words, the need to postulate asocial and ahistorical meanings falls away. Meanings are not objects of any sort.[116] We train people to use words. We start talking about the meaning of words when we want to explain to someone how to use a word.[117] Such explanations can take many forms (give a synonym, show a picture, point at something, train participation in a new language game). We start talking about the meaning of what someone has written or said when we don't know how to go on reading, listening, or talking in the ways in which we have been trained. Explaining (interpreting) the meaning of an utterance or text consists in removing the barriers to understanding, the barriers to going on, whatever they might be. The number of such barriers seems unlimited and thus the interpretive task is always a function of a historically specific, contextually located problem of understanding.[118]

That we can talk about words having meanings does not require assuming that there are necessary and sufficient criteria for their semantic application, that there must be Frege's concepts, Husserl's *noema*, Russell's universals (Platonic forms). Historically developing social customs of linguistic use and training are all that is required. Things do not have to share some supposed common metaphysical essence in order for them to share a common name. They may only share family resemblances and bear the same name because of the historical use of that name in grouping things.[119] As Wittgenstein points out, there is no conjunctive or disjunctive set of properties that any game must have in order to be called a game, and there is no set of such properties that guarantees that it will be called a game.[120] What is true of the word "game" is true of all words. One can appreciate how damaging this claim is to all postulations of unchanging meanings when one applies this interpretation of words to the philosopher's vocabulary. What are named by the word "property" only have social and historical identities. So are the "things" named by the words "word," "sentence," "language," "meaning," "what was said," "assertion," "belief, "desire," intention," "feeling," "thought," "true," "number," "identical," "different," "similar," "simple," "complex," "justify," "prove," " know." Even the philosopher's battle sword "contradiction" has only a social and historical identity. As Wittgenstein writes, "Civil Status of a contradiction, or its status in civil life; there is the philosophical problem."[121]

In order to emphasize the social character of linguistic pragmatics, Wittgenstein points out that one can account for the phenomena of understanding what someone says, and of reading with understanding, without postulating any mental images or Husserl-type private intuitions of meanings or rules to follow.[122] People simply go on doing what they have been socially trained to do, training that involved correcting the learner's linguistic behavior so that it conforms to existing social customs of usage and approvals/disapprovals of usage. It is useless to postulate private rules to account for observable behavior because these rules also can be misapplied and only social norms can separate correct from incorrect application. The explanation for our ability to suddenly understand the meaning of a linguistic expression (without making an observational study of social usage and approvals of usage) lies with such understanding consisting of knowing how to do things with words, how to go on, and with barriers to such skillful use sometimes being suddenly removed by any number of different techniques.[123]

Perhaps one of Wittgenstein's most significant contributions to the strengthening of an interpretation of language and thought as social through and through comes from his discussion of our talk about the pains we and other people have. Pain talk is social in two senses of social. First, it is social in being governed by social norms.[124] Because there is a natural correlation between being in pain and exhibiting pain behavior, the latter can get used socially as unquestioned indicators of the presence of the former. This correlation is natural but not necessary, thus permitting people who know at least some of the pain language game to pretend they are in pain when they are not and to pretend not to be in pain when they are.

Second, pain talk, like all talk about "mental" events and acts (thinking, imagining, intending, remembering, feeling, etc.), is parasitic upon interpersonally encountering people. "Being in pain" is an observable characteristic of people. When we see a child lying in the street, screaming and bleeding with a broken leg after being hit by a car, we do not infer she is in pain; we see a child in pain.[125] We do not see only nonpersonal behavior and then infer personal actions or psychological states; we do not see only nonpersonal characteristics and then infer the presence of people. We see people and we see them doing things and undergoing experiences. We do not hear mere noises or see mere ink marks; we hear people talking and we read what they are saying. We come to be persons in a context of interpersonal encounters and we are trained to use our vocabulary of persons, actions and experiences just as we learn all of our vocabulary. Non-personal vocabulary has no privileged status such that all other vocabulary is constructed out of it. Encounters with nonpersonal objects is not privileged over encounters with people. The behaviorists are wrong in assuming this. Philosophers who would reduce all language about people, actions and experiences are wrong when they think that some language about nonpersonal physical objects is the primitive language to which the languages of personal life, history, the social, and the religious must be reduced. We form opinions about stones, but Wittgenstein writes, we are not of the opinion that the people we encounter are people; rather we live with attitudes toward these people that are attitudes towards a Soul.[126] In a Wittgensteinian interpretation of language and rationality, social practices and interpersonal encounters replace asocial and ahistorical meanings and structures as the inescapable factors present in human linguistic and rational life.

B.   HEIDEGGER'S DESCRIPTIONS OF EXPERIENTIAL MEANING

Heidegger goes even further than Wittgenstein in his interpretation of the undeniable social pragmatics of meaningful human life and understanding. Although in his later writings, as I interpret them, Heidegger is trying to find a way of writing which could express his encounters with the other to social rationality, I find in his early writings a rich body of insights that can deepen the Wittgensteinian interpretation of human understanding presented in the previous section. Dialogue with Heidegger's texts is well worth the strenuous effort demanded of the reader of his texts. Even his early texts are hard to read because of Heidegger's introduction of a host of new technical terms that he believes are necessary to prevent his interpretation of human understanding from being reduced to just one more modernist, metaphysical theory.

Heidegger writes that all of our writing, speaking, thinking, and understanding of personal and nonpersonal beings in the world are matters of participation in an interdependent, holistic set of contingent, historical, and social practices. He is a Hegelian who has listened to Kierkegaard, seeing all objects and subjects as socially constituted in interdependence, and seeing all understanding and misunderstanding as aspects of and definitive of practical, living, existential modes of subjectivity. Given his interpretation that anything that is for us "a being" is something that is socially constituted, and that all conceptualizing, perceiving, asserting, interpreting, and theorizing are participations in social practices and presuppose practical, existential understanding, it is not surprising that logical positivists, such as Carnap, found meaningless his talk about Being and Nothing. Carnap never recognized that Heidegger is seeking to overcome all traditional metaphysical interpretations of beings, Being, and Nothingness.[127] Carnap never recognized that Heidegger was attempting to fatally replace all modernist epistemological interpretations of understanding as being merely a matter of intellectual and theoretical propositional beliefs.

Our understand of beings, Heidegger claims, consists primarily in knowing how to live with them, how to do things in socially trained ways with them (hammer nails, have a picnic in the shade under a tree, sweep up or hide the useless dust under the bed).[128] Our primary relationship to objects is being absorbed in a nonthematic way in coping with and skillfully manipulating the beings available for us to deal with, given our socialization. It is not the representational intentionality of which Husserl wrote. What the tree in our backyard means to us is not primarily what is said about trees of a certain kind in a theory in botany. It is that which we sit under, that whose leaves we rake up, that from which our son fell and broke his arm, that through which the early morning sun shines into our kitchen window. It is only when there is a total breakdown in a people's practical absorption in dealing with things that they merely gaze at them as objects or, if they live in a scientific culture, theoretically detach themselves from practical absorption in order to discover their "objective" characteristics and explain their causal properties.[129] Our primary understanding of the meaning of things is located in our ways of dealing with things. We show our understanding of a screwdriver by screwing screws with it. This understanding present in our practical coping skills is part of a whole set of holistically interdependent skills we have acquired by being socially trained to live in a certain way with culturally constituted objects. Beings, including human beings, are in the world in the same manner that screwdrivers and carpenters live in a culturally specific world of carpentry and that teams and sportswriters live in an American, Japanese or Puerto Rican world of baseball. These are historical worlds that only bear family resemblances to each other.

Gazing and theorizing are parasitic on the absorbed exercise of socially trained skills. Theoretical objects require objectification, the decontextualizing of the life world in which we act. Theorizing then requires recontextualization, and thus all scientific data reports are theory laden. Interpreting things as objects in a world of spatial, temporal, and causal relations, "objectively" knowable by any and all people located in any and all social and cultural worlds, requires seeking to remove all variable social and cultural factors, an activity which itself requires participation in a certain set of highly disciplined social practices. The seemingly universal applicability of the formal necessities of mathematics, which so concerned Frege and Husserl, is dependent on the development of the modern social practices of objectifying things and mathematizing the world in such a way that Newton could begin to talk of free failing bodies when left to themselves.[130] As Kierkegaard had written, objectivity is a mode of subjectivity; a secondary mode presupposing the more primary mode of absorbed practice and participation in the social and cultural practices of objectifying and theorizing. As Wittgenstein has written, what we say or write, what we believe, presupposes historically and socially specific language games and forms of life. Experiences of things in our world are not passive perceptions of "external" objects but are socially trained acts of living with culturally constituted objects. Likewise, believing and desiring are themselves the exercise of social and cultural practices, and thus actions are not simply the causal result of beliefs and desires. We live with practical understanding, and sometimes for some people in some social worlds this involves knowing how to objectify, gaze, theorize, and construct causal explanations.

Our understanding of the meaning of beings, therefore, cannot be gained by the bracketing procedures recommended by Husserl. For

Heidegger, as for Wittgenstein, meanings are not objects available for simple inspection and description. The meaning of the tree I see in my backyard is not simply present in my observation, ready for mental inspection and description once I focus my attention properly by bracketing out nonessential characteristics. We can understand this meaning only by interpreting our interdependent, socially trained coping skills (one of which is my seeing of things like trees) and the interdependent world of cultural objects we live with in daily life (the tree I see is one such cultural object). To articulate my understanding of the tree I see in my backyard, I must interpret my entire social and cultural world, something which can never be made explicit because trying to do so presupposes the exercise of skills that always remain silently in the background. Likewise, no interpretation can ever be total because each is made from a point defined by unexamined background presuppositions and each has its own practical orientation. Our understanding can only be "lighted up" by various interpretations; it cannot be exhaustively presented in an all-encompassing, explanatory theory, whether that theory be scientific or metaphysical. At different times in his philosophical career, in order to do different sorts of things, Heidegger provides different interpretations of the twentieth century, North Atlantic world in which he found himself. Sometimes he focuses on our use of cultural artifacts, tools. At other times he focuses on our efforts to control things, on the way social practices come to be, on human efforts to exercise power over things, or on our efforts to live without understanding the merely social character of the constitution of all beings and understanding.

Throughout most of his philosophical life, Heidegger is concerned with the meaning of Being and with reawakening understanding of the question of the meaning of Being.[131] What does it mean for hammers, dust under the bed, and people to simply be? He distinguishes his concern about the meaning of Being, however, from the traditional metaphysical project of using the principle of sufficient reason to locate in the necessary existence of a necessary being (Aristotle's unmoved mover, Aquinas's God, Hegel's Absolute) the reason why all contingent beings are and are as they contingently are. Such metaphysical projects are labeled by Heidegger as "ontotheological.[132] Ontotheologians assume that all contingent beings must have some common characteristic in order for them simply to be. For contingently existing beings, this supposedly is the characteristic of being necessarily caused to be by a necessarily existent supreme being who is the ultimate reason why anything is and is as it is. Being necessarily existent, this supreme being is taken to be the cause of its own existence. For Hegel, this ultimate ground of being and value was Absolute Being itself, the rationally necessary law of the historical development of social and cultural practices.

While maintaining Hegel's interpretation of the historical and holistic, social character of all beings, including human beings, Heidegger rejects the Hegelian idea that the history of the social constitution of beings is governed by a rational law of necessity. Being, Heidegger writes, is free.[133] Social and cultural practices exist contingently. They could have been different. There is no ultimate metaphysical reason why they are as they are. They just are. They rest on nothing. Furthermore, they might be different in the future. Poets might let new worlds come to be through their poeticizing.[134] By creating new ways of conceiving things, new vocabularies, poets create new worlds in which people can live and beings can be meaningful to them. Interpretation, exemplifying dialogical listening, might add to the meaning of things.[135] Ruptures in the historical life of social and cultural practices might occur.[136] While the meaning of Being is always tied to people's social ways of living, these ways can change and in that sense Being is free.

In Heidegger's interpretation of Western social and cultural history, however, the dominant trends in that history have been massively influenced by ontotheologies. For most thinkers the answer to the question of the meaning of the Being of beings has been so obvious that they lost the ability to genuinely ask the question. Even the development of modern scientism, with its secular abandonment of ontotheological explanations, with its positivistic faith in the autonomy of scientific thinking, with its usefulness to those who wish to technologically control things, still retains the old metaphysical understanding of the meaning of the Being of beings. This is shown by the way it treats all beings as mere objects of perceptual gaze, theoretical inquiry, and technological domination. Abandoning ontotheology, however, has produced major changes in modern Western social and cultural practices. Having been trained for so long to expect metaphysically ultimate explanations and justifications, modern life is heavily influenced by the experience of the absence of such ultimates, by the experience of the nothingness upon which everything rests, by the experience of the death of the metaphysical god. Even as a man's life can be dominated by his experience of the absence, at the dinner table or in the backyard or in his bed, of his wife who had died after living with him for forty years, so people in the modern world anxiously respond in various ways to the sense of loss that haunts modern life. New forms of nihilism have arisen; new forms of religious fundamentalism have attempted to reestablish ontotheologies on grounds of faith rather than reason.

Heidegger's transformation of Hegel's ontotheological theoretical holism into a practical holism without a metaphysical absolute does maintain that understanding the meaning of the Being of all beings involves a living appreciation of the contingent, social, and historical character of all beings, of our understanding (and misunderstanding) of them, and thus of our understanding of ourselves. This does not mean, however, that, for Heidegger, beings now are to be seen as the creations of people rather than some supreme being. It does not mean that he is endorsing that sort of humanism.[137] Beings are socially constituted, not created. Even as a nation-state comes to be through the acceptance in practice of a constitution, so beings come to be beings for people through the social constitution of such beings and people. Trees, chairs, photons, cars, and Coca-Cola bottles exist for us only because in our society they are thought about, seen, and dealt with in a certain way. In the movie *The Gods Must Be Crazy*, what we moviegoers see as a Coca-Cola bottle being thrown out of an airplane is seen by a native African as a gift from the gods. Coca-Cola bottles had not been constituted in his world as objects to be seen. The constituting of beings usually is not done deliberately by individuals, even as most social and cultural practices are not the products of people following a conscious plan of action adopted after deliberating about what to do. Furthermore, people too are socially constituted, and so are the desires and reasons they use in their deliberations. The social and the cultural gets to us before we can get to them. Adults train and nurture new generations to participate in existing practices. In this manner the social and the cultural reproduce themselves. In Heidegger's language, people are thrown into social and cultural worlds and find themselves engaged in social practices: classifying, differentiating, individuating, seeing things in a certain way; desiring, fearing, prizing, and hoping for certain sorts of things; living as and understanding themselves to be a certain sort of person (black, female, American, handicapped, poor, homosexual). We, our concepts, the beings we perceive are all socially constituted.

Being inescapably social in this manner does not, however, make people into mere robots or social functionaries. Our social training enables us to cope with things in a variety of ways, dealing with implements as various sorts of things (under a variety of aspects), being startled when breakdowns occur, and dealing deliberately with things as objects when breakdowns do occur.[138] Since the social and cultural practices that we inherit often conflict with each other, it is not possible to be merely a social functionary just doing what one has been trained to do. Each individual person has to make a living endorsement of some parts of her or his inheritance while rejecting other parts. Some individuals, understanding the social and historical character of the Being of all beings, can let themselves be poets through whom new practices may be initiated. Some individuals, such as Heidegger, may draw upon their pretheoretical understanding of their world and upon marginalized practices in their world in order to criticize what are seen as the dominant tendencies in their world. (These criticisms will be examined in the next chapter.) That there may be dominant tendencies in a specific social and cultural world, thereby giving to this world a historical destiny, does not mean that a social and cultural world is so determined that a predicable future is inevitable. Social practices continue from generation to generation only if older generations keep participating in dominant training practices and if new generations continue to give such practices continued life by participating in them.

Social change can come from a variety of sources. Giving a living endorsement to marginalized practices can lessen participation in current, dominant practices. Also, if dominant tendencies are due to a cover up of important aspects of our pretheoretical understanding, and perhaps due to a coverup of the coverup, then a critical interpretation might expose these coverups and end for some participation in the dominant practices. Finally, some people might let their understanding of Being allow them to become poets through whom new worlds are created, new vocabularies, actions, attitudes, and moods are produced.

In the interpretations of meaning provided by Wittgenstein and Heidegger, neither linguistic meanings nor the meaning of beings in the world or the Being of beings are seen as asocial and ahistorical. Meanings are not objects at all. Explaining the meaning of something is enabling someone to do something: to use words in a certain way, to cope in a certain way, to understand how to act, feel, live. Interpretations of the meaning of texts, historical situations and actions, or social and cultural practices are motivated by breakdowns in our understanding. These interpretations are aimed at restoring our understanding, our ability to go on reading, listening, responding, acting, living. Frege and Husserl charge that one must postulate asocial and ahistorical meanings if people are to be able to say the same things or to understand what things mean to other people. Saussure charges that one must postulate universal and timeless syntactical values (relations) in order to account for the synchronic character of language. Wittgenstein and Heidegger attempt to show that no such necessities exist. Shared social practices and practical understanding or know-how is all that is required.

A major question seems to remain unanswered by this Wittgenstein/ Heidegger interpretation of meaning. People in different places on Earth and people at different times in different histories have had and still do have different social and cultural practices, different ways of understanding things, different vocabularies. How can we account for people in one social/cultural world, in one historical era, being able to understand people in different worlds and different eras? As different as people's social worlds may be, some cross-cultural understanding does seem to occur. At least we understand that there are people with different social and cultural practices.[139] Must we not postulate asocial and ahistorical meanings to account for people in one social/cultural world having some understanding of people in other worlds or historical eras? As difficult as it is for most of us to read Plato's *Dialogues* or Japanese Zen poetry, some understanding seems possible. How is this to be explained except by postulating asocial, ahistorical meanings and reader's abilities to transcend their social, cultural, and historical idiosyncrasies to know these meanings? Let me offer the following two-part answer.

Wittgenstein's interpretation of the natural conditions that form the necessary background framework for human understanding and reasoning provides the first half of the explanation. There are natural correlations between being in pain and exhibiting pain behavior that are common to all human beings and many animals. Before we have opinions about each other, we just do live with each other interpersonally. We treat other humans, and things that look like them, as individuals with sensations and feelings. In addition, there are regular reactions that almost all human beings have to certain sorts of training (looking in the direction at which one is pointing, learning to follow arithmetical rules). Without these natural regularities there would be none of the rule-following involved in any of the many, different social and cultural practices that people have constituted.[140] There are also virtually universal social regularities (such as what Heidegger called "the mathematization of the world") that make certain sorts of rule-following activities possible. "Without the interest our culture has in discrete entities and their numerical comparisons, the natural numbers and the rules for their use would not play the central part they do in many of our everyday practices."[141] No matter how different the linguistic and other social practices are of a group of people, we see them as people having sensory reactions to their environment and as acting in socially trained ways. Therefore, Wittgenstein writes, "The common behavior of mankind is the system of reference by means of which we interpret an unknown language."[142] Common behavior and not transcendent meanings is what enables people to begin to understand people in different social and cultural worlds. It is only a beginning, however, for there still remains the problem of living in one social-cultural world and interpreting people's actions in another world.

Hans-Georg Gadamer, a student and close associate of Heidegger, has attempted to tell the second half of the story by presenting an interpretation of understanding literary texts and human actions that accounts for crosscultural understanding without postulating such asocial, ahistorical meanings or transcendental knowledge. Whenever I previously wrote about dialogue, I was appropriating Gadamer's position. He has pointed out that all understanding and interpreting is done by someone who possesses a background framework, a set of socially acquired abilities and dispositions as well as natural regularities, a set of practical, living prejudgments (prejudices). The modern, Western Enlightenment tradition had a prejudice against prejudice, and thus sought in a pragmatically self-refuting way to find a point of view from which to interpret human life that would transcend all social, historical, or individual variability. In the prejudgments, prejudices, of the Enlightenment is the modern Cartesian taken-for-granted that judgments and interpretations are unjustified unless they can be proved using justifying reasons.[143] Gadamer sides with the pragmatist in claiming that all judging begins with taken-for-granted, traditional reasons, prejudices, which are used until reasons are present for doubting them.[144] One must separate overhasty judgments (prejudices in the bad sense of the word) from taken-for-granted judgments that have not yet been shown to be unjustified.

Since all human actions are performed against a background of prejudgments, how can one person, performing interpretive acts against one background, know what another person is doing, saying, writing when that person is acting against another background? Well, we can't know historical actions and their cultural products (literary texts) the way scientists gain knowledge of chemical reactions. Human actions have meaning to those acting but chemical events have no meaning to the chemicals reacting. Gadamer denies that the authors of actions have privileged access to the meaning of their own actions or the texts produced.[145] They too must be interpreters of the background world out of which their action or text arose. Questions of meaning only arise when background taken-for-granteds are not sufficient for going on acting, responding, reading, listening, when acts of interpreting are needed. The meaning of an action or text, therefore, is always a function of what it means to the interpreter. Interpretations by the actor's contemporaries, who share much of the same background as the actor, also are not to be privileged. However, not only may actions and texts mean different things to interpreters in different worlds and eras, but cultural and historical distance may make possible critical interpretations that contemporaries found impossible, given their prejudgments.[146] Although the meanings of actions or texts remain a function of what they mean to interpreters, this meaning is not just anything an interpreter reads into the text. Interpreters need to be open in their interpretations and must not simply be forcing actions and texts into Procrustean beds structured by the interpreter's own background prejudices.

For Gadamer, dialogue is the key to crosscultural understanding.[147] I let the actions and words of people from other worlds and times say something to me. I do not reduce differences to something the same as what obtains in my own world. I come to a text prepared to hear something, something new, something challenging my own way of understanding things. When I hear something strange being said or done, I don't try to reductively translate it into my current way of understanding things; I let the strange challenge my taken-for-granteds, my prejudices. I, of course, don't throw away my whole background. I couldn't succeed even if I wanted to try. I don't have to become a sixteenth century samurai in order to gain some understanding of him. Of course, dialogue also is a matter of talking back as well as listening. I judge what I hear as well as let it judge me. Crosscultural dialogue is possible, not only because of universal human regularities, but also because languages and social-cultural worlds are not unchangeable prisons and because texts are in a sense contemporaneous with all readers. I read what Plato and Confucius and Heidegger have to say to me. My vocabulary can change. My background taken-for-granteds can change. I acquire an openness to experience.

If one opens oneself up in the manner that dialogue demands, one cannot predict what one will hear, how one's background prejudgments will change, what one will become. Dialogue and cross-cultural understanding require taking that "dangerous" risk. It is through such dialogue that poetic ruptures in social-cultural history occur, that the Being of beings exhibits its ungrounded freedom. Interpreting is ontologically productive. The meaning of Plato's world or Shakespeare's texts is a function of what they mean to those engaged in interpretive dialogue with them. Such meaning is subject to historical growth and modification. It is neither an object transcending the social and historical nor a fixed condition in the mind of an actor or author. The meaning of a text or historical act itself is historical. What Hamlet means is a function of what it has meant to all the people who have read and interpreted it and what it will mean to future readers with their unpredictable backgrounds.

It is against such a background of historical meaning that one needs to interpret failures to understand and misinterpretations. Failures occur when one refuses to interpret things in any way other than what is made possible by one's current prejudgments. One just can't make sense out of what has been written or is being done. Interpretations can be labeled as misinterpretations by other interpreters and by the original interpreter at a later time when it can be pointed out that large portions of the text or set of actions are being ignored or that the interpretation offered just doesn't maintain internal coherence. According to Gadamer, neither failures to understand, misunderstandings, or crosscultural understanding necessitate asocial and ahistorical meanings.

By interpretive dialogue with the texts of Wittgenstein and Heigegger, I have been constructing an interpretation of the social nature of human rationality. There is much more that can be added to this interpretation that will strengthen the claim that it is not necessary to postulate asocial and ahistorical meanings in order for human discourse, thought, and experience to exist. Next, by dialogically engaging the texts of so-called "poststructuralists" such as Derrida and Foucault, we can uncover powerful additional considerations for endorsing a social interpretation of human social rationality.

C.   POST-MODERNISM AS POST-STRUCTURALISM

Saussure claims that one can separate diachronic (historical) interpretations of language as a system of signs from synchronic interpretations, which focus on what the syntactic relationships between linguistic signs in a system are like at any given historical moment. He also claims that one can and should separate an analysis of the idealized material aspects of signs (signs as signifiers) from the idealized conceptual aspects of signs (signs as signifieds). Derrida challenges both of these claims as well as a host of other claims about the possibility of dealing with language ahistorically or of identifying nonmaterial objects such as meanings, concepts, propositions, intentions, or claims. Foucault charges that a synchronic interpretation of language as a system would not be adequate to account for the historical development of various forms of discourse given that such forms of discourse are produced by the historical exercises of power producing the domination of some groups of people while benefiting other groups. Derrida and Foucault write on other issues that will be considered in later chapters, but here I will focus on their critiques of the claim that there are asocial and ahistorical structures and meanings. The challenges presented by Derrida and Foucault apply not only to Saussure's form of linguistic structuralism but to all the other forms of structuralism modeled on Saussure's work in linguistics. These two thinkers charge that supposedly structural relationships cannot be totally separated from the supposed content in such structures. Relationships and the identity of individuals so related cannot be isolated from their historical past or their future possibilities. All linguistic and human worlds are material and historical through and through.

V. DERRIDA'S DECONSTRUCTION OF MODERNIST THEORIES OF SIGNS

Derrida's deconstructive critique of Saussure's texts makes it difficult, even indecent, to attempt to summarize or paraphrase Derrida's critique. One of the goals of Derrida's deconstructive rhetoric is to aid his readers to understand that there are no ahistorical, nonmaterial concepts, ideas, propositions, claims, positions, or critiques to be reproduced by translations or paraphrases. There are, therefore, no Derridian ahistorical propositions or positions (abstractable from the actual texts he has written) to summarize or paraphrase. One can only write for one's own rhetorical purposes in response to Derrida's writing. Derrida emphasizes the extreme difficulty involved in writing a general and systematic interpretation of writing and language.[148] Any such interpretation would be historically tied to what had been written about language by people such as Frege, Husserl, and Saussure. It would have to use words written by them and interpreted by their readers, who would be heavily influenced by these writer's metaphysical efforts to subordinate writing to oral speech and oral speech to asocial and ahistorical thoughts, concepts, and meanings. Furthermore, readers, with expectations influenced by their readings of earlier metaphysical, ontotheological interpretations of language and meaning, would come to Derrida's texts expecting to be able to abstract the essence of his interpretation, the central idea which they take for granted must be the organizing principle of his interpretation. However, it is just these ideas of an essence and an organizing principle, this logocentrism, that Derrida, in his interpretation of language, wants to show to be unstable.

When one carefully reads and interprets texts embracing or not resisting ontotheology or logocentrism, Derrida writes, one can discover that the inescapably historical and social materiality of all language, and thus of those texts, stands in conflict with any ontotheological, logocentric reading of them. When carefully interpreted, such texts deconstruct themselves. Many of the texts that Derrida has written consist of interpretations of the texts of Plato,[149] Rousseau,[150] Hegel,[151] Husserl,[152] and Saussure[153] presented with the rhetorical goal of letting these texts deconstruct themselves. In all of his writing about language and writing, Derrida is struggling to find literary styles to use which will enable him to resist the ontotheological and logocentric inheritance that he claims contaminates all writing about language. Sometimes Derrida seems to be writing that all language, not just philosophical texts, is contaminated by this inheritance so that one can never escape the need to do ever new readings of one's own last writings so that they too can deconstruct themselves.[154]

This, however, seems to attribute to philosophers far more power over human language than they actually exercise. Focusing on the actual pragmatics of the vocabulary of writing, speaking, thinking, conceiving, etc., as recommended by Dewey and Wittgenstein, would allow us to interpret ordinary language as endangered but not totally enslaved by the metaphysical spinning of linguistic wheels.[155] Also, as will be developed in chapter 5, focusing on saying and writing, rather than on what is said, as Emmanuel Levinas recommends, would allow us to find even philosophical texts that are not enslaved by ontotheology and logocentrism. The interpretation of Derrida's texts which follows, therefore, sees such texts as rhetorically directed efforts to remove barriers to the reader's understanding of the historically and socially material character of all language and rationality, an understanding that never has been slavishly tied to metaphysical, epistemological, ontotheological, and logocentric claims about language, meaning, or interpretation. I believe there is enough pragmatic sameness between what Derrida is writing, what I am presenting as my interpretation of his general interpretation of language, and what my readers will be interpreting as my interpretation to make Gadamer-type dialogue possible between all of us.

One place to begin an interpretation of Derrida's deconstructive reading of Saussure is with the reminder that Derrida has read and listened to Heidegger's practical, holistic interpretation of human understanding. One can even hear resonances of such practical holism in Saussure's claim that signs have no identities in and by themselves because signifiers and signifieds are what they are only because of their functional relationships within a socially established system of signs. Saussure, however, had great difficulty in maintaining this claim because of his further claim that language primarily is a tool for communicating knowledge of speakers" thoughts and concepts to listeners. Heidegger had interpreted speakers and speaker meanings as being functionally located in a historically developing, practical, holistic world. Saussure, however, seems to slip into an interpretation of subjects, concepts and speaker meanings that resonates less with Heidegger's socially constituted thinkers and meanings than with Husserl's subjects, meanings, and transcendental egos that have transcendental meanings present and available for intuitive inspection.

Derrida, therefore, begins by challenging Saussure's claim that language is primarily a tool for communicating ideas or thoughts from a speaker to a hearer. He writes that for Saussure "communication presupposes subjects (whose identity and presence are constituted before the signifying operation) and objects (signified concepts, a thought meaning that the passage of communication will have neither to constitute, nor, by all rights, to transform)."[156] Before language can be a communication tool, however, it has to be a socialization tool that is used in training people how to participate in linguistic practices, a tool used in constituting speakers as the social subjects that they are. Besides, language also is a performative tool used to constitute social roles and institutional verdicts, as Austin wrote.[157]In addition, language is a plaything in the hands of writers and poets. Interpreting speaker meanings is always a matter of interpreting a speaker's participation in a whole social and cultural world of practices in which the words the speaker uses have only historically developing, socially functional identities.[158]

In Derrida's interpretation there are no transcendental signifieds, no purely ideal thoughts, ideas, concepts, propositions, identifiable without reference to contingent, historical, and social conditions, knowledge of which can be gained by hearers by way of communication from one person to another through the use of words. Derrida seeks to deconstruct all texts in which there is claimed or presupposed a metaphysics of presence, a metaphysics which holds that there are self-contained objects (Aristotle's sensible particulars, British empiricism's copies of sensory qualities, Husserl's meanings) simply cognitively present to a self-contained subject. Subjects and objects, whether objects of perception or meaning, are socially constituted and are knowable only through participation in historical and social practices of understanding and interpretation.

As Derrida reads him, Saussure's very distinction between the signifier and signified aspects of language, and his prioritizing of speech over writing, are due to the contamination of his text by a metaphysics of presence.

> The maintenance of the rigorous distinction…between the *signans* and *the signatum*, the equation of the *signatum* and the concept…inherently leaves open the possibility of thinking a *concept signified in and of itself,* a concept simply present for thought, independent of a relationship to language.… By leaving open this possibility…Saussure accedes to the classical exigency of what I have proposed to call a "transcendental signified," which in and of itself, in its essence, would

refer to no signifier, would exceed the chain of signs, and would no longer itself function as signifier.[159]

Saussure, for essential, and essentially metaphysical, reasons had to privilege speech, everything that links the sign to *phone*.[160] *Phone*, in effect, is the signifying substance *given to consciousness* as that which is most intimately tied to the thought of the signified concept. From this point of view, the voice is consciousness itself. When I speak, not only am I conscious of being present for what I think, but I am conscious also of keeping as close as possible to my thought.... Not only do the signifier and the signified seem to unite, but also, in the confusion, the signifier seems to erase itself or to become transparent, in order to allow the concept to present itself as it is.[161]

Signifiers and signifieds, for Derrida, were he to use this vocabulary, are inescapably interdependent and possess only historical, social identities. The social identity of signifiers can wander (deliberately or accidentally) because of the material family resemblances between signifiers within a discourse or language game and between different discourses and language games. Consider the relations holding between "proper," "property," and "propriety" or between "author" and "authority" or "subject," "subjected," and "subjective." The nomadic journey of words as signifiers produces wandering, nomadic journeys for the uses of such words, for what they signify. Derrida grafts into his interpretation of writing Levi Strauss's term "bricolage," the borrowing of expressions from the texts of one's heritage.[162] The actual usage of homonyms, homophones, and homographs may accidentally or deliberately feed off of each other. One might talk of tears in the fabric of our lived world in a way inseparable from the tears of suffering produced by such tears.[163] Signifieds also wander because of people's rich use of metaphors and because of the way their associations of things affect the relations between signifieds. No clear line of demarcation exists in our linguistic practices between using words and associating things, using words literally and using them metaphorically, idealizing signifiers and idealizing signifieds.

Interpretations of thought and oral speech, Derrida writes, would do better if they were modeled on interpretations of writing rather than having writing interpreted as a degenerate form of oral speech or thought. Chronologically, we may learn to speak orally before we learn to write, but the very thing that metaphysicians of meaning don't like about writing (its historical and social materiality) may be inescapable characteristics of speech and thought also. While constantly warning about the dangers of metaphysical uses of the word "science," Derrida attempts to give an alternative to Saussure's science of language with his own grammatology, his own interpretation of the general character of writing, and thus of speech and thought.

Derrida substitutes the word "gram" for the word "sign." Grams are material/ideal functional units in a practical holistic system of writing (speaking, thinking, experiencing) functioning always against a background of skills and social practices. They can be known only by interpreting for a practical purpose their place in social historical worlds of writing and living. Grams are iterable (usable again and again) and they can be grafted into new contexts, discourses, language games, thus attaining changing identities.[164] No interpretation of a gram can be complete because its functional identity is tied to a constitutive outside, to constituting supplements, to that which is absent from either immediate inspection or any given interpretation. Grams are marked by "differance": the gram's identity is supplemented by things it differs from and it is tied to things in the past it differs to, traces of the past that mark its present identity, traces that one must interpret by tracing them back through a record of the gram's use, its wandering historical identity, an interpretation that is never exhaustive.

If one is to think trace, one must think it before metaphysical oppositions take over. It is not ambiguous between two self-contained ideal senses. One's tracing of traces is always marked by traces. It is not a metaphysical thing, fact or principle. It is pluridimensional and not locatable on a metaphysical linear time line on which all things happening to metaphysical self-contained things can be located. No science or discipline can metaphysically represent it and explain it. The gram "trace" can only be interpreted. The same holds for the gram "differance."[165] This gram also is not a sign with an ahistorical, asocial signification that simply can be present. In writing an interpretation of writing, one can write that differance is the presupposition of all grams, but this does not make differance into some metaphysically representable property of grams. This "gram" has nonmetaphysically synonymous substitutes: "arche writing," "arch trace," "spacing," and "supplement," with each substitute having a place in a pragmatically slightly different rhetorical strategy of deconstructing writing contaminated by ontotheology, logocentrism, and metaphysics of presence, and their prioritization of one alternative over its supposedly categorically different opposite. (Thought over oral speech; speech over writing; the ideal over the material; mind over body; the unchanging over the changing; the necessary over the contingent; the essential over the accidental; the selfsame over difference, outside, other; presentation over interpretation; ultimate explanation over irremovable mystery; the literal over the metaphorical or mythical; truth and knowledge over rhetoric.) Deconstructing such writing is not a matter of reversing these priorities but of showing the need to dissolve all metaphysical absolutizing of these oppositions. Deconstructive writing aims at interpreting all language, thought, assertions, beliefs, desires, experiences, things, qualities, relations, events, and processes as subject to differance, trace, and supplementation. They are all socially and historically constituted.

Derrida's deconstructive reading of Saussure's theory of linguistic structures is extended by him to cover all structuralist theories. The social theories of structuralists are modeled on theories in chemistry. In chemistry, characteristics of compounds are given explanations by analyzing compounds into a systematic description of the elements making up the compounds and of laws governing the relations between different elements and between a set of elements and compounds of such elements. The identities of such structures depend upon a principle (a logos) that limits the range of variations in such structures. Structuralists want to be social chemists. Social structures, as interpreted by structuralists, have a center (a central defining logos) but this center, this central principle, is itself not a part of the structure. Thus, structuralist theories are logocentric metaphysical theories. The history of metaphysics, Derrida writes after the manner of Hegel's interpretation of different historical epochs of understanding, is the history of different principles constituting differently structured human worlds. These theories of structured worlds all are motivated by a desire to limit variations, to get beyond anxiety by guaranteeing reassuring constancy and certitude. A rupture, however, Derrida writes, occurred in the historical development of structural accounts when people like Kierkegaard, Nietzsche, Heidegger, and Freud began to think about theoretically structured worlds, about the desire for such accounts, about the absence of any accounting in the account for the central principle organizing the structured world. Once ontotheology is over, the principle of sufficient reason cannot be applied to the structure's center. Understanding one's way around social worlds is always a matter of more or less skillful participation in social practices; interpretation always is a matter of aiding such understanding by developing interpretations rhetorically serving to remove particular barriers to understanding. The structuralist, Levi-Strauss, found it impossible to maintain an absolute separation between nature (the universal, free of normative ordering) and culture (that dependent upon norms which vary from society to society); the incest taboo, it turns out, is universal, spontaneous, and normative.[166] Similarly, Derrida finds what we take to be the world of objects of nature to be socially constituted, needing the same kind of understanding and interpretation as linguistic texts. Everything is a text needing reading and interpreting.

VI.   FOUCAULT'S INTERPRETATION OF DISCOURSE

Language as a set of social practices in which people are trained and disciplined to participate, Michel Foucault writes, needs to be interpreted as part of a whole set of disciplinary practices that result in some groups of people benefiting from other groups of people being subjected to dominating power. In the next two chapters, we will examine in more detail Foucault's interpretive critique of the dominating power produced through disciplinary practices. Here I want to focus only on Foucault's writings about the social character of language as disciplined discourse and about the social practice of labeling certain users of language as authors.[167] Saussure interpreted language as a tool for communicating knowledge of speakers" meanings, a tool whose character at a given moment of time can be presented as an abstractable, ahistorical synchronic system of syntactical relationships. In his texts Foucault points out that such an interpretation fails to deal with the historically changing social practices that control who can use certain forms of speech and when the use of such discourse is permitted. Not only are classification systems and vocabularies socially constituted in terms of group interests, but so are entire types of discourse (economic discourse, legal discourse, criminal justice discourse, medical discourse, mental illness discourse, linguistics discourse, philosophical discourse, academic discourse). Foucault's use of "discourse" bears significant family resemblances to Wittgenstein's use of "language games," except that Wittgenstein did not attend to the relations of power that produce such discourses and which are reenforced by this production. Language for Foucault is not an undifferentiated system available as a tool usable by any and all speakers. Linguistic practices are socially organized into overlapping sets of discursive practices, organized in such a way that not any speaker at any time can use any set of words.

Saussure's interpretation of language results from his sharing of an ancient traditional desire to think and write without thinking about the practices and institutions of discourse in which language users are participating. This desire is based on the assumption that language is a nameless voice, a transparent, infinitely open medium. In contrast, according to Foucault, "…in every society the production of discourse is at once controlled, selected, organized and redistributed according to a certain number of procedures, whose role is to avert its powers and dangers, to cope with chance events and to evade its ponderous, awesome materiality."[168] In Foucault's interpretation, discourse is a social object that is subjected to controls. Speaking becomes such a social object, becomes discourse, when some speaking is excluded as improper. Engaging in speech and discourse is exercising power, getting others to do things. It is often treated as a dangerous exercise of power. Since the changes in the history of discourse are subjected to chanciness, such changes will be treated as threatening by groups benefiting from the conservation of established discursive practices. Language as discourse is material and not transparent. It is the product of social forces that sometimes are difficult to mold or change, and it exercises awe inspiring power, producing objects, subjects, domination, and resistance to domination.

Foucault, in his interpretative description of the social practices that control speech, classified such practices into three sets of sets, with, of course, no absolutistic boundaries separating such sets. First, there are three types of exclusionary practices. (a) Some people are prohibited from saying certain things by being denied the right to have their speech taken seriously. The speech of radicals on the right and the left is denied access to serious political debate in the United States. The speech of pedophiles is too gross to even be entertained. (b) The speech of some members of certain groups is not even included in common, understandable discourse; the speech of the "irrational," the "mad," the "crazies." (c) Often excluded in the traditional Western world and much of the new "global" world is speech not produced in an effort to represent "facts" as they supposedly are independent of all the social and historical variability of knowers, "facts" as present to the mind of an ontotheological god and meeting the possibility demands of some logocentrism. Excluded is speech that inspires respect or terror, speech which is the interpretive reading of a text rather than a representational report of what is just "seen." This last set of exclusions is supported by a vast array of social practices and institutions: pedagogical practices, a publishing industry, libraries, and laboratories obediently serving a will to metaphysical truth;

a literature based in "true" discourse that places beyond question scientific representations and sincere expressions; economic practices codified in a theory of wealth and production (whether capitalist, Marxist, neo-capitalist, neo-Marxist), a penal code of rights validated by knowledge claims in sociology, psychiatry, and medicine.

Second, there are three sets of disciplinary, normative practices that aim at maintaining control within established discourses. (a) In controlling what it is proper to say, appeals often are made to tradition, to a master narrative grounded on repeating an authoritative origin for speech in this discourse (a religious text, a political constitution, a history of judicial interpretations and decisions, a set of commentaries on the meaning of original texts). (b) What new statements can be made within a discourse is often controlled by professionalizing speech into an academic discipline's discourse. Only certain objects may be talked about in a given science at a given time; only certain definitions and rules of inference are permitted; only certain methods can be used in determining "true" claims; only speakers with certain credentials are authorized to make serious claims or raise serious questions; only certain techniques and tools can be used. Academic disciplines are disciplinary; they discipline apprentices to use disciplinary discourse properly. (c) Depending upon whether certain forms of speech are responded to as dangerous or not, some texts (the dangerous ones) get unified into a social object by appealing to a common origin and a single seat of coherence, by treating them as the work of an "author" who can be held responsible for these texts. As opposed to such questionable texts, the others are treated as being transparent. In the sixteenth and seventeenth centuries, theological texts were treated as transparent and left anonymous while scientific texts were attributed to authors. In the twentieth century, scientific texts are treated as transparent and left authorless while literature is tied to authors. Sometimes authorhood is attributed to the originators of a theory, a tradition, or a discipline, such as Homer, Aristotle or Hippocrates, or to the originators of whole forms of discourse that make possible and regulate speech and the writing of books, such as

Marx and Freud.[169] Since authors are not socially immaterial subjects with ahistorical intentions, such intentions cannot be the deciding factor in determining the meanings of texts. Attributing authorship and interpreting authored texts are always interest serving actions.

Third, control over discourse also is attained through four different techniques (technologies) for controlling the conditions under which discourse may be used. (a) Rituals are instituted governing the use of various kinds of discourse. Religious rituals, judicial rituals, academic professional meeting rituals are used to say who may speak and under what circumstances they may speak. (b) Doctrines not allowed to be questioned are used to require all speakers to recognize the same "truths," thus allowing for a division between orthodoxy and heresy. These doctrines often are the sort which require one to adhere to the defining ideology of some class, social or racial status, or nationality. (c) Educational practices are used to control means of access to and the distribution of discourse. "Every educational system is a political means of maintaining or modifying the appropriation of discourse, with the 'knowledge' and power it carries with it."[170] (d) Writers and readers of a certain form of discourse often end up in "fellowships of discourse" whose function is to preserve or reproduce discourse in such a way that it will circulate only within a closed community, according to strict regulations, without those in possession being dispossessed by this circulation.[171] These groups might be formally organized as professional associations circulating "secrets" among each other, or they might be informally related as writers of literature, with their acts of writing being institutionalized as they are today, creative acts performed singularly and separately to an anonymous set of readers.

The social constitution and control of discourse is not simply a second-story layer of social structure built on top of a ground-floor set of syntactical and semantical structures. Given a Wittgensteinian interpretation of talk about the meaning of what someone says or writes, explanations of meaning aimed at enabling one to go on with one's listening or reading often require locating such speech and writing within a form of discourse. Understanding the discursive character of language is crucial to understanding how words have been used or can be used. The discursive character of language is part of the pragmatics of language that make semantic and syntactical relationships possible. Foucault's interpretation of discourse (and authorhood), therefore, makes a significant, independent contribution to the plausibility of a thoroughly social interpretation of language and human rationality.

Both Derrida and Foucault are critical interpreters of the texts of Nietzsche and Heidegger. Their critiques of Saussure's theory of signs and linguistic structures can be interpreted as continuations of Nietzsche's critique of modernist metaphysical and epistemological projects and Heidegger's critique of Husserl's theory of asocial, ahistorical meanings. When taken together with the critiques written by Kierkegaard, the early pragmatists, and Wittgenstein, the case in favor of interpreting human rationality as social gets stronger and stronger. One final set of texts will be now be considered, the texts of the neopragmatists, Richard Rorty and Richard Bernstein. They not only add strength to a social interpretation of rationality but they also isolate very clearly some of the major problems that arise when such a social interpretation is endorsed.

VII. NEOPRAGMATISM'S CHALLENGES TO MODERNIST THEORIES

Just as Dewey had critically interpreted and reconstructed in a pragmatic fashion Hegel's accent on social history, so current pragmatists such as Richard Rorty and Richard Bernstein are doing the same to the writings of twentieth century European philosophers. They add additional persuasive texture to a social and historical interpretation of rationality. They both weave their Deweyan/Wittgensteinian critique of recent American and English attempts to redefend the epistemological project with their interpretations of the European critiques of ontotheology, logocentrism, and metaphysics of presence. Rorty directly takes on the late-twentieth-century defenders of the epistemological project whereas Bernstein concentrates on critiquing its presence in the writings of social theorists. They both critically knit the general interpretations and criticisms of late-twentieth-century cultural practices given by recent European philosophers into the pragmatic tradition of social criticism authored by Dewey, attempting to show that practicing social criticism does not require postulating asocial and ahistorical norms.

In the dialogues by Rorty and Bernstein with the texts of Heidegger, Gadamer, Derrida, and Foucault, they not only listen and endorse but they also talk back and criticize. Their criticisms take two forms. First, they seek to recover something of Hegel's optimism[172] about the Western adventure of increasing the possibilities for more human freedom and happiness. They seek to defend current Western social and cultural practices against the existentialist, Marxist, and "postmodern" calls for radical critiques of the supposedly pervasive, dark, enslaving tendencies in such practices. Bernstein sees more in such "dark" critiques than Rorty does, but he too defends a hopeful use of existing rational practices of criticism. Both are political liberals seeking to defend such liberalism without any appeal to moral norms which transcend the social and historical. Since many defenders of the asocial and the ahistorical do so because they think that moral criticism of social practices is impossible without them, Rorty's and Bernstein's interpretations of social criticism will make an invaluable contribution to the interpretation of social rationality being offered here. How "dark" that criticism should be will be examined in the next chapter.

The second criticism that both Rorty and Bernstein address to the recent European philosophers they are reading is directed at what they see as the mystical and religious tendencies present in some of them. Rorty and Bernstein seek to remain thoroughly secular and humanistic, rejecting as useless all talk about anything other than the social and historical. Here Rorty and Bernstein agree with the ontotheologians who claim that religion is dependent upon belief in the existence of the philosopher's god, that supreme being that is the source of all being and value. Believing that this god is dead, Rorty and Bernstein find no alternative to their social secularism. They claim that there is no other to social rationality and those who think there is are nihilistically threatening such rationality that does exist.

In examining the critiques by Rorty and Bernstein of recent defenders of the epistemological project, we can find a good resting place for this chapter's social interpretation of rationality. Rorty's criticisms of the "dark" interpretations of the Western social and cultural practices that constitute Western social rationality provide a profitable challenge to the interpretations that I will present in chapter 3. Rorty's and Bernstein's opposition to what they see as nihilistic critiques of the self-sufficiency of social rationality will present a challenge to the ethical and religious use of such critiques that I will present in chapters 4 and 5.

Listening to the texts of Rorty and Bernstein, we are forced to ask the following questions: Is social criticism possible without postulating asocial and ahistorical norms? Is it possible to make social criticism so radical that it critiques social rationality itself? Can this be done without falling back upon the traditional metaphysical and epistemological projects? How is "radical" social and cultural criticism to be critically interpreted? Is it possible to keep space open in our interpretations for not allowing social rationality to exhaustively blanket human life? Is it possible to keep space open in our lives for comporting ourselves to some other to social rationality without falling back into ontotheology?

Rorty directs his criticism at recent interpretations of the episte-mological triad: the mind, the world, and the supposed relations of the first to the second in representation and truth as correspondence. Rorty again and again writes that people and their language, thoughts, and worlds are social through and through.[173] People are not to be seen as Cartesian mental substances possessing representations and knowledge of nonmental substances.[174] People are only biological organisms[175] that have networks of beliefs and desires.[176] Likewise, in his interpretation, rhetorically aimed at aiding his readers to opt out of the epistemological project, Rorty recommends that we stop talking about the Mind's epistemological counterpart—the World; something supposedly independent of the mind but capable of being represented and known.[177] Rorty, of course, is not recommending that we stop talking about such worlds as the worlds of baseball or finance or that we stop asking people, especially scientists using technical language, what they are talking about when they use a word like "quark." Neither is he suggesting that there weren't continents, oceans, plants, and animals before there were people who could talk about them. Part of our constitution of them as objects we can talk about is the understanding that they could have been around even if Homo sapiens did not yet exist. Such ordinary talk and beliefs, Rorty insists, are not dependent upon the talk of epistemologists about worlds or facts corresponding to our representations or upon the talk of those philosophers who want to be metaphysical realists rather than some other kind of metaphysician.

Rorty's most sustained criticisms have been directed at various theories about the semantical relations supposedly holding between Minds and Worlds (the way things are in themselves, independent of any relations to us), the semantical relations of representation and truth as correspondence. Beliefs, Rorty claims, get related to beliefs when offering justifications of beliefs open to challenge and beliefs are causally related to many different kinds of items in the universe. There are relations of aboutness between socially constituted people and socially constituted objects, but there are, he writes, "no relations of representation."[178] Nothing gets explained when one talks about concepts representing objects that are determinate independent of being represented. "Determinate" cannot be given a use and there is not and cannot be any test of the accuracy of a representation independent of our successful use of words, using social standards of success.[179] In a similar manner, nothing really gets explained, Rorty charges, when one says that beliefs are true because they correspond to the way things are in themselves, independent of any relation to believers, or when one says that such independent facts make beliefs be true.[180]

Rorty wants us to abandon all these epistemological claims and the modernist projects tied to them. He, therefore, joins common cause with those European philosophers who are trying to end metaphysics, ontotheology, the metaphysics of presence, and logocentrism.

On the epistemological issue, Bernstein agrees with Rorty. Bernstein gives his pragmatic project several labels: "Non-Foundational Pragmatic Humanism"[181] and "Dialogical Rationality."[182] From the time of his earliest writings he has accented "praxis," living practical reason and rationally skillful action, as the key to understanding human rationality.[183] Again and again he has attempted to demonstrate the social, historical character of human rationality and life. He tells us that "social institutions are the medium of human life,"[184] that "men are what they do..." (that) social *praxis* shapes and is shaped by the complex web of historical institutions and practices within which they function and work.[185] "Intersubjectivity lies at the very heart of human subjectivity."[186] He endorses the pragmatic "theme of the social character of the self and the community... [in which] the very idea of an individual consciousness that is independent of shared social practices is criticized."[187] He criticizes current mainstream social science because "the only image of human beings that makes sense to many mainstream social scientists is one where individuals are exclusively motivated to maximize their private wants, desires, and interests, whatever they happen to be... There has been a persistent tendency in mainstream social science to neglect, suppress, or underestimate the essential feature of social and political practice."[188]

Bernstein also claims that our social subjectivity is thoroughly historical. "For I agree with Gadamer that we belong to traditions before they belong to, and are appropriated by, us."[189] He endorses those who interpret scientific rationality in terms of "an ongoing historical tradition constituted by social practices" and who are aware that "the criteria for evaluating and validating scientific hypotheses and theories that are abstracted from existing social practices are threatened with a false rigidity or with pious vacuity..."[190] He points out in addition that existing social practices and historical traditions of rationality are fractured and variable. He joins in "The postmortem celebration of contingency, fragmentation, fissures, singularity, plurality, and ruptures (that defy reconciliation)."[191] It is an illusion to think or expect that there can be a final reconciliation that integrates all ruptures and differences... For our everyday experience is one of a fractured totality."[192]

There are no "fixed universal ahistorical rational standards of critique," Bernstein writes, and there need not be any because we have a whole "bricolage" of "strategies" for criticizing affirmations and practices—"argumentation, narrative, imagining new possibilities, articulating visions of what we take to be desirable."[193] He focuses on these strategies, when they are pursued under the guidance of the regulative ideal of achieving a rational consensus,[194] an ideal of open and undistorted dialogical engagements.[195] Bernstein joins Gadamer's effort to avoid being trapped into choosing to be either an "objectivist" or a "relativist" while still remaining able to criticize social practices. He praises Foucault's critique of existing social practices, but he criticizes Foucault for failing to have any justified norm to defend social criticism.[196] This is a charge that I will examine in the next two chapters. Bernstein is very sympathetic to the project of social and culture criticism being carried out by Jurgen Habermas (which I also will examine in the next chapter), but he assigns to Habermas's ideal of undistorted communication in a dialogical community only the pragmatic status of being the best way of doing justice to a pragmatic interpretation of human understanding and praxis as being social, historical, fragmented, pluralistic, fallible, and revisable.[197] He objects to the Kantian, transcendental character of Habermas's attempts to justify this ideal. Instead, Bernstein sees this ideal in a pragmatized Hegelian manner as "a *telos* immanent in our communicative action... not to be understood as a *telos* that represents the inevitable march of world history... but rather as 'a gentle but obstinate, a never silent although seldom redeemed claim to reason,' a claim to reason that 'although silenced again and again, nevertheless develops a stubbornly transcending power.'"[198] Bernstein criticizes Rorty for not attending carefully enough to the problem of justifying social criticism.

Rorty writes that it is neither possible nor necessary to have any justifications for seeking undistorted communication and the maximum freedom possible for self creation (final values for Rorty) other than the convictions embedded in the postmodern world of bourgeois liberalism in which procedure is prized over product, in which the "true" and the "good" are taken to be whatever is the outcome of conversation and dialogue, and in which such dialogue revolves around the issue of how best to balance the peace, wealth, and political freedoms needed to attain freedom for self creation.[199] The best we can do is tell a narrative of the rise of liberal social and cultural practices that have "no purpose except freedom[200] and which "were designed to diminish cruelty, make possible government by the consent of the governed, and permit as much domination-free communication as possible to take place."[201] (Liberals) are the people who think that cruelty is the worst thing we do.[202] Liberal practices incorporate the West's "increased ability to tolerate diversity...to be comfortable with a variety of different sorts of people, and therefore with an increasing willingness to leave people alone to follow their own lights.[203] "The Kantian identification with a central transcultural and ahistorical self is thus replaced by a quasi-Hegelian identification with our own community, thought of as a historical product.[204] Rorty admits that this is a sort of ethnocentric position, but he claims there is no alternative. "We have to start where we are—..." but (this) "is the ethnocentrism of a 'we' ('we liberals') which is dedicated to enlarging itself, to creating an ever larger and more variegated *ethnos*."[205] This is a liberalism that "already contains the institutions for its own improvement...a free press, free universities, and enlightened public opinion."[206]

Rorty is a reformer and not a revolutionary. He does not think that we need any more conceptual revolutions in our moral/political vocabularies or in our cultural practices of the sort advocated by thinkers like Marx, Nietzsche, and Heidegger.[207] He does not see any widespread, deeply entrenched contamination of existing liberal practices that might warrant a despairing abandonment of our liberal heritage for supposedly being counterproductive, for being a real barrier to the freedom it professes to be seeking. He shares Dewey's social hope[208] and not the pessimism of those who are convinced that liberalism's "hopes for greater freedom and equality which mark the recent history of the West were somehow deeply deceptive."[209] He does not want to transform the social constitution of people but merely wants people "to notice and understand people they passed on the street... to turn their eyes toward the people getting hurt, notice the *details* of the pain being suffered, rather than needing to have their entire cognitive apparatus restructured."[210] He thinks that novelists and ethnographers are particularly good at helping us notice such suffering. Rorty wants to expand our chances for being kind and for avoiding the humiliation of others.[211] The problem, Rorty contends, is not faulty liberal practices but rather greedy, stupid, shortsighted conservatives.[212] People and not social structures are what need changing.

Bernstein gives more weight to what Marxists and existentialists have to say about defects in our social practices. He thinks that greed, selfishness, the desire to dominate, and shortsightedness may have deeper motivations than are first apparent. Social practices may be contributing to their presence, and even the best of intentions may be unable to prevent the cruel production of suffering, oppression and domination unless practices are changed. "[Marx] showed the possibility and the importance of asking and trying to answer questions... concerning the origin and nature of social institutions that pervade and shape human life."[213] Bernstein praises the neo-Marxists who have "relentlessly sought to highlight the 'dark side' of the Enlightenment legacy and indeed all of social and cultural modernity."[214] Existentialists "stand as a penetrating challenge to any solutions to the problems of human alienation."[215] Bernstein praises

Foucault for revealing "the dark possibilities that can erupt in history" even as he criticizes him for failing to thematize the ethical-political perspective that informs his critique.[216]

Bernstein criticizes Rorty for failing to seriously listen to the charge that bourgeois culture and economics stand in conflict with liberalism.[217] Rorty, Bernstein claims, neglects "social facticity, that is, the cruel social realities and the human suffering of the affluent liberal societies that Rorty celebrates."[218] (Rorty) never seriously asks what it is about rich lucky liberal societies that enhances greed and makes us so cynical about political life. Bernstein chastises Rorty for eliminating from his interpretation of Heidegger any consideration of Heidegger's radical critique of our age.[219] He challenges Rorty to specify in detail what kind of cruelty and humiliation the liberal wishes to prevent, given the socially and culturally specific character of cruelty and humiliation. He challenges him to show that the privatizing of self-making, together with the restriction of the political to issues of procedural protections of differences, would not increase cruelty and domination.[220] In spite of their differences, Bernstein, the pragmatist, praises Rorty, the pragmatist, for challenging social and cultural critics to show in detail how to find a way of justifying one's criticisms and ideals without appealing to metaphysical or epistemological foundations.[221] Responding to this challenge, and to the debate over the dark side of our social and cultural practices, is what will organize the reflections presented in the next two chapters.

Rorty and Bernstein do share the conviction that all writing about something other than social rationality is something to be rejected. They may disagree on what humanism comes to, but they are both pragmatic humanists who want nothing to do with writing that seeks to point at some other to the human world of beliefs, desires, social practices and their socially constituted objects. "There is just us..."[222] They both share what they see as a constitutive characteristic of pragmatism, that human inquiry is to serve practical purposes: "to reweave beliefs,"[223] to "make us happier by enabling us to cope more successfully with the physical environment and with each other,"[224] to be an ironist redescribing through the use of new vocabularies, which are never taken as better metaphysical representations,[225] to criticize and politically reconstruct human praxis.[226] Bernstein wants a kind of radical criticism that critiques the dark side of current social practices. Neither he nor Rorty, however, want the kind of radical critique that challenges the autonomy, self-sufficiency, and exhaustiveness of the social itself.

Rorty has no sympathy with what he sees as Heidegger's and the early Wittgenstein's writings about "an Other to reason."[227] He sees Heidegger's talk about language being a gift of Being as a matter of slipping back into old metaphysical talk, and he sees his desire "to retain a sense of humility, or a sense of gratitude, toward something which transcends humanity" as simply a self grandizing desire to make himself "into a world-historical figure, "the first postmetaphysical figure," a desire that in fact only turns him into one more "ascetic priest" by setting himself apart from his fellow humans.[228] Bernstein sees great danger in Heidegger's critique of our age's practices of rationality and Heidegger's claim that we can only continue to let things go downhill all the way or "prepare to be prepared for the manifestation of god." This tells us nothing, Bernstein writes, "about what human praxis means here and now in our concrete historical horizon."[229] "Heidegger's silence is resounding, deafening, and damning," Bernstein charges, because the dignity that Heidegger wants to guard for meditative people graciously waiting for the gods to speak is a dignity that is "blind and impervious to mundane suffering and misery, victimization and mass extermination."[230]

On the one hand we should not be surprised by this pragmatic opposition to even consider seriously challenges to the self-sufficiency and exhaustiveness of human social rationality. Since Peirce, pragmatists have restricted themselves to considerations of what is useful to human, rational practice. That goodness might transcend rationality, that comportment toward the ineffable might be a vital part of human living, is never entertained as a possibility. On the other hand, that these two pragmatists do not consider this possibility is surprising.

Rorty's liberal utopia accents respecting differences and an alternative world constituting vocabularies. Yet he shows no respect for all those religious vocabularies that point to the ineffable and criticize human efforts to make the human into a self-sufficient god. Rorty rejects efforts by European philosophers to indict the rationality and existing practices of ordinary people, but he indicts, marginalizes and excludes from consideration the religious language games and practices of millions of ordinary people in many different cultural worlds. Such people, he seems to suppose, are still trapped in historical backwaters and psychological infancy while the progressive march of history has moved on to secular humanism. Both Rorty and Bernstein emphasize the primacy of open dialogue in establishing rational practices, but they seem unable to listen to those religious writers who would point to the finite character of such rationality. They seem convinced that such religious speech and writing is distorted, that the death of the ontotheological god legitimates the exclusion of all religious voices from the dialogue. Do we find present in both of these thinkers remnants of the positivism that Bernstein finds present in Rorty's refusal to judge between alternative vocabularies?[231]

The dismissal by Rorty and Bernstein of all writing about some other to social rationality presents a major challenge that I will deal with in chapter 5, where writings about social rationality's other will be critically interpreted, writings by philosophers like Levinas who claim that encounters with such otherness is presupposed by all social rationality and *praxis* and that such encounters issue forth in an ethic and religiousness that accent the uniqueness of every person and our responsibility for every person, especially the most vulnerable—the orphan and the widow. Bernstein's pragmatic commitment to secular humanism seems to prevent him from interpreting Levinas's writings about that which is other than Being in any manner other than as writings about people who are different people (but still the same as us in being socially constituted people) or people with different social and cultural characteristics.[232] Although acknowledging the value of Levinas's claims about "the radical incommensurable *singularity* of the Other,"[233] he does not deal with Levinas's claim that this really is acknowledging the other to social rationality and that this does open the door to a nonontotheological approach to religious life.

Rorty's and Bernstein's strengthening of the interpretation of the social character of rationality being presented in this chapter sets the stage for the next two chapters. In chapters 3 and 4, I will investigate the use of social rationality while engaged in social and cultural criticism. In chapter 5, I will attempt to show that social rationality is not autonomous, self-sufficient, and exhaustive of human life.

—✦— CHAPTER THREE POSTMODERNISM'S PASSION FOR PERSONAL FREEDOM AND BEAUTY

Social rationality is an ocean undulating beneath an empty sky and over a floor of bottomless mud, lapping away at shifting and unchartable sandy beaches. Within it are eddies of social and cultural specificity. Among the many currents moving within it are those of social and cultural criticism whose historical identities are maintained through their changing forms by virtue of continuing family resemblances. For a long time critics swimming in these currents have attempted to dive down to the ocean's floor in search of solid foundations or to fly up above this dynamic ocean to some brilliant, beautiful, and fixed star, hoping thereby to legitimate their critiques, but succeeding only in disturbing and weakening these critical currents with their rhetorical foam. Since the mid nineteenth century, however, many critics have rejected and radically critiqued these would-be divers and fliers. They have found that their own individual particularity and the intersubjective character of these critical currents are sufficient to allow them to sustain and at times redirect these critical practices. The next two chapters will consist of a series of dialogues with these critics.

Until the nineteenth century, what was taken as unproblematic by most critical thinkers in the West was the practice of leaving uninterrogated the working presumption that there are asocial and ahistorical criteria of rationality and morality that can and must be used as reasons for indicting some social and cultural practices and for justifying others. I suggest, however, that this presumption can and should be dropped and that a pragmatic approach can produce radical forms of not unjustified social and cultural criticism. As with beliefs, actions need justification only when there is some reason for thinking that acting that way is wrong. Freedom of action, like freedom of belief, needs no justification; only restrictions on freedom have such a need. Many actions simply remain not unjustified. Only some of them are judged to be unjustified.

Many actions are cases of participating in social practices of rationality, and they consist simply of doing well what one has been trained to do. Sometimes such actions are matters of skillfully reasoning instrumentally in selecting among alternative means to some goal. Sometimes these actions are matters of skillfully exercising traditional techniques for finding operational resolutions to problems of conflicting interests and rationales. (Labor and management turn to professional arbitrators to resolve differences.) At times, when some types of actions and some social and cultural practices are judged to be problematic for good reasons, it is because they are in conflict with other practices and ways of acting that are left unquestioned. These are the occasions on which reflective social and cultural criticisms arise. Sometimes such problematic actions and practices are judged to be justified, all relevant factors considered, and at other times they are judged to be unjustified. In both cases the employment and endorsement of merely historical and social norms are all that is required.

Before engaging in dialogue with those critics who see themselves as fully immersed in social and historical currents of rationality, however, it is important to remove one possible misunderstanding. I am not suggesting that no significant social and cultural criticism existed prior to the attack on Hegelianism in the nineteenth century by critics such as Kierkegaard, Marx, and Nietzsche. On the contrary, I am suggesting that those currents of critical reflection in the West, which stretch from the ancient Greeks through the Enlightenment, contain valuable resources that can and should be preserved after they have been separated from the ontotheological and epistemological pollution by which they have been contaminated and weakened.

I am suggesting that the resemblance which locates almost all Western critics up to the present time in a single historical family of critics is the similarity of their efforts to resist dominating and oppressive power and to minimize nonconsensuality. They have been trying to enable people to understand that dominating relations of power do not have to be the way they are and thereby empower people to resist such domination. The Western classical, medieval, modern, and "postmodern" projects of criticism are best understood when they are located in their specific historical settings and when they are interpreted as voices for resistance movements, for freedom fighters, for intellectual practitioners of freedom.[1] No matter how important it is for us to redirect the traditional Western currents of criticism, there is much in our historical inheritance that we cannot dispense with because this is what makes it possible for us to do our critical reasoning today. Only as swimmers, heavily influenced by historically changing eddies of economic and political practice, can we redirect the critical currents in our inescapable ocean of social rationality. Besides, there is much in our critical inheritance that we would be fools to throw away because the types of oppressive power that earlier critics resisted are still present in our worlds in all too similar and dangerous forms.

I. POSTMODERNISM'S APPROPRIATION[2] OF EARLIER FREEDOM FIGHTERS

Socrates protested against the popular educational practices of the Sophists who taught Athens' young aristocrats how to be successful participants in the Athenian democracy by acquiring power through the use of deliberately misleading and manipulative rhetoric and ruthless expediency. Socrates may have called for a search for universal and timeless definitions of various virtues in order to legitimate his protest, but one need not attempt to make such a flight out beyond social practices in order to have reason to endorse his protest. Even he didn't need the definitions for which he was searching. The Greek dramatists of his era provided more than enough material to warrant his protest. Socrates' opposition to being manipulated and to being sacrificed on the altar of expediency is something every opponent of oppression and exploitation can and should endorse. Merely living as a specific individual in a world of power relations, which often are asymmetrical relations of domination, is sufficient to provide a rationale for doing that. In the case of Socrates, such oppressive relations existed not only in neighboring Sparta but also in the slaveholding world of his own Athens. That his condemnation of the educational practices of the Sophists was not extended to a condemnation of the slavery practices of his class of Athenian aristocrats shows the historically situated character of his protest and that it was not derived from the application of definitions of supposedly universal and timeless virtues and norms. What he did oppose, of course, still can receive our rejection.

Plato criticized the "democratic" practices of Athens that led to the "unjust" conviction and execution of Socrates. He argued that this kind of democracy provided no protection for critical dissidents such as Socrates. Here again, we can endorse his desire to protect such dissidents without endorsing either his recommended substitute for democracy or his defense of that recommendation. Plato was convinced that the Athenian majority who voted to condemn Socrates to death made a mistake because they did not possess the kind of freedom necessary to make reasonable judgments. The rational capacity of most people to make not unjustified judgments, Plato claimed, is incapacitated by shortsighted and imprudent bodily and economic desires and by blind, passionate attachments to existing civic institutions and practices. It is just such desires and passions that were being pampered by Sophist educators. Plato attempted to justify his defense of Socrates and his criticism of Athenian democracy by claiming that the sovereign warrant to rule politically should be granted only to those whose lives are governed by knowledge of the unchanging, universal character of human nature and virtue. In the ideal Republic that Plato offered as an alternative to the Athenian Democracy, not being free from ignorance and irrationality is sufficient warrant for being subjected to the rule and power of those "rational" persons who do know what is best and who thus know how to set people truly free by making them rational or willing to follow directions given by rational leaders. Those floundering in a sea of historically shifting social practices, Plato contended, are unable to understand their own slavish practices and thus unable to resist them or swim free of them. Plato's critique, however, does not need that kind of flight from the social and historical. Neither does the claim that the power of democratic majorities must be institutionally restricted so as to protect the freedom of dissidents and minorities to express beliefs unpopular at the time. In order to endorse Plato's opposition to lives dominated by unguided passion, one need not endorse his call for guided obedience to a "rational" elite. One only needs to point out that although in times of battle one may need the unquestioned passionate loyalty of warriors to their civic commanders, this does not hold for citizens in general. As Socrates demonstrated, without a questioning of existing practices and policies, one removes the whole point of exercising critical rationality in political life. Critical and self-critical democratic debate permits the governed to identify and remove threats to living freely and well in their social worlds. Likewise, in order to endorse Plato's opposition to an individualistic, often imprudent attempt to satisfy bodily and economic desires without concern for the long-term effects upon oneself or others, one need not endorse his call for "philosopher-kings" who would paternalistically control efforts to satisfy existing desires and direct an educational effort to inculcate into future generations one set of socially nonconflictual desires. Prudence is a virtue in virtually all worlds of social rationality, although it is seldom the sole virtue. So likewise, worlds of social norms always restrict satisfying desires that have been found to affect others detrimentally. The social world also usually tends to support social stability and its own reproduction (often too much so). If the minimization of nonconsensuality is our goal, then a social world in which there is a minimization of restrictions on desires and on efforts to standardize desires, rather than Plato's Republic, should be our goal. Also, as modern democracies have discovered, institutionalized protection for freedom of expression by dissidents is compatible with democratic rule by majorities. Plato's Republic is not the only alternative to Socrates' Athens. Majorities in democracies with built-in protections for dissidents will still make mistakes, but such mistakes then can be criticized for being stupid, shortsighted, racist, sexist blunders in the hope that new majorities will change things. The best protection possible for dissident voices is the recognition that all reasoners and knowers are finite, fallible, historical, socially constituted persons, not transcendent philosopher-kings but persons whose rhetoric, always interest-colored, is at its best when it seeks to minimize domination and oppression.

Augustine, drawing upon those resources deposited in the Greek/Roman world after merging its traditions with Middle Eastern religious currents, criticized his Greek inheritance for failing to recognize the radical nature of the ignorance of finite persons and its power to render people incapable of coming to know themselves or the worlds in which they live. As he interpreted human propensities, people aren't just failing to maintain rational control over their desires and passions; they are passionately denying their finitude in their very attempt to maintain rational control. By refusing to hear any call from the finite's other, from the nonfinite, from the infinite, they are turning the finite into a self-contained, self-sufficient absolute, a god. For Augustine, only when finite human reason is exercised in faithful obedience to the infinite is it noncorruptive. When Platonists think that there is a form of reasoning that can enable them to fly out of the ocean of social rationality, they usually are willfully ignoring the historical, social, interest-driven, finite character of all reasoning and they are doing so out of a desire to avoid listening to anything other than themselves, out of a desire to be an independent, all-sufficient being. People are willfully ignorant in such a way that this willfulness contaminates all their desires, passions, and social rationality. Augustine turned the Platonic account of ignorance into the Christian account of sinful, willful, disabling ignorance and rejection of God's existence and commands. In turn, he transformed the Platonic authorization for the rule of rational and knowledgeable philosopher-kings into the Christian authorization for the rule of the faithful, knowing, saving Christian Church over all matters of faith and morals, and for the "earthly" rule of civic rulers anointed by this knowing Church.

Augustine's radicalization of Greek and Roman currents of social and cultural criticism added dimensions of breath and depth that deserve preservation and expansion. One need not endorse Augustine's own ontotheological positions to endorse his understanding that beliefs are the product of willful actions and interest-driven rhetoric. Pragmatists have said the same thing. One need not endorse his interpretation of the infinite as a supreme being in order to endorse his interpretation of the human condition as involving denials of human finitude and refusals to listen to or be faithful to the call of the infinite. As we shall see, this is the thrust of Kierkegaard's appropriation of Augustine. One need not share Augustine's conviction that the Christian Church is the authorized translator of the call of the infinite in order to endorse the claim that the finite's other calls us not to deify anything finite, including the ocean of social rationality.

All of the major Western critics from the time of the sixteenth-century Renaissance through the eighteenth-century Enlightenment battled against practices restricting individual freedom of thought and action, which presumed that the Christian Church was something other than another finite, human institution, that it possessed unique authority to determine the correctness of matters of belief and action, and that it can pass on to monarchs of the new nation-states the sovereign authority to rule over the citizens in these states. This opposition can be endorsed even while one laments that these same opponents turned to various forms of metaphysical humanism to legitimate their battle against domination. One can also lament that they ignored Augustine's warnings about deifying forms of human rationality by seeing themselves as self-sufficient, and his warnings about not remaining faithful to social rationality's infinite other.

Renaissance artists and writers, in order to resist Church domination, drew upon their memory of Greek and Roman practices, marginalized for centuries by the domination of Christian institutions. Although many of these creative cultural critics substituted a new humanistic rhetoric to replace the Church's rhetorical claims to special divine inspiration and authority over all matters of faith and morals, the manner of resistance of these Renaissance masters did not need such rhetoric and would have been better off without it. Merely recognizing that the marginalized can exist as a worthy aesthetic alternative to dominant practices would have been sufficient to undercut Church efforts to legitimate its own practices of domination and provide alternative options for individual artists and writers. Merely remaining faithful to the unclassifiable particularity of artists and the individuals they are creatively encountering would have been sufficient to undercut Church authority. There was no need to deify human social rationality. Abandoning all talk about transcendent aesthetic standards and recognizing that only a multitude of incommensurate social standards exist would have gone even further to minimize nonconsentuality in the creative work of artists and writers. The choice by renaissance artists of preferring faithfulness to their own individual inspiration, over faithfulness to a Church's supposedly faithful interpretation of a divine inspiration, did not require them to try to do the impossible—leap beyond the world of social rationality.

Protestant religious resistance and reformation movements roared through gates in the dams opened up by the Renaissance artists. Empowered by new economic and political currents, Protestant reformers challenged established religious powers by pointing out that Christianity does not have to be the way it then was practiced. Luther read and interpreted Augustine and Paul on his own and proclaimed the priesthood of all believers. Zwingli went even further and endorsed the sovereignty of each individual interpreter of the Bible and of each congregation of worshipers that has a shared faith. Sameness produced by submission to a single institutional authority was replaced by differences between worshiping communities and individuals. Even as renaissance artists could and should remain faithful to their individual inspirations, so individual Christians and communities of Christians could and should remain faithful to their personal encounters with the infinite, no matter how much they had to draw upon social resources to think and talk about such encounters. The young Luther protested against the whole marriage of early Christian practical religious understanding to Aristotelian and Scholastic ontotheological theoretical understanding. Although many Protestant theologians were not able to free themselves from the rhetoric of Greek/Christian ontotheologies, this rhetoric was not needed. Their prioritizing of individual faithfulness to personal encounters with the infinite over acceptance of Church-sponsored claims did not require any legitimation from such metaphysical theories. No encounter with the nonfinite other to the finite social world can ever be legitimated because legitimations always consist of movements within the finite world of social rationality. As we shall see, this is what makes Kierkegaard the most Protestant of Protestant critics and reformers, because he recognized so clearly that faithfulness to the infinite has to appear absurd to those seeking to judge even the infinite with finite social concepts and norms. It should not surprise us, therefore, that Heidegger found so much motivation for his critique of ontotheologies in his early reading of Luther and Kierkegaard.[3]

The creators of the scientific revolution of the sixteenth and seventeenth centuries followed their artistic and religious counterparts in protesting against existing restrictions on their individual freedom to make investigations of physical phenomena and to individually construct theories that they believed explained these phenomena. Sovereignty was shifted from Church or ancient authorities to individual investigators as it had been shifted to individual artists and worshipers. The investigations and theories of the new modern scientists challenged a great deal of the accepted wisdom of the day. What was not to be questioned was questioned and revolutionized in such a way that appreciating the importance of historical actors in a social world became unquestionably primary to all cognition. The scientific revolution began when Copernicus rejected the generally unquestioned Aristotelian presumption that people are first of all passive in the perception of physical objects, merely taking pictures of such objects which then only need theoretical classification and explanation. Copernicus taught us that, instead of merely trusting our eyes as we see the sun move through the sky, we need to understand that observers contribute to such appearances by their own rotation on the surface of the earth as it and they revolve around the sun. Knowers actively contribute to the cognitive situation. Later investigators kept expanding this Copernican revolution by identifying more and more that observers contributed. Galileo and Locke pointed to the sensory contributions that people make so that sets of colorless, tasteless, oderless atoms can appear as sweet smelling purple lilacs and sour, green dill pickles. The Romanticists pointed out the culturally specific contributions that are made to the conceptual component in all perception.

By replacing an earth-centered, Ptolemaic astronomical world with a heliocentric solar system, the Copernican revolution denied people the status of being that valued center and point and purpose of the universe that metaphysical and theological theories had assigned to them. In the Copernican world, people are just biological creatures spinning on a small planet revolving around a rather small sun/star in a physical universe of billions of such sun/stars. If it makes any sense to talk about significance from the standpoint of the physical universe, and if size determines significance, then in the Copernican world people are very insignificant. What the Copernican revolution took away with one hand, however, it gave back with the other. It elevated individual persons to the status of being the active beginning points of all knowledge of the physical world. Not long afterward, as we shall see, individual persons were elevated to the status of being the beginning and end point of all other forms of significance.

The scientific revolution of the sixteenth and seventeenth centuries also elevated the status of the community of scientists over that of the Church or the ancient "authorities." When the claims of one scientist are challenged by those of another, the challenged scientist has to present good reasons acceptable to the community of scientists for rejecting that challenge or for justifying the claims made in spite of the challenge. Scientific criticism thus becomes one of the main currents in the Western world of social rationality. The settled opinions of the scientific community become the taken-for-granted background of prejudgments of individual scientists whose inquiries and theoretical explanatory work receive their point and purpose from the anomalies that are experienced given that background. As Dewey pointed out, scientific inquiry begins when conflicts appear within the world of scientific opinion and practice and it reaches its goals when what is problematic in the scientific community is rendered unproblematic. The scientific revolution was a battle waged by practitioners of freedom against established traditions and institutions in the name of the sovereignty of individual scientists and the objectivity found in the fallible, settled but revisable opinions and practices shared by such scientists.

The epistemologists (theorists of knowledge) of the seventeenth and eighteenth centuries also swam in these modern scientific waters, even as they attempted as philosophers to avoid drowning in the roaring currents of modern science that threatened to sweep away all other forms of cognition. The epistemologists presented themselves as deep sea divers who could uncover the indubitable foundations that their skeptical excursions supposedly proved that science needed. These epistemologists also were caught up in the individualism of the modern era. Rationalists and empiricists alike claimed that all knowledge begins and ends with the individual. Whereas the new scientists could acknowledge the social origin of their prejudgments and the social character of scientific objectivity, the epistemologist shared the Platonic distrust of the contingencies of historical and social currents. Individual experiences or ideational intuitions, not social training, were claimed as the sources of all representations. Individual, incorrigible experiences or ideas that are clear and distinct to individual calculators were claimed as the ultimate justifications for scientific claims. Nothing social or historical could stand between individual believers and what is knowable. By making these episte-mological claims, philosophers attempted to resist being excluded by scientific popularity from the theoretical cognition industry.

One can be critical of the epistemologist's failure to appreciate the social character of all ideas, experiences, and justifications while also praising them for their endorsement of the scientist's resistance to the power exercised by the Church and classical authorities over human inquiry. One can appreciate the efforts of philosophers to prevent themselves from being thrown out of work, without endorsing the means they chose for doing this. It is not epistemology that physics lacks but needs. Rather, what physicists do not attempt to do, but people need, is to present the kind of general, critical interpretations of the human worlds in which they find themselves, worlds in which scientific inquiry and theorizing are located. It is by moving within the historical currents of social and cultural criticism that philosophers will always find work to do. Interpreting the epistemological project as a historical resistance movement to established power relationships permits us, therefore, to endorse much of what it opposes while still affirming that human rationality is social through and through.

All of the modern artistic, religious, scientific, and epistemological resistance movements were taking place in a context of powerful political and economic currents of domination and resistance to domination. Each of these resistance movements influenced and reenforced all the others. The individualism accentuated in artistic, religious, and cognitive practices became even more pronounced in the rhetoric about individual political, economic and moral rights that became the defining mark of the modern Western social and cultural world. Utilizing the feudal vocabulary of duties that serfs had to pay to their lords and the services that each social station had a right to expect from the other, and using the language of being bound (obligated) by the oaths lords swore to their kings, the rhetoric of rights was utilized to resist the ruling political and economic order. In the name of the moral sovereignty of individual persons, the absolute authority to exercise state power, which monarchs supposedly received from an ontotheological god via the Christian Church, was challenged. Even Hobbes' effort to justify the monarch's possession of absolute power had to be made in terms of the prudential well-being of the

individuals being governed.[4] One need not endorse the ontotheological rhetoric of natural moral laws and rights, which was offered
by Hobbes and Locke as a replacement metaphysical legitimation for
talk about the divine right of kings, to endorse modernism's claim
that political restrictions on individual freedom must be justifiable
to the individuals involved. An appreciative understanding of the
importance and limits of the rhetoric of individual rights is best
gained by locating that rhetoric historically in the dynamics of the
political, economic, social, and cultural power relations that gave to
modernity its distinctive character.

Once it had gained political recognition in the Roman world,
the Christian Church felt empowered by being able to bless royal
thrones and their claims to unquestionable control over state power.
In turn, emperors in a threatened Roman Empire and kings in the
newly emerging nation-states sought the power that came from
being legitimated by such a blessing. This blessing was sought and
attained by the new kings while they were in the process of trying to
overpower a landed aristocracy that had acquired great power during
the centuries after the fall of the Roman Empire. Resistance to royal
power, however, was present from the first moments of acquiring
such power and legitimation. The Magna Carta was a product of
resistance by the lords of the British landed aristocracy and it became
an extremely valuable cultural deposit in Western currents of social
criticism. In the seventeenth and eighteenth centuries, this cultural
wealth was withdrawn and reinvested by a new British class whose
economic power came from commerce and industry rather than
ownership of land. This new class sought to legitimate its resistance
to the power of the working partnership that had developed between
the throne and the landed aristocracy by utilizing the very rhetoric
that these aristocratic lords had used to force the king into such a
partnership. It did so by grafting into English political and economic
language the rhetoric of artistic, religious, scientific, and epistemological individualism swirling through the era's currents of resistance
to domination. Democratic liberalism was born.

Exercises of state power that restricted individual freedom, it was claimed, had to be justified to those persons whose freedom was being restricted. In Locke's language, all authorizations for the exercise of state power had to come from the individuals being governed.[5] Political sovereignty lies with the individual citizen and state authority exists only when citizens delegate such authority to the state's governmental agents. Liberty itself needs no justification; only its restriction does. One need not endorse Locke's metaphysical claims about natural rights to endorse his accent on the primacy of individual liberty. The pragmatics of justification imply that individuals need not justify their actions until there is a good reason for thinking that they are doing something wrong. Liberty takes precedence over indictments and justifications. That is the very liberty the lords claimed for themselves in the Magna Carta. In eighteenth-century England it became the centerpiece of Locke's democratic liberalism. Individuals remain at liberty to do as they choose until they have good reason to surrender such liberty. As Locke understood things, only to gain protection for one's individual life, liberty, and property from domestic and foreign threats do citizens have good reasons to delegate such authority to governmental agents executing the wishes of an elected parliament. When not facing such threats, individuals have a right to be left alone by their governments. Only for the protection of liberty and individual rights should liberty be limited.

One can endorse such political individualism and the rhetoric of negative rights (the right to be left alone by one's government) without endorsing all of the ways it was applied by Locke and the class for which he spoke. Locke went from political individualism to economic individualism. By claiming that state-protected property rights are acquired only when individual labor is involved,[6] Locke offered a legitimation of the economic power of the new class of merchants and industrialists as they resisted the efforts by the landed aristocracy to use its partnership with the throne to exercise control over their commercial and productive activities. One need not endorse the laissez faire capitalism, which profited from Locke's call for a governmental hands-off approach to market dynamics, in order to endorse representative democracy and restricting the power of government agents so as to protect artistic, religious, and scientific liberty and the freedom of expression, which is the key to representative government and a necessary condition for the existence of a domain of private life.

The new class of capitalists, however, could no more control the flow of the vocabulary of rights in the currents of criticism than the old landed aristocracy could control the rhetoric of the Magna Carta. In the centuries since Locke wrote, rights talk has been employed in strategies and tactics of resistance to domination and oppression in ways that he and his class never imagined. Universal suffrage was demanded. On grounds of an individual right to the means necessary for the exercise of the rights to life and liberty, welfare state advocates and the UN Declaration of Human Rights extended rights talk beyond negative rights to positive rights and thus to the duty and obligation of government agents elected by the people to empower them by guaranteeing income, work, education, health care, and protection from social and econmic discrimination. The use of talk about moral rights to legitimate restrictions on governmental actions was generalized far beyond the arena of state actions, and it became the primary vocabulary used in many cultural and social worlds to oppose anyone's restrictions of someone else's personal liberty. Such extensions of rights talk need not deny the importance of guaranteeing negative rights in the political realm in order to assert that such a guarantee is not sufficient to minimize nonconsensuality in general. One can endorse the principle that governments should not unduly restrict freedom of expression while also endorsing the principle that the people working through elected governments should work cooperatively to organize economic life so as to give people the power to live freely. Since no omniscient, omnipotent planner controlled the manner in which the rhetoric of rights flowed in Western currents of criticism, one should not be surprised that all sorts of conflicts appeared in the use of such rhetoric. Positive rights face a problem in representative democracies that negative rights do not face. Negative rights against the government are guaranteed when government agents don't interfere, when they do nothing, but positive rights require government action. This usually means that tax monies must be spent in order to empower people. However, in a representative democracy, taxation and expenditure policies are determined by majority rule. When a majority doesn't want to spend tax money to empower individuals, saying that someone possesses a positive right is only saying what a majority "morally" should do and it is not asserting any kind of state guarantee that the individual will be empowered. Although talk about positive rights may still have some persuasive political power, it also is the source of a great deal of frustration when governments fail to provide what people think they have a positive right to receive. Also, utilizing rights talk to say what people ought to do through their government to empower other people often is counterproductive. It reinforces the power that the rhetoric of rights has in general, power that those profiting from oppressive economic practices can utilize in branding, as violations of private property rights, efforts by democratic governments to minimize such oppression. Groups calling for their positive rights to empowerment are labeled as merely special interest groups seeking to unjustifiably use state power to take away private property that its owners have a right to have protected and not confiscated by the government.

Similarly, huge problems develop when rights talk is extended beyond the context of restrictions of governmental interference with personal liberty so that it becomes the primary moral rhetoric in a culture. First, claiming a right is introducing a trump card that supposedly takes precedence over other considerations. Governmental efficiency must take a back seat to the negative right to freedom of expression. Making rights claims against other individuals, however, is usually met with claims to competing rights. Often there is no social consensus on how to resolve such conflicts between competing claims, and thus the conflict is tossed into government courts, and the horror of a social world of constant litigation is born. Second, rights claims in the political realm of negative rights are made by adult citizens who have legal duties, but when rights talk becomes the general form of moral rhetoric we end up talking about society's rights, the rights of young children who have no duties, the rights of fetuses, the rights of the dead, the rights of future generations, animal rights, and the rights of trees. We end up in hopeless metaphysical debates about the characteristics a being must have to possess moral rights. We end up being cultural imperialists as we try to force rights talk into the moral discursive practices of people living in other social and cultural worlds

Although problems exist in the current practice of rights talk, this does not mean that one should try to abandon it. Since rights talk is going to be the primary moral language for many people for a long time to come, it becomes even more important to historically situate it, to understand its social pragmatics, to see how in the West it can be blended to good effect with other forms of moral rhetoric that rights talk marginalized, and to see what can happen when it is placed in dialogue with non-Western forms of moral rhetoric (Confucian, Buddhist).

All of the resistance movements that we have just briefly examined have claimed that freedom and liberty can be enhanced and nonconsensuality minimized by having people gain a broader or deeper understanding of themselves and the social and cultural worlds in which they live. The forms of domination being resisted and the strategies and tactics of resistance may have been different, but all were engaged in what became known as the enlightenment project. I have been suggesting that this project can be endorsed even though one rejects the metaphysical, ontotheological, epistemological, and rhetorical aspects of the mode of understanding offered for enhancing freedom.[7] In the dialogues that follow, I shall be treating all these critical interpreters as participants in an enlightenment project. I suggest that by locating their critiques in the appropriate historical currents of social rationality, we can increase the effectiveness of their strategies and tactics of resistance. The best of seventeenth- and eighteenth-century modernism is strengthened when it is allowed to flow into the currents of post-Hegelian social and cultural criticism. There are three such historical currents that I will separate out for critical interpretation, even though they are constantly influencing each other. One set of critics (Kierkegaard, Nietzsche, Heidegger, the later Foucault, and Zizek) focus on the need to care for oneself so that one does not become an uncritical social conformist. The second set of critics (Marx and the neo-Marxists, Habermas, Foucault, Gouldner, Iris Marion Young, and Cornell West) focus on the need to resist and modify the social practices in which one participates. The third set of critics (Kierkegaard, Levinas, Zizek, Mark Taylor) focus on the need not to absolutize the social, the need to live faithfully to encounters with the social's other. All three sets of critics endorse a thoroughly social interpretation of human rationality although many of them claim that human living involves much more than the use of social rationality. The first two sets of critics will be examined in this and the next chapter and the third set in the last chapter.

II. KIERKEGAARD AS SOCIAL/CULTURAL CRITIC

If human rationality is social through and through, then how does one avoid becoming nothing but a social conformist acting as one's socially inculcated roles, norms, ideals, desires, expectations, fears, and hopes prescribe? What is the value of the political and economic freedom of individuals, if these individuals use this "freedom" only to do what one has been socially nurtured, trained, and channeled into doing? These questions played major roles in giving birth in the nineteenth century to the existentialist movement. They were closely tied to the concern that existentialists had over reaffirming the significance of individual human lives, even though rationality, because of its social and situated character, could not be interpreted as providing an ontotheological ultimate that guranteed such significance, and even though the merely social always concerned itself only with the significance of types of people and not with people in their particularity. Kierkegaard, Nietzsche, the early Heidegger, the later Foucault and Zizek all present critical interpretations of how people are living as socialized persons and recommendations for how people are to care for themselves. These critiques are aimed at calling for people to take responsibility for their own lives so that they can find a significant way of living beyond being mere social conformists. A critical issue, therefore, becomes one of explaining how people who always are swimming in social currents can be more than mere waves in those currents, how social and cultural critics can make sweeping indictments of the very social and cultural currents without which they cannot function.

Kierkegaard's critique of the world in which he found himself in the 1840s is radical in two interrelated senses. First, it critiqued the quality of the social and cultural practices of his present age, practices painfully similar to those dominant in our own age in their curtailment of human freedom. Second, it critiqued the presumed self-sufficiency of the social and cultural world itself, and that sense of self-sufficiency for social rationalities and identities that give to the social and cultural practices of these present ages their distinctive and dangerous qualities. In this chapter Kierkegaard's first critique will be interpreted. In chapter 5 I will examine his call to go beyond mere social worldliness and to live faithful to encounters with social rationality's infinite other.

Kierkegaard shared much in common with Augustine in that both claim that people need to free themselves from the inept and fractured socialized selves they end up with when they uncritically participate in the social and cultural practices that previous generations have instituted and which their own actions sustain. Social and cultural criticism for Kierkegaard always is a matter of self-criticism, and such self-criticism always involves critically interpreting one's social and cultural environment. What must be resisted is what one finds oneself to be when one simply participates in a pattern of life dictated by all too common social and cultural ways of acting, feeling, thinking. As was pointed out in the last chapter, Kierkegaard shared much with Hegel in spite of his opposition to the Hegelian metaphysical system. Kierkegaard accented the social and historical character of human subjectivity and rationality. He also accented the conflictual character of the social world that produces fractured persons despairingly trapped at the intersection of different currents. The traditional social practices that determine so significantly our social identities were interpreted by Kierkegaard as both obstacles to personal freedom and the very materials that must be appropriated and reconstructed in order to critique and diminish their power as obstacles.[8] It was from within the social and historical that the quality of life found there was critiqued by Kierkegaard in the name of the particularity of persons who always remain social and historical even though their particularity is never just their social individuality.

In what he offers as a review of a novel entitled *The Two Ages*, Kierkegaard presents his critical interpretation of his modern age.[9] He begins by criticizing the general population as well as philosophers and theologians for being social conformists who merely go along with current cultural fashions. Most people in the present age, he charges, just *reflect* the social norms and expectations of the social worlds into which they happen to have been thrown. That it is normal in the "modern" world to accent individual artistic, religious, political, and economic freedom does not guarantee to the people normalized in such a world the empowerment needed to individually help determine what they will be. Kierkegaard critiques both the manner in which such modern "freedom" is acquired (conforming) and the quality of such "free" lives (living despairingly).

Kierkegaard charges that all social worlds take on a life of their own (like a demon at work) primarily functioning to reproduce themselves and not to provide space for persons to live with a particularity and singularity that is other than the fulfillment of some social role or obedience to some social norm. Regardless of what different sets of social roles and norms are accented in different social and cultural worlds, people are socialized and normalized to be normal, proper reflectors of those norms. Over and above socializing people in culturally specific ways, people are socialized to be conformers. However, Kierkegaard claims, only by being enabled to endorse or reject portions of one's social and cultural inheritance does one become able to take personal responsibility for one's own life and thus become more than a mere social functionary. Social practices in his modern age, Kierkegaard claims, rather than enabling people to take personal responsibility for their lives, in fact make it very difficult for people to do anything but go along with the "modern" way of life. Ironically, the modern accent on individual freedom becomes freedom's enemy because the modern world does not appreciate the significance of the social practices that give to people their social subjectivity and individuality. I can be free and responsible for my own life only if I can refuse to be any one of the things I have been socialized to be, although, of course, I cannot and will not refuse to be all of these things. I can make such a refusal if and only if I understand that my individual subjectivity (concepts, beliefs, desires, feelings, values, taken-for-granteds) is social through and through. Enlightened understanding here can make possible greater individual freedom.

With respect to the specific content of his modern world, Kierkegaard claims that the present age is *leveled* down into socially safe and unbearably bored and boring conventional ways of living and being a person (bourgeois, middle-class, churchgoing, proper). People say and do what is "publicly" proper, reasonable, or normal, or they rebel in socially standard ways (don't be old-fashioned; be new-fashioned). People function with feelings of self-esteem and personal identity based upon using publicly common criteria of comparative worth (attractive in the eyes of others, smart, successful, popular).[10] Fear of being different along with envy and resentment of those seen as being comparatively better dominate their lives. In addition, unless they come to recognize that they are more than mere social functionaries, these people, constituted as they are by the process of leveling, cannot reform the process because for them "reform" is defined by the process (make the system work better). The process of leveling creates and is sustained by the press and the "public" it claims to speak for and to. The "public," humanity leveled down in this way, is part of the problem and is incapable of being part of the solution. Existential enlightenment is required to know how social practices should be changed, and the best of social engineering will not eliminate the need for individuals taking personal responsibility for their lives.

Furthermore, Kierkegaard claims, many of the leveled down reflectors in the general population unfortunately (and fortunately) experience despair over their inability to live successfully as the social conformists they are. This very despair indicates a kind of understanding that such conformism doesn't really work. Nurturing conformity ignores crucial dynamics of social life. There are multiple, incommensurate, and conflictual elements within all persons' social inheritance. People cannot really avoid the project of prioritizing these different conflicting elements. Furthermore, since in any social order there are different social and personal ways of living remaining open as possibilities (socializing people is not programming robots), people must in a kind of willfulness throw away the opportunity to endorse such alternatives in order to live merely by reflecting leveled-down customs. Therefore, Kierkegaard concludes, unless and until one personally gives an unlimited (infinite), passionate living endorsement to a set of priorities, to a way of living, one's life will neither be one's own or at peace with itself. One will be only a fragmented social functionary who is merely living within the conflictual social roles and unstable socialized mode of subjectivity into which one has happened to fall. Thus, the first major choice confronting every person is the choice of being either a mere reflector trying just to go along or of being personally involved by endorsing (choosing) what kind of social individual one will be. This, Kierkegaard charges, is the ethical call to choose to will one thing. *Either* take responsibility and define oneself *or* fail to take responsibility and merely live as what the social system and chance (with all of their conflicting and oppressive elements) make of one.

This ethical disjunction is closely tied to a second disjunction. To take responsibility for one's life is to focus one's attention on one's own kind of subjectivity, something that does not happen if one is living with an objectivistic mode of subjectivity, a way of living focused on objects in the world around the person rather than a way of living focused on that person's way of living. Therefore, one always faces the choice of living with an object-oriented or a subject-oriented way of thinking, feeling, and living, either focusing on our way of relating to objects or focusing only on objects themselves. The social practices dominating life in the "modern" world, Kierkegaard charges, train people to live by an objectivistic mode of subjectivity. This inoculates people against living an existentially concerned, responsible, and free life because such a life is gained only when it is understood that subjectivity is the truth, that being primarily concerned about how one relates to things in the world is the mode of subjectivity, the way of existentially living in the world, that is the one that frees and empowers. It does not work to attempt to escape being merely social and historical by striving to transcend all personal and social subjectivity through an appeal to an asocial and ahistorical realm of objectivity. This was Kierkegaard's objection to Hegelianism and to most of the philosophers and Christian theologians of his age. In the last chapter we examined Kierkegaard's criticism of the claims of the philosophers of the ahistorical and asocial. Here we need to examine a different kind of criticism, one Kierkegaard directs at the people making these objectivistic claims and at their motivation for asserting what they do.

In *Philosophical Fragments* and *Concluding Unscientific Postscript,* Kierkegaard charges that these philosophers and theologians lack the radical form of critical self-interpretation needed to liberate themselves from being merely social functionaries giving expression to the spirit of objectivism dominating the age. The philosophers of his age, mimicking the physical scientists, had fallen into a customary approach to things, a customary set of background practices, assumptions, beliefs, and values, a customary mode of subjectivity that focused exclusively on objects and sought "objective" beliefs about such objects, objective in the sense of having erased all influence from variable social and cultural practices and personal commitments. In their conformism with objectivism, they failed to see any other alternative. They did not even sense the possibility of a subjectivistic mode of subjectivity, a way of living focused on one's way of living. By attempting to totally transcend the finite, however, these objectivistic metaphysicians, episte-mologists, and moral theorists were not providing an alternative to blind social conformism and unexamined traditionalism. They were in fact functioning with an uncritical endorsement of current fashion and established tradition. Furthermore, their efforts to rationally transcend the finiteness of the socially variable and the historically changing is not just an innocent failure to recognize the social character of the rational, but it is an attempt to deny their own finiteness, to claim for themselves the status of an unassailable god. It is an attempt to serve the self-interests of philosophers by seeking to exercise dominating power over all other intellectuals by claiming that they alone know the ultimate explanations and justifications. As Kierkegaard interprets things, their efforts are ethical in character (making a choice for which one cannot escape responsibility) and they always fail to escape despair, given the social and historical finiteness of human rationality.

Likewise, to Kierkegaard, most theologians of his age also were mere social conformers, continuing to presume the objectivistic mode of life which had been contaminating Christianity since its unholy alliance with Greek ontotheologies. These theologians were still attempting to see the God of worship and prayer as one more object, a superobject, a supernatural being, who supposedly has objective properties, of whom one can have objective knowledge (or at least beliefs that one by faith can hold to be objectively true), and in terms of whom one can give transscientific (metaphysical) explanations of and justifications for everything being as it is and not otherwise. As a radical critic of such customary theology, Kierkegaard, through the voice of Johannes Climacus, rejects all talk about God being an object which falls under some social concept or about which one can have beliefs that satisfy some social criteria for being "objective." He wrote, "…an objective acceptance of Christianity is paganism or thoughtlessness… Christianity protests every form of objectivity… Objectively, Christianity has absolutely no existence."[11] Although Kierkegaard does affirm that success in self-building can be found only in Christian faithfulness to the call of the infinite, he insists that such faithfulness does not consist in beliefs about an infinite being that has objective characteristics. The objectivistic mode of social subjectivity, seeking as it does to transcend social rationality, does not work. The task confronting the social critic, according to Kierkegaard, is one of radically critiquing the social and cultural without attempting to transcend the social through a fetishized objectivistic mode of rationality that blinds itself to its own subjectivistic and social character.

Before looking at Kierkegaard's critical interpretation of specific types of modern life that fail to escape despair, it would be well to keep in mind two other general critical claims that Kierkegaard makes. First, he claims that the aesthetic, religious, scientific, political and economic changes taking place in his present age will not enable people to live free from domination or despair. Existentially caring for one's own individual mode of subjectivity is a necessary condition for practicing freedom. Focusing on the nature of one's individual mode of subjectivity, of course, does not exclude being concerned about the nature of existing political and economic practices or about gaining objective scientific knowledge of scientific objects. Refusing to endorse metaphysical ontotheology or positivistic scientism and refusing to find salvation through mere social and cultural reformations or revolutions can be parts of a project of practicing freedom that includes being scientific, reformist and revolutionary. Besides, if social practices could be instituted that would nurture people to be non-conformists and critics exercising care for themselves, this might aid people to take personal responsibility for their own lives although even such nurturing can never eliminate the hard work needed to gain self-understanding, freedom, and empowerment.

Second, Kierkegaard claims that it is possible to live in despair without being conscious of this condition. Therefore, an individual's actions, manner of life, and mode of subjectivity can be understood only when it is interpreted in the light of that individual's history and his or her whole social, cultural, and historical world. Extreme social conformists may appear to be living without desperation, but this may be due only to their good (and bad) fortune of not yet having experienced those dramatic ruptures that reveal what always has been latent beneath the surface. For example, ontotheological objectivists may appear to have escaped from despair, but their very belligerent defensiveness reveals their deep-seated anxieties and desperate attempts to maintain control over the uncontrollable. As Nietzsche stressed, we must treat words, actions, conscious feelings, and moods as symptoms that need to be critically interpreted by locating them in a much larger historical and social setting. As Kierkegaard interprets things through his appropriation of Augustine, the conformist and the ontotheologian are willfully ignorant and willfully deceiving themselves about their ignorance and its coverup.

Freedom from willful ignorance, self-deception, and despair requires electing to exercise passionate attention to the character of one's life and to take responsibility for molding a way of life that works. Merely choosing to take responsibility to selectively endorse parts of one's social and cultural inheritance while refusing other parts, however, is necessary but not sufficient to guarantee a mode of living free of despair. One's refusals and endorsements have to produce a workable combination. Kierkegaard claims that there are many ways to fail in the project of self-making and that it is very difficult to succeed.

Kierkegaard identifies a number of these ways of failing in the project of taking responsibility for one's life. There are people, he claims, who are trying to be responsible and care for themselves who nevertheless still are failing. Kierkegaard points out that not everyone is part of the general population trapped in the "public." For example, there are people living aesthetic, moral, and religious ways of life who find themselves alienated from the conforming public and who are searching for an alternative but who fail to find a workable alternative.[12] Although many among the alienated nonconformists will fail in their projects of self-making, it is from among them that the critical interpreters of the human world must come. Also, even the philosophical and theological ontotheologians are opposed to "mindless" conformity; that is why they recommend objectivistic modes of subjectivity as alternatives. This choice, however, also does not work. As Kierkegaard critically interprets the human condition, taking responsibility for one's form of life, one's mode of subjectivity, requires doing more than just trying to avoid the boring boredom of the leveled-down life of the extreme social conformist. Practicing freedom so as to minimize coercive social control and to maximizing personal power over one's own life requires self-understanding and self-discipline. For a way of life to work, some very demanding criteria have to be satisfied. In order to interpret Kierkegaard's criticisms of the failing ways of life in his age, it is necessary to understand the criteria of "working" that he uses in his critical interpretation of these modes of subjectivity.

In *Sickness Unto Death*[13] Kierkegaard writes through a pseudonym, Anti-Climacus, and presents an interpretation of the many ways in which people fail in the ethical task of taking responsibility for their lives. Anti-Climacus contends that a workable mode of subjectivity must be one that allows people to live in full recognition and acceptance of the ramifications of the dual nature of all human beings. On the one hand, people are *determined, finite,* and *temporally changing.* On the other hand, people are *free, infinite,* and *unchanging through time.* People are determined by biological, social, and cultural structures, practices, and institutions, with each person possessing one specific biological and social inheritance and living from moment to moment in a changing world as a changing individual. People also, however, are free and able to endorse and reject aspects of their social and cultural inheritance, to creatively modify the practices they will leave as their legacy to the future, and even to be a particular person living in faithfulness to that which is other than anything and everything social. People are able to conceive of infinite possibilities. They can conceive of social and cultural alternatives to their actual inheritance and alternative ways of molding inheritances into individual lives. They can conceive of the general possibility of alternative social practices and individual lives that cannot yet be conceived in any determinate way by the finite persons now existing. People also can live with an unchanging self-determined identity through all the changes in their lives.

People constitute themselves as specific persons by relating themselves to these two sets of factors and by relating themselves reflectively to their manner of relating these factors, with such reflections modifying the specific character of the factors involved. Thinking you are not free to do something can guarantee that you are not free. Not recognizing that subjectivity is truth and that one first needs to focus on the character of one's mode of subjectivity will guarantee that one will never even begin the spiritual quest required for successful living. Personal identity is gained through the successful completion of a spiritual project of self-understanding, self-acceptance, and creative self-constitution. Leveled reflectors are never successful in life because they never really get started in this project. They live at war within a conflictual inheritance and with living denials of one or more of the inescapable existential factors of human life.

Anti-Climacus labels the various sorts of failure in the activity of self-constitution as different forms of despair. That despair is possible can be seen as proof that people are not merely beasts or socialized robots or puppets. Talk of failure makes sense only where success is possible. In the case of despairing failures, rather than succeeding in creating and maintaining an unchanging self through the changing moments of its life, it is only the failure that is unchanging and gives continuity to their lives. Such people are eternally dying and this is what Kierkegaard labels as a spiritual sickness unto death.[14] Many people, Kierkegaard charges, live lives that show no consciousness of the need to constitute themselves as persons and thus of their failure to do so. They are the spiritless people who "poo-poo" all talk about spirit or self-making or who find distractions so as not to consider the issue of self-making. Some merely accept good fortune or blame bad luck and thus try to avoid dealing with the issue of the quality of their spirit. Some people avoid conscious self-making by identifying with some abstract universal (the state or nation). They live failing lives of despair without consciousness of their failing or their despair. These are not just personal failures. Existing social and cultural practices in the "present age" nurture people not to engage in this kind of critical self-interpretation, and thus social and cultural criticism is needed to succeed in blending the inescapable conditions of human life.

Whether conscious of one's failure or not, the failure is always due to accenting one of the existential factors to the exclusion of the other. Sometimes the finite gets accented at the expense of the infinite. There is a lack of movement to new possibilities beyond what is given by one's social/cultural inheritance and by chance. Thus, one remains as simply one more example (a repetition) of what one does in a given society and culture. Sometimes the infinite dominates the finite. One seeks unlimited, transhuman knowledge (rather than simply the not unjustified beliefs of a finite person in a specific contingent context of vocabularies, beliefs, and doubts). Sometimes necessities succeed in denying living space to possibilities. People get lost in fatalisms and determinisms or nihilisms in which all possibilities are seen as so petty and trivial that it doesn't make any difference what one does or what kind of self one makes of oneself. In other cases, sometimes concern for possibilities drives out recognition of real and limiting necessities. People despairingly wish to be what their concrete limitations make impossible or they melancholically freeze in inaction because of concern over unlikely fearful or dreadful possibilities. In a similar manner, the temporal, changing character of human life sometimes gets sacrificed by accenting the eternal and unchanging, or the eternal gets sacrificed by accenting the temporal and changing. Neither people, nor their minds, nor their ideas, nor their spirits totally transcend the temporal, historical, determinate, finite, biological, social, and cultural. Neither, however, Kierkegaard insists, need people be merely temporal. They can develop a quality of spirit that gives to themselves an unchanging character by passionately willing one thing.

Some people are only too conscious of their continuous failings, and this intensifies their failing and their despair. Some people fail because they knowingly don't try hard enough.[15] Despairing over the earthly, they think that the task is too demanding given what they "are." They live merely wishing they were someone else. They weakly let misfortune stop their efforts at self-making. "I've just had a string of bad luck." "I'll try again when my luck changes." Conscious of their continuous failing, they might seek forgetfulness in sensuality, in diversion in some "great" earthly project, or in seeking comfort from others by parading before them their own failures (only to hate themselves for being so weak as to tell others about their failings).

Failures in the project of self-making can be classified in various ways. Consider, for example, Kierkegaard's identification of the following three ways in which people fail in the project of self-making even though they strive to be more than a mere social conformist. First, there is the aesthete who aestheticizes everything, including other people's lives and feelings, striving to avoid all social forms of propriety by avoiding all commitments to others or oneself and by trying to live each moment as if the whole of infinity were contained in it. Kierkegaard examines the implications of such an aesthetic way of life by writing in *Either/Or* through a series of pseudonyms (Victor Eremita, A. Johannes the Seducer, Cordelia the Seduced). He points out the self-defeating character of the aesthetic project. Would-be aesthetes must diligently and continuously discipline themselves if they are to avoid making commitments and thus live totally involved in the aesthetic quality of each passing moment. Neither being committed to any "this" nor to any "that" mocks oneself because then one is no one.[16] Also, were one able to carry out this impossible task, the result would not be a life but only a series of chance occurrences, many of which would not be aesthetically praiseworthy. The aesthetic choice is no choice at all.[17] Trying to live as an individual totally free from the social and historical and with only a set of aesthetic momentary experiences does not work.[18]

Although the aesthete's project fails, it is understandable why the attempt is made, given the aesthete's limited perception that this is the only way to avoid all the other objectionable alternatives. The aesthete wants nothing to do with the lives of the aristocrats who are bored with their lives and nothing to do with the social roles of the middle-class bourgeoisie who bore others and themselves.[19] Neither is the aesthete willing to live as the comic and blind romantic who falls in love, expecting it to last for a lifetime all on its own.[20] Also unacceptable and impossible in the eyes of the aesthete is the life of one attempting to live primarily in obedience to and out of respect for "abstract" rules, laws, or imperatives. The aesthete shares Johannes Climacus's understanding that such a Kantian attempt to define oneself primarily as a moral individual whose essence lies in its respect for the imperatives of "pure practical reason" is an unworkable project. Only by abstracting away everything that is sensuous and socially contingent, everything human, can such purely formal imperatives seemingly be isolated, but then they are useless to humans, especially since they ignore the social status of the abstractor and the social status of the criteria of formal independence.[21] The aesthete and Johannes Climacus also agree that attempting to live as a mere social functionary doing one's duty, as Hegel recommended, will not work. In the lives of humans one never reaches Hegel's last stage of historical development in which people are freed from alienation from their social roles or freed to live peacefully in nonconflictual roles.[22] The aesthete is pushed toward an affirmation of the life of aesthetic immediacy by the rejection of everything social and by seeing such immediacy as the only alternative to total surrender to social normalization. In endorsing the possibility of being something other than merely a leveled down reflector, the aesthete is very close to that truth of subjectivity that produces success in the project of self-making.

Missing is a recognition that affirming infinite possibilities can never be divorced from endorsing specific aspects of one's social inheritance and one's interpersonal situation.

Being responsible for oneself requires refusing to be a mere social conformist blind to the infinity of possible life options. It also requires affirming one's inescapable finiteness. Some people, therefore, might assume that they as self-makers must attempt by themselves to relate themselves as finite, historical self-makers to this infinity of possibilities so that they might give to themselves individual identities that remain intact throughout their lives. Kierkegaard identifies two ways in which such rugged individualists might try to be responsible for their lives by trying to carry out the project of self-making all by themselves. These are the final two ways of failing, according to his classification scheme.

People, refusing to be mere social conformists, might acknowledge both their socially determined finiteness and the infinity of life options open to them and then attempt to give themselves an unchanging personal identity by striving to live faithfully as a moral person. As interpreted by Kierkegaard, persons in the moral form of life attempt to commit themselves without reservation (infinitely) to a set of lifetime commitments to other people. Appropriating Hegel's ethic of social role fulfillment, Kierkegaard illustrates this moral form of life with the totally devoted husband and committed judge who takes personal responsibility for his occupancy of these social positions and their place in the social world. He makes an unlimited commitment to be the husband and the judge he is.[23] Moral persons seek to live with infinite commitment to fulfill their duties to the other social individuals to whom they are related (wife, citizen) and who have proper expectations, given their social status and the commitments of the moral person.[24] Kierkegaard's communitarian ethic is presented as superior to Kant's formalism, which is seen as leaving out the inescapably concrete and finite details of the lives of human individuals. It is also presented as superior to a Hegelian ethic of role fulfillment because in Kierkegaard's moral form of life people are not just social functionaries or robots but are involved in personally endorsing (choosing) a subjective mode of subjectivity in which they commit themselves to other individuals in accordance with the requirements spelled out in their social inheritance and mutual agreements and contracts as social individuals.[25] Through unlimited, infinite commitment, the finite moral individual attempts to give to the social, cultural, and historical world of people the status of autonomy and self-sufficiency.

This moral form of life, Kierkegaard charges, when it is treated as autonomous and self-sufficient, fails to work as a living mode of subjectivity for a number of reasons. First, reifying any finite social morality by being infinitely committed to it is filled with danger. Objectivists such as Socrates and Plato found in this danger motivation for attempting to transcend the finite by postulating eternal standards and ideals that could be used in critiquing existing social practices. As we shall see, Nietzsche and Marx, while endorsing the social character of all standards and ideals, also introduced similar critiques of our all too human moralities.

Second, being infinitely committed to anything finite will always leave people in despair. A finite person needs a motive for making an infinite commitment to the moral order existing in a certain social world. Even Kant, with his accent on the autonomy of pure practical reason, recognized this. He acknowledged that people insist that moral virtue be paired with personal happiness, either one's own or that of others. The world in which this moral order exists, however, is not a world in which worldly happiness is guaranteed to the morally virtuous or those they care about. Therefore, Kant claimed, people are motivated to be morally virtuous only by postulating both a life beyond their finite lives and a perfect and omnipotent being transcending the finite world and guaranteeing the needed pairing between virtue and happiness. Making such postulations, however, reduces finiteness again to mere appearance. In this life, people will despair over the huge disparity existing between virtue and happiness. The innocent and the good too often suffer and the moral failures are worldly successful, enjoying the fruits of life.

Third, even love for others cannot provide the motive needed for making an infinite commitment to morality. The infinite commitment definitive of love can conflict with the infinite commitment to morality. An infinite commitment to a person whom one loves will produce a wish that, in the conflictual relationships that inevitably arise between lovers, one's lover will always be in the right morally and one be in the wrong. However, this wish often conflicts with what one cannot help but recognize to be the case, and that is that sometimes, given the moral implications of existent social roles, one's lover is in the wrong.[26] It is to the particularity of individual people that we are related in love, but it is to social individuals of a kind that we are related by moral obligations. Finally, we know all too well that we continuously fail to live up to the demands of morality, both in carrying out the duties definitive of our present social roles and in reforming oppressive social roles. The more we sincerely try to be moral the more we feel guilty about our all too apparent failures. Thus, Kierkegaard concludes, even choosing to be a moral individual, the best kind of social individual one's social world permits, is not sufficient to avoid existential failure and despair. Of course, it does not follow that one is free to be immoral simply because social morality, when treated as self-sufficient, doesn't avoid existential failure. Our interpretation of Kierkegaard's understanding of the proper place of morality in human life will have to wait until the last chapter, when we consider the place of morality in the life of the person faithfully living in response to encounters with social rationality"s radical other—the not finite, the infinite.

The final way of failing in the project of responsible self-making that Kierkegaard identifies involves people who become knights of resignation. They go through life lamenting that they will never gain what they and all other people desperately want, a union of righteousness and happiness or at least a nondespairing life. At the same time they continue to want what they have no hope of gaining. They despairingly abandon all projects aimed at getting what they want. They live wanting without hope of getting. They remember everything, but the memory is precisely the pain. In infinite resignation they are reconciled with their existence as people wanting but always failing to get a harmonization of the finite, determinate, and changing aspects of their lives with the infinite, free, unchanging aspects. They wear a shirt spun with tears. For Kierkegaard they are the closest to and the furthest from succeeding in caring for themselves and practicing freedom.[27] Their understanding, according to Kierkegaard, lacks one crucial element. They don't understand that finite people cannot on their own create themselves by relating themselves to the infinite. As determinate, finite, social, and historical individuals, they need to let the infinite other to all social finiteness first call to them so that then they can respond to this call with a faithfulness that will give to their lives an unchanging character. Letting the call of the infinite other to all social rationality be heard, however, requires understanding that with us there is an infinite otherness to all our describable traits. More about this in chapter 5 when we put Kierkegaard and Levinas in dialogue with each other and with Hindu and Buddhist understanding of the otherness to all finite things that is central to human life.

It is crucial not to draw unwarranted conclusions from Kierkegaard's focus on the responsibility of persons to take a hand in creating themselves out of the social and cultural materials they have inherited and the possibilities left open by those materials. Although he does contend that social reforms and scientific or technological discoveries cannot eliminate the need for existential responsibility, he need not deny that social and cultural reforms might remove some of the barriers making it unnecessarily difficult for individual persons to accept such responsibility. Kierkegaard surely is not denying that his own texts can weaken some such barriers. Some of what he is doing might become an established cultural practice. This already has happened in some educational circles. Similarly, his opposition to objectivistic modes of subjectivity does not imply opposition to science and technology and what they can do to lessen or prevent human suffering. They cannot eliminate the need for existential self-examination but there is no reason to oppose them, although there are excellent existential reasons for opposing objectivistic scientism.

III. NIETZSCHE'S CRITIQUE OF SOCIAL/ CULTURAL BARRIERS TO FREE LIFE

Kierkegaard's despairing conformists, philosophers, theologians, aesthetes, moralists, and resigning nihilists appear in Nietzsche's texts as a herd of nihilistic, fearful, envious, resentful slaves and dominators of those few potentially free spirits who are trying to celebrate life in spite of its unjustifiable suffering and who are trying to be masters over their own lives. Using a wide variety of literary forms (aphorisms, speeches, dialogues, poems) and rhetorical tropes (ridicule, satire, hyperbole), Nietzsche presents a critical interpretation of the oppressive social and culture world in which he found himself in an effort to empower the few who were able at his historical moment to understand and resist being dominated in that world. The few life-affirmers retain this ability in spite of the efforts of the many life-negators to overpower these few potentially free spirits. Through their practices and institutions, especially their use of their objectivistic, ontotheological, and moralistic rhetoric, life-negators either seduce life-affirmers to give up their freedom and power or they exclude and marginalize them as mad, irrational, and dangerous.

Readers seeking to appropriate Nietzsche's texts face two difficult tasks if they are to enter into dialogue with these texts because of the literary and rhetorical style Nietzsche uses in an effort to empower life-affirmers to resist the life-negators. First, since Nietzsche is challenging the presuppositions of the metaphysicians and epistemologists of his age, presuppositions still held by many in our age, readers are required to take great care to avoid forcing upon Nietzsche's texts interpretations that would reinforce the prevalent practices and rhetoric which he is trying to weaken through his writing. Second, presenting the kind of general interpretation of Nietzsche's texts that I am attempting here always leaves one with the worry that one will thereby sap his texts of their rhetorical power. Needless to say, nothing can substitute for reading Nietzsche's own words. Given that many of his friendly and hostile readers, however, have become so fascinated with the apparent trees in his forest that they fail to see the forest, this critical interpretation perhaps can aid some readers to make the hermeneutically circular journey to the whole that is necessary for interpreting the parts.[28]

Nietzsche's freedom-serving, holistic, critical interpretation can be analyzed into three interrelated parts: (1) An interpretation of interpretation as the appropriate approach to use in gaining an understanding of the social and cultural worlds in which we live and of ourselves who have been nurtured, trained, and coerced to live in them. (2) An interpretation of the problematic character of being what we are and living in the worlds in which we find ourselves, especially given the herd's understanding (misunderstanding) of its world. (3) An interpretation of how people who desire to live as free spirits in their human, all too human, worlds are to go about caring for themselves and practicing freedom. In what follows I will present my appropriating interpretation of each of these parts.

Again and again throughout his texts, Nietzsche proclaims that the best that knowers can hope for is to be "interpreters of experience."[29] He acknowledges that his own proclamations also are interpretations.[30] Acknowledging this, and that other interpretations are also possible, however, provides him with no reason for not being firmly committed to his interpretation.[31] As a falliblist, Nietzsche, of course, admits that he might someday discover that he was wrong, although as he wrote he certainly didn't think so. Furthermore, Nietzsche claims, all interpretations are offered in service to specific interests. All interpretations are made from a particular point of view determined by such interests, and thus they present only such an interest-colored perspective. Nietzsche's interpretive perspective is determined by his interest in enabling potentially free spirits (including himself) to lessen the power of the masses to control the subjectivity and lives of such spirits. The experiences that are to be interpreted perspectivally are not the uninterpreted passive perceptions of Aristotle or the sense data of Locke that can serve as some "objective" foundation for knowledge. Nietzsche is not that kind of empiricist. There are no neutral, interest-free, unconceptualized data that different people view from different perspectives. All of our experiences and actions are what they are because of the vocabularies we use in conceptually constituting these experiences and actions, vocabularies that are culturally variable, historically changing, and interest-directed. Interpreting experiences and actions, therefore, requires interrogating them.

The vocabularies of the masses, Nietzsche charges, are constructed out of fear, envy, and resentment and serve the interests of these slaves to freedom-restricting concerns. The critical interpreter, therefore, must function as a physician trying to interpret experiences and actions as symptoms of social and cultural illnesses.[32] The symptoms, however, can be interpreted only if they are located in the worlds in which they are occurring. As a physician, therefore, the interpreter must function as a chemist analyzing the social and cultural whole down into the specific practices that are producing the overall effects manifested in the symptoms being interpreted.[33] Once identified, these practices have to be classified according to the type of illness they exhibit.[34] Furthermore, physicians do their interpreting of symptoms and analyzing and typing of social and cultural practices as healers striving to promote spiritual health by warring against social and cultural illness, living misunderstandings, and flawed forms of subjectivity. Nietzsche calls upon his physicians to philosophize with a hammer, rhetorically making use of two senses of this phrase. First, as a hammer hitting a tuning fork sounds out false notes, so criticism can be used as a hammer sounding out the hollowness of social and cultural practices. Second, as a (sledge) hammer can be used to smash false idols, all available rhetorical devices are to be employed in smashing down the cultural walls being used to enslave potentially free spirits and to turn such spirits from being among the few life-affirmers into being among the many life-deniers.[35] Because life-affirmers have the strength to confront the misfortunes of life with their eyes wide open and without trying to explain away suffering and chance, when they get seduced by the metaphysical, religious, and moral rhetoric of the life-deniers, they are the ones who have the strength to be the most self-disciplined among the life-deniers—the ascetics and priests.[36]

In Nietzsche's interpretation of the human situation, reference repeatedly is made to three general factors that play major roles in conditioning human experiences and actions. It is against this background that he diagnoses the problematic character of the way the common herd lives. First, Nietzsche sees life as filled with unpredictable chances and accidents. "Over all things stand the heaven Accident... the heaven Chance..."[37] Second, he is convinced that most people see life as a problem[38] because it is filled with chanciness and accidents and because it is filled with suffering that has no obvious justification.[39] Misfortune hits everyone[40] and little moments of human happiness cannot justify human suffering.[41] The third conviction that frames Nietzsche's interpretation is that human behavior consists of at least five different exercises of power.[42] Some people act spontaneously, affirming life, giving form to experiences without conscious planning.[43] Other people react out of envy, resentment, and fear of what others are or are doing.[44] Some act to eliminate chance and to explain away or justify suffering.[45] Some act to overpower others so as to get them to serve the actor's interests and emotional needs.[46] Finally, there are those few who act so as to be a master over themselves by resisting efforts by others to turn them into slavish conformists and life-denying ascetics.[47] In interpreting Nietzsche's project of social and cultural criticism, therefore, we need to foreground his specific writings against his background understanding of chance, suffering, and power.

Nietzsche makes a very sweeping indictment of his age's social and cultural world. He indicts the nihilism that he sees contaminating just about all of the religious, moral, philosophical, artistic, and political currents of his world. For most people, he claims, life is a problem. For no apparent or good reason, misfortune strikes individuals whom people see as innocent and undeserving of the suffering of the pain, terror, and humiliation that they experience. Furthermore, much of this misfortune seems to occur by sheer accident and chance, and thus one cannot prevent it or prepare oneself for it. Most people's lives, Nietzsche claims, are filled with the fear that such misfortune will occur to them and their loved ones. This fills them not only with great anxiety but also with a deep sense of nihilism, a sense that life is not fair, that life is meaningless, that life doesn't care, that it is evil, that it has no intrinsic worth in and by itself, that living is worthwhile only if life can gain significance by being related to something other than what it appears to be. Their nihilism, born out of fear of uncontrollable suffering, is reinforced by their modern post-Copernican scientific understanding that identifies people as tiny creatures moving on the third rock from the sun, which is a mediocre star in a sea of billions of stars.[48]

This anxiety and sense of nihilism, however, Nietzsche charges, can not be tolerated by these life naysayers. Therefore, they religiously and/or philosophically postulate the existence of some world or being beyond the world as it appears in their everyday life.[49] They postulate a supernatural god or an ultimate reality that can provide an explanatory and justificatory reason for everything (including misfortune) being as it is, even if the reason is only known by a god whom we have to trust as having such knowledge. They then fetishize their own creation by forgetting that they had postulated this ontotheological realm and by covering up the nihilism, anxiety, and fear that motivated the postulation. They declare that life does have meaning and value in spite of appearances because it is related to this ontotheological realm. They furthermore claim that anyone who rejects this ontotheology is in fact a nihilist denying that life has value. They believe that only with ontotheology can life have significance. Nietzsche directs his rhetorical efforts at attacking all forms of nihilism and ontotheology motivated by such nihilism. Not surprisingly, ontotheologians have branded Nietzsche a dangerous nihilist giving voice to human despair, attacking the very foundation of the meaningfulness of human existence, and eroding all motivation for respecting other people or oneself. Nietzsche charges that life doesn't need any foundation. It simply is. People can live cheerfully while all the time being fully aware of all the vicissitudes of life.

Nietzsche's critique of ontotheological nihilism is not set forth, however, as just an expression of his disinterested interpretation of his world or as merely a defensive response to the charge that he is a nihilist. His rhetoric is not primarily directed at the herd of nihilists who are slaves to their fears and uncritical conformists to the ontotheological socialization and acculturation they have received. Nietzsche does not believe that most people in the herd are able to understand what he is trying to write.[50] Not everyone, however, he believes, is a fearful, slavish member of the herd. There are a few who are able to say "yes" to life with their eyes wide open to its chanciness and potential for pain and suffering.[51] There are a few who do not need some grand justification for life itself, do not need to think that there is some cosmological point, plan, or purpose for all the joys and pains in life in order to joyfully sing and dance their way through life fully aware of its uncontrollable chanciness and suffering. These noble and potentially free spirits, free from merely conforming to herd dispositions, are the one's to whom Nietzsche directs his rhetoric.[52]

Although Nietzsche contends that these few noble people have the power to affirm life, he sees his rhetoric as playing a vital role in their lives. It can provide them with the empowerment they need not to be seduced any longer by the ontotheological or moral rhetoric of the nihilists. The nihilists use their rhetoric in an effort to control or exclude from the human community these joyous, nonconforming life-affirmers. The herd, slaves to fear and anxiety, further enslave themselves by (1) their envy of the life-affirmer's freedom from such anxiety and fear, (2) their resentment of these people who have the power to affirm life and live without finding some cosmic meaning for human life, and (3) their fear that the life-affirmer's rejection of the nihilist's whole reactive way of life will undermine the effectiveness of the ontotheological edifice constructed by the nihilists to persuade themselves that life isn't really chancy and that misfortune is really only an appearance of ultimate significance. Therefore, out of such envy, resentment, and fear of the life affirmers, the nihilists construct life-denying and freedom-controlling norms of rationality and morality.

Using these norms, life celebrators are marginalized, branded as naive, simple-minded, and irrational, and are controlled or excluded by being branded as evil and dangerous. The morality being pushed by the ontotheological nihilists, who look to the unchanging for protection from chance and to a supernatural world for guarantees that suffering is justified, is one that denigrates the bodily and natural life that is joyfully and spontaneously affirmed by those who have no fear of life. Unfortunately, many persons, who are able to be masters of their own lives of joy and suffering, become enslaved by the slavishly fearful naysayers to life. This happens when celebrators of life internalize the slaves' ontotheological and moral rhetoric.[53] It is in order to break the hold of the nihilist's rhetoric over life-affirmers that Nietzsche directs his rhetoric to these few potentially free spirits. He laughs at the nihilist's rhetoric. He ridicules it. He interprets its genealogy and motivations in order to show that one can free oneself from the power of its seductive rhetoric and become a free spirit returning to a joyous affirmation of life, fully aware of all its attractive and unattractive aspects.

Nietzsche claims that he is writing at a time when there is good reason to believe that his rhetorical hammer could successfully sound the hollowness of all of the nihilist's ontotheological and moral claims. In the minds and moods of many people, the ontotheologian's god, in all of its metaphysical, epistemological and moral variations, is dead, killed by people who find ridiculous all of the metaphysician's pretentious claims.[54] The growing awareness in Western Europe in the nineteenth century that there is no metaphysical God nor any ultimate explanations or justifications magnified the fear, anger, and resentment of the nihilists who see their whole way of life under attack. They had banked everything on having metaphysical and epistemological ultimates provide the security and significance they found lacking in their fearful lives. Faced with the threat of existential bankruptcy, some slaves to fear wallowed in their nihilism[55] while others reacted defensively with even more intense hatred of celebrators of life who laughed to death their metaphysical and epistemological crutches.[56] However, the argumentative attacks by Hume and Kant on speculative, metaphysical explanations, the literary ridicule coming from the pens of writers such as Voltaire and Dostoyevsky, and all the criticisms of Hegel's attempt to include history in a metaphysical system had created a cultural climate in which celebrators of life could be empowered by Nietzsche's genealogical rhetoric to become spirits free from the herd's seductive metaphysical, epistemological, and moral theorizing. Employing a kind of Hegelian dialectical analysis, Nietzsche sees that the conflicting social and cultural forces of his age had created space for critics such as himself to place under question the basic presuppositions of the metaphysical, epistemological, and moral currents of his age. He did not have to appeal to asocial and ahistorical norms to condemn these presuppositions and to celebrate living without them. He and critics like himself only had to be physicians motivated by an interest in people living well enough to celebrate life, wise enough to interpret the age's symptoms of illness, and artistic enough to provide the rhetoric that can empower some people to heal themselves.

In his attempt to empower potentially free spirits, the rhetoric that Nietzsche uses is very easy to misinterpret. Many of Nietzsche's opponents have done just that to his call for life-affirmers to go beyond the slave's morality of good and evil, to live spontaneously, to become authors of their own values, and to be masters living dangerously. Nietzsche's writings about the death of God similarly have produced a great deal of misunderstanding. Nietzsche has been branded as an amoralist, as a moral relativist, as advocating actions (war) and attitudes (elitism) that would be condemned even by life-affirmers who were free of the nihilists' seduction. Nietzsche has been condemned as an enemy of all religion. If one is to critically interpret and dialogically appropriate Nietzsche's texts, it is important, therefore, to attend to the things Nietzsche wrote that provide good evidence for labeling as misinterpretations the readings Nietzsche's opponents give to his rhetorical attacks on the nihilist's metaphysical gods, the epistemologist's ultimate grounds, and the slave's morality born out of envy and resentment.

Although there are times when Nietzsche writes as though he is rejecting all moralities,[57] there are many places in his texts in which he writes of multiple moralities[58] and calls for ranking some moralities as being better than others.[59] He proposes going beyond the slave morality of good and evil, motivated by fear and resentment,[60] to the life-affirmers' morality of good and bad.[61] Goodness for the life-affirmers is found in their affirmation of life and in their rejection of any restrictions on the freedom of life-affirmers simply because slaves to fear, envy, and resentment are opposed to their lifestyles or actions.[62] Because social moralities have thus far been constituted primarily by fearful and resentful nihilists, life-affirmers are going to have to create a new morality free of restrictions on the many different not-unjustified forms of joyous living. This new morality will be free of prohibitions on human freedom not required to protect the freedom of all life-affirmers and free spirits.[63] Only the protection of freedom will warrant restricting freedom. It will not only tolerate but prize the many different kinds of prized and valued lives that free spirits will artistically create. It will not be relativistic because it will contain universal condemnations of infringements on such freedom. After all, this is the core of Nietzsche's indictment of the nihilistic life-denier's whole social and cultural world.

Nietzsche simply radicalizes the modern age's opposition to restrictions on personal freedom.[64] In the new freedom-endorsing morality of the life-affirmers, one must not even use force to require nihilistic slaves to abandon their ways of living, as ridiculous and laughable as they appear to life-affirmers. Nietzsche charges that one must never attack individuals or blame them for the social and cultural currents in which they are trapped.[65] For those unable to profit from the cultural physician's rhetorical medicine, the best thing to do is simply to go one's own way and pass them by, even if that means that they still keep applying their nihilistic morality to themselves.[66] Nietzsche is only claiming that no one should do what the nihilists are doing, forcing their nihilism, ontotheology, and morality upon those able and willing to live differently, celebrating life while fully aware of the suffering and chanciness it contains. It is the social and cultural world of nihilism and its offspring, especially its efforts to seductively deceive and thus control potentially free spirits, that Nietzsche calls life-affirmers to war against. When Nietzsche writes that free spirits "will the eternal reoccurrence of war and peace," he is pointing out that, since free spirits renounce all asocial and ahistorical absolutes while still living in the midst of the herd, they will repeatedly have to war against conformity to the herd and live peacefully with the result that they attain.[67]

Recommending that his readers rhetorically pass by those unable to profit from his writings does not imply that Nietzsche is indifferent to the suffering of other people. Nietzsche urges kindness to all people,[68] a kindness that was other than a self-serving pity which saw others only as pitiful victims to be paternalistically controlled. Nietzsche also acknowledges that life-affirming and freedom-practicing spirits will have to pay a price for gaining and maintaining their noncon-formity.[69] Nietzsche promises that the pain of accepting the physician's interpretive medicine and recreating oneself would be more than made up for by the freedom and joy attained.[70] The herd, however, often increases their suffering by not letting such spirits live freely,[71] especially when those spirits are members of their family or once were counted as their friends. To the extent that the herd does hear something in what Nietzsche writes, they may bring upon themselves the additional suffering that results from seeing their gods dying off and their world of fetishes and rationalizations collapsing. In love and kindness, Nietzsche aims his rhetoric at those capable of becoming free spirits who would find the freedom and joys gained worth the price of the surgery required, linguistically passing by those not yet capable of listening to his critical interpretation of their world. Nietzsche is a kind of elitist, but his elitism consists only of two not-unjustified positions. First, he affirms that for him and other free spirits a life free of fear of life, free of fetishized metaphysical and theological rationalizations, and free of envy, resentment, and fear of difference is better than the all forms of nihilistic living. Second, he claims that, as he critically interprets the Western social and cultural world, a whole herd of people are living out the consequences of metaphysical, theological, and moral interpretations adopted out of fear and resentment, interpretations that would not be endorsed in the absence of such fear and resentment, as the lives of free spirits demonstrate. Nietzsche's elitism is the elitism of the physician toward the patient, of the educator toward the unknowing, of the social and cultural critic toward those who misunderstand and misinterpret. Given Nietzsche's commitment to freedom and his use of his critical interpretation of social and cultural worlds of his day as a critical weapon in warring for such freedom, it is not at all inappropriate to locate Nietzsche in the Enlightenment tradition, even though he radically critiques modernity's epistemological, metaphysical, and religious practices, and even though he focuses on undermining cultural practices and on aiding some people to care for themselves rather than on changing political and economic practices.

The new values of the life-affirming free spirits have various dimensions to them. First, cheerful lives lived in joyful celebration of life are commended to all able to live them.[72] Free spirits are to float, dance, and play.[73] They are to be dancers at a Dionysian festival feeling an orgiastic overflowing of life in an unchanging world of change.[74] Living free from slavery to social and cultural convention, however, does not mean trying to do the impossible, casting off all traditional ways of doing things. Rather, it means dialogically listening to the past and then talking back; it means appropriating the past so that one can sing old melodies in one's own fresh way.[75] Second, living freely and cheerfully requires that one move beyond being what one has been made to be by the herd and that one become a master of oneself. Freedom does not happen accidentally. Rather, it takes great effort to become free.[76] Taking care of oneself requires artistic vision of the life one would live and then personal discipline in order to remove from oneself everything that stands as a barrier to achieving that goal.[77] Becoming a free spirit requires exercising artistic control; it does not mean simply letting oneself go.[78] It does not mean stupidly abandoning oneself to one's instincts or passions, which can conflict with each other, but it means taking responsibility for oneself as one prunes oneself into a living, Dionysian work of art.[79] Nietzsche reminds us that staggering around is not dancing.[80] Nietzsche invites people to so live their lives that, when they are about to end, these people can will to live them over again and again, that living this way could stand timelessly, eternally, beyond indictment.[81] Finally, Nietzsche claims that if one takes care of oneself and frees oneself from the seductive efforts of the nihilists and for joyous affirmations of life and freedom, then one will be serving the common good because one will be prizing freedom for everyone and cherishing all not-unjustified differences.[82]

Just as Nietzsche's opposition to nihilistic slave morality does not exclude the possibility of proposing a moral pluralism of freedom and prizing of difference, so his opposition to metaphysical gods does not exclude the possibility of proposing nonontotheological forms of religion.[83] His radical critique of all social and cultural threats to the particularity of free spirits who create themselves by deciding what to endorse and what to reject from their inheritance is quite similar to Kierkegaard's critique of fetishizing the socially finite and of preventing oneself from listening to the silent voice of the social's other. Again and again, Nietzsche proclaims that life is other than the divisions and individuations that human conceptualizations produce. He proclaims that there is nothing more awesome than the infinite, unchartable sea of no-thingness which is other than the hard land mapped out by social concepts.[84] He praises what he interprets as the original understanding of the Israelites in which their worship of Yahweh is an expression of their "natural" power, joy, and hope, a naturalness not reducible to any participation in social practices. He condemns how Israel's priests falsified this earlier concept of God.[85] He praises the manner in which the eternity of life is experienced religiously in the Dionysian festivals and becomes a holy way of living.[86] Although he interprets Buddhism as being nihilistic (an interpretation I will challenge in chapter 5), he praises Buddha for going beyond good and evil, for being a physician to those depressed by suffering and chance in life, for prizing the living particularity of persons over the impersonal world of social conceptualization.[87] Finally, while he is blasting what the Christian Church and its ecclesiastics have done to what he interprets as the original Christian faith, he nevertheless praises this faith, this Christian way of life. He calls Jesus a "free spirit" who, like Sankara in Hinduism and Lao-Tzu in Taoism, experienced life as something that is outside all social concepts or knowledge. Nietzsche claims that it is in Jesus' faithful way of living that one encounters God because Christianity is faithful living and not a set of doctrines.[88] Kierkegaard could have endorsed all of this. Kierkegaard sees his knights of faith as unique and indescribable persons giving identity to themselves by living faithfully to the call of the indescribable, infinite other to the symbolizable world of social rationality. The pleasure and joy of Nietzsche's Dionysian dancers also defies reduction to the states of finite objects and subjects in the world of social rationality. Their lives are not that different from those of Kierkegaard's knights of faith walking in the deer park.[89]

IV.   HEIDEGGER ON REVOLUTIONIZING DECADENT WESTERN CULTURE

Three examples, Martin Heidegger, Michel Foucault, and Slavoj Zizek, will be sufficient to illustrate the manner in which the currents of critically interpreting the relationship of people to their social/ cultural environment continues to flow and swirl in the twentieth century. Heidegger appropriates Husserl's phenomenology as a hermeneutics of "everydayness,"[90] and Aristotle's practical reasoning as one of knowing how to use tools, which social practices have constituted with proper uses and locations.[91] He does this within a context formed by his appropriation of Kierkegaard's call to take responsibility for one's own life by living within a certain kind of subjectivity, one that Heidegger describes as opening itself to radically new possibilities by listening to the representationally silent other of all beings. For Heidegger the call to assume responsibility for one's way of living within the social practices in which one has been socialized is a call from one's own "conscience" to accept one's social and bodily finiteness without totally losing oneself in the social practices of one's age or in nihilistic anxiety about one's impotence to free ourselves from one's historical inheritance. Michel Foucault's ethic of practicing freedom and caring for oneself is produced out of his appropriation of Heidegger and Nietzsche. "For me Heidegger has always been the essential philosopher... Nietzsche alone did not appeal to me—whereas Nietzsche and Heidegger: that was a philosophical shock.... I am simply a Nietzschean."[92] In the space of freedom opened by a Nietzschean-Heideggerian genealogy of the present, Foucault sketches what is involved in disciplining oneself in using such freedom to achieve the life one has chosen for oneself. Slavoj Zizek appropriates Jacques Lacan's psychoanalytic appropriation of Freud and Heidegger's interpretation of human life in order to show how individual failures to successfully relate to social rationality and its "other" not only result in individual trauma but also produce and are reenforced by the racism, nationalism, and conflictual neocapitalist popular culture prevalent at the end of the twentieth century. He spells out what is involved in caring for oneself when this consists in going beyond adjusting oneself to social proprieties, what is involved in accepting the inescapable, nonsubstantial void at the center of each person's and each culture's life. Heidegger's phenomenological hermeneutics, Foucault's interpretive analytics,[93] and Zizek's personal, social, and cultural criticism produce radical critiques of twentieth-century social and cultural practices, and they do so without encountering any need to appeal to asocial and ahistorical norms to justify their critical interpretations.

Heidegger worked as a cultural critic from his earliest days as a Roman Catholic theological student in 1909-1911, endorsing then and until 1916 a neoscholastic criticism of a modern world held captive by objectivistic presuppositions and a reductionist rendering of the religious in terms of a psychology or sociology that left no room for a Christian way of living or for Eckhart's Christian form of mysticism.[94] By the end of World War I, however, Heidegger had discovered the writings of the young Luther and Kierkegaard and had become a free Protestant endorsing, along with Protestant theologians like Karl Barth[95] and Rudolf Bultmann,[96] a criticism of both the modern secular world and scholasticism's burial of "original" Christianity under medieval and Greek ontotheologies.[97] In many direct and indirect ways these early Christian concerns (as well as his later interests in Taoism and Buddhism) heavily influenced Heidegger's critical interpretations throughout his life. His criticism of most people's lostness in their worlds sounds very much like these religions' condemnation of the sinfulness or blinding cravings of the world as it exists. His call for people to release themselves from worldly living into a radical kind of meditative thinking is a call for adopting attitudes of self-surrender, care, trust, and patience that resonate with these religions' calls for people to prepare themselves for radical liberation. During the 1920s and early 1930s, people in the West generally and for the most part, and certainly reflective people like Heidegger, sensed an alienation from the whole world of traditions into which they had been thrown.[98] This alienation, manifested in a mood of boredom with social, worldly life in general and in a mood of anxiety, not over anything in particular but rather over life's contingencies, was one that all the traditional ways of living seemed impotent to handle. From the beginning to the end of his career, Heidegger's criticism of the social and cultural practices of the West is radical in the sense that he judges that these practices are so thoroughly infected with anti-human tendencies that they are irredeemable and need to be replaced with practices of a radically different kind. His texts continuously present analyses of what is wrong with Western civilization (objectivistic, ontotheological, calculative, technologistic, will to dominate, fear of contingency) and what can be done to precipitate a radical social and cultural change (distinguish beings from Being, resolutely face death, be the shepherd of being, guard the fourfold of the earth, the sky, the mortals and the divinities). As he interprets the human situation, Western civilization is dangerously close to falling into a living hell, and it is his task to play a decisive role in preventing this disaster by deconstructing this world and opening the door for the construction of a different kind of world.

Heidegger's critical interpretation of the human way of living, and thus of his own act of interpreting this way of life, is sweeping, but it is always done as a finite person living in a world of contingent social and cultural practices. Socialization, he claims, is inescapable. The Western pattern of socialization, however, is fortunately not inescapable, although people in the West generally and for the most understand themselves and the worlds in which they live in terms only of the possibilities that circulate in the actual average Western public understanding of things.[99] Most people become dominated by a public realm of practices, with the realm of the private only being an ineffectual withdrawal from the public.[100] As Nietzsche points out, however, the times are such that a small group of people, in which Heidegger includes himself, are able to do more than live as dominated victims or as mere dropouts and copouts.

In order to critically interpret the way people live and understand things, Heidegger appropriates the phenomenological approach of Husserl and the nonontotheological aspects of Aristotle's philosophy, especially his accent on nontheoretical, practical judgements in *The Nicomachean Ethics*.[101] To Heidegger in the 1920s, the phenomenological slogan "Back to the things themselves" was an imperative to make a critical interpretation of human "facticity," human everyday life, which, in opposition to scientistic and metaphysical objectivism, did not presume either that people primarily are theoretical knowers of objects or that they are merely objects to be theoretically known. Thus, in *Being and Time* he accents the primacy of the practical understanding that finite, historical, and social people have of tools ready-to-hand, of objectified beings now merely present-on-hand, and of themselves as people (Dasein) thrown into a world of social and cultural practices which people in the past constituted and people in the present sustain, a world which through socialization gives them a social identity and traditional ways of acting, thinking, wanting, feeling, and hoping. This pretheoretical mode of understanding, Heidegger charges, is permeated by frustrating self-deception and misunderstanding. Fortunately, however, Heidegger continues, even as people throw themselves into publicly endorsed ways of living and giving priority to an objectivism that accents theoretical knowledge and technological control, there still remains within people a still, small voice of conscience rejecting such a way of taking things.

Beyond their practical activities of using tools, people are, and in some manner never can totally forget that they are, the creators and sustainers of the practices that are responsible for the constitution of toolish beings ready-to-hand and theoretical objects present-on-hand. Even though people get lost in the worlds in which they live, they still possess a pretheoretical understanding of themselves and their world that never gets completely or permanently buried.[102] They are people who moment by moment give meaning to their past by focusing on what it makes possible in the future. They are people encountering the earth as well as living in socially constituted worlds. Even when people try to think of themselves as mere objects, they still also resist being reduced to constituted theoretical objects or human resources in some contingent social world. People live with a sense of homelessness and the uprootedness of all beings, the kind of alienation Marx found defining the history of the modern age, a finding Heidegger appropriates.[103] These tendencies, Heidegger claims, will determine the destiny of the West unless they are resisted and deconstructed. It is still open to people to disobey what they hear as this call of destiny; they are free to prevent it from becoming their inescapable fate.[104] It is always up to people themselves whether any constituted world and its historical tendencies are going to be a blessing or a curse,[105] whether it is going to be a free space preserving the freedom for new worlds to come into being or it is going to be a blind alley.[106] It is in resistance to dominant historical tendencies that there surprisingly arise in some rare people the ability to criticize what they are and what their social world is like.[107] Such criticism enables people to imagine that things could be different, and it enables them to take care of themselves so that their resistance might be strengthened and that space might be opened for new possibilities to come to fruition.

Heidegger repeats Kierkegaard's call for people to take responsibility for their lives, acknowledging that they can begin critical self-reflecting only within the social and cultural world into which they have been thrown. He also insists that it is open to them to either endorse, reject, reassemble, modify, or creatively add to this worldly inheritance as part of their own personal project of living out the rest of their rather short lives. People, Heidegger claims, care about themselves; they comport themselves toward themselves in a practical, moral manner, making Kierkegaardian ethical determinations of which possibilities open to them are to be actualized.[108] People know that there is more to themselves than can be captured by any set of descriptive categories into which objectivists might try to pigeonhole them. Their significance is more than the utility value that might be assigned to them by those who would treat them only as tools or raw material (producers, consumers). Tools ready-to-hand and objects present-on-hand are what they are only because of their inescapable ties to the social practices constituting their identities and describable natures. These are social practices founded and sustained by people, people who are always more than their socially describable identities. Worlds are always and only people's worlds. Again and again, throughout *Being and Time*, the Being of all identifiable beings, including human beings, is inescapably tied to historically changeable social practices and moments in which individual people give meaning to their past by responding to the possibilities for the future that it frames.[109]

In spite of what people cannot escape from being, Heidegger claims, they seek to flee from themselves out of fear of their own freedom and out of anxiety about the contingencies and indeterminateness that frame human life. People generally and for the most part seek refuge in a public mode of life in which they focus on, cling to, and are ensnared by beings. They do not step back and gain a reflective understanding of the socially constituted character of all beings or of the contingent and historically undetermined character of such social constitution.[110] At first Heidegger makes this point by saying that people in the public mode of life do not distinguish between beings and the Being of beings.[111]

Heidegger defines the notion of "Being" as possibility. The possibility that Heidegger is talking about is not one of the possibilities or potentialities of constituted beings. It is the possibility of different beings being constituted, of sets of social and cultural practices being established that would be different from those now operating in the Western world. It is the possibility of people living lives that would be radically different from current public and private lives, of people being different kinds of people.[112] Our tools, our cultures, our nation-states, our selves all might not have been and some day might be no more. To understand the Being of beings, one needs to understand these radical possibilities. Later, in order to make the point that there always were, are, and will be alternative possibilities to any world of social practices and identities, Heidegger contrasts such social worlds to the not yet socially constituted earth, with the world grounding itself upon the earth and the earth always jutting through the world with possibilities that worldly identities, differentiations, actions, and feelings can never exhaust.[113]

There are various ways, Heidegger claims, in which people lost in the public become ensnared by beings and thus cringe before idols from which they need liberation if they are to be fully human and free to entertain possibilities not dreamed of in their current worldly life.[114] First, they remain trapped within traditional ontotheologies in which contingent and historically undetermined social and cultural history is ruled out and Being is not seen as possibility but as a supreme, necessarily existent Being causing things to be as they are. This metaphysical, ontotheological interpretation of Being prevents most people from considering the possibilities that were closed off when such ontotheologies were first begun thousands of years earlier.

These are possibilities that now can be reconsidered only if today's dominant public ontotheological way of traditionally taking things is destructured.[115] Because most people's thinking works only with the representational ideas of beings that are contaminated by a two-and-a-half-thousand-year-old ontotheological tradition, merely working with such ideas will not be sufficient to produce the kind of radical change needed.[116]

Second, people get trapped in the twentieth-century worship of scientism, thinking that there are only scientific objects (beings present-on-hand) and besides that nothing. They do not recognize that such beings also are socially constituted and thus presuppose people, social practices, and even toolish beings ready-to-hand with their instrumental environment, none of which are reducible to scientific objects.[117]

Third, people get so lost in the practical life of producing and using tools that everything becomes "enframed" in a technological ethos in which nothing is allowed simply to be, nothing is excluded (including people) from being interpreted and treated as standing reserve available to be ordered up for use.[118]

Fourth, people get "captivated, bewitched, dazzled and beguiled" by the prevalent practice of calculative thinking.[119] This is the kind of thinking present in science, technology, metaphysical "proofs," and talk about reforming worlds and rationally engineering social and cultural life. Captivated by calculative thinking, a form of humanism is endorsed in which people take themselves to be gods, the lords of Being,[120] determining what is possible in social and cultural history. These people act as though they are the shapers and masters of the worldly practices, such as language, which give to all subjects and objects their social identities.[121]

In accenting these four ways of getting lost by conforming to what had become traditional ways of understanding and living, Heidegger is endorsing Kierkegaard's and Nietzsche's radical critique of traditional Western social and cultural practices. He, however, gives his own "quasi-religious" spin to their critiques. Scientism and the ethos of technological enframing are the twentieth-century historical offspring of ontotheologies dating back to the Greeks, and all are grounded in a fearful anxiousness about uncontrollable social and cultural possibilities and in a demonic effort to maintain godlike control over everything.

What does Heidegger see as the undesirable and dangerous effects of such lostness in the public life of the West? His general concern is that we will not be free (able) to be faithful to all that each of us is and we will not be able to let others be free to be all that each of them is. In Heidegger's eyes, nothing could be more dangerous than this.[122] Not only will we always be miserably at war with ourselves, but consequently we will sustain practices that result in being inhumane to others. This is so for many reasons. As Kierkegaard points out, trying just to do what "one does," what "they do," doesn't work. Traditions only define future possibilities to those choosing how to live in the present. In Heidegger's words, there is an inseparable tie between the *futural,* the *having-been,* and the *moment of vision* in its time.[123] Besides, traditional social and cultural proprieties do not coexist harmoniously; choices must be made and responsibility for those choices needs to be acknowledged, especially since many such choices produce oppressive domination disguised as inevitabilities. In addition, no matter how much it is surrounded with social proprieties, people cannot completely erase their understanding that each person dies singularly alone stripped of all social masks, an inevitability not understood by those lost in the public until it is painfully revealed at a time when one cannot rewrite the narrative of one's life and only feelings of regret remain. Since only people can anticipate the possibility of no more possibilities for them as individuals, people and only people die in this existential sense, something that makes people different from all "objects" of scientific study.[124]

Heidegger, echoing Kierkegaard's and Nietzsche's diagnoses of the nineteenth century, points out that twentieth century people, conditioned by an ontotheological rhetoric of ultimate explanations and justifications but increasingly aware that there are no such ultimates, experience an anxiety about everything resting on nothing, which produces all the personal and social illnesses and disasters that Kierkegaard and Nietzsche had pointed out.[125] If one elevates theoretical knowledge into the highest form of understanding and one sees Being as a Supreme Being and not as radical possibility, then it is understandable that one would see all beings as merely scientific objects once such a Supreme Being is dead in one's life. Heidegger charges that trying to treat people as just one more kind of theoretically understandable, scientific object prevents us from respecting ourselves or others as the unique individuals that we are, as the beings playing a crucial role in the constitution of all beings, as the beings who have the ability to so care for themselves that different worlds can originate through them. Just as people understand that they are more than the social masks they wear, so they sense that they are more than just instances of general scientific categories of which there could be duplicates. They cry out, "Here I am. Deal with me. Don't pigeonhole or stereotype me."

Heidegger recognizes that it is a small step from treating people as nothing but theoretically understandable objects to mistreating them as technologically usable objects, mere human resources available for use in carrying out established social policies. Objectifying beings and theorizing about them, Heidegger claims, is not done just to satisfy innocent theoretical curiosity but in order to produce and utilize tools in service to a project of seeking more effective control over the materiality of one's environment and oneself. Having argued for the primacy of practical understanding over theoretical understanding, Heidegger proceeds to criticize the increasingly common practice of so generalizing our practical, instrumental understanding of tools that the whole earth becomes nothing but a standing reserve of raw materials available for human use, with people themselves becoming mere human resources to be used to gain ever-greater efficiency in our lives as tool-users. In this technological mode of subjectivity, Heidegger charges, instrumental practices take on a life of their own, ever-striving to become more effective in sustaining and reproducing themselves. People become deluded into presuming that they really can gain complete mastery over nature and people.[126] Greater and greater frustration arises as it is discovered that nature and people actively resist being reduced to mere useful tools or usable materials, with this frustration motivating people to apply greater and greater power in an effort to overcome this resistance.

Given that ontotheology, scientism, and the ethos of technology are the major traditions in which people are losing themselves in the West, these are the traditions, Heidegger charges, which will turn a historical tendency (a destiny) into a totalizing fate unless people can care for themselves in such a way that they gain the ability to assist in letting radically new possibilities for social and cultural life appear. Were this historical tendency to become the closed fate of the West, it would not be possible for there to exist artists and poets opening up new possibilities.[127] It also would prevent any sense of the nonutilitarian, precious holiness of the earth/world to arise, a sense of the holy that would make it possible for the silent voice of the divine infinite to issue injunctions to people for living faithfully and harmoniously with radical possibilities, natural regularities, and other mortals.[128] Given the present strength of these tendencies, Heidegger at one point prophesied that only a god could save us.[129] By this he does not mean that a supernatural, supreme being would have to magically alter human history. He means that people must cease seeking to control social/cultural history and must stop trying to march over everything. Instead, people must take off their shoes, recognize the holy sacredness of the ground on which they stand, and thereby release themselves and their worlds to possibilities that at present they cannot even imagine.

What can people do to produce the kind of radical cultural and social revolution that Heidegger judges to be necessary? In his 1929 lecture "What Is Metaphysics?" Heidegger claims that revolutionary cultural change requires liberating people from the idols they have erected to protect themselves from the radical contingency and indeterminacy of the constituted worlds in which they live.[130] He claims that people not only have representational knowledge of objects present-on-hand and practical knowledge of tools present-to-hand, but they also have an understanding of the whole of beings, an understanding that is present in some of their moods. Sometimes they are astonished that anything at all exists. Sometimes they are bored to death with everything. Sometimes, far beyond liking a person's looks and personality, they feel overwhelmed with joy at the bare existence of the person they love.[131] Finally, as Kierkegaard and Nietzsche point out, most of the time they are anxious about the contingency and indeterminateness of the world even though it is only at rare moments they consciously sense such anxiety, usually having successfully turned themselves away from such contingency and having lost themselves in their lives with the beings in the world. People sense anxiety when they sense that their flight from contingency gets nowhere and that, other than constituted beings and the possibility that such beings might not have been and might not continue to be, there is nothing

The nothing that Heidegger contrasts to the Being of beings needs to be understood in several ways. Sometimes, saying that everything rests on nothing consists of denying ontotheology by saying that there is no ultimate explanation or justification for the beings that are or for their being as they are. It consists of saying that there is not anything that grounds everything. There is no supreme being that accounts for the being of all beings. Sometimes, however, the term "nothing" can be used in speech as a contrasting term to all terms used to speak about beings and the Being of beings in order to indicate that one has encountered and responded to the no-thingness of the nonfinite, to the unique specificity of individual people that can never be captured by any social categorizations, to the infinite indeterminateness of the earth that can never be totally imprisoned in any human worlds, to the free character of the Being of beings, the free character of the history of radical possibilities.[132]

How does the understanding embodied in these moods aid people to gain liberation from their idols? People experience anxiety over the contingency of the world. This anxiety, Heidegger claims, can enable people to look back to when earlier generations first founded our theoretical, objectivistic, and technological set of social practices and recognize that our social/cultural ancestors could have taken a different path and thus our world could have been different. With this as a springboard, people could try to creatively appropriate into their current way of life some aspects of what had been closed off by past selections.[133]

Social/cultural critics have two tasks. First, they must analyze what is inescapably involved in existing as a human being who constitutes and lives with other beings. Second, they must present an interpretation of cultural and social practices that exhibit people's alienation from such a way of existing. Critical interpreters, like Heidegger, can appropriate the traditional ways of understanding things that produce such misunderstanding and alienation so as to reveal the possibilities closed off by such misunderstanding and alienating self-denial. Believing that the public's misunderstanding and alienation is a result of or expression of traditional philosophers' theoretical presumptions and claims about the nature of the Being of beings, Heidegger sees the philosopher as uniquely equipped to aid people to overcome their alienation and misunderstanding and thus to be free to comport themselves fearlessly toward radical contingency and possibility, to hold themselves out into that nothing that frames everything.[134] The philosopher, who is able to do reflective thinking, can aid people to care for themselves by teaching them to do such thinking for themselves. In his destruction (deconstruction) of the present, Heidegger wants to break the hold on our thinking that is possessed by current practices of solidifying traditional ways of interpreting canonical philosophical texts, and he wants to do so in order to examine these texts to see what possibilities were closed off by these standardized interpretations.[135] By recognizing that traditional, anticontingency philosophical texts once upon a time were placed in the philosophical canon while alternatives were excluded, people can come to recognize that all social practices once upon a time came to be by excluding alternatives that now could be appropriated for current life. People thus could come to recognize that the dispositions of our current destiny need not be taken as fated necessities and that people now could make a founding choice of a radically different nonalienating way of life, if they would prepare themselves to be such radical world creators.

How does the critical interpreter, however, get enough people to be sufficiently enlightened and free to revolutionize existing social and cultural practices, given that generally and for the most part they are so lost in the public's misunderstanding and self-alienation that they cannot hear the voice of such an interpreter? Appropriating Plato's disdain for the democracy of those chained in caves of ignorance, Heidegger charges that elections and parliamentary legislation are not the answer because they only reinforce public stances and do not revolutionize them.[136] Also, writing a book such as *Being and Time* hardly seems sufficient to produce the change desired. A much more radical means is needed if a whole new social/cultural world is to be constituted. In 1933 and 1934, Heidegger tragically thought he had found this means in Hitler and National Socialism's promise of a radical revolutionizing of decadent Western civilization.[137] By getting a whole nation to be passionately committed to a single Führer who is one of those rare persons able to stand outside the West's current decadent practices, and by getting a whole educational system obediently following the dictates of a single, enlightened critical interpreter of the human condition and the philosophical and cultural history of the West (Heidegger), one world could be ended and a new world could be constituted through the new social and cultural practices established. In his eagerness to achieve radical change, Heidegger tragically loses sight of the whole point of seeking revolutionary change and thus ends up endorsing means that had no hope of achieving the ends he is seeking. The goal is to free people's understanding from alienating traditions in order that they can take responsibility for their lives, and this hardly can be achieved by coercing or training them to be uncritically obedient to the supposed wisdom of a national Führer or a philosopher-king. Being enslaved by new political or philosophical idols is no way of overcoming the public's slavish adherence to traditional idols in order to avoid facing radical contingency. National disasters such as mass rioting, war, and genocide may produce deep and widespread social and cultural changes, but there is every reason to doubt that they will produce more responsible people continuously free to choose among a wider range of options in a historical context of wide open possibilities for social and cultural change.[138]

Heidegger soon realized that the specifics of his chosen means would not achieve his desired ends. The German educational establishment had too strong an institutional and professional investment in the old traditions to be willing to obey Heidegger and his call for change. National Socialism, with its thirst for personal, party, and national power and its effort at a total (totalitarian) treatment of people as mere resources to be used in pursuing such power, turned out to be just another example of the problem that needed a revolutionary solution. Heidegger saw Nazi Party functionaries abandoning radical cultural change and supporting his educational opponents because the Nazi leadership wanted scientific and technological research that would support their power objectives and not a poetic and mystical world full of possibilities for continuous social and cultural change. Having experienced this failure in producing the revolutionary change that he continued to believe was necessary, Heidegger from 1935 until his death concluded that no one using any means could willfully produce the changes needed.[139] Cultural and social worlds cannot be deliberately constituted in terms of carrying out an engineering blueprint. The best that people can do is to reflect upon the things they are doing that prevent the needed cultural revolution from occurring, and then patiently and trustingly wait for a new world to creatively emerge even as any worldmaking work of art emerges.[140]

Radical creativity, Heidegger concludes, will require more than attempting in an Apollonian rational way to put the old pieces together into a new pattern. As Kierkegaard points out when he claims that people cannot on their own relate themselves to that which is other than the worldly finite, so Heidegger charges that socialized individuals cannot force something radically new into human social and cultural practices; people cannot at will create new cultures. What people can do, however, is care for themselves in such a way that they remove themselves as obstacles to something new occurring. People must discover that the place they can call home is that place near to Being, near to radically new possibilities.[141] People are not all-powerful lords who determine what is possible; they are to be shepherds taking care that radical change remains possible, taking care of themselves so that space remains open for new possibilities.[142] New ways of living need to be constituted by people. However, trying intentionally and deliberately to create a new world requires forming intentions with old concepts and deliberating with old rationales. People must move beyond calculative thinking, drawing inferences from established classification and individuation schema, and from old ways of thinking about how to use objects. They must begin to practice a different kind of thinking that both allows new vocabularies to be born and allows people to trustingly wait for new cultural practices to be established.[143] People can continue in the old ways and thus prevent anything radically new from being constituted, but the best that people can do to assist the arrival of the new is to get out of the way. People will constitute new practices but not by an act of a controlling will. The poem must write itself in the poet; the thought must seize the mind of the thinker. Poets and thinkers become world creator by letting new ways of understanding things arise within them. One must let die off the old self and world in order that one can gain a new life and world, trusting in a nonnihilistic way that one will be thankful for the results of letting things be free of human efforts to control.[144] As Nietzsche would put it, one must trust life enough not to seek to control things, theoretically or practically. Alternatively, in Kierkegaard's idiom, one must respond faithfully to the call of the nonfinite if one is to find a workable way of living as an alternative to an anxiety-ridden, objectivitistic, and technological mode of subjectivity. Trustingly letting things be does not consist in giving up the spirit of criticism of new social and cultural practices but rather consists in constantly sounding out the new to test for the presence of hollowness, the hollowness of new futile efforts of people to evade contingency and chance.[145]

The quasi-religious character of Heidegger's concern about the salvation of decadent Western civilization is apparent. Dialogically appropriating Heidegger's texts, however, requires talking back to them. Three aspects of Heidegger's project require special critical attention.

First, without rejecting the idea that unexpected ruptures occur in history, one certainly can question the utopian notion that a whole "decadent" inhumane social/cultural world can be replaced in one fell swoop by an entirely different, truly human, freedom-serving world. As we shall see, it is just this kind of revolutionary wholesale replacement of social and cultural practices that Foucault rejects when he claims that total liberation from the forces of evil is beyond historical possibility and that only local resistance is possible. This, of course, is a significant possibility because it can enlarge space for personal freedom. Seeking heaven on earth is not the only rationale for social change; making life a little less hellish for certain people at certain places at a certain time is extremely significant for those involved. Once one recognizes the continuing role that the will to power plays in human lives, then one can appreciate even more fully how important it is to preserve and strengthen governmental institutions protecting negative freedom, the freedom to be left alone, even to be left alone in our ignorance by those who would enlighten us, save our souls and the world. The whole world might need radical transformation if freedom for really new possibilities is to be opened up, but that goal of maximizing possibilities cannot be attained by denying people the freedom to reject the means chosen by someone else to achieve that transformation. In the classical Christian theodicy, even an omnipotent, omniscient, loving god had to let evil occur in order that human freedom can be preserved. The later Heidegger would have been well served to have paid more attention to his earlier writings on the overriding significance of the specificity and uniqueness of individual human beings, a significance that supposedly is to be served by any revolutionary change in social and cultural practices and certainly is not to be sacrificed for the sake of his desired revolution.

Second, without rejecting the claim that human freedom is threatened in all the ways identified by Heidegger (and many others), one can also accent and even expand Heidegger's early emphasis on the freedom-enhancing practices still available in spite of the threatening and destining tendencies in Western life. That rare "reflective thinkers" like Holderin, Kierkegaard, and Heidegger do appear suggests that in spite of decadent tendencies there also are saving practices, marginalized as they may be, which can be deliberately appropriated for the purpose of deconstructing these decadent factors and of constructing homes close to radical contingency. Gadamer draws upon Heidegger's early appropriation of Greek philosophy, and he calls for us to enter into dialogue with past traditions in such a way that our current prejudices get challenged and unpredictable changes occur. Also, one need not reject Heidegger's accent on people as tool-users and agents responsibly and resolutely facing their mortality in order to point out that people have many other characteristics that empower them to resist the freedom-threatening tendencies in Western social-cultural life. People often are prevented from acting by being forced to endure starvation, disabilities, disease, pain, and suffering. Not only does the requirement to be such a suffering patient call upon freedom fighters to seek to lessen such burdens, but it is just such suffering that draws some people out of their narcissistic pursuits of personal power and relates them to other people, not merely as fellow tool-users but as people compassionately bound together interpersonally.[146] Similarly, one can appropriate Heidegger's claims about social-cultural worlds always being inescapably tied to the earth in order to make a major attack upon placing nature and culture or body and mind in warring conflict. One thus can attack the many Western paternalistic efforts to keep men and women in conflict, with virile men finding their home in culture while women are treated as less than persons because they are so tied to natural processes. The relation of mothers, fetuses, and placenta to each other might give us much better models of subject/object and subject/subject relations.[147] Heidegger's analyses of the fallen character of people is not so much wrong as it is incomplete. The meagerness of Heidegger's analysis of human facticity shows up in his presentation of only two options to people. Either seal the fate of the West by thinking only with decadent representations and calculations, or think in silent, self-sacrificing, thankful, patient meditation. Here we will be better served to remember Wittgenstein's interpretation of the many different language games (ways of thinking) people are involved in and how all of them presuppose the primacy of interpersonal relationships that prevent any totalistic enframing by an ontotheology or a technological ethos.

Finally, one can endorse Heidegger's critique of the ontotheological character of much of Western philosophy and its canonical texts while also criticizing Heidegger for exaggerating the power of such texts to dominate Western social and cultural practices. Heidegger is still too Hegelian, seeing history as primarily intellectual history and intellectual history as primarily the history of philosophy. Heidegger might have done better developing his accent in *Being and Time* on the primacy of human practice over human theory. Foucault will point out that often major ruptures in human social/cultural history occur as unintended and unpredictable consequences of changes in apparently insignificant minipractices, especially when they are exploited by groups benefiting from asymmetrical power relations of domination. The move from Heidegger to Foucault is the move from a cultural revolutionary to a freedom fighter resisting minipractices underpinning oppressive domination. In seeking freedom, Small probably is better than Big. It is by no means obvious that deliberate attempts to modify minipractices might not significantly increase human freedom. Certainly, feminists, environmentalists, people of color battling racism, neo-Marxists, and democratic socialists such as Dewey believe such efforts have proved to be significant. Had

Heidegger not prioritized so highly his life as a critical interpreter of metaphysical texts, he might have recognized the existence of many social practices, interpersonal relationships, nontechnological encounters with nature (like his own life in the Black Forest), and nonontotheological religious encounters with the nonfinite that sustain people's resistance to objectivism, scientism, and the technological ethos.

V.   FOUCAULT'S ETHIC OF SELF-DISCIPLINE IN THE PRACTICE OF FREEDOM

Although Foucault does not believe that there is any one practical project of social change that people can undertake to end once and for all human domination, he does present a critical interpretation of the social and cultural practices that are producing such domination in the Western world in the late twentieth century. He also sets forth a set of concrete proposals for resisting such domination, for practicing freedom in spite of current social tendencies. Producing critical interpretations is one such exercise of the power to resist the powerful currents producing domination.

The ultimate norm that Foucault uses in critiquing current practices and in evaluating alternative possibilities is the minimization of nonconsensuality, and in that sense the maximization of both negative and positive freedom.[148] Foucault's critical interpretation and his strategies and tactics of resistance will be examined in the next chapter, where I reflect upon what practices need change and what methods can be used to make the changes deemed desirable. In this chapter I want to focus on what Foucault has to say about how we are to take care of ourselves, how we are to discipline ourselves in exercising such freedom as we are able to secure for ourselves. I need to proceed cautiously here. I don't want to give the impression that people can separate the task of fighting for space for freedom from domination, from the task of caring for oneself in the space free from nonconsensuality that has been secured. The space of freedom exists only as long as one continually practices freedom, increasing one's freedom from domination and disciplining oneself in pursuit of one's personally chosen goals. Since reducing domination usually requires resisting being the person one has been socialized to be, only by reducing one's own complicity in being dominated can pursuing personally chosen goals be a matter of practicing freedom. Nevertheless, even though caring for oneself in one's exercise of freedom can never be separated from critiquing and modifying social practices producing domination, in this chapter I will concentrate only on the former.

Foucault draws a distinction between morality and ethics.[149] Morality governs what one may do; it consists of social prohibitions, requirements, and permissions for exemptions from these mandates. Ethics for Foucault has to do with what one is to be, with how one is to relate to oneself and care for oneself. Actions are to be morally mandated only when this is necessary to minimize nonconsensuality for everyone. (I will defer until the next chapter the problems of just distribution that seem to arise here, since some freedoms seem more important than others and since it seems one may be forced to choose between giving great freedom to a few rather than a little freedom to many. For now let me simply say that in Foucault's analysis of dominating power and the power to resist such domination, power and freedom are not items to which a theory of distributive justice can apply its calculations.) [150]Although one must take care of oneself so as to resist practices and institutions producing domination over oneself and others, one also needs to care for oneself so as to take advantage of the material possibilities opened up in the space of social freedom so as to make of one's life a beautiful work of art in the eyes of oneself, others, and future generations.[151] Foucault acknowledges that in his ethics he is simply functioning as a Nietzschean who is aestheticizing one's care and discipline of oneself once the moral demands of resisting unnecessary domination are met.[152]

Foucault's ethic of self-care requires that we answer four interrelated questions that we need to put to ourselves. (1) What sort of being do I want to be? What is my desired *telos?* (2) Why am I seeking this goal? What legitimates in my own mind the pursuit of this goal? What is the rationale to which I am *subjecting* myself? (3) What aspects of myself do I need to work on in order to change myself from what I am into what I choose to be? What is the material *substance* of myself that needs to be reworked in order that my life will have the form specified in my telos? (4) What training techniques do I have to apply to myself to move from what I am to what I seek to be? What *ascetic* of self-discipline do I need?

Obviously this is a very general and abstract ethic of self-care. All the details depend on what the person is like who is answering these questions, what the concrete possibilities are that remain open in the space of social and cultural freedom in which the person is located, and what *telos* the person has chosen on the basis of that person's legitimating rationales. There are many different kinds of beautiful lives at which people can aim and they can do so for many different reasons. There are many different kinds of socialized individuals living in many different kinds of social and cultural environments. Furthermore, these details are subject to continuous historical change as resistance increases or decreases and thus possibilities expand or contract, as rationales and legitimations get critiqued, as the person's ascetic succeeds or fails, as one's *telos* gets fine-tuned, as the person changes, as the social environment changes, as unexpected contingencies arise. Along with loyalty to one's ascetic of self-discipline, a critical interpretation of one's social and cultural environment must be continuous, as must self-examination and criticism.

The thrust of Foucault's moral call for a minimization of nonconsensuality is the call to avoid limiting, and to aid increasing, possibilities for oneself and others. In that sense we are called to understand the vastly different ethical tasks confronting different people and to respect and cherish the many different forms of life people choose and seek to create, sometimes—to some extent—successfully. This understanding of differences, and the moral and ethical demands that this understanding makes on us is a result of the project of interpretive analytics that Foucault carries out from within the social and cultural world into which he is thrown, with the rhetorical discourse that he founds serving his interest in minimizing nonconsentuality. There seems to be no need to justify such an interest, since everyone always is engaged to some extent in resisting some form of domination. Furthermore, there does not seem to be any rationale anyone can give to a person pursuing an interest in minimizing non-consensuality to legitimate a restriction on that person's freedom to do so. Foucault is in his own way simply adding another chapter to the Enlightenments's commitment to freedom.

VI.   ZIZEK ON WORKING THROUGH OUR CRAVINGS FOR UNITY AND ENJOYMENT

Although Nietzsche and Foucault invite us to make our lives into beautiful works of art, they do not reflect upon key factors that are presupposed by such an invitation or on what might be psychologically involved in accepting that invitation and undertaking such a project. Critically examining this invitation generates a host of troubling questions. First of all, works of art usually are expected to possess a kind of formal unity and completeness such that every element, and every relationship among the elements in the artwork are needed while no other elements or rearrangements have to be added. Is it really possible, however, to attain such unity and completeness in a human life? Furthermore, we need to consider what dangers are involved in seeking for unity and completeness. Second, how do we discover or decide what we want to be, what our desired telos is or is to become? Is it not necessary to examine the nature and logic of wants and desires in order to answer this question? Third, don't our legitimating rationales themselves need critical analysis if our freedom is to be maximized? How do they originate? How are they related to our desires, especially to the desire to have a beautiful, unified life?

Finally, how can we learn to discipline ourselves so as to transform the material "substance" of what we are into what we want to be unless we make a critical analysis of what people generally are and are not and what each of us as a particular person is, is not, might be, and cannot be? To what extent can we distance ourselves from our socially inherited subjectivity? To what extent are we and can we be artistic agents creating our own lives?

Slavoj Zizek, with an explosion of publications in the last decade of the twentieth century, shows how difficult it is for people to follow Foucault's advice to practice freedom by ethically building beautiful lives and politically resisting dominating oppression, given what is involved in the formation of people's desires, fantasies, and senses of self-identity and self-worth, and given how our social and cultural practices both influence and are influenced by such psychological factors.[153] Appropriating the psychoanalytic theories of Jacques Lacan and certain aspects of various Marxian critiques of economic oppression and domination, Zizek presents a critical analysis of people and their social and cultural worlds, which concludes that practicing freedom requires that we acquire and exercise three interrelated abilities.

(1) We must learn how to "work through" the social practices currently embodying social fantasies, ideologies, fictions, and fetishes that produce and sustain domination, oppression, and our complicity in their continued life.

(2) We have to learn how to "work through" the desires leading us to absolutize our social symbolic order, which is structured so as to control our enjoyments. Doing this requires learning how to "work through" the fantasies we construct to cover over felt flaws and gaps in the social order and our psychic lives. Antagonisms always exist within the social order and among our desires. The social order never can thoroughly control enjoyment, and desires are such that they never are satisfiable. Our psychic lives never can be fully unified or complete because at their core there always will remain an unfillable void even as the objects of those desires always contain antagonistic elements resisting unification.

(3) Once we have "worked through" our absolutizing desires and our concealing and unifying fantasies, then we have to learn how to commit ourselves to some one specific form of social life without absolutizing it. If we are going to minimize nonconsensuality, Zizek claims, we have to learn how to have faith in a political form of democracy that evacuates any locus of power and in which the fate of society is permitted to depend upon the contingent and unpredictable outcome of elections.[154]

Zizek charges that although it sounds noble for Nietzsche and Foucault to call for tolerating, respecting, and cherishing nonoppressive social and cultural differences, doing so requires something much more than simply being a cosmopolitan, egalitarian, unengaged liberal standing above all particular social worlds and letting all cultural differences be mere differences (not that Nietzsche or Foucault endorse such liberalism). It is going to require recognizing and working through the fears, envies, fantasies, and ideologies involved in racism and ethnic hatreds. It is going to require recognizing and politically acting to change the antagonistic forces in our current social political economy that so much of current culture is engaged in covering over. It is going to require being a committed particularist passionately involved in some specific and concrete world of social practices.

In Zizek's appropriation of Lacan's appropriation of Heidegger, the psychological implications of the social constitution of human subjects is spelled out in such detail that a crippling and perhaps fatal blow is struck against all theories that would interpret the social as merely a product of the activity of already functioning individual selves. While accenting the primacy of social practices over the subjectivity of individual people, the Zizek/Lacan position, however, denies the claim that everything is social "all the way down." There is something other than the social even if it can only be named and not described (given that all descriptive vocabulary is social).[155] Analyzing breakdowns in the life of the symbolic order (the world of social rationality with all of its conceptualizing and reasoning) shows that there is something present in people's experience more "Real" than the socially constituted reality of beings and events. The socially constituted is what Zizek calls reality. The fractured character of this reality points to something other than reality. Zizek/Lacan call this the Real. The Real consists of a dimension of enjoyment that cannot be socially contained, although the whole symbolic order and reality are constituted to keep such enjoyment under the control of social law and order.[156] What is true of reality is also true of our subjectivity. Analyzing the logic and conflictual character of any subject's desires shows that at the central core of any subject is an empty void that the social constitution of subjectivity cannot remove.[157] There is an irremovable "Real" that our entire conscious and unconscious symbolic apparatus can't account for or control. This void at the heart of social rationality produces in people a craving to fill it up, to unify ourselves as subjects and to unify our constituted social world. Learning how to care for oneself and to relate oneself to the social requires understanding these cravings. It requires understanding why people disastrously fail to deal with these cravings and what is required in order to successfully work with and through them.[158]

Again and again, Zizek, echoing Lacan, asserts that the very movement of Homo sapiens from presubjective animal existence into being human subjects is a movement molded by social and interpersonal factors operating in accordance with a logic of desire. A presubjective need for an object with use value is transubstantiated into a demand that some person supply us with a socially constituted object that has exchange value. These demands for constituted objects generate desires that the persons of whom we make the demands have certain positive attitudes toward us, have a willingness to meet our demands. In turn, this desire that others look favorably on our demands generates in us a desire to satisfy the desires of other people so that they will have a favorable attitude toward our demands and thus they will desire to satisfy our demands.[159] Our desires, therefore, are always desires that others have certain desires toward us,[160] and these desires are always socially, linguistically coded in a culturally specific way.[161] Desiring that others have certain desires towards us requires that we have some sense of ourselves as specific selves. Children arrive at a sense of self-identity only when another person (functioning as a mirror reflection) offers an image of unity to the emerging human subject.[162]

Thus, in a complex set of interdependent intentions (demands and desires) whose objects themselves ultimately are intentions (attitudes and desires), subjects are constituted in a network of interpersonal and social relations. In addition, a demand can become an autonomous striving demand (a drive) to sustain a demand that some person supply our needs. More important, people can become driven to sustain the enjoyment of making such continuing demands. We so enjoy making demands that we feel anxiety when we get too close to having our needs and desires met, our enjoyment of demanding ended.[163] It is the enjoyment of demanding that fuels a will to power that Zizek sees located at the heart of all psychic and social life. At the dawn of all human worlds is this social and interpersonal drama of enjoyable demanding and never satisfiable desiring. There are three reasons why our desires will never be fully satisfied. (1) We don't desire them to be satisfied; we enjoy too much willfully making demands on others. (2) Other people also enjoy willfully exercising power over us and therefore are not willing to be mere satisfiers of our desires. (3) Other people and the social order, whose desires we seek to satisfy so that they will look favorable on us, are fractured and do not have a unified set of desires that we could satisfy.

It is Zizek's analysis of unsatisfiable desires tied to a will to power that helps us understand one of the most difficult dimensions of the Lacan/Zizek interpretation of human psychological and social life; that is the claim that there is something more "Real" than the reality of socially constituted objects in the symbolic order. The "Real," Zizek tells us, never exists as an object that falls under a concept. It cannot be described.[164] From the viewpoint of socially constituted beings, it is a void.[165] Only retrospectively, through an analysis of the conflicts and voids in the social symbolic order, do we discover that this order is not exhaustive or all-inclusive and that something is left over.[166] This "Real" that the world of social rationality can't govern, says Zizek, is pure willing and the pure enjoyment of pure willing, the enjoyment of willing to will, of demanding to demand, of desiring to desire, of enjoying such enjoying.[167] Not describable bodily needs but the enjoyment of contentless willing creates space for there to be subjects with free wills not colonizable by social rationality.[168] These subjects have, from the point of view of the symbolic order, an unfillable void at the center of their being. Their freedom from the social depends on the existence of that void.

Experiencing the social world as having a leftover is always traumatic because it consists of encountering a "hard kernel" that can't be described or explained in terms of the symbolic order. It is a traumatic derailing of orderly, daily life.[169] In order to cover up the existence of that void, many people, under the influence of the social practices subjectifying them, use fantasies to turn this leftover, which it is impossible for the symbolic to contain, into an area of prohibited willing and enjoying.[170] When Wittgenstein ends the *Tractatus* by charging, "Whereof one cannot speak, thereof one must be silent," a traumatic impossibility is being transformed into a mystical, spiritual imperative.[171] Of course, only socially constituted subjects reflecting with socially constituted languages upon their socially constituted desires, fantasies, and ideologies could point out that there is a nameable (though indescribably) other to the world of socially constituted beings. Only critically thinking people can understand that the symbolic is an island in a yolk of enjoyment.[172]

The birth of the subject begins with a passage from need and enjoyable demanding to the social, symbolic world.[173] The whole world of social practices, the entire symbolic order, becomes in fact the intentional object of our demands, desires, and drives. Its order of priorities provides us with our ego ideal (what we are to be like to be likable to this "other" whose desires we desire to meet so that we will be liked by it).[174] Desiring to be socially conventional is a constitutional part of our very subjectivity. It is only because of the antagonistic and nonunifiable character of these conventions that we can gain the distance needed for agency and the ability to resist and make unique contributions to our individuality. Our entire conceptual and belief system is colored by this "logic" of desire. Most of our beliefs (as behavioral dispositions) are unconscious (although social) and primarily revealed in our practical procedures.[175] It should not be surprising then that the desires, which are so central to what we are, often are best revealed in our dreams. We are more Lao-tzu's free and beautiful butterfly encountered in dreams than the craving, analytical, prosaic and frustrated persons who usually dismiss our dreams in our waking moments.[176]

Our desire to satisfy the desire of our other, in order that it would desire to be favorably inclined toward us, becomes, according to Zizek, a craving to find a harmonious unity in this other and thus in ourselves. This craving manifests itself in many different ways. The whole ontotheological enterprise in all its variations is an attempt to provide to the entire symbolic world of social rationality the unity we so desperately crave for it to have. As Zizek puts it, an other is sought for the incomplete, fractured, conflictual symbolic order that is ours. A master signifier is sought after. We introduce some sort of puppeteer pulling hidden strings and making everything meaningful.[177]

When this enterprise fails, as it always does, we individually create fantasies out of socially available elements in a further desperate effort to attain such unity and consistency in ourselves and our social world.[178] In our imagination we fantasize about what we really are like in an effort to unify our lives as desiring beings, something we sense as being necessary if our desiring is to make sense.[179] "We're really good people having a terrible run of bad luck." We fantasize about what history, the ecosystem, our nation, race, or ethnic group really are like so that we ourselves, everything that happens to us, and everything that we do is meaningful relative to our demands, desires, and drives.[180] Ideologies feeding off of such fantasies are used in efforts to treat as harmonious unities the social orders in which we live. There is "manifest destiny," "the white man's burden," "saving the world from communism," "the law of supply and demand." We lose ourselves in such fantasies and ideologies motivated both by the enjoyment they give us and by the anxieties about ourselves and our world that make them needed.

Similarly, our perception of socially constituted objects as metaphysical substances is motivated by a craving for unity, consistency, and dependability. From the beginning of our linguistic activities, we work with rigid designators that tie linguistic expressions to their referents through social naming or baptism practices, treating such referents as unified and unique substances even though no set of descriptive characteristics could ever give them such unity.[181] Also, our earliest social training gets us to take socially constituted institutions and roles and treat them fetishly as substantial realities existing independent of the social natures we assign to them.[182] Nations, governments, schools, churches, contracts, currencies, laws, courts, policemen all become metaphysical substances. The results are often tragic, as when a group of people (the Jews, the Japanese) are taken to have some hidden, inner, unifying core that explains why they all have what we see as undesirable characteristics, in spite of all the exceptions to such generalizations and stereotypes that we encounter daily.[183] In fact, Zizek claims, the social unity of a group is always a matter of a shared enjoyment, an enjoyment that always exceeds its social structuring and therefore remains an enigma to the members of the group.[184] Our racial and ethnic biases and hatreds are grounded always in three factors: (1) a fear that these "others" will steal our group's enjoyment, our way of life; (2) an envious craving to bite into the socially and culturally ordered enjoyment of these strange foreigners, an envy that we have to hide from ourselves, given that it reveals that our way of ordering enjoyment is never experienced by us as adequate; and (3) a blaming of these others for the inability of our way of life to provide us with nonconflictual enjoyment and satisfaction (thus a hatred of our own enjoyment).[185]

The unity, however, for which people crave, from the moment at the mirror stage when they first form a sense of self-identity, is a unity, Zizek claims, that never is attained in spite of the mighty efforts of people to achieve that result. An unfillable, unsatisfiable void always remains at the center of all subjectivity, symbolic order, and social rationality.[186] The demanding and enjoying that are at the heart of human life obviously attract us, but they also fill us with guilt because demanding and enjoying always remain as uncaptured renegades to the symbolic order that tells us as subjects what is right and what is wrong.[187] This failure to attain psychological unity is inevitable given the role that people's desires play in the constitution of their self-identities and given the fractured character of the social, symbolic order whose favorable approval people so desperately seek. I can never satisfy my desire to satisfy the desires of the social world to which I cravingly desire to conform because there is no unified and consistent set of commands that it gives to me[188] and because my demand to keep demanding would be dealt a death blow were such commands ever unified.[189] Given the ethnic, racial, and national identities, mythologies and ideologies now socially constituted, and the antagonisms constitutive of these identities, there is no harmony or unity in our current historical world. Irreconcilable conflicts develop between our efforts on the one hand to live in a secular world of science, politics, and economics that gives no unified meaning to life, and our efforts on the other hand to profess belief in a supernatural, spiritual (often superstitious) world that supposedly gives meaning to our lives. Given the inherent contradictions in the world's current global neocapitalistic economic system (it never has sufficient markets for its necessary overproduction), one cannot meet all its commands no matter how much one would desire to do so.[190]

In addition to the "Real," which never can exist within reality as constituted by the symbolic order, there are also interpersonal encounters of void-centered subjects with each other. Presupposed by all the social rules of vocabulary, syntax, and usage is the use of speech merely as a password alerting listeners to the presence of speakers and listeners in such interpersonal encounters.[191] Infinitely prior to the world of people being socialized into playing roles or participating in

practices, there is this world of interpersonal encounters. Our encountering other people beyond the social masks they wear is, according
to Zizek, encountering the enjoyment of these people that is other
to any symbolic order; such encountering is always traumatic.[192] Of
course, one cannot traumatically encounter such enjoyment unless
one encounters describable, socially constituted subjects (whose
psychological lives are organized around a center that is indescribable
because it is a void). Therefore, it still remains true that, considered
psychologically, people are individuals only because of the encounters
that give them a mirrored sense of personal unity and because of the
conflictual social practices that produce them as fractured subjects
lacking unity.

Zizek points out that a whole host of contradictory proverbs has
been created in an effort to do the impossible—unify our terrestrial
life and its enjoyments with something beyond it. It sounds deep to
say that one should forget about the afterlife and live life fully here
and now, but it also sounds deep to say that one must escape the
illusory and vain pleasures of earthly life and think about eternity. It
sounds as deep to try to combine the two positions by talking about
bringing eternity into daily life as it does to proclaim that heaven and
earth can never be combined. It sounds deep to focus on the cognitive
problem raised here by saying (1) that life is an enigma too difficult to
understand and thus that one must accept the unfathomable mystery
of things, or (2) that one should avoid false mysteries because life
basically is simple in that there is no reason for things, or (3) the
mystery of life lies in the simple fact that there is life.[193]

What then is one to do? Our subjectivity is the product of our
demanding, our enjoying, our desiring, and the social world subjectifying us. The social, symbolic world is fractured and can never deal
with all of our demanding and enjoying. We have a void at the center
of our subjectivity and the "Real" of our demanding and enjoying
is more in us than our selves as socially constituted subjects.[194] We
fetishize, we fantasize, we mythologize, we hegemonize, and we
dominate and oppress in order to satisfy our cravings for power,

enjoyment, and meaningful unity. What is to be done? Zizek gives a many-part answer, advising us what to do psychologically, culturally, politically, and religiously.

First, we need to understand in such a way that this understanding is incorporated into all of our desiring, believing, and living that a void will always exist within ourselves and that antagonisms will always be present in our world of social practices.

Second, even though in our practices and our intentional expectations we will continue to treat social fictions as though they are substantial objects (we still will treat money and the courts as something very "real"), we need to defetishize them and recognize that such treatment is grounded only in incomplete and incompletable shared social practices.

Third, even though we will continue to construct personal fantasies to cover over the void at the heart of our lives and the antagonisms in our social order, we need to "go through" or "work through" these fantasies, recognizing that they are only our creative way of making our lives work.[195] As a corollary to respecting in a nonfetishizing way our own fantasies, we need to accept the ethical imperative to respect as much as possible other people's fantasies, other people's particular absolute, other people's particular way of organizing their universes of meaning. We need to do this because, Zizek claims, residing in this fragile, helpless particularity is the dignity of every particular person.[196] We can work through our fantasies and avoid invading the fantasy space of others only by gaining some distance from our own fantasies, that is by recognizing their ultimate contingency even as we use them.

Fourth, we have to cease relying on the big other, recognizing instead that it is not unified, that it is filled with irremovable antagonisms, that it can't (thank heaven) provide accounts for everything. We have to recognize that the inexplicable "Real" will always keep popping up.[197] We have to choose the terror of living without everything being meaningful and socially rational and thus we have to stop hoping for symbolic harmony.[198]

Fifth, we have to oppose all forms of oppression and domination by engaging in "authentic political acts." These are not acts performed within the currently existing set of social relations and what they make possible. They are instead acts that currently seem impossible because they will change the parameters of what is possible.[199] "Authentic political acts" challenge, disturb, and seek to erode the motivating energy of the social mythologies, ideologies, and operating state and civic apparatuses producing oppression and domination. In particular, Zizek charges, it is necessary to challenge the neocapitalist illusion that economic practices are to be freed as much as possible from political practices. It is necessary, he claims, to endorse instead the Marxist insight that freedom from oppression and domination requires an authentic political act of repoliticizing the economic.[200]

Sixth, we have to oppose all forms of totalitarianism by supporting faith in a democracy in which the locus of power has been evacuated and in which everything is allowed to depend upon the unpredictable contingencies of elections.[201] No one is to speak for "the people" because only oppressive and dominating power can produce the illusion of there being a unified, harmonious "people" for whom someone can claim to speak.

Seventh, we have to prize people's passionate commitments to various forms of group life and shared enjoyments precisely because such commitments resist symbolization. As Paul did in helping form Christianity, we have to make an unjustifiable but not unjustified commitment to something that is for us a "truth event" in faithfulness to which a social form of life is constructed. An event is for us a "truth event" precisely because faith in it produces a social group and order to which we are attached.[202] We have to do this in a way that continuously recognizes the unfillable void that still remains after such a commitment and the contingency of all social ways of organizing enjoyment. Doing this takes us beyond the liberal abhorrence of commitments to contingent, social particularities while also avoiding the fundamentalist tragedy of attempting to justify such commitments in terms of some ontotheology, big other, or master signifier.[203] We have to come to know in a living way that understanding our culture or the culture of some other group is a matter of finding out and letting stand what is enigmatic in that form of life.[204] While striving to respect the fantasy space and social attachments of others, we have to recognize that advocating a universal imperative to do so (which is thus added to the ruling symbolic order) may be counterproductive because it produces one more "must" that gives perverse enjoyment to its erring appliers and enforcers. Respect for the particularity of others is better protected if one dares people to be free of all master signifiers and thus free to perform authentic political acts that make and create unjustifiable but not unjustified social attachments and personal fantasies.[205]

Zizek has appropriated much from Kierkegaard, Nietzsche, Heidegger, and Foucault through his dialogical readings of their texts. His rejection of all master signifiers is their rejection of all ontotheologies and metaphysical humanisms. His location of the Real, the symbolic world's other, at the heart of fractured social reality and personal subjectivity resonates with Kierkegaard's charge that every person must deal existentially with the infinite and the finite to find a workable form of life. Zizek provides a psychological/social account of Nietzsche's will to power and Nietzsche's diagnosis of our all too human craving for unity. Zizek calls for us to work through our cravings and fantasies, and Nietzsche calls for us to enjoy living with our eyes wide open to its unpredictable and uncontrollable chanciness. The Zizek/Lacan "Real" is strikingly similar to Heidegger's earth that juts up throughout our socially constituted world. Heidegger's charge to take responsibility for one's life inspite of its limited finiteness and Zizek's call to commit oneself to a specific way of life and to remain faithful to it illuminate each other. Zizek's call also fleshes out what is involved in Foucault's call to discipline oneself to achieve one's chosen *telos*. These are five writers worth entering into dialogue with again and again as we try to make sense of our lives and as we try to live free and beautiful lives.

Zizek also shares with Kierkegaard, Nietzsche, Heidegger, and Foucault the position that radical criticism of people's relationships to their social environment is possible without appealing to any asocial and ahistorical absolutes. When these thinkers focus on what people should be like as they relate themselves to the social order as it is, they also invariably critically evaluate that social order and offer recommendations for changing it so that oppression and domination are lessened and so that individual persons can acquire the power to relate themselves to the social in the ways recommended. Critical existential analysis of the lives of individual people is tied to critical social-cultural analysis. Let's now turn our attention directly to those critics who have focused on the unjustifiable character of the social, economic, and political practices prevalent in much of the world during the past two hundred years.

⊹ CHAPTER FOUR
POSTMODERNISM'S RESISTANCE TO SOCIAL OPPRESSION AND DOMINATION

The social currents in which people must swim are currents that people themselves have constructed, often as unintended consequences of the activities in which they are involved. These currents are powerful, not only in the way in which they limit the power and freedom of the people swimming in them, but also by the fact that these currents channel the way in which one generation of swimmers nurtures and molds the next generation by inculcating in them desires, beliefs, self-images, norms, ideals, and rationales for acting. When these currents are polluted with social practices producing domination and oppression, the people swimming in these currents themselves become contaminated. In spite of what we might think about ourselves or how we might rationalize our actions, we often are responsible for the continued existence of practices and institutions whose net effect is the strengthening of economic exploitation, political authoritarianism, racism, sexism, homophobia, and the unjust treatment of the aged and the disabled.

Even as people have constructed and perpetuated these oppressive and dominating practices, so they can reconstruct them. Doing so, of course, is going to require hard and at times painful work, requiring extensive cooperative enterprises carried out persistently over a long period of time. Specific problems have to be identified and specific programs of action aimed at solving or lessening the effect of these problems have to be conceptualized and put into practice. Merely having intellectuals do social and cultural analysis and criticism certainly is not enough. Nevertheless, such analysis and criticism is also certainly a necessary condition if practical reformers and reconstructionists are to know what needs reforming and reconstruction and why change is required. Sometimes it is the social critic who starts the process of changing the direction of social currents. Although it is true that many times the critical interpretations presented by social analysts are motivated by popular resistance movements already operational, social critics still play valuable roles in focusing the direction of the new currents and in legitimating and thus strengthening them. The social critics to be examined in this section play both of these roles and they do so without appealing to ahistorical or asocial conditions, norms, or ideals.

I.   A POSTMODERNIST MARXIST CALLS FOR THE DEMOCRATIZATION OF ECONOMIC PRACTICES

Marxism still? Oh yes! Neocapitalism at the beginning of the twenty-first century may be quite different from the capitalism that Marx analyzed, criticized, and organized opposition forces against in the 1840s, but this new brand of global, transnational corporate capitalism still is producing economic oppression and domination that needs to be resisted. One hundred and fifty years of experience interpreting Marx's texts can teach us a great deal about what we can and should appropriate from his analysis and critique and what should be rejected, given our experience over the past century with communist nation-states that have attempted to legitimate their regimes with Marxist rhetoric.

The collapse of the Soviet empire and the abandonment in China's social practices of Marx's revolutionary project make it doubly important that we remind ourselves of how much we can learn from the Marxist tradition, if for no other reason than the fact that the defenders of neocapitalism are so successfully using these two historical events in an effort to close off all serious consideration of Marxism, contending that the bankruptcy of the Marxist critique is now self-evident. Even such a strong critic of the selfishness and sadism present in current capitalistic economic and social practices, as Richard Rorty, contends that Marxism no longer has anything practical to say to the current world, having become merely an intellectual toy being played with by university academicians.[1] Only a dialogical reading of the analysis and critique presented in this postmodern Marxist interpretation , however, can decide the issue of whether it has anything to say. Without denying that some people empowered by capitalistic economic practices are selfish and sadistic, the issue remains whether neocapitalism is operating in such a manner that domination and oppression result even when the owners and managers of economic institutions try not to be selfish or sadistic. I suggest that so much of Marxist discourse has been appropriated by contemporary interpreters of our social world, even by Rorty, that many interpreters overlook its presence in their own work and they underestimate its continuing rhetorical power to counter the rhetoric of current defenders of global capitalism.

Two aspects of Marxism can be appropriated in order to support the primary thesis of this chapter. These are the Marxist understanding of the social character of all people and the Marxist goal of seeking to maximize freedom. Marx is the first major thinker in the West to emphasize the historically contingent and materially social character of people. As one of his critical interpreters puts it, "Marx's view of human nature is now so widely accepted that a return to a pre-Marxist conception of human nature is unthinkable."[2] As a corollary to the appropriation of his understanding of people as social is the almost universal appropriation of the Marxist understanding that history must be interpreted in terms of social practices and institutions, especially economic ones. Marx is one of the first Western thinkers to challenge the adequacy of democratic liberalism's accent on political freedom and negative freedom from government interference in the activities of individuals,[3] demanding instead that such negative freedom must be supplemented with the positive freedom that empowers one to act, a freedom that can be attained only when economic and social democracy is added on to political democracy. It is this demand for positive freedom that has been appropriated by many of the reform and revolutionary movements in our recent history: the feminist movement, the post-civil rights movement among people of color, the environmental and ecological movements. The idea of people modifying their social inheritance in order to leave as a legacy a social environment maximizing freedom and minimizing nonconsentuality is a Marxist goal we should appropriate.

Marx repeatedly claims that human life and rationality are social through and through. Already in 1844 he writes that "...just as society itself produces man as man, so is society produced by him...The individual is the social being... Established society produces man in this entire richness of his being."[4] The following year he adds, "But the essence of man is no abstraction inherent in each single individual. In its reality it is the ensemble of the social relations."[5] Furthermore, "the difference between the individual as a person and what is accidental to him (or her) is not a conceptual difference but a historical fact."[6] Although Marx certainly has appropriated Hegel's accent on the social character of human life, we must be careful not to underestimate the transformation that takes place when Marx gives a materialistic rather than an idealistic reading of Hegel's interpretation of the social character of people. The materials that Marx accents are the contingent economic, political, and cultural practices sustained by the people participating in them and within which ever-new generations are trained to live. It is this contingency, and the need for constant active sustaining and training, which guarantees that people are not merely socialized robots functioning in a grand metaphysically developing movement.

Marx on this matter stands with Kierkegaard as both of them affirm in the 1840s the contingent and social character of people as historical agents. While both call for people to avoid being merely social conformists, Kierkegaard calls for people as agents to individually blend the finite and infinite aspects of their subjectivity while Marx calls for them to band together to revolutionize the social environment that is their finite inheritance. "Men make their own history, but they do not make it just as they please; they do not make it under circumstances chosen by them, but under circumstances directly encountered and transmitted from the past."[7] These are circumstances in which their social subjectivity is formed and within which they live, but these circumstances can be historically changed and revolutionized. Marx presents a general critical interpretation of his social world and its historical tendencies (in Heidegger's language, its destiny if it is not revolutionized). This does not imply that people cannot change their world. Marx's call for revolutionary thought and action is a call coming from one historical agent not trapped by his social inheritance to other agents to exercise their potential for revolutionary agency. Marx's world was filled with just those important conflicting and antagonistic tendencies that Zizek emphasized. This is why Marx, as a critic, could find space from which to level his revolutionary critique.[8]

In order that Marxism can be interpreted freshly, a number of misinterpretations need to be eliminated. Many of those who today summarily dismiss Marxism interpret it only as a program for the nationalization of private property. They fail to recognize that Marxist theory is primarily concerned with criticizing existing social conditions and not with presenting a blueprint for organizing future social life. Already in his early 1843 essay, "For a Ruthless Criticism of Everything Existing," Marx writes that "… the designing of the future and the proclamation of ready-made solutions for all time is not our affair."[9] He urged his readers not to try to prefigure the future but to focus on critiquing private property, existing "liberal, representative government," people's theoretical existence (science and religion), and their very consciousness and self-consciousness. In *The Economic and Philosophic Manuscripts of 1844*, Marx writes that "communism as such is not the goal of human development—the structure of human society."[10] Repeatedly throughout his writings, Marx refuses to speculate about what social life would be like after capitalistic oppression and domination end. Freedom for Marx meant freedom for people to collectively and democratically decide what their social and economic practices and institutions were going to be like, and thus what they themselves were going to be like. Given the freedom that comes to socialized people when they rationally regulate their interchange with nature and each other,[11] people can become accomplished in many spheres of activity.[12] One cannot predict which options free people will choose among the many that will be available to them.[13]

Marx's accent on the importance of empowering people with positive freedom, and on the insufficiency of merely granting negative political freedom, has led many critics to falsely accuse him of sacrificing such negative protection from government domination and oppression. Marx does claim that bourgeois political freedom is not enough to produce human freedom. He does claim that, when fused with capitalism and the view that such political freedom is sufficient, it becomes in fact the enemy of empowerment. In such a bourgeois world, man leads a double existence. "He lives in the political community, where he regards himself as a communal being, and in civil society where he acts simply as a private individual, treats other men as means, degrades himself to the role of a mere means, and becomes a plaything of alien powers."[14] By legally protecting the "private" owners of the means of production from any democratization of economic practices, workers are rendered powerless to organize and control their productive activities so as to avoid the devastating and alienating effects of the "free" market. It is the power to be authors of their working lives that people need. It is freedom from the effects of the "free" market that working people need, not just freedom from abusive exercises of state power. People need the power to dominate chance and circumstances and not to be dominated by them,[15] and economic democracy is a necessary condition for the acquisition of such power.

Although negative freedom and political democracy are not sufficient, Marx acknowledges as early as 1843 that they constitute a significant achievement and great progress. "It is not, indeed, the final form of human emancipation, but it is the final form of human emancipation within the framework of the prevailing social order."[16] Thirty-two years later he reaffirms his defense of certain areas of privacy free from government interference. "Everyone should be able to attend to his religious as well as his bodily needs without the police sticking their noses in."[17] Furthermore, he affirms that pursuing economic democracy is aiming at the goal of providing to all people maximum possible control over constructing their whole way of life and not just control over their laboring hours.[18] Given that some people are willing to take more risks than other people and are willing to exert more effort in their economic activities, differential economic rewards probably will be needed to maximize people's opportunities to control their lives.[19] Finally, Marx recognizes that economic democracy could not be achieved in one or two nation-states while the rest of the world's economy remained under the domination of capitalistic authoritarianism, especially when the holders of economic power are allied with politically authoritarian nation-states.[20] As he foresaw, the owners seeking to maximize profits would flee nation-states seeking to democratize their economies to other nation states where labor time could be cheaply purchased through low wages, miserable working conditions, and environmental neglect and where people had little or no collective economic or political power to define the quality of their own lives. Only if the workers of the whole world united could they lose their chains and gain democratic economic power.

As Marx critically interpreted his social and cultural world, two great evils were being produced by the capitalist economic practices that played such a dominant role in his world. These are the evils of alienation and misery. Alienation means loss of control in defining one's life; the effect of such alienation in a capitalist world is misery. Marx tells us that industrial laborers, who sell their labor time as a commodity, are alienated from the product of their labor because it becomes a hostile object increasing the profits and thus the oppressive and dominating power of those "buying" their labor time.[21] Workers are also estranged from their own productive activity, which no longer defines their lives but now is only a means to gain money either to maintain their merely animal existence or to gain free time after work to begin living. Workers are estranged from their own uniqueness as individuals because they now are just units (usually interchangeable units) in an industrial machine. They are alienated from their communities because they now must act solely as individuals selling their labor time. They are alienated from other people because all of them must now compete with every other person in their efforts to sell their labor time.[22]

The misery, exploitation and oppression that resulted from such alienation in the laissez-faire capitalist world in which Marx lived is spelled out in great detail in his masterpiece, *Capital*.[23] Impossibly long working hours, dangerously unsafe working conditions, oppressive and humiliating domination of the lives of workers and their families, low wages barely sufficient to sustain life and replenish the pool of those able to sell their labor time, an army of unemployed guaranteeing competition for available jobs paying the lowest possible wages, and the exploitation of child workers. As Marx interprets things, this alienation and misery is the result of the capitalist system which requires the maximization of profits, no matter the cost. Were owners to substitute compassion for exploitation and domination, competitors would soon put them out of business. Capitalists, workers, the unemployed, and their families all experienced alienation, but a few have the wealth to sugarcoat their alienation while the many have misery to intensify it.

Capitalism, of course, has changed greatly since the nineteenth century. Analyzing four sets of such changes should help us see that the Marxist call for economic democracy is as relevant at the beginning of the twenty-first century as it was in his day. The first major change has been the move from mostly uncontrolled laissez-faire capitalism to government supported capitalism. This change was motivated by the rise of monopoly and oligopoly capitalism during the late nineteenth century. The overwhelming majority of the owners of businesses recognized that government regulation was needed to prevent the destruction of their chance to compete in the market by those who would use their wealth to drive out competition or to corner the world's gold or money supply. This new attitude toward business-government relations can be compared to the attitude toward sports. You can't have football or capitalist competition that will produce winners unless there are rules that guarantee real competition.

This toleration of government involvement in capitalist economic practices, of course, is not completely new. The whole game of capitalism cannot be played unless the state's police and judicial practices are used to establish how legal rights to "private" property are acquired and transferred. Soon, however, businesses found more and more places where government involvement could aid capitalistic practices. Government monetary policies could help soften the effect of economic depressions and inflation. Since government income depended on taxes on business profits, it became mandatory that government do everything it could to help businesses maximize those profits: build highways and airports, fund scientific research that businesses could use in developing new products, processes, and technology that would increase business profits. Finally, government itself became one the "private" sector's biggest consumers of products and services: government office buildings and equipment, high-tech products and services, prisons and military material, plus everything purchased by the millions employed by the government. In 1913, US government spending was 8 percent of gross national product but by 1995 in was 33 percent. In this new business-government partnership, it has been crucial for business to maintain control over government so that economic democracy could not replace authoritarian control aimed at maximizing profits. This it has done all too successfully through domination of election campaign financing, lobbying, and maintaining a cultural hegemony legitimating this capitalist supporting partnership.

The second major change in the capitalist system occurred when it switched from accenting production to focusing on increasing consumption. Marx had predicted that overproduction would become a major problem in the capitalist practices of his day, but he did not anticipate the capitalist response to this problem. Business owners eventually recognized, often under worker and government pressure, that it was in their own best interests to increase consumption at home and abroad. They introduced new tactics to increase consumption. Industry-wide increases in workers' wages were introduced so that overall purchasing power would be increased without one business in the industry being put at a competitive disadvantage. Minimum wage laws were accepted as was the welfare state, with its provisions for unemployment compensation for laid-off workers, welfare payments for unemployable persons, and social security payments and Medicare to the elderly because this guaranteed the continued presence of purchasing power. In spite of their tactical benefit to the capitalist system, these changes along with increased government consumption were accepted only grudgingly, and efforts continuously have been made to strengthen the capitalist system in other ways: privatize public education, prisons, Medicare, and social security.

To further enhance consumption, new markets were opened in "underdeveloped" countries. China in the nineteenth century was forced to open its doors to consumer products produced in North Atlantic capitalist countries. Economic imperialism changed its face. Instead of just stealing gold and slaves and exploiting natural resources such as oil and rubber, the new imperialism also aimed at establishing and controlling overseas markets.

At the center of neocapitalism's accent on consumption was the introduction of sophisticated programs of advertising and market research aimed at increasing consumption. At first advertising was used only to secure for a business a larger share than its competitors of the existing market for products meeting consumers' felt needs. Soon, however, advertising and market research techniques were used to increase overall consumption. New needs were created in the minds of consumers. They were convinced that they absolutely needed cosmetics and hair spray, the services of hairstylists and real estate agents, the latest styles in blue jeans, Nike shoes, and high-tech equipment, two-week vacations and tickets to football, baseball, basketball, and hockey games. New values were instilled in people so that they could purchase and consume without guilt or shame. Old values that accented working, saving, and not borrowing were replaced by a value system which said it is perfectly all right to spend (even if it puts you in deep debt to your credit card bank) and it is perfectly all right (even obligatory for psychological health) to enjoy yourself. New identities were given to people as they became convinced that self-fulfillment could be gained and could only be gained by purchasing certain products: a certain car, certain cigarettes, certain clothes, certain furniture, certain sorts of unusable antiques and collectors' items.

In this push for ever-increasing consumption, soon symbols were being sold for consumption rather than products for use. People were convinced that success means having what others do not have: a big boat, a second home on the lake, two weeks in Florida or a trip to Europe, membership in a country club or health club or civic organization. Decency means having at least as much as what others have: a little motorboat, a mobile home at the lake, five days at Disneyland, playing golf or tennis at public parks. Advertisers sold symbols of masculinity, femininity, health, family togetherness. McDonald's and Burger King ads do not sell hamburgers but a family-friendly environment for a family outing. Next, market researchers and advertisers began identifying and selling models of products so that simulations of the models could be produced for purchase.[24] For example, market researchers found that people wanted to buy big, plump chickens, but since ordinary chickens do not look like the ads in newspapers, genetic engineers worked on producing bigger and plumper chickens and then butchered chickens injected with water so that they would look like the pictures. The final product was a simulation of a simulation.

The third major difference between nineteenth-century capitalism and current capitalism is its movement from accenting factory production of products to accenting providing services for consumer consumption. Two examples should be sufficient: the development of leisure industries and communication industries. More and more people now find their life in what they do after work rather than in what they do during work. They work in order to earn the money needed to start living during their leisure hours. Huge new industries have arisen to meet the felt needs of people for products and services to be used in their leisure hours. People "need" TV sets and productions, stereos and disks, computers and computer games and Internet services. They "need" concerts of classical and pop music. They "need" every imaginable kind of spectator sporting event. They "need" sporting equipment and places to bowl, jog, hunt, fish, ski, sail, do aerobics, and play golf or tennis. They "need" gardening and home remodeling supplies, restaurants and fast-food places, and Jiffy auto service centers. They "need" highways, gas stations, airports, airlines, travel agencies, hotels, and motels so that they can travel, travel, travel.

Perhaps even more revolutionary in consequences in neocapitalism has been the development of the communications industry. Instantaneous communication has made it possible for a global capitalist system to develop in which it is profitable to decentralize production and consumption while centralizing authoritarian management. Production can be located in developing nations where production costs can be minimized, but data on production efficiency and productivity can be monitored instantly in London or New York, where management can instantly communicate orders to modify procedures. Products, services, sales, and advertising techniques can be modified to meet the specific felt needs in different societies and cultures. Whole new industries have developed that sell communication and market research services to other industries. A global market has developed for the consumption of TV programming, movies, and records that permit businesses to develop the needs, attitudes, values, and sense of self-worth that will best serve the profit interests of all capitalist businesses.

The fourth and final change in capitalism that I want to mention here is the blurring of old class lines and the erasure of active revolutionary opposition to the neocapitalist system. Many ordinary workers individually have purchased stock in profit-seeking businesses. Labor unions manage huge worker retirement funds so as to maximize the return from their purchase of stocks. Most workers have purchased on credit homes, cars, and a host of other consumer products and are as interested as big businesses in keeping down interest rates on borrowed money. The alienation of skilled craft workers, which played such a powerful function in Marx's age, has been greatly minimized as they have gained a degree of control over their apprentice training system and over their working conditions within the overall demands set up by management. The alienation of intellectuals (What would history have been like if Marx had secured a university teaching position or if his journalistic efforts had succeeded?) has been greatly minimized by giving them high-paying jobs in industry with a significant amount of freedom to pursue their intellectual interests and by giving them secure university teaching and research jobs with decent salaries and health and retirement benefits. Karl Marx became a revolutionary activist when he could not secure a university teaching position and his journalistic efforts became financial failures, while today the leading American Marxist intellectual, Frederick Jamison, holds a high-paying endowed chair at Duke University. Even as the landed aristocracy in classical China bought off all the leaders of peasant revolts prior to Mao, so capitalists now have learned how to buy off possible threats to their authoritarian power control of economic practices.

These many changes in the form of capitalism have been matched by many changes in Marxist critical interpretations of existing capitalist practices. Accepting the challenge of the early Marx to carry out a ruthless criticism of everything existing, new generations of "Marxists" began to criticize Marx for what was not accented or sufficiently appreciated by him and they leveled damning criticisms of the 1889 Second Communist International and of Soviet communism for what it was accenting dogmatically and in contradiction to Marx's spirit of ruthless criticism. Three examples can aptly illustrate this critical development in Marxism.

First, many neo-Marxists have claimed that Marx failed to appreciate the significance of forms of domination and oppression other than economic. He didn't attend to the marginalization and misery experienced by people of color, by religious and ethnic minorities, by the disabled, by the elderly. Marxist feminists have charged that Marx ignored the labor of women in the home, the labor of homemakers in reproducing new generations of productive laborers, the manner in which men, proletarians and bourgeoisie alike, were dominating and oppressing women. He failed to realize that socializing property and seeking economic democracy might do little to end the mistreatment of women or to empower women or democratize the home. Proletarians and communists often have been sexist. These critics of Marx still remain Marxists in that they appropriate his discourse of ruthless criticism of domination and oppression and his insight that no forms of domination and oppression can be weakened without economic empowerment and increased democratization of the economic practices, and without opposing a capitalist economic authoritarianism that singularly pursues the maximization of profits.[25]

Second, Western neo-Marxists leveled a series of major criticisms against the Second Communist International, which was founded in 1889 and functioned as the "official" voice of Marxism for the next 25 years. The "official" interpretation worked with an oversimplified model of the relationship existing between economic practices and other political, social, and cultural practices, with the former serving as a substructure thoroughly determining the character of the others in its dependent superstructure. It claimed that the inherent conflicts and antagonisms in a capitalist world would lead to capitalism's own self-destruction; one simply needed to wait for history to reach its own causally determined end (economic crises producing proletarian class consciousness producing revolutionary spirit and praxis producing a worker's seizure of state power producing a withering away of the state and the end of domination and oppression).

Karl Korsch[26] and the Frankfurt school of social theorists[27] in Germany, Georg Lukacs[28] in Hungary, Thorstein Veblen[29] in the United States, and Antonio Gramsci[30] in Italy all argued for a more Hegelian, organic, and holistic interpretation of the capitalist world in which linguistic, cultural, legal, political and economic practices are seen as interdependent.[31] In 1923, Korsch, a leader in the Communist Party of

Germany, until he was expelled in 1926 for attacking Soviet imperialism, criticized what he called the "vulgar" socialism of the Second International for failing to recognize that all social and cultural practices are as objective as economic practices and need to be ruthlessly criticized and revolutionized. Lukacs, again in 1923, argued that capitalist society in all of its economic, political, and social life is thoroughly stained by a reification of commodities in its economic and political practices and in its cultural vocabulary, beliefs, and values. Such commodification of both working and leisure time cannot be treated simply quantitatively but must be interpreted, as Wilhelm Dilthey had pointed out, using a Hegelian organic model in which commodities are located in a social whole distinctively marked by the near universalization of commodification of the functional elements within it.

Already in 1899, in his *Theory of the Leisure Class,* Veblen attacked the dogmatic optimism of American Marxists of his time by pointing out that worker class interests often lost out to worker class consciousness. Workers adopted a value system in which wealth meant to them social propriety and authority. Workers tried to mimic the wealthy leisure class by practices of conspicuous consumption. These were values and practices inculcated in them by the wealthy capitalists who exercised hegemony over culture through their control of schools and the media. In interpreting the capitalist world, these cultural practices as well as other nationalistic and militaristic practices need to be considered along with economic practices in order to understand what is going on.

Gramsci accented the manner in which the holders of economic power reinforced and legitimated their power through control of government machinery and a cultural hegemony consisting of control over schools and intellectuals. The power gained through such hegemony is so significant, Gramsci pointed out, that social revolutionary action requires the development of counterhegemonic intellectuals, institutions, and practices (worker and peasant schools, open universities, newspapers, journals, book publishers, institutional grouping,s and attachments). The general point made by all these

Marxist critics of "vulgar" Marxism is that social practices of many different sorts (economic, political, social, cultural) are interrelated in an organic whole with no one set of practices either dominating the others or functioned unaffected by the others. Therefore, domination and oppression may exist in any set of these practices, and increasing freedom in any one area requires revolutionary changes in all areas.

The basic charge against the theoreticians of the Second International is that it did not appreciate the effect of the so-called superstructure upon the class consciousness of the proletariat and the owners of the major means of production. Neo-Marxism in a sense was born when the economic crises in the last two decades of the nineteenth century, which Marx had predicted, did not produce revolutionary consciousness or actions by the proletariat. A unified class consciousness did not develop because workers were never just workers; racist, sexist, ethnic, national, and religious differences separated them and pitted them against each other. In addition, any hope for revolutionary worker class consciousness was destroyed by consumerism and the development of a culture in which self-fulfillment was felt to come through consumption and participation in leisure time activities because life began when work was over. After World War I it was authoritarian fascism and not communism that won worker loyalty with its nationalistic symbols and its promise of authoritarian order and the good life for consumers. Economic factors influenced racist, sexist, and nationalist practices, but it was these cultural practices and what they meant to people that also influenced the significance of the economic.

Although unified worker class consciousness was not created by capitalism's economic crises, a sort of unified owner class consciousness did arise. Neither Marx nor the theoreticians of the Second International foresaw that capitalists would modify the competitive and laissez-faire character of capitalism in order to deal with economic crises and in order to weaken the threat that they saw in worker discontent. As already mentioned, ruthless individualistic competition was replaced by competition within government enforced rules. Increased wages, shorter work days and weeks, and the welfare state were accepted in order to defuse worker discontent and to create huge new markets for consumer products. In addition, cultural hegemony was established through schools, mass media, and the successful politicians who received from the business world the huge amounts of money needed to campaign for office in the mass media era and who moved back and forth from government jobs to high-paying management and consultant positions in the business world. Interest in maximizing profits and the value of stock investments of businesses in general took precedence over any other interests that might divide this owner class. Racism, sexism, and marginalization of the disabled and the elderly were tolerated when profitable and opposed when they became unprofitable. War materials were sold to potential national enemies until huge profits could be made by selling them to one's own government as one's nation went to war. National corporations played cities, states, and regions against each other, and global transnational corporations played nations against nations. In neocapitalism it is domination over the entire social, cultural, political, and economic world that is fostered in order that businesses in that world can continue to maximize profits. Neo-Marxists charge that it is only by increasing the democratization of this entire world that this domination and its concomitant oppression can be lessened.

Marx's spirit of ruthless criticism of existing practices in service of overall democratization also became embodied in a group of thinkers critical of what Lenin was doing to Marxism to drive democracy out of communism. The Second International had predicted that economic crises in capitalism would produce a worker revolution. In the 1880s and 1890s, however, crisis after crisis occurred, but no revolution occurred. Lenin concluded that communism would not arrive through a passive waiting policy. He proclaimed that a disciplined communist elite, a vanguard party, would have to be formed to initiate and control the revolutionary movement. In 1903, Trotsky warned about the danger that a dictatorship of the proletariat could become a dictatorship over the proletariat by the Communist Party, and then by the Central Committee of the Communist Party, and then by the general secretary of the Communist Party,[32] exactly what happened in the Soviet Union under Stalin. Trotsky's prophecy had been prefigured by Michael Bakunin when, at the Hague Congress of the Communist International in 1872 (prior to being expelled from the congress), he rejected Marx's proposal to seize the state and establish a dictatorship of the proletariat. Bakunin predicted that uniting authoritarian economic power with authoritarian state political power would merely replace a bad dictatorship with an even worse dictatorship.[33] In 1904, Rosa Luxemburg charged that what Lenin was proposing was not worker economic democracy but a military, bureaucratic style of dictatorship over the workers.[34] In 1923, Korsch attacked Lenin for establishing a dictatorship over the proletariat rather than permitting the proletariat to democratize the Russian economy and state.[35]

In addition, neo-Marxists became very critical of the Soviet-dominated Comintern, which required all communists to obey its directives that seemed only to be furthering the national interests of the Soviet Union and not the world interests of communist democratization. They also became critical of the Soviet Union's identification of the socialization of property (the democratization of the economy) with state nationalization of property. This, the neo-Marxists charged, only produces state capitalism with its own forms of domination and oppression. Besides, the concentration of all economic power in the hands of a small dictatorship and bureaucracy controlling political power inevitably creates tyranny and unimaginable misery.

Neo-Marxists have made a host of recommendations for resisting neocapitalist efforts to dominate the social world. First, they have attempted to carry out an integrated project of social and cultural interpretation and criticism of our neo-capitalist world. They seek to expose consumer fetishes and the unsatisfying quality of the lives of people captured by consumerism. They have critiqued identifying one's life with one's leisure activities and have attempted to show that this narcotic numbing of us during our working hours can never gives us a free and desirable life because such a life requires that we have significant personal control of our productive activities and our social and cultural environment. They have attempted to expose mass media-induced desires and the sense of self-fulfillment with which they seek to provide us, by revealing how seeking to fulfill these desires makes us slaves to others rather than persons creating beautiful lives for ourselves. They have attempted to show how vocabularies and forms of discourse (rationally accepted forms of speech, institutionalized regimes of truth and knowledge) are more powerful even than ideologies in producing forms of subjectivity that lead such subjects to end up being subjugated (marginalized so they do not even have a voice that can attract attention).

Second, neo-Marxists have worked to build up counter hegemonic practices and institutions. Gramsci set up worker schools in Italy. Stuart Hall established open universities in London so that radical social-cultural critics would not be silenced by the vocabularies and modes of discourse dominating the higher educational establishment in England. Noam Chomsky helped establish South End Press in Boston so that radical critical writers could get into print ideas that established, market-driven presses wouldn't consider. Cornell West and Bell Hooks speak through African-American Christian churches in order to have an institutional base for counterhegemonic efforts. Feminists and people of color have created women's studies, black studies, and ethnic studies programs in universities and consciousness raising sessions outside the formal academic world, again aimed at weakening oppressive hegemonic domination.

Third, neo-Marxists are calling for people to engage in a unified critique of all forms of domination and oppression and to show the inseparable interconnections between such forces. Identify and criticize all practices that have the effect of producing docile and useful servants of the holders of dominating and oppressive power. Form rainbow alliances of urban factory and service workers, the permanently unemployed, feminists, people of color, the disabled, the elderly, and gays and lesbians so that each member can identify with all the other members as resisters of domination and oppression in whatever form it appears, thus producing a new kind of group consciousness and unity without destroying not unjustified differences.

Fourth, neo-Marxists are seeking to identify and weaken the new, deadly class structure that has arisen in neocapitalism. The major division in the neocapitalist world is between the group of people who give orders and the group of people who almost always and only take orders. It is this latter group of people who are alienated from their work activities and from others who compete with them for the same jobs and who are exploited, marginalized, and silenced. This division exists in the local workplace and in the global marketplace, where managers in central headquarters in the First World give orders, and governments and workers in the Third World either obey or face economic ruin. Neo-Marxists call for resistance to such domination by seeking for ways to democratize the workplace so that workers, managers, and consumers are mutually involved in determining work procedures and the disposition of earned profits. Democratize the whole economic system by holding corporations accountable for social disruption because of industrialization or relocation. Expose the character of transnational corporations. Resist letting them divide workers by nationality, race, or sex. Seek to build a unified worldwide labor union system to confront transnational corporations. Have unions focus on worker influence in determining working conditions so that they can live while working rather than thinking only of benefits which allow them to live after the workday ends. Experiment with nonstate forms of socializing property. Encourage the development of co-ops and worker-owned industries. Use the tremendous power of worker retirement funds in stock investments in order to oppose domination and oppression and not just to increase the size of the fund and the financial benefits it will give to workers when their work life is over.

Finally, many neo-Marxists are calling for dropping the impossible dream of final and total liberation from all domination, oppression, and social antagonism. Instead, they urge developing strategies and tactics for resisting domination and oppression in specific cases in specific ways. Drop the illusion that there is one big thing that one can do to end once and for all time all alienation, misery, domination, and antagonism. Instead, do a lot of little things to resist. Consciousness-raising here or there. Changing practices, rules, and customs in this place or that. Don't trap yourself in the false dilemma: either we seek heaven on earth or it is not worth trying to do anything. Instead, choose as one's goal in life to make life a little less hellish in my family, my workplace, my city, my nation. Build a beautiful life by remaining loyal to a commitment to do whatever one can to resist any and all forms of domination and oppression wherever and whenever they occur.

Marxism, whatever else one can say about it, consists of a ruthless and massive criticism of existing social practices. Furthermore, it can do so without assuming an asocial or ahistorical, nonrhetorical standpoint from which it carries out its criticism. From within a social world filled with antagonistic conflicts it constructs critical interpretations of that world and the place within it of its own efforts to carry out this critique and revolutionary changes of existing practices. What guides its criticisms, rhetoric, and resistance efforts is its passion for freedom and democratic empowerment. If we focus on the "material" character of its dialectic and not get misled by attempts by "vulgar" Marxists and defenders of capitalism to saddle it with metaphysical theories of economic determinism, then Marxism remains as a prime illustration of our ability to do criticism of our social environment and historical situation from our material and contingent location in that environment and situation.

II. POSTMODERNIST ELEMENTS IN HABERMAS'S SEARCH FOR A DEMOCRATIZING OF GOVERNMENTAL POLICYMAKING

The Institute for Social Research was established in Frankfurt, Germany, in 1923. Its distinctive project of critical theorizing was crystallized by Max Horkheimer, who served as its director from 1930 until 1953, and Theodor Adorno, his colleague and the institute's director from 1953 until 1969. Allied with the institute were Walter Benjamin, Herbert Marcuse, and Erich Fromm. Due to their attack on fascism, they had to flee Germany in 1933 when Hitler came to power and only reestablished the institute in Frankfurt after their return from the United States at the end of the Second World War. Critical theory's most prolific and influential spokesperson at the end of the twentieth century is Jurgen Habermas.

All of these critical theorists searched for a way to critically and ruthlessly interpret social practices without assuming that critical theorists can ever escape their social, cultural, and historical situatedness. (The claim that Habermas is an exception to this tendency will be examined below.) Horkheimer calls for using an interdisciplinary approach to understanding historically developing human social and cultural worlds because such worlds, although never complete, fully unified or final, still need to be approached holistically, as Hegel and Dilthey had pointed out.[36] He charges that at the heart of any critical interpretation of existing social practices there has to be an immanent critique of the ideology of bourgeois ideas of justice, equality, and freedom because these ideas conflict with bourgeois practices dominating our current world. Bourgeois individualism, Horkheimer claims, is counterproductive of individual freedom because its effect is the production and reinforcement of coercive social conditions. Ideological enlightenment is necessary, even if not sufficient, for human liberation. This is because the subjectivity of free human beings requires that the subject's perception of its social world not be distorted by oppressive social conditions. Originally, Horkheimer had thought that because the proletariat's passion for freedom would lead to its willingness to destroy itself as a class (along with all other classes), it could speak universally for the emancipation of all people. After World War II, however, Horkheimer had less and less faith in the proletariat, given the manner in which it had been bought off by a commodity culture.

Adorno also appropriates Hegel in a materialistic manner and focuses on the radical consequences of taking a holistic approach to understanding the phenomena we encounter when those phenomena are located in larger frameworks that socially are never unified or complete. These historically contingent phenomena are and must always be taken as symptoms of social and cultural worlds that are contaminated by practices hopelessly striving to control nature and other people through the use of merely instrumental forms of rationality.[37] He advocates the use of a practice of negative dialectics in which critical analysts reject any simple, empiricist theory of representational perception of particulars. Critics need to negate the adequacy of any such perceptions because such particulars must be interpretively located in a larger theoretical framework. The analyst then proceeds to reject also the adequacy of any presentation of such a framework because all frameworks are contingent, incomplete, and contaminated. The goal of negative dialectics is to undermine all perceptions of socially constituted objects and subjects and all theoretical systems seeking to understand such objects. It does so in order to preserve that uniqueness of particulars that transcends all social constitution and conception and in order to keep alive the possibility of continuous, ruthless criticism of both particulars and systems and the possibility of continuing constitution and reconstitution of social and cultural practices. Adorno constantly seeks to defy the norms of established language by writing in hyperbole and with irony. He advocates the utilization of a socially committed form of art and music in which form is accented over content and in which art and music are not realistic, naturalistic, expressionistic, utopian, or avant gardism. This would allow artists and composers of music to resist the desire of the wealthy for a freshness and newness to make up for the boredom of bourgeois life. Appropriating the texts of Marx and Kierkegaard, Adorno's art would turn its back on the sufficiency of social rationality and point instead to that unique particularity which is the other to the whole world of social rationality.

Horkheimer and Adorno, in their masterful 1944 study of the Enlightenment,[38] attempt to enlighten their readers about the totalitarian dangers (fascist, Stalinist, capitalist) inherent in that Western movement known as the Enlightenment. They charge that the Enlightenment began with noble intent of using scientific knowledge to liberate people from fears generated by unwarranted superstitions and from the disasters resulting from preventable diseases, famines, floods, etc. Unfortunately, they contend, the Enlightenment became historically linked to practices that turned scientism, technological mastery of nature, and efficient control of people into unquestioned absolutes to be accepted and ruthlessly pursued. They point out that a whole culture industry has developed in order to enhance such efficient control and unquestioned acceptance. It is important to remember that it is only certain features of the "Enlightenment movement" that Horkheimer and Adorno are attacking. These are: (1) ignoring the concrete uniqueness of particulars in the West's mathematization of objects for scientific study and technological control; (2) ignoring the holistic character of the world in the West's movement toward positivistic empiricism; (3) focusing only on an instrumental form of rationality in an effort to gain progress in controlling nature and people. They themselves acknowledge that their critical interpretation of the historical situatedness of the Enlightenment movement is presented in order to enlighten people so that they can become free to change these tendencies and practices and prevent the effects being produced.[39] The financial support that Horkheimer, upon Adorno's urging, had the Institute for Social Research give to Walter Benjamin in the 1930s probably was due to Benjamin's focus on the materially inexhaustible richness of particulars, which no concepts or theories could exhaust, and to his analysis of how art, once part of the ritual practices constituting an historical tradition, had become, in this age of museums and mechanical reproduction, primarily exhibition art serving the political interests of those controlling the consumer industry.[40]

The voice of the Frankfurt school in the last quarter of the twentieth century has been Jurgen Habermas, who appropriates the writings not only of the early members of the Institute for Social Research but also those of the neo-Marxists, Freud, American pragmatists such as Charles S. Peirce, social theorists such as Dilthey, Max Weber, and Talcott Parsons, developmental psychologists such as Piaget and Lawrence Kohlberg, speech Act theorists in the tradition of Wittgenstein and John Austin, and neo-Kantians such as Karl-Otto Apel. Of the multitude of issues on which he has written in the hundreds of articles and books that he has published, focusing on just three will serve the purpose of this chapter—showing that social rationality need not lose its historical and social status in order to carry out social criticism of the social environment in which it is embedded. Habermas presents an ideal test case for this thesis since he does argue that there is a universal and ever-present criterion for judging norms that can be used in carrying out social analysis and criticism. The three themes to be investigated here are: (1) Habermas's conception of the task of critical theorizing, (2) his attempt to justify his general normative claims by using "weak" transcendental arguments about the conditions necessary for the existence of language, and (3) his critique of our current social-economic-political world and his recommendations for changing it. I will attempt to show that his notion of critical theory has much to recommend it, that his "transcendental" arguments in support of universal normative claims are not a return to metaphysical efforts to transcend the historical and social, and that much can be learned from his critique of our current social world even when one disagrees with his goal of seeking to maximize consensus among people.

Habermas seeks to present a comprehensive interpretation of the human situation and its historical development.[41] Habermas's interpretation is as comprehensive as the sweeping metaphysical theories of Aristotle and Hegel, but one would misunderstand his project if one saw him as presenting just one more grand, a priori description of how things generally are, one more metaphysically "final" explanation of why everything is as it is and not otherwise, or one more "ultimate" justification of some moral principle. Habermas insists that there are no uninterpreted facts to describe and explain[42] and that the relation of language and thought to what they are about is always practical.[43] He writes that there is no "pure reason," either in the realm of theory or practice,[44] and rather than ultimate justifications of moral norms or principles there is just a pragmatic, context situated procedural test that rules out certain actions and norms as unjustifiable.[45]

Drawing very heavily upon Peirce's contention that all beliefs are plans of action and that the pragmatics of language and thought take precedence over its semantics and syntactics, Habermas interprets all discourse as serving human interests.[46] Our natural and biological descriptions and explanations, he claims, are forms of productive labor that serve our interest in controlling the material resources of nature.[47] Our hermeneutical interpretations of historical events, social practices, and cultural productions serve to arrive at and maintain mutual understanding and self-understanding, thus serving our interest in maintaining and reproducing our social and cultural identity.[48] Appropriating Hegel and Darwin, Habermas asserts that social groups have a dominant interest in maintaining the ongoing life of the social whole; service to this interest determines the evolutionary development of social history. Human labor and production, including human cognitive activities and personal interactions, are aimed at serving our most basic interest, meeting the material requirements needed for life and reproduction.[49] Human symbolic life, with all of its beliefs, interpretations, and norms, provides what is required to maintain social-cultural forms of life and psychological modes of subjectivity that give identity to holistic social groups and their members. At the heart of such symbolic activity, Habermas claims, is the linguistic activity of justifying descriptive, explanatory, normative, and expressive claims when such claims come under challenge.

As part of his comprehensive account of how everything hangs together, Habermas presents a master narrative of social history. His account of the dialectical evolution of social history is one that draws upon the texts of the neo-Marxists in order to attach to Marx's narrative of the economic interplay between the forces and means of production a more Hegelian account of the dialectical development of human symbolic life (human cognition, human discord, and consensus on normative claims about what beliefs are true and what actions are justified).[50] He further claims that the historical evolution of social practices and institutions is mirrored at the individual level in the development of a person's subjectivity from infancy to adulthood.[51] Although he strives to be as comprehensive as possible, still he claims that his account is only his own fallible, historically and socially situated interpretation backed up by the justifying reasons he finds sufficient to answer his real and anticipated critics.[52] Furthermore, he contends, his interpretation always remains a rhetorically committed "critical" reflection, not disinterested but rather serving our human interest in being emancipated from acting under the duress of coerced opinions that one cannot justify to oneself or others. Such critical reflection serves our interest in strengthening our personal autonomy.[53]

Habermas demonstrates that interpreting and theorizing can be massively comprehensive and general while still being pragmatic and situated. Appropriating his emphasis on the pragmatic and historical character of his project does not mean, however, that one must endorse all the specific claims Habermas makes in his interpretation. For example, followers of Buddhism, Taoism, Henry Thoreau, Martin Buber, and Martin Heidegger would critique Habermas's accent on the human effort to control things. They would call instead for people to go beyond these efforts to dominate and instrumentally control raw materials in nature and instead to simply and respectfully let nature be. They seek to produce poetic characterizations of nature expressive of such respect. They could endorse Habermas's account of our instrumental relation to nature as an account of how things unfortunately are generally and for the most part, while still claiming that people can escape such a historical "destiny" by transcending our socially inherited craving to reproduce our social world and our social identities.

One also might commend Habermas's desire to tell a story about how things generally hang together but still reject with supporting reasons his grand narratives of social history or personal development and his commendation of efforts to seek a single, unified master description of how things are and a single general explanation of why they are that way. The Lacan-Zizek interpretation of psychological development, as we have seen, accents the importance of the non-symbolic (enjoyment) and the imaginative instead of Habermas's emphasis upon the development of social cognitive skills and consensus. Also, as we shall see, Foucault's interpretation of historical change differs from Habermas's heavy accent on the centrality of productive, technological control and symbolic coherence. Such an accent, Foucault claims, leaves out of the story the role of the mini-practices of exercising dominating power that make economic and political power possible and symbolic consensus seem desirable. Jean-Francois Lyotard, differing from Habermas but echoing the position of many historians, claims that it is not possible to justify any master historical narrative; one can only write many different mini-narratives in the areas of the different sciences, different areas of art and literature, different areas of economic, political, and military life, different religions and areas of cultural change.[54] Similarly, as we have seen, Rorty and Kuhn accent the not unjustified use of multiple, incommensurate vocabularies and explanatory frameworks in science when it is engaged in revolutionizing its disciplinary practices and paradigms. These differences from Habermas in the content of their interpretations should not cover over their common agreement with Habermas on the pragmatic, historically situated, and interpretive character of our understanding of the human situation.

It is on the pragmatics of all speech acts that we must concentrate if we are going to understand Habermas's interpretation of the nature of our claims about the correctness ("validity") of the descriptions, prescriptions, and justifications that people produce. Seeking here again for a single, comprehensive, integrated account of the pragmatics of speech acts, Habermas presents a theory that he has called "universal pragmatics"[55] and "formal pragmatics."[56] Although Wittgenstein had claimed that there are only family resemblances between language games, Habermas reductively treats this as simply a result of Wittgenstein's restriction of himself to a merely therapeutic project of weakening the presumptions of aprioristic metaphysicians and epistemologists.[57] He does not share Wittgenstein's appreciation of how radically different language games can be, how different, for example, religious language games are from either scientific or psychological language games.[58] Habermas claims that all speech acts can be classified in terms of just three pragmatic functions (represent the world, express a speaker's mental states, and establish legitimate interpersonal relations).[59] Although at times Habermas's effort to be comprehensive makes it seem as though he is presenting a god's-eye view of what communicative speech acts are like and how they are to be judged for correctness, it is important to read through this appearance in order to see how thoroughly pragmatic and situated he interprets all speech and writing (including his own). Had he remained even more pragmatic, he perhaps would have seen that his three-part schema for classifying pragmatic functions had only a certain kind of pragmatic utility. Others, for other purposes, can and do classify language games very differently, often in order to accent the relative independence of religious, poetic, and interpersonal linguistic practices.

In Habermas's comprehensive interpretation of things, all claims about what is the case or what ought to be the case take place in socially "lived worlds" of shared practices, vocabularies, beliefs, and norms.[60] Similar to what was pointed out in chapter 2, Habermas claims that it is only when specific breakdowns occur in the cohesiveness of such a shared world that questions about the correctness or justification of these claims or practices even arise.[61] Still, Habermas does claim that, in spite of their situatedness, any and all speech acts do have certain general conditions necessary for their very existence; they have certain inescapable presuppositions.[62] People can and often do misuse words and speak ungrammatically (talking or writing in an incomprehensible way). They often speak and write deceptively, lying to others and to themselves about their beliefs or desires or intentions and deliberately getting people to misunderstand them. People often do fail to comprehend or understand what other people are saying. Habermas claims that these are only possible because they are the exceptions to and parasitic upon the general case.[63] Generally and for the most part, we use words as others use them and approve of their use; we share the beliefs common in the groups socializing us; we try to get others to understand what we are saying and to agree with our beliefs about what is the case and what ought to be the case (using commonly shared justifying reasons to defend our beliefs when others disagree); we truthfully express our beliefs, desires and intentions. Understandability and comprehensibility, Habermas claims, are inescapable presuppositions of all our speech acts.[64] Also inescapable are the use of shared norms calling for truthfulness and a shared attempt to reestablish through conversation a social consensus when conflicts arise among beliefs.[65]

The criteria governing comprehensibility, however, Habermas points out, are also pragmatic and situational. People generally use words in ways that are similar enough to keep conversations going, although the use and meaning of such words are not in any metaphysically absolute sense identical.[66] Similarly pragmatic are the criteria governing our claims that our descriptive assertions are true; the vocabulary of truth has a use only in the context of disagreements and arguments about what to believe.[67] Interpreting truth claims in a counterfactual manner not unlike Habermas's, I claimed in chapter 2 that when one reasserts a claim by saying it is true, one is committing oneself to saying that one either will always continue to assert it or one will drop it and admit that one's earlier belief was mistaken. Habermas's own insights into the pragmatics of truth claims, however, sometimes get unnecessarily covered up by his desire to systematize things. He says that a commitment to truth is presupposed by all descriptions[68] whereas all that the pragmatics of the term "truth" seems to require is a commitment to claim truth when our descriptions are in fact challenged.

Habermas also gives a pragmatic and situated interpretation of justification. Providing justifications for beliefs or actions is required only when they have been actually challenged. Again, however, Habermas seems to overstate his case in his effort to construct a comprehensive formal pragmatics. He claims that all claims about what is the case or what ought to be the case presuppose a commitment to justify such claims,[69] whereas the pragmatics governing the use of the term "justification" seem to require merely that justifications get offered only when justified challenges to a claim have been introduced. This distinction is important for a number of reasons. First, the pragmatics of 'justification' show that the burden of proof in the case of claims lies with the challenger of a claim and not with the initial claimant; doubting always needs reasons, but believing only sometimes does. Second, although fallibility is always possible, certain sorts of first person claims (I am in pain, I see paper on the desk, I remember turning on the computer a little while ago) are generally reliable even though they could only be justified by claims of the same sort. To doubt a pain report is to doubt the truthfulness of the reporter or that the reporter knows how to use the word "pain." Doubting someone's personal perceptual or memory reports requires reliance on someone else's perceptual or memory reports, as every trial lawyer knows.

The third reason for keeping this distinction between universal justifiability and situation specific justifications may be the most important because it challenges Habermas's claim that all speech acts presuppose pursuing the ideal of seeking universal consensus in our descriptions and in our procedures for judging moral norms. He claims that social maxims are invalid if they would not receive assent from all free and informed persons who might be affected by them.[70] Habermas argues that when engaged in disagreements about the correctness of claims we have only three choices. Either (1) we can continue giving commonly accepted justifying reasons until a consensus is reached among uncoerced and informed persons, or (2) we can resort to "strategic reasons" (offering bribes or threats to produce agreement), or (3) we break off the encounter by retreating to skepticism or the exercise of blatant force.[71] Restricting us to these three options, however, fails to recognize the possibility that people may be working with different and incommensurate vocabularies, ontologies, and moralities. It also fails to recognize that conflictual encounters between such people may be handled by either (a) simply letting basic differences be basic differences, or (b) by creating operational agreements that each party to the agreement interprets and justifies to themselves in radically different ways, or (c) by creating new vocabularies, ontologies, or moralities that both sides to the disagreement endorse as they both become new kinds of social persons living in new social worlds, even as they probably remain basically different in other uncontested areas.

Secular humanists and religious theists don't talk the same language, think of nature in the same way, tell the same kind of historical narratives.[72] Only reductionists, who could not justify themselves to their opposition, would deny that such differences are not unjustified. Similarly, different people might work with different kinds of moralities (rules, virtues, compassion for the uncharacterizable uniqueness of people). When people working within different moralities encounter each other and discover difficulties in knowing how to go on, reaching operational agreements is all that is needed, with each side interpreting the agreement in its own way and using its own morality to justify the agreement to itself.[73] Habermas contends that the operational agreement must be justifiable as rationally acceptable, as justified from an "objective" point of view to which all participants to the agreement must adapt their separate, socially distinct "moralities."[74]

When considering the problem of basic moral disagreements, however, the best model to turn to may not be philosophical ethical theories that treat moral rules as though they were legislated requirements and prohibitions and moral principles as though they were constitutional mandates, even if seen only as procedural mandates. A better model might be the Confucian model, which treats moral rules as precedent or tradition warranted injunctions that often need to be creatively interpreted and reconstructed when traditional warrants come in conflict because of unforseen implications or changing situations. Sometimes consensus on norms governing actions often can not be discovered but needs to be created by those embodying certain social virtues, especially the Taoist and Buddhist virtue of respecting the indescribable uniqueness of particular persons.[75] At other times, that same kind of respect calls for letting socially specific moralities and ways of proceeding simply be different.[76]

As Habermas elaborates on the pragmatic and situational nature of justification, many of his claims about universality and the need to pursue the ideal of consensus begin to lose their absolutistic appearance. He tells us that the requirement for universal consent applies only to those engaged in discursively testing a contested norm[77] and it covers only cases that hold out the prospect of reaching consensus through the giving of reasons.[78] Furthermore, from the criterion of normative validity, the ideal of universal consent, one cannot sit alone in an armchair and deduce or discover any specific norms because only through dialogically produced consensus can new norms be introduced.[79] In addition, for Habermas this procedural criterion determines only what is right (normative requirements and prohibitions) and not what is good (the many different cultural ways of living a good life).[80] Furthermore, Habermas stipulates that he will call something a case of being convinced only if the person adopts the view on the basis of established reasons,[81] that he will call something a communicative interaction only if the participants coordinate their plans of action consensually on the basis of shared reasons,[82] and that he will call something a communicative action (which presupposes the norms of truth, rightness, and truthfulness) only if it is motivated by reasons open to the test of universal consensus.[83] Narrowing the domain of the application of the universal consensus criterion in this manner tightens its inescapability but it leaves unaddressed the examples mentioned in the last paragraph. In the next chapter we will examine the position of Emmanuel Levinas, who contends that there is a form of moral responsibility that is presupposed by all speech, not just argumentative discourse, and that covers all the cases covered by Habermas's criterion and the cases it leaves unaddressed.

Habermas does help us understand how assertions can have undeniable presuppositions. As I pointed out in chapter 1, assertions and claims as the products of speech acts have two different kinds of necessary conditions. On the one hand, there are certain conditions that assertions must satisfy in order to be true. On the other hand, there are certain conditions that obtain in order for the assertion to exist. As I interpret things, I would argue that the existence of language is only one of many necessary, undeniable, inescapable presuppositions of any and all assertions. Other conditions would be the existence of people, the existence of social practices, the dependency of deception upon truthfulness, the reliability of perception and memory. Showing that such a condition is necessary, of course, requires locating it in a general, comprehensive interpretation of the nature of language and assertive speech acts. At best it is contingently necessary. The correctness of claiming that some particular assertion is undeniable is dependent upon the correctness of the interpretation of which it is a part. Because his claims about inescapable presupposition are embedded in his comprehensive interpretation of things, Habermas claims that he is defending a weak form of transcendental argumentation.[84] Furthermore, as we have seen, he is calling for only a very narrow application of his transcendental argument. Habermas is only writing about the presuppositions of communicative speech acts being performed in a mode of argumentation aimed at "convincing" any and all possible participants in this argumentative interaction that a certain contested norm of action is or is not morally binding on all of them. As I would put it, playing the game of offering justifications necessarily involves trying to justify what one has asserted to anyone who has plausible doubts about the matter. This requires using the doubter's reservoir of reasons when justifying oneself to that doubter. In that sense it requires reaching a consensus with such doubters.

In the next chapter, in my examination of Levinas's writings on ethics, I will attempt to show that Habermas's form of transcendental arguments embedded in comprehensive interpretations is stronger than he thinks because language itself, and not just its argumentative use, has ethical presuppositions, presuppositions that take ethics beyond argumentative consensus on universally binding norms and locate it in interpersonal encounters where one is called to responsibility to respect people in the radical otherness of their unique singularity.

Regardless of what one thinks of his comprehensive interpretation of our relation to nature or of his claims about the undeniability of our obligation to seek normative consensus, Habermas's comprehensive critical interpretation of contemporary economic, political, social, and cultural life is extremely rich and suggestive in its own right.[85] In his critical analysis of the way our current economic and political systems are operating, he charges that people have lost democratic control over these vital dimensions of their lives. Furthermore, if people were to become aware of how these systems really are operating, then those systems would lose the legitimation they need in order to continue operating. As Habermas sees it, the central element in the democratic process resides in deliberative procedures that guarantee that political policies represent a public consensus on how to compromise competing interests within an ethical-political understanding of what is the correct and justified way of doing so.[86] Advanced global capitalism and the modern administrative state, together with a culture dominated by consumerism, careerism, vocational privatism, leisurism, moral skepticism, and positivistic instrumental reasoning, however, have greatly diminished any democratic determination of public policy.[87] Here is the source of the legitimation crisis that modern social life faces and that is responsible for the drastic drop in political participation by average citizens.

In analyzing our modern Western social world and the ways people's lives are integrated within it, Habermas distinguishes (1) spheres of private and public practices, which provide the cultural requirements (worldviews, values, ideals, norms) needed to maintain and reproduce this social world, and (2) systems of integrated economic and political effects (often unintended) of efforts to meet the material requirements for maintaining this social form of life. Habermas distinguishes the public sphere, constituted by agreements reached through communicative action (after discussion and debate in forums, assemblies, and arenas), from the private spheres, where differentiations in family, religious, and aesthetic values and lifestyles are sometimes respected but often merely tolerated.[88] This division into public and private spheres occurred at the time of the liberal-bourgeois revolution, when issues of religion and taste were privatized and when agents of the state were limited in their control over the capitalist economic system and private property. The boundaries between the two spheres are porous, however. Deliberation and argumentation often is present as agreements are reached in families, churches, or private clubs, and a public consensus reached through argumentation often produces general educational practices aimed at training children to participate in and accept the results of free and open argumentation, even in the private realm.

The division boundaries in the modern social world between our advanced, global economic system and our nation-state political system (especially its administrative system) is likewise porous. The state administrative apparatus protects, regulates, and supports privately owned businesses, which in turn provide much of the data and many of the personnel needed to run the state apparatus. In a similar manner, as we would expect given Habermas's holistic conception of social worlds, a great deal of interaction takes place between the public and private spheres on the one hand and the economic and political systems on the other. State actions impact on what gets counted as family, what support goes to a family in terms of tax deductions, welfare payments, and social security benefits, how the state involves itself in family life (child abuse, spouse abuse), and state administrative distinctions become internalized norms through the actions of schools and welfare and juridical systems. The private sphere impacts on state systems by having internalized norms like gender and individualism influence welfare policy and structure juridical and administrative law practices and by having discursive practices become institutionalized in state practices (mental health, sexual deviance, criminal delinquency). Public sphere debates help determine political legislation with the state administration providing most of the data for such debates. Also, the citizens voting for political leaders are often also employees of the state (civil service and military personnel) and clients receiving services from the state (male social security clients and female domestic failure clients). Likewise, public sphere debates can modify both consumption and economic practices. The media, in which many of these debates are conducted, are huge, private economic enterprises that have tremendous control over what gets discussed in the mass media. Finally, the private sphere and the economic system continuously influence each other. Employees in the system are also private consumers and consumerism often buys off worker dissatisfaction. Worker treatment influences family life (who cares for children, who has power in the family) and family life impacts on economic activity (the wife/mother and the independent child as the primary consumer decision-makers, the family role of women restricting women to "women's jobs").

Habermas's major criticism of our current Western social world is that democratic control of political policy is threatened because the public sphere is less and less able to determine what our political policies will be. Because democratic control is threatened, the legitimation of our economic and political systems faces crises. Legitimation is effective at all only because the nature and significance of our loss of democratic control is partially hidden from the people.[89] The loss of democratic power is due to economic, political, and cultural changes that have occurred in the past century. As we have already noted, crises in traditional laissez-faire capitalism led to an authorization of state management interventions (bank crises, business cycle crises, worker safety crises, collective bargaining crises, unemployed persons crises). The need for government management of the economy destroyed any mass loyalty to the ideology that the market could all on its own produce a just society. Mass discontent with classical capitalism was only diffused as people came to believe that they now had the power to democratically control through their government the undesirable effects of such capitalism. It is just this belief, Habermas contends, that will disappear if people become informed about what is really happening today in our political and economic systems. The state administrative apparatus has become more and more independent of democratic control as an anonymous civil service becomes increasingly influenced by a bureaucratic mentality aimed at reproducing itself and by a therapeutic presumption that they, as experts in providing social services, know what is best for their citizen clients, and as the administrative apparatus becomes dependent on the economic system for its data and personnel.[90] Furthermore, the rise of huge corporations less susceptible to market factors and the development of a global economy less controllable by the political decisions of any single nation have additionally eroded any democratic political control of the economic system. The public, however, has been effectively prevented from focusing on the significance of these losses in democratic power by the ability of current systems to foster in people mass loyalty to the nation and passive client dependency on experts by getting people instead to focus only on careerism, consumerism, and leisure rather than on participation in determining political policies.[91]

Finally, there has been a massive depletion of the cultural resources available in the sphere of public debate to foster the critical emancipatory analysis and judgment needed to foster a democratic settling of the social norms and goals to be used in reconstructing economic and political systems. Science, technology, industry, and political administration have become interlocked in a circular reinforcing process continually seeking to increase technical control over natural resources and efficient management of human resources.[92] The operational accent on instrumental reason is ideologically reinforced by a rising skepticism about the place of knowledge in determining human goals and by positivism's denial that there is any such knowledge. Political thinking often thinks only strategically about how to get control of governmental power by getting support from a constellation of interest groups, and it does not raise questions about the legitimacy of the actions of these interest groups. [93] Modern law is often seen as either mere commands or as strategic moves in service to interest groups, thus respect for law itself is greatly weakened.[94] The very success of social welfare programs to alleviate suffering caused by laissez-faire capitalism has led to a strengthening of a neoconservative ideology that would cut back political management of the economy and thus would diminish democratic political control of the economic system and its effects.[95] Expectations of governmental services for client-citizens have risen just when global market dynamics make it more and more difficult for governments to manage the economy and provide the services demanded. In order to reduce client expectations and the cost of legitimating the "free market" through government management, neo-conservatives today too successfully preach supply side economics, with its hardly justifiable ideology that all have an equal opportunity to hit the jackpot, and with its accent on the ungovernability of big government, on national patriotism, and on uncritical bourgeois religion (sometimes "modern" and sometimes "evangelical fundamentalism").[96]

Habermas's whole critical theorizing is aimed at showing that one can and should work in the public sphere to get agreement on norms which can be used in publicly critiquing and then democratically reconstructing our political and economic systems. His texts aim to serve this emancipatory interest. It is by changing governmental policies and practices that unjustifiable situations are to be corrected. It is through public argumentation about what is justifiable that people become empowered to give informed and uncoerced consent to the continuation or reformation of existing practices. Just as one need not appropriate everything in Habermas's account of social history and personal development in order to appropriate his account of the social and pragmatic character of comprehensive accounts of human life, so one need not endorse everything in his analysis and critique of the modern Western advanced capitalistic and bureaucratically administered welfare state in order to endorse his effort to present a merely pragmatically warranted indictment of the social world in which we are located. Habermas, by his very effort to be so comprehensive in his explanations of things and in his defense of democratic rule by a free and informed public, serves as an excellent illustration that ultimate justifications in terms of ahistorical and asocial conditions or norms are not needed in order to do social criticism.

III. FOUCAULT'S CHALLENGE FOR LOCAL RESISTANCE TO THE SOCIAL PRACTICES MAKING DOMINATION POSSIBLE

Foucault has written that he laments that during his philosophically formative years immediately following World War II he never had even heard of the work of the Frankfurt school and Habermas, especially on the history of rationality and the critique of the Enlightenment idea of context and interest-free rationality, given the many similarities between their writings.[97] Although the similarities are interesting to note, it is on the differences between Foucault and Habermas that I want to focus because in Foucault we find an even broader and deeper analysis and critique of our social practices, one which will accent even more radically the social and historical character of all rationality. I will focus on three differences. First, the general norm that Foucault uses in doing social and cultural criticism is the minimization of nonconsentuality rather than Habermas's goal of justifiablity through possible rational consensus. Second, Foucault moves beyond focusing on unjustifiable economic and political practices to an analysis of the many disciplinary minisocial practices producing dominated groups of people, minipractices that make economic and political domination and oppression possible. Third, Foucault claims that minimizing nonconsentuality will require something more than just the critique of ideological beliefs and the reformation of governmental policies; it also will require changing the minipractices producing our existing forms of social rationality (our categorization of things, our discourses, our taken for granted beliefs about things, our institutionally established "truths" about things).

As we saw in the last chapter, Foucault only calls for the minimization of nonconsentuality and not for the maximization of consentuality. The former needs no justification and the latter often is not justifiable. Given a pragmatic interpretation of them, justifications need to be offered to someone only when there is a reason for thinking that one is doing something wrong. In the absence of a specific indictment, acting freely needs no justification; infringements on freedom, however, are always open to a demand for justification. Seeking to minimize cases of people being coerced to suffer or do something to which they do not give their consent is seeking to maximize the freedom of people to choose what will happen to them and what they will do. Since justifying oneself requires justifying oneself to those issuing complaints about infringements of their freedom, only in the name of greater freedom (positive and negative) can lesser cases of freedom be restricted. This does create the problem of distributing freedom fairly among all people concerned, given that one must measure both the numbers of people involved and the importance to these people of the options being weighed. Still, reaching a consensus on the measuring formula to be used in weighing these two factors is justifiable only by the need for such a consensus in order to minimize nonconsentuality. If one were not to keep the pursuit of consensus subservient to minimizing nonconsentuality, one might very well end up with the rather narrow range of free choices that everyone could agree on, thus restricting the freedom of those who wish to do unpopular sorts of things even though such actions do not restrict anyone else's freedom of action.[98]

Furthermore, the imperative to minimize nonconsentuality directs us to seek to remove barriers to freedom of which we who are being constrained are not even aware (commonly accepted uses of words, labels, beliefs, and criteria of knowledge, decency, and reasonableness; the sense of self-identity and self-worth that we have been socialized and enculturated to possess; hosts of seemingly innocent everyday practices that we have been trained to participate in as something that one simply does). Seeking to minimize non-consentuality may require empowering people to refuse to be what they are,[99] whereas seeking to maximize consensus may involve leaving people who are their own worst enemies reaching a consensus which increases the problem of coercion rather than maximizing the power of people to resist coercion and to have increased control over what they are and what they can choose to do.

The power existing in the modern world, Foucault claims, differs significantly from earlier forms of power.[100] It is different from the power that owners had over their slaves because such owners simply wanted to appropriate the bodies of their slaves and did not focus their attention on what slaves thought or felt about such ownership. Modern power also is different from the power feudal lords had over their vassals who, out of identification with the manor or out of fear of physical violence or loss of place for one's family in the feudal manor, had to be productive and to participate in the rituals expressing submission to the right of the lord to rule. It is also different from the power employers had over their servants, dominating their wills and getting them to perform their duties out of fear of losing their jobs. The modern exercise of power, on which Foucault focuses his interpretive analysis, is the power present in a system of social practices that result in people being socialized, acculturated, and trained so that they will control themselves, so that they will be law-abiding citizens, productive workers, normal people with healthy, rational and scientific minds, healthy bodies, and normal sexual practices. The modern system for controlling people has the great virtue of minimizing resistance because there is no apparent show of power that would motivate increased resistance. People often are not even aware that they are being controlled, dominated, and oppressed or that others are profiting from a system greatly restricting the possibilities open to them.

In order to understand Foucault's analysis of the systemic relationships of power existing in our world, it is crucial to remember what Marx had taught us, which is that the presence of domination does not depend upon the existence of evil people intentionally dominating and oppressing people. Although there surely are people consciously trying to dominate other people, it is the system that is the basic problem because it would produce its undesirable effects as unintended consequences no matter what were the conscious motivations of those profiting from the system. Foucault is claiming that we end up being controlled, overpowered, dominated, and oppressed because of a system of power relations between people that does not depend upon evil intentions to produce its effects.[101] Since this power that produces subjugated subjects and dominated and oppressed people is distributed throughout this whole system of power relationships between people, it is not a commodity that can be possessed by some king, government, or economic class and thus taken back as one's own possession by overthrowing such supposed holders of power. Government agents and holders of economic power may increase their control of things by taking advantage of such power relationships but merely substituting new agents or merely socializing property will leave the underlying power relationships, and their effects untouched.[102] The power present in this system of power relationships is not just repressive power keeping people from doing things. It is also productive power producing subjects of a certain sort, producing discourses, producing institutionalized sanctioned regimes of supposed truth and knowledge, producing even pleasure.[103] The power that modern governments, capitalists, sexists, and racists exercise over others is dependent upon a system of power relationships that produces what these groups can use but which they cannot possess, although they certainly might try to make it more effectively meet their vested interests.

It is crucial not to misunderstand what Foucault is saying about this system of power relationships and our position within it. He does claim that (1) all people are caught up in this system that produces domination and oppression, (2) our very subjectivity and sense of social identity is heavily influenced by this system, and (3) we cannot seize from some possessor the power present in this system. This does not mean, however, that people are only products of and social functionaries within this system, that they have no agency (no power or ability to act), or that they are fated to hopelessly remain subjected to domination and oppression. Foucault is neither a social determinist nor a fatalist. Yes, there always are power relationships between people. These are relationships, however, between people who as agents are actively engaged in doing things, doing things to other people that result in domination and doing things that consist in resisting such domination.[104]

People are always trying to get other people to do things that people in the first group want people in the second group to do, and people in the second group are always resisting doing what others want them to do when they don't feel like doing it. People are always doing things by habit or choice, which has the unintended effect of getting caught in situations in which they are required to do something, out of fear of consequences or out of a guilty conscience, things that limit their own options while increasing the freedom of action of members of some group benefiting from this requirement. These same people are also always acting so as to resist such requirements, often at the price of living with a warring conscience.

Power relationships between agents are not always and are not only relationships in which someone ends up being dominated. Power relationships become relationships of domination only when a rather stable, persistent, asymmetrical relationship of power exists.[105] When John usually gets Sally to do what John wants, and Sally seldom gets John to do what she wants, then John is dominating Sally. When the power relationships between John and Sally are continuously reversible, then no domination is present although people are still getting each other to do things. When a system of social practices exists which is usually getting me to do things that restrict my freedom of action and which is usually benefiting someone else, then I am being dominated in that social world. When people live within a system of social practices in which people get each other to do things, but these people have significant power to constitute and modify those practices, then domination is not present. Relationships of power are not always relationships of dominating power.

Neither are power relationships producing domination only domination relationships. Whenever we end up being dominated, either by the intentional acts of others or because of the unintended effects of the social practices in which we are involved, we always resist. We always seek to minimize the effectiveness of these actions and practices to limit our freedom.[106] Slaves became masters of the art of obeying orders in their own way so as to preserve some sense of dignity for themselves. Servants become very skillful at getting around the excessive demands of their employers. People in the modern world learn tactics for maneuvering themselves through their everyday world of rules and regulations without giving in completely. Our subjectivity is never so subjugated that we become deaf to what is still being said in opposition to "official" discourse, no matter how much these opposition voices are marginalized by being labeled "irrational," "ignorant," "old fashioned," "insane," "sick," "degenerate," or "evil." If there were no such marginalized voices still around, and if no one were able to hear them, there would be no need for the system of practices producing domination. The presence of resistance shows that agency never dies off, that people are never turned into mere robots, that it is people, resisting people, who are dominated, and not that they are mere robots or computers being programmed. The presence of marginalized, subjugated practices and discourses shows that hope for increasing the freedom of dominated people is not illusory.

It would be well to recall here Kierkegaard's claim that it is always difficult to preserve realism without falling into determinism and fatalism, to preserve hope without deluding oneself with rose-colored romantic wishes for the impossible.[107] Foucault attempts to show that resisting domination may be much more difficult than Kierkegaard ever imagined, but that there is still space for hope. In order to understand Foucault's interpretive analysis of the problem of domination and to appreciate the strategic and tactical challenge that it presents to resistance freedom fighters, it is necessary to see how he critically analyzes both the system of minipractices producing domination and the manner in which these local practices are globally colonized by the state, business owners and managers, racists, sexist men, and homophobic men and women. In developing his analysis of dominating power relationships, Foucault builds upon the work of Nietzsche and Marx.

Foucault calls himself a Nietzschean[108] and four major aspects of his program seem to find their origin in Nietzsche's writings. Previously we saw how Foucault used Nietzsche in constructing an ethic calling for people to create in themselves living works of art. Also, Foucault's accent on asymmetrical power relationships can be interpreted as an elaboration of Nietzsche's talk about the "Will to Power," about power being the law of gravity in human relationships. Similarly, he expands Nietzsche's warning about the dangers present in a social-cultural system that is an expression of a "Will to Truth" by writing about the dangers present as our world suffers under a "Will to Knowledge." Finally, he further develops Nietzsche's use of genealogical analysis as an intellectual tool to be used in resisting domination, in enabling people to refuse to be what they are, enabling them to recognize that what is presented as necessary is really open for reconstruction. Let's postpone examining genealogical analysis as a weapon available to resistance movements and first examine how a "Will to Knowledge" can strengthen dominating power relationships.

At first it seems irrational, or at least paradoxical, to claim that a will to know can produce domination. Isn't all education about trying to come to know the truth? Haven't we been taught again and again that we should seek the truth because the truth will set us free (from superstition, from preventable disasters). Haven't we been taught that knowledge is power and that it will give us the power and positive freedom to create good and meaningful lives, the power to use technology to do things we otherwise would be unable to do? Foucault, of course, is not denying that we should seek to find those beliefs that we are willing to claim are true when others challenge them and which we are willing and able to justify as knowledge by showing that there are no reasons good enough to doubt them.[109] What he is warning about are practices that are trying to do more than this. He warns us about the all too common practice of presenting certain claims as THE TRUTH that everyone should be brought to believe and never to question, claims that social groups and governments can use to legitimate other social practices that create dominated and oppressed people.[110] Foucault wants us to critique all REGIMES OF TRUTH, all EPISTEMES, and all KNOWLEDGE DISCOURSES, not in order to produce universal skeptics who believe nothing (an impossibility), but in order to empower people to question what is often presented and accepted as being "known beyond all question." Critique religious and political discourse and regimes, if their claims are treated as sacrosanct. Critique dogmatic discourses and epistemes pretending to be science but refusing to recognize the pragmatic, fallible, and self-critical character of all scientific descriptions and explanations. Foucault's critique of the will to knowledge is twofold. First, he points out that dominating relationships of power cannot be "established, consolidated, nor implemented without the production, accumulation, circulation and functioning" of certain sorts of discourses and regimes of truth. Second, he claims that in the case of human beings, certain sorts of discourses and epistemes can exist only because people are subjected to dominating power relationships.[111] Dominating power and the promulgation of this sort of supposed knowledge reinforce each other.

Foucault is concerned particularly about the inflated claims made by dogmatists in the human sciences who refuse to admit the pragmatic, rhetorical, and interpretive character of our understanding of human beings. He presents critiques of the knowledge claims of the so-called experts in the fields of language, economics, medicine, psychiatry, psychology, criminology, and social welfare.[112] These are the knowledge claims that masses of people are trained to accept as unquestionable truths, a training and acceptance that produces dominated and oppressed people, especially when this training is used by the state and those profiting from our economic system. In order to see the feedback character of dominating power and institutionally sanctioned knowledge claims, one needs to appreciate how discursive practices and knowledge training are dependent upon nondiscursive practices that produce domination. Foucault describes these disciplinary practices that produce dominated people and that turn them into individual objects which can become thereby the objects of study in various human sciences.[113]

First, modeled after modern army life, people in factories, schools, and hospitals are trained to be organized so there will be a proper place at which each of them is to be located at each assigned time of the day, week, and year so that they will move through bodily movements and assigned activities in the most efficient way possible.

Second, the movements and activities of people will be observed by their supervisors. Are they absent or late? Do they take unauthorized breaks? Does their activity show inattention, lack of zeal, negligence?

Third, these observations will be examinations. Are they doing what they should be doing? Do they have the appropriate beliefs and know-how? Have they been properly normalized?

Fourth, in the case of nonconformity there will be applied either micropenalties such as petty humiliation, coldness, indifference, or, in case these little penalties fail, the nonconformists will be fired, expelled, or denied medical treatment.

Fifth, the expectation will be created that one always is being gazed at and that one always might be caught and punished.

Sixth, giving each person a proper place to be at an appropriate time and giving each person proper things to do, and then observing and testing each person's behavior, allows individual files to be created on each person, files that often remain with that person for life, files that allow people to be turned into individual cases that can become the objects of study by the human sciences.

The human sciences can exist only if the freedom of agents is sufficiently restricted by dominating practices so that they can be turned into objects that can be "objectively" studied. The human sciences are sciences of individuals and they can exist only because statistical data can be gathered on such individuals: birth and death certificates, school records, employment and job performance records, medical and psychological case studies, military records, tax records, criminal records. Dominating power is a necessary condition for the production of "knowledge" in the human sciences.[114]

The supposed knowledge of human individuals gathered in the human sciences often becomes institutionally established regimes of truth and discourses of knowledge, which serve to strengthen a system of dominating power relationships. They make possible the classification of people individually and in mass. The standards of truth and knowledge used in the human sciences, hiding the dominating power creating their objects, are presented as though they are as objective as those present in the natural sciences, even though rocks and atoms don't resist but people do. They are used to separate who is rational from who is irrational. The science of linguistics supposedly tells us when we are speaking meaningfully and when we are talking nonsense. Economics supposedly tells us who is a useful, productive worker and who is lazy, a bum, a vagabond. Medicine supposedly tells us who is healthy and who is sick, who is able-bodied, disabled, or no longer able-bodied. Psychology and psychiatry supposedly tell us who is normal, abnormal, mature, immature, healthy minded, perverse, deviant, insane, and responsible for their actions. Criminology supposedly tells us who is a criminal, a delinquent, law abiding, and dangerous.

Having helped divide the normal from the abnormal, the successfully normalized from the failures in the disciplinary training program, the human sciences also purport to tell us what to do with the abnormal, how to marginalize or exclude them so as not to disrupt the whole system of normalizing people to be docile and useful workers and citizens.[115] The human sciences tell us how to exclude the failures temporarily while they are being treated, reformed, or retrained, and how to exclude the incurable "failures" permanently by condemning them to physical death through capital punishment or to permanent living death as prisoners, inmates in mental hospitals, supervised dependents in a state welfare system, or as crazy poets, philosophers, or mystics condemned to wander around the outer margins of normal life.

We have only told half the paradoxical story about our search for truth and knowledge, Foucault claims, when we have pointed out how dominating power and institutional validation of truth and knowledge claims reinforce each other. The second half of the story concerns the resistance power that is present in pointing out the threatening relations holding between dominating power relationships and discursive and knowledge validating practices in the human sciences. Resistance power is gained by coming to recognize that these relationships and practices are not necessary. The genealogical studies Foucault carries out are done as part of his practice of freedom, are done in service to people seeking to resist domination.[116] They are aimed at showing how the present, with all its supposed normalities and necessities, need not be the way it is.[117] Foucault recommends that we approach institutionally validated discourses and epistemes (acceptable vocabularies, beliefs, values, standards of meaningfulness and correctness) not as a polemicist seeking to disprove such beliefs but as a Nietzschean social physician diagnosing a social system by interpreting such discourse as symptoms of a system of power relationships producing subjugated discourses and subjects, subjects who are (but need not be) implicated in their own subjugation as they uncritically participate in the practices they have been trained to follow.[118]

Foucault attempts to show what had to be excluded and marginalized in order for the present to be as it is. He attempts to use the remnants of the marginalized as a means for resisting the current system of practices producing domination. That his genealogy of the present is possible shows that normalization has not been totalized and that subjugated discourses can be tools for resistance. Foucault admits that, in doing genealogical interpreting, recovering, and participating in subjugated and marginalized discourses, there is real danger that these discourses, once brought to light, also might be co-opted and subjugated once again. That something is dangerous, however, is no reason for not doing it, especially when all other options also are filled with danger; it is only a reason for doing it cautiously.

Practicing freedom, as Nietzsche taught Foucault, is always filled with danger.[119]

It is as a participant in the discourse of Marx who does not ever quote Marx[120] that Foucault helps us understand why we must not ignore global political, economic, and social-cultural forms of domination even though these global forms depend upon an interwoven network of localized minipractices, a microphysics of power. These practices are something on which Marx did not focus his critical eye but which Foucault in the spirit of Marx adds to Marxist discourse. Foucault does not let us forget that there still exists the domination and oppression produced by the colonization of these minipractices by the state, the managers of economic institutions, and the heads of patriarchal families.[121] These are the colonizers who operate on the unquestioned conviction that it is possible and desirable to have a totalization of a normalization that produces docile and useful citizens and bodies,[122] the human versions of robots, and which excludes from society as abnormal the cases when normalizing training fails.

Foucault reminds us that it is very useful for the holder of global forms of dominating power to get most people to focus on individual criminals and delinquents and not on the injustice and inhumanity of a system making such dominating power possible. Street crime is not a threat to the system. It usually is a matter of the poor attacking the poor. Besides, fighting wars on crime is big business. It is useful for those profiting from dominating relationships to have people focus on mentally ill patients and not on the madness and insanity of current practices dehumanizing people. It is useful for them to have people focus on sexual perverts and thus not see the perverse pleasures of domination, the pleasure gained by gazing at other people's pleasures and pains, other people's confessions of their "abnormal" behavior.[123]

In opposition to the ideal of totalization of normalization, Foucault offers the critical norm of minimization of nonconsentuality. He emphasizes the extent to which domination and oppression in the contemporary world depend upon a subjugating of subjectivity that is derived from a sense of propriety instilled in people by regimes of supposed truth and knowledge. Since such regimes focus on individuals created by disciplinary practices, Foucault instead focuses on the singularity of persons, a singularity that is other than being merely a socially constituted individual, and he calls for minimizing the restrictions on their power, restrictions produced by practices producing dominating power.

In opposition to Marx, Foucault charges that social and cultural practices do not produce domination primarily through ideological indoctrination of beliefs but rather through discursive and other disciplinary practices that produce subjugated subjects.[124] Ideology, he claims, is a latecomer on the field of power battles. Before there is the dominating power of ideological beliefs there is the dominating power of discourse and discipline, the organization of man's space, time, and movements, the production of vocabularies, criteria of rationality and truth, and socially constituted subjects. That is why merely entering into polemics with colonizers' ideologies is not enough to resist domination. Polemics is not sufficient and it can exacerbate the problem. Any new global story one offers as a replacement for a "false" ideology very probably will be co-opted and used to support further domination by the global colonizers because the microphysics of power that supports such colonizers has been left intact. It is the microphysics of dominating power itself that must be resisted.

Disciplinary practice must be sabotaged and local resistance movements must be organized. Genealogical studies of the present can show that what currently seems necessary really is not necessary at all. Echoing Heidegger, Foucault points out that once current practices didn't exist, and when they were being established there were live alternatives that were then pushed aside but which can be appropriated and reconstructed today. Social cultural critics must be symptomologists and teachers empowering people to enlarge the space of the possible in their lives. The uncritical acceptance of the human sciences must be challenged. Subjugated discourses must be demarginalized. New discourses must be founded. People must live poetically in the world. New nondominating power relationships must be built up. What is required, Foucault claims, is patient labor and the impatience of freedom.[125]

In addition to his criticism of the overreliance by many Marxists on the effectiveness of ideological criticism, Foucault has a second but related criticism to make of traditional Marxism. He is opposed to all grand schemes aimed at the total liberation of people from domination and oppression. He charges that domination and oppression are problems that will never be erased totally from human life. One cannot gain liberation from them in the way that Europe gained liberation from the armies of Nazi Germany. One can only do what the French did during the German occupation, join in resistance movements aimed at minimizing current nonconsentuality. These resistance movements in the first instance will have to be local, although at times they can be coordinated, even on a global scale, as is now occurring with the women's movement and the environmental movement. Global liberation movements, like global efforts to replace current ideologies, most likely will be co-opted by the current colonizers of the currently operating microphysics of power. Increased freedom can be gained only by the patient labor of practicing freedom while remaining impatient with current unnecessary restrictions on freedom.

Foucault sets forth seven principles for patiently practicing freedom.

(1) Free political action from paranoia that seeks to unify and totalize.

(2) Proliferate actions, thoughts, and desires rather than organizing them in a hierarchy.

(3) Prefer the positive, multiple, different, and changing rather than the prohibiting, unifying, and solidifying.

(4) Militantly fight abnormalization by recognizing, along with Zizek and Levinas, that enjoyment and desire are the real that must not be covered over by representations.

(5) Don't use thought to ground political practice or use political practice to discredit lines of thinking, but use political practice to intensify thinking and use analytical, genealogical thinking to multiply the social domains and practices where political action can introduce resistance.

(6) Move from accenting the "rights" of socially constituted individuals to accenting practices that will deindividualize such socialized persona by multiplying and diversifying the social masks that people wear.

(7) Do not fall in love with overpowering other people.[126]

As a Nietzschean genealogist and quasi-Marxist freedom fighter, Foucault interprets his project as part of the modern, Western enlightenment project.[127] He insists that he is not part of any program endorsing epistemological or ethical relativism or irrationalism. He is opposed to the current institutionalized division between the rational and the irrational, but he still wants to make statements that he can claim are true when they are challenged by others and he wants to be able to challenge other beliefs by declaring them to be false. He persistently tries to justify his beliefs when there are reasons for doubting them, just as he also tries to show that other beliefs are unjustifiable. He does not endorse modern forms of a metaphysical, epistemological, and ethical humanism that postulate that there exist, in some nonhistorical, nonsocial, and nonpragmatic realm, things called meanings, norms, values, or an essence for human beings. He does, however, want to be classified as a modernist. For Foucault, modernism is about being ruthlessly critical about everything in the present, especially about being critical of oneself, in order to minimize coercion and maximize one's ability to be a creator of oneself as the beautiful work of art that Kierkegaard and Nietzsche called us to be. It is in his ethic, which I commented on earlier, that Foucault spells out what is involved in being a self-reconstructor in the space opened up by one's efforts as a resistance freedom fighter.

IV. AMERICAN INTELLECTUAL FREEDOM FIGHTERS

Foucault always interpreted his intellectual work as an integral part of his life as a resistance freedom fighter. It was not only, however, by having his writings show that things don't have to be as they are, and thus that domination does not have to be tolerated, that Foucault practiced resistance. Throughout his life, in addition to his writings, Foucault was actively involved in efforts to empower prisoners, incarcerated mental patients, university students, workers in Poland resisting their communist government, and homosexuals.[128] Foucault's efforts to deconstruct and reconstruct social practices through the use of intellectual and other tactics and strategies have been continued by many other critics who have appropriated his texts and his activities. In this section I will introduce only a few Americans who have been influenced by his discourse and example in their resistance to sexism, racism, and intellectual pretentiousness. Since all of these critics and freedom fighters reject the possibility or necessity of ahistorical or asocial critical norms, examining their texts and actions can supply an appropriate exit from this investigation of social rationality's critical power.

A. ALVIN GOULDNER

Foucault repeatedly expressed concern that social scientists generally lacked awareness of the dominating power being used to constitute their objects of study and of the unintended effects of their practices in reinforcing such domination and its legitimation. This concern also was at the center of the texts written by the American social critic Alvin Gouldner. Not only social scientists but the whole modern class of intellectuals, Gouldner charges, whether they be economic or political bureaucrats, members of the technical intelligentsia, sociologists, or critical social critics and revolutionaries, have class interests that are often allied with the interests of other classes, interests that these intellectuals usually do not acknowledge but which influence their ideas and practices and that contribute to domination and oppression. Gouldner claims that critical rationality, with all of its language and norms, can be understood only when it is historically located within a developing culture of critical rationality (CCR).[129] Writing as a historian, sociologist, and social theorist and critic, he presents a genealogical account of the origin in the modern world of a diverse class of intellectuals unified by their mutual sharing of the culture of critical rationality.[130] He also constructs a detailed historical analysis of the development of Marxism and critical theory, with their critiques of capitalist ideology and their blindness to their own ideology and to the interests of the rising class of intellectuals that they serve.[131] Although sharing with Foucault the conviction that ideologies gain their power from the environment of minipractices in which they are historically located, Gouldner more than Foucault focuses his attention upon the modern ideologies that have been used to build functional coalitions among different interest groups. He does so because he believes that critical theorists and critics, as intellectuals, can engage in significant resistance to domination by critiquing such ideologies, a resistance that would be strengthened if intellectuals were aware of their own ideology and their own class interests validated by that ideology.[132]

Gouldner's general narrative of the formation of Western intellectuals into a class of their own is a thread within an overall story of the historical appearance of a bourgeois capitalist social and cultural world.[133] Similar to economic entrepreneurs who wanted freedom from control by the throne and the landed aristocracy, so intellectuals wanted freedom from the censorship of tradition and Church. Both groups seized upon a grammar of rationality, which rejected sacred authority or coerced beliefs. Reasons justifiable to all participants in a discussion must be given to warrant a conclusion. Gouldner demonstrates that the rise of the intellectuals as a class, with a common interest in ownership of cultural capital, is intimately tied to six other trends: (1) the rapid growth of mass means of communication (books and newspapers) and the creation of a reading public; (2) the utilization in the mass media of vernacular languages rather than the elitist languages of the clerics; (3) the end in the arts of the patronage system; (4) the rise of an anonymous and highly competitive market for the printed word; (5) the competitive demand for intellectuals by the nations of Europe, which produced easy immigration for them and the rise of cosmopolitanism; and finally (6) the development of public schools that kept supplying the increasing number of intellectuals needed in this modern world.[134]

What began as a common effort between economic entrepreneurs and intellectuals to break free from royal and clerical control developed eventually into a series of conflicting and competing classes. As the new bourgeois holders of economic power themselves took over political power from the old aristocracy, they attempted to secure their status by seeking to buy off intellectuals and to gain hegemonic control over intellectuals, the mass media, the schools, and the general public. The liberal demand at the political level for freedom from traditional authority became incorporated into ideologies specifying natural property rights, free contracts freely arrived at, the unquestioned merit of increasing gross national wealth, the sacredness of national identities, and the appropriateness of using African slave labor to enhance economic growth and capital accumulation. In spite of the success that the holders of bourgeois economic power have had in remaining in power, tension always has existed between these economic powers and the various factions within the new class of intellectuals.

The owners of economic capital need the scientific and managerial technical intelligentsia, the economic and political bureaucrats trained to effectively achieve the goals set by the owners, and they need the creators of cultural capital who can provide the ideological materials needed to exercise hegemonic control. All these intellectuals resist having beliefs and actions violently forced upon them; that is why effective hegemonic specification of desired goals is the only mechanism open to the bourgeois holders of economic and political power. Bureaucrats have to be bought off with the security of routines and employment (even if bureaucratic red tape proves economically counterproductive) and with a culture of consumerism (which does aid in producing an expanding market). The technical intelligentsia have to be bought off by giving them the professionalism they desire and the ability (to some extent) to continue working on the intellectual and technical puzzles that so captivate them. Some humanistic intellectuals also were turned into technical puzzle addicts while others were rendered relatively harmless by the holders of economic and political power through their ability to control the media and schools through which intellectuals can communicate and reproduce their ideas.[135] In his historical analysis of Marx and Marxism, Gouldner points out how Marx's inability to secure a university teaching position and his inability to succeed economically as a journalist led to his alienation from the whole bourgeois world. In Eastern Europe, where an economically bourgeois and politically liberal revolution never had taken place, the rising class of intellectuals saw in socialism a chance for themselves to directly realize their potential as the proper class to control not only culture but also economic and political power.[136]

Gouldner sees the new class of intellectuals as a potentially significant force for resisting domination, even though it is a flawed class. It is significant because of its culture of critical rationality and it is flawed not only because it contains intellectuals who have been bought off by security, consumerism, and protected enclaves of professional autonomy, but, more important because it conceals from itself its own class interests and their impact on how the culture of critical rationality is utilized by them. Gouldner finds Galbraith's treatment of the new class, as benign and trustworthy,[137] as ignoring the specific class interests of the new class itself. He finds that Bakunin's excessive fear that the new class will become one more elite master class[138] is grounded in a failure to appreciate the way that the power of the new class is limited by the holders of economic, political, and bureaucratic power and by Bakunin's failure to appreciate the positive potential for this class to resist unjust uses of such power. This failure to appreciate the conflicts that exist between the interests of intellectuals and these other classes (with the ruling economic class seeking hegemony control while the intellectual class sought autonomy and equality) is the basis of Gouldner's criticism of Talcott Parsons' dream of the new class serving to uplift the old ruling class and turn it into a genteel elite[139] and of Noam Chomsky's fear that the new class is nothing but a tool of the old ruling class.[140] For Gouldner, the flaws in the new class must not be covered over but neither should we fail to appreciate the potential for resistance that is present in its perennial conflicts with the ruling powers.

In order for intellectuals to function as resistance freedom fighters it is necessary for them to remain continuously engaged in critical self-reflection without permitting this to immobilize them. Because it is so easy for their own class interests as intellectuals to stand in conflict with the project of resisting domination and oppression in all its forms, self-analysis always is necessary even though it is never sufficient because it is no substitute for action. It can enable critically minded intellectuals to transcend, from time to time, their own class interests. Drawing upon their common culture of critical rationality, it can enable critical theorists and some of the technical intelligentsia to unite, from time to time, in resistance efforts.

Gouldner specifies a number of actions that intellectuals as intellectuals can take in their resistance practice of freedom. Since those benefiting from current asymmetrical power relationships want to reinforce those relationships by maintaining cultural hegemony so as to legitimate the present system and to diffuse efforts to change those relationships, intellectuals must engage in counterhegemonic activities. Reveal the oppression and domination. Show the contradictions in the ruling ideology. Don't allow those benefiting from these asymmetrical power relationships to define social reality or exclude the news hostile to their hegemonic control, an exclusion practice needed to make what is present seem good, normal, natural, necessary, and inevitable.[141]

A whole body of American social theorists has been trying to follow Gouldner's advice. For example, Paul Bove in his books[142] and his editorship of the journal *boundary 2* has continuously focused attention on the unjust power relationships reinforced through literature presupposing the ideology of modern humanism. Edward Said in his writings has focused on the manner in which entrenched power has attempted unjustly to define social reality and diffuse the critical power of intellectuals.[143] Perhaps some of the most promising work by American intellectuals engaged in resistance freedom fighting is to be found in the writings of American feminists and African-American critical theorists.

B.   IRIS MARION YOUNG

An excellent example of feminists who are appropriating Foucault's work in their resistance to domination and oppression is the work of Iris Marion Young.[144] Young strengthens Foucault's position by providing many amplifications and much reflective support for his call to minimize domination and oppression. She also uses Foucault's analyses of recent practices of punishment and sexuality to support her policy recommendations for public approaches to pregnant drug addicts and family identities. Rejecting the notion that someone (a philosopher) can sit in an armchair and discover through pure reflection a universal, universally justifiable, impartial norm of justice, Young claims that moral norms are social constructs arrived at by free and open dialogue among those to be governed by the norms.[145] Finding fault with general principles of justice, which supposedly specify how one should distribute benefits and burdens, Young develops the Foucaultian notion that justice requires one to reject all forms of domination and oppression, forms that can be identified only by looking in detail at the practices present in each different social and historical locality. Projects based on the assumption that the problem of justice is simply a distribution problem are doomed both to fail and be counterproductive.

Why do efforts to work with an abstract, supposedly neutral distribution principle fail to produce justice? Young charges that this failure is due to three factors: (1) It is impossible to distribute rights because these specify relationships within institutional settings (employers-workers, parents-children, husbands-wives, police-citizens), and such relationships cannot be distributed equally to all persons. (2) It is impossible to distribute self-respect because self-respect is a function of attitudes towards oneself, one's situation, and one's prospects, *and* it is a function of cultural and social practices producing advantaged and disadvantaged people. (3) It is impossible to distribute power because it is not a material people do or do not possess, but it is an interpersonal relationship between people, especially between people in groups who are oppressed and dominated and people in other groups who benefit from these power relationships.[146]

Why is the effort to seek justice through the search for and application of supposedly impartial principles of distribution counter-productive? Why does it actually contribute to injustice? Young gives two answers. First, by seeking to merely redistribute benefits and burdens within the existing social and cultural practices and relations, we tend to see such practices and relations as natural and inevitable, thereby reinforcing them, when in fact they may be unjust because they produce oppressed and dominated groups of people, with people in other groups benefiting from this oppression and domination. Second, by viewing power as a distributable possession, we fail to attend to the structural relationships producing oppression and domination independent of the intentions of the people in the groups involved *and* we fail to see the widely dispersed microphysics of power that produces victims who too often are unintentionally complicit in their own oppression and domination.[147]

Young offers an alternative understanding of justice. Justice is the absence of oppression and domination. Although individuals might be engaged in oppressing and dominating other individuals, freedom fighters need to focus on groups being oppressed and dominated and other groups benefiting from such oppression and domination because it is there that one finds the major locations of injustice in the world. What is a group? Groups, Young informs us, are not merely aggregates of people (like the people in Times Square on New Year's Eve) or associations of people (such as churches or clubs constructed by contractual agreements among their members). Groups are what give us our social identities. We often identify ourselves in terms of how others group us (woman, Jew, gay, black). We are members of a number of changing and sometimes conflicting groups (women, black, poor, Christian, student) and thus we have multiple group identities and no fixed, unified social self. That idea that we are autonomous, self-made, unified persons prior to our involvement in the social practices that locate us in groups is a myth.[148] People are oppressed and dominated[149] because of the practices that locate them in social groups while other people benefit from such victimization because those same practices locate them in other profiting groups. This becomes very evident once we examine the nature and varieties of oppression and domination.

Young, like Foucault, characterizes domination in terms of people acting upon people. When one is dominated, one is prevented from determining one's actions and the conditions that need to be satisfied in order to act. When dominated, self-determination is constrained. Oppression occurs when self-development is constrained, when the ability of people to develop and exercise their capabilities and express their needs, feelings, and thoughts is inhibited by the actions of others and by the social practices that exist. Social injustice occurs when there exist institutional constraints on self-determination and self-development. Young adds great specificity to Foucault's talk about minimizing nonconsentuality by distinguishing five different varieties of oppression.

(1) Exploitation occurs when the beneficial results of the labor of people in one group are transferred without appropriate compensation to people in another group. The exploitation can be economic (when workers lose material benefits, control over their laboring activities, and self-respect) or patriarchal (when

men get freedom and power and women give care and sexual benefits while receiving little back) or racial (when people of color overwhelmingly end up as servants or doing auxiliary work while receiving little or no recognition).

(2) Marginalization occurs when people in certain classes are expelled from useful participation, denied freedom, made to feel useless, bored, and devoid of self respect.[150]

(3) Powerlessness occurs when people in certain groups never give order to others but always end up having to take orders.

(4) Cultural imperialism occurs when the dominant meanings in a society render the particular perspectives of people in certain groups invisible while at the same time stereotyping people in that group and marking them as other than normal (crazies, weirdos, irrationals, sickies).

(5) Violent oppression occurs when individuals in a certain group are subjected to systematic violent treatment because they are members of that group. The unconscious motive for such violence often is the fact that the violent person's own identity is threatened by the mere existence of the other group, given that the violent person's own identity (as white, male, heterosexual) is socially constituted as being other than the group being despised.[151]

Young, like many other feminists and African-American appropriators of Foucault's work, focuses on cultural imperialism as the source of injustice in America that intellectual critics can most successfully attack. Overt and conscious forms of tyrannical racial and sexist domination and oppression have to a large extent been ended and replaced by forms of cultural imperialism tied to the social marking of people by placing them in groups on the basis of bodily features (black, female, old, disabled, fat) and then dealing with them as irrevocably degenerate and not respectable. Xenophobia is present, finding the bodies of members of some groups as ugly, horrifying, disgusting, and loathing. Unconscious patterns of aversion behavior are present, but, in the current climate of acceptable discourse, victims and critics of cultural imperialism are not even allowed to say what they are sensing or observing without being charged with either over-reacting or reverse discrimination.[152]

As an integral part of these practices of cultural imperialism is an ideology of assimilation and formal equality that attempts to legitimate the marginalization of resistance practices and discourse. The United States today, Young charges, is operating under ideals of assimilation and formal equality that are perversions of earlier liberal ideals of liberating people from domination and oppression, perverse ideals that are neither workable nor desirable. Moving to formal principles of equality, where everyone supposedly is treated equally regardless of group locations, does not work because it does not eliminate existing groups or group oppression and domination. Seeking assimilation is undesirable because doing so results in members of certain groups being disadvantaged. Ignoring group differences ignores the reality of current social practices and their effects, and it perpetuates and exacerbates oppressive inequalities. Acting in terms of an ideal of universal humanity blinds beneficiaries of current practices to their own group specificity, and this perpetuates cultural imperialism. For example, the major problem with seeking to provide equal economic opportunity to women and blacks is not the presence of discrimination, the absence of formal nondiscrimination, but the oppressive presence of the myth that group neutral merit criteria can be used to measure job performance or predict the likelihood of excellence in job performance. None of the four necessary conditions for a just merit system, however, currently exist. Such a system would need: (1) culturally neutral qualifications specifiable in terms of skills and competencies needed to achieve specified tasks; (2) specifiable skills and competencies that would be indicators of excellence of performance; (3) the actual judging of the competencies and perfor-mances of individual persons; (4) the availability of measures for ranking predicted and actual performance that would be independent of and neutral with respect to culturally variable values.

For most jobs in the modern economy, Young charges, none of these conditions needed for justice can be satisfied. Jobs are too complex and multifaceted to be able to both precisely identify tasks or measure level of performance of tasks. It is impossible to specify each worker's contribution to huge team efforts, the primary mode of modern labor. Many workers do not produce directly but exercise discretion as they supervise or prevent something from going wrong, and we can't predict what will go wrong or what skills are needed to prevent or repair damage. Writers of job descriptions and most evaluators of job performance often have never done the jobs themselves and don't know what is involved, with the result being that evaluations usually are of worker attitudes and comportment, evaluations that are culturally specific. Experts admit that there are no value neutral criteria for measuring leadership, initiative, cooperation, judgment, creativity, and dependability. What usually gets evaluated is conformity, the smooth reproduction of established, culturally specific ways of doing things. Furthermore, it is sheer mythology to contend that educational performance and standardized tests are both culturally neutral and effective predictors of job success. Current educational practices do not equalize, but they reproduce inequalities when they ignore significant group differences, often ending up in blaming students and parents for lack of success. Besides, there is little correlation between education success and occupational success because current schools primarily teach cultural values and social norms and not technical skills. There is little evidence that standardized test success correlates with job success. Tests themselves are a culturally specific phenomena that accent working alone and being competitive.[153] Therefore, Young calls for the democratization of all practices specifying criteria for evaluating competencies and performances by making explicit and public the values being pursued, by choosing criteria that do not exclude any group but rather lessen oppression and domination, and by letting workers, peers, clients, customers, and representatives of oppressed groups choose the criteria.[154]

As part of her project of resisting social practices, including discursive practices, which support cultural imperialism, Young advocates celebrating the positive values of group differences because these are liberating and empowering. This would recognize the social and cultural specific character of values so that the culture of the beneficiaries of current power relationships would no longer be taken as universal, natural, and inevitable. Also, it would promote group solidarity because it would no longer be necessary to abandon one's own group in order to make it in the dominant culture of the current beneficiaries of oppressive power relationships. It would allow people to say "I am black," "I am gay," "I am physically challenged," "I am old," "I am dependent," and be proud of it. At the political level Young presents a whole series of specific actions that groups in the United States might take to fight against injustice beyond simply participating in the current system of two-party politics.[155]

C.   BELL HOOKS

The attack on cultural imperialism and other forms of oppression leveled by Young, a white feminist, parallels a similar attack by bell hooks, a black feminist. Hooks claims that, in her attempts to resist the cultural imperialism producing racism, sexism, and oppressed economic classes, she has become increasingly appreciative of Foucault's critique of social and cultural practices producing dominating power relationships.[156] Rejecting all attempts to seek asocial and ahistorical norms because of their strengthening of dominant and oppressive social practices, hooks presents case illustration after case illustration of the possibility and necessity of being a historically and socially situated resistance freedom fighter.[157] She attacks the practice of attempting to elevate some socially situated beliefs into absolute truths and she seeks instead to restore for consideration certain forms of subjugated knowledge. In support of such restoration projects, she calls for doing a Foucaultian genealogy of black art.[158]

Again and again, hooks reaffirms the holistic character of social and cultural practices by insisting that one can neither understand nor resist one form of oppression when one isolates it from other forms of oppression. Phallocentric and homophobic sexism, racism, and classism are all interconnected and all must be resisted by all freedom fighters, even though such fighters might focus for tactical reasons on just one of these forms at a time.[159] She shows how white men's sexual abuse of slave women served their interests in strengthening their dominating power more than their interests in sex.[160] She charges that the project of white women seeking equality usually meant to such women equality with upper-class or middle-class white men and not equality with black nurse's aids or single mothers on welfare. Racist and class oppression remained unaddressed in their pursuit of economic and social empowerment.[161] In their very restricted pursuit of "equality," white women remain nauseated by having their white male movie heros having sex with black women.[162] White feminists often became antifamily, seeing families as restricting their freedom. This blinds them to the fact that black women often see their families as the least oppressive institution in the current world.[163] Focusing primarily on improving their position in the current class system, many white women ignore the feminization of poverty occurring in the United States.[164] Our white supremacist, capitalist, patriarchal, homophobic society, hooks charges, prevents the development of an educational program that will produce in students a critical consciousness of the interconnected forms of domination and oppression existing in this country.[165] Attempts to produce racial assimilation, legitimating it with the liberal rhetorical valorization of individualism and formal equality, subvert the development of the critical black consciousness needed to resist this entire holistic nest of oppressive practices.[166] Economically successful black men get sucked into raging against poor black people.[167] Black men in all economic classes succumb to the homophobia so common across racial lines in this country.

Hooks calls for freedom fighters to resist domination and oppression in whatever form it shows its face. The attack must be total even though the tactics used must be localized to specific forms of oppression, and, as Foucault pointed out, one must never expect total liberation but only gradual lessening of injustice in one area in order to better practice freedom in that and other areas,[168] Because each of us is located in so many groups, we never can possess nor should we want to possess a unified self or a consensus driven, flattened out form of subjectivity.[169] Regardless of one's sexual orientation (heterosexual, homosexual, bisexual, autosexual, celibate), one can insist that the government get out of the business of attempting to regulate whether or how people secure genital pleasure.[170] Even though each of us has our primary location in different parts of our social and cultural world, and even though none of us possess any unified self, still we can experience solidarity in our common opposition to all forms of domination and oppression.[171] We can do this without postulating any ahistorical or asocial norms other than maximizing freedom. Resistance in the name of freedom can take the form of loving our similarities (blacks loving blackness) and our differences, with such love being the protector of freedom.[172]

D.   LUCIUS OUTLAW AND MICHAEL ERIC DYSON

There are a host of black male intellectuals who are sounding the same themes as bell hooks and drawing inspiration from the work of Michel Foucault. Lucius Outlaw rejects all false universalizations and abstract essentialism in order to accent the finitude of all human understanding.[173] He calls for deconstructing all absolutistic metaphysics and epistemologies[174] and other modernistic tendencies that would prevent people from recognizing the significance of the play of differences.[175] Outlaw does so in order to preserve a place for race in the context of democratic pluralism.[176] Building on Foucault's claim that all discourse is action-guiding and attitude-molding, Outlaw wants to appropriate the project of the black studies movement that always had liberation as its goal[177] and to develop it into a field which he calls Africology. This would consist of a Foucault type genealogy of the discursive formations at the heart of the way of life of a people named for their origins,[178] a people whose lived experiences are marked by their membership in racial groups and the oppression such people have experienced.[179] Outlaw thinks that it is crucial to conserve a place for race in the context of democratic pluralism.[180] As an intellectual, Outlaw thinks that it is possible for him to make an important contribution to this resistance conservation project by carrying out a Foucault-type analysis of prevalent epistemes of race, of the rules for the formation of race as an object of study.[181]

Michael Eric Dyson is carrying out just such an analysis of contemporary American cultural treatments of race.[182] He says that as a black social critic fighting against injustice, he wants to baptize Foucault and other postmodern analysts by dipping them in the waters of American racial cultural practices in order that they can be reborn as voices relevant to the unjust treatment of blacks by whites and blacks by blacks.[183] As such a critic, Dyson examines the discursive rules governing racial talk by whites and blacks, rejecting all essentialist treatments of the vocabularies of race and insisting that the analyst examine three crucial aspects of such discourse: (1) the context surrounding racial discourse, the material realities of black economic poverty and educational impoverishment; (2) the subtext of racial discourse to see its different forms, subtle shapes ,and disguises; (3) the pretexts of rationalizations and arguments used in efforts to justify racial oppression.[184] The analyst needs to map out the existing racial ecology in order to see how racial identities are constituted,[185] and in order to appreciate the power that racial discourse has and the lack of unity that exists in black identities.[186] Such an investigation, Dyson claims, will help us see how political liberals often fail to contextualize their racial discourse and how such decontextualization makes their discourse dangerous and ready for neoconservatives to co-opt and use their discourse to strengthen racial domination.[187] It will help us, Dyson claims, to become aware of the devastating effects on current practices in the criminal justice system and the social sciences of the hypervisibility of black youth.[188]

Dyson provides hosts of examples within the black community that corroborate Foucault's analysis of the disciplinary practices producing domination and Foucault's recommendations of strategies and tactics for combating such domination. Since these practices focus on controlling people's bodies, Dyson endorses the way that blacks are engaged in redeeming the use of their bodies "by employing it in rites of sanctification, rituals of purification, and acts of celebration."[189] He urges that blacks recover the exotic use of bodies from exploitation by whites.[190] Recognizing that the body always remains as "other" to all social practices, and thus as "other" to oppressive racial practices, he argues for the establishment of a theology of eroticism,[191] and for the celebration of the union of pleasure and rage found in hip-hop music.[192]

Dyson rejoices in the postmodern celebration of difference by black youth, especially as found in the life and music of Michael Jackson.[193] Although critical of gangsta rap's treatment of women and violence, Dyson praises the prophetic rage found in current black rap music, just as it was found in earlier rhythm and blues music.[194] He finds in such music a powerful tactic for resisting racial injustice. All too aware of Foucault's caution that liberation can never come in one fell swoop, Dyson points out that resisting racism will be a perennial struggle.[195] He also charges that the fact that practicing freedom and resisting domination is an inescapable part of living is no reason for nihilistically surrendering to despair. It is possible to join rage to exotic enjoyment, as suffering blacks always have learned to do.[196]

Resisting injustice, Dyson points out, is something blacks must also carry out within their own communities. At the current time that means attacking black juvenocracy, grounded as it is in self-defense and the cultures of crack and guns.[197] Resisting injustice always needs institutional instruments through which one can work, and for Dyson this instrument is the black church, which has always united religious celebration pointing beyond social practices with political involvement in resisting oppressive practices.[198]

E.   CORNELL WEST

The ideal writer for drawing to a close this chapter, while also opening the door for the issues discussed in the next chapter, is Dyson's teacher, Cornell West. As a social and cultural critic focused on the plight of poor people of color, West has creatively and critically appropriated and applied insights from most of the writers dealt with in the past three chapters while also remaining an engaged intellectual deeply involved in the practical projects of resisting economic exploitation, state repression, bureaucratic domination, and cultural subjugation. As a product of, critic of, and voice for Afro-American Christian churches, West has argued for the need for an ethical and religious response to the existential crises of nihilism, despair, and hopelessness generated by the socioeconomic and cultural inhumaneness of the present age. Thinking and speaking from within the historically shifting, polluted streams and sands of current social and cultural practices, West attempts to show how freedom fighters can maintain both realism and hope by utilizing helpful even though marginalized traditions already present in these environments, and by relating oneself existentially to that which is ethically and religiously other than social practices, institutions, and subjectivities.

West is a pragmatist who endorses the efforts by a string of American thinkers, beginning with Emerson, to evade the assumptions and presuppositions of German and British epistemologists and metaphysicians seeking ideal vocabularies, ultimate justifications for beliefs, or ultimate explanations for the way things are believed to be.[199] While appropriating Rorty's attacks on traditional North Atlantic philosophy and its privileged representations, correspondence theory of truth, and socially transcendent subjects of self-reflection, West wants to do what Rorty is suspicious of doing—carry out a genealogical study of our present age as part of a general theoretical narrative of how various kinds of power have produced current curtailments on freedom.[200] As a genealogist, West appropriates major portions of Foucault's project and, as a theoretical analyst of the misuse of power, he draws heavily upon the texts of neo-Marxists, feminists, and the prophetic voices of African-American secular and religious writers and preachers of the past century.[201]

West defends a holistic, pragmatic understanding of truth in which religious truth claims are tested by the value of such claims to provide insights, illuminations, capacities, and abilities to honestly confront and effectively cope with the inevitable vicissitudes and unavoidable limit-situations in life.[202] While approving efforts to construct synoptic narratives and overarching vocabularies that provide enhancing self-images and enabling coping techniques[203] he sides with the Wittgensteinians and postmodernists in calling for us to get rid of metaphysical projects that hide and conceal their social background conditions.[204] Ontologies must always give way to our histories and epistemology to our social practices.[205] Pragmatism at its best, West affirms, would follow Dewey's lead[206] and combine the historicism of Rorty and Bernstein with moral vision, social analysis, and political engagement and thus be (1) prophetic, (2) critically tempered, (3) courageously analyzing social causes of unnecessary forms of social misery, (4) promoting outrage, (5) organizing constituencies to resist and alleviate such misery, (6) having faith in democracy, (7) combating despair, dogmatism, and oppression, (8) loving the uniqueness of individuals, and (9) being loyal to one's community.[207]

West charges that one cannot understand racism in the United States unless one understands its relationship to the economic exploitation of people of color during the industrial, monopoly, and multinational phases of American capitalism.[208] While rejecting any crude Marxist attempt to reductively see racism as only working-class exploitation in capitalist systems, West endorses the position of W. E. B. Du Bois, who asserts that racism does have a life of its own but that it cannot be separated in our world from forms of capitalist injustice and Eurocentric imperialism.[209] West claims that racism as well as nationalism, gender oppression, homophobia, and ecological devastation cannot be understood without the insights of Marx's historical and economic analyses, Georg Lukacs' theory of reification, and Antonio Gramsci's conception of hegemony.[210]

West believes that there is a progressive form of Marxism that can and should be appropriated by Christians seeking to revolutionize the world in faithfulness to Christian ideals.[211] West calls for the establishment of a Christian form of socialism in which the application of the Christian norms of individuality within community and democratic participation in the decision-making process lead to a mixed economy. In such an economy, the state will own the industries of basic producer goods. There also will be local self-managed socialist enterprises, cooperatives, small businesses run by self-employed entrepreneurs, and self-employed artists, writers, plumbers, and farmers.[212] Still, West finds Marxism as inadequate as it is invaluable, for two reasons. First, it does not recognize the need for a religious orientation to meet human existential needs and it is blind to the power residing in Christian narratives and symbols to give meaning and depth to suffering and love, to deepen tragedy, and to highlight at the same time joy, laughter, and gaiety.[213] Second, it needs to have its analyses of power supplemented by Weber's analysis of the domination produced by the manner in which private and public bureaucratic organizations are regulated by impersonal rules aimed at efficiency and self-perpetuation,[214] by Habermas's analysis of the repression caused by the dissolving of public space where the common good can be advocated by the use of public funds to sustain centralized economic power,[215] and by Foucault's analyses of discourse, truth regimes, subjectification, and disciplinary practices.[216] West is a dialogical listener and a creative appropriator.

West has continuously made use of various aspects of Foucault's critical project. He has argued for the importance of doing a genealogical study of racism and human practices of classifying people by race and he has emphasized the need to do an analysis of the discourse in which racism is conceptualized.[217] He has praised Foucault for his study of marginalized people[218] and for the model he provides of intellectuals who are skeptical of regimes of truth and seek to disrupt and dismantle them, and who are always mindful of how they as intellectuals are themselves socialized and acculturated.[219] West also shares with Foucault an appreciation that human life is filled with struggle, that humans always remain finite and fragile, and that although utopian energy must always be maintained, still the kingdom of God is only a regulative ideal guiding our daily practice of freedom.[220]

West does state a number of objections to the Foucaultian project, as he interprets it, objections that would be telling if the interpretations of these "objectionable" aspects were unavoidable dimensions of the project, something I think Foucault has denied to be the case. Responding to these objections not only will further clarify Foucault's project but it will also remove any potential threat to West's appropriation of the rest of Foucault's project. West is concerned that Foucault's quasi-Kantian inquiry into the necessary conditions for the existence of certain discourses will take us back to more metaphysical transcendentalism.[221] As earlier discussions of Foucault and Habermas have pointed out, however, such an inquiry is always located within a fallible and historical interpretive scheme and is only identifying contingently existing social practices without which the discourses could not exist.

West is also concerned that Foucault's replaces human agency with the operation of impersonal forces[222] with his accent on exercises of power that are not reflectively and consciously directed. This concern, however, is needless since, as was pointed out earlier, Foucault always interprets power relationships as holding between agents who are acting on others and resisting such influence. Although such actions often result from skills and habits instilled by socialization and training and do not require reflective consciousness to be carried out, these are habits that can be broken by the kind of reflective awareness gained by doing things such as genealogical investigations of such socialization.

West interprets Foucault's project as being too narrow in scope, focusing only on the subjugation that results from the social and cultural subjectification to which people are subjected, thus failing to address the exploitation, repression, and domination produced by economic, state, and bureaucratic practices.[223] Foucault, however, admits that he is not studying all forms of power or domination but that he is focusing on the previously ignored social and cultural microphysics of power that make economic and state domination and oppression possible. Foucault claims that he is doing this in order that people become further empowered to resist all forms of domination.

Finally, West charges that Foucault is only advocating resistance and rebellion and not the kind of reform that can lessen the power of dominating forces.[224] While Foucault does warn that all reform movements are dangerous, in that they can and often are co-opted so as to strengthen domination, he does not advocate running away from such danger. Instead, he calls for the utilization of such strategies and tactics of governmentality that can reform conditions and thus strengthen resistance, always remaining alert to the new dangers present in the reformed conditions. This warning seems to be just the warning that West issues to those utopians who think that human life can ever be anything but a continuous struggle for freedom. For West, the Christian, history is a battleground between the forces of good and evil.[225] Foucault calls it a battle between freedom and domination.

West's powerful addition to the projects of Marx, Weber, Dewey, Habermas, and Foucault is derived from his critical appropriation of the traditions and institutional agency of Afro-American Christian churches. This is a tradition that sees the world through the eyes of the victims of the global life-denying forces operating in our world. This is a marginalized tradition that can be recovered. It can allow us to understand our own relative victimizing and victimization. It can instill realistic hope and it can encourage collective action to resist the forces o f domination.[226] By sustaining him through the absurdity of being an American and a person of African descent,[227] West finds in Christian prophetic pragmatism the hope and resources needed to hold at bay the nihilism and despair of the absurdity of life without denying the presence of the tragic.[228] Part of the tragedy in the present age, West contends, is that dominant Eurocentric and secular ideologies and practices of capitalistic liberalism or neo-orthodoxy invariably lead to cynicism, nihilism, and despair.[229]

In order to fulfill its prophetic potentiality, West claims, the Afro-American church itself needs critical reexamination and reconstruction so that its religious focus on oppression can remain a source of struggle for liberation in this historical situation and not just be an opiate pacifying the oppressed while waiting for some "other world" form of deliverance.[230] He recognizes that there are economic, political, and spiritual crises in Afro-America, given the unemployment and underemployment of African-Americans, given the captivity of many Afro-American leaders to the Democratic Party, given the class divisions developing in the Afro-American community, given the invasion of drugs, the replacement of family and church influences with those coming from the mass media. Especially dangerous, he thinks, is the tendency by the power-elite-controlled mass media to use sex to provide stimulations that will keep a lid on potential nihilistic explosions in young people.[231] Nevertheless, West has faith that the Afro-American Christian community has the resources needed not only to deal with its own crises but to become a leading agent for change for those freedom fighters seeking to resist all forms of oppressive injustice. Out of its years of resisting slavery, segregation, and overt and institutional racism, and through the development of its unique form of Protestant Christianity, the Afro-American community possess the deep moralism, principles, and strength needed for a protracted struggle against personal despair, intellectual dogmatism, socioeconomic oppression, and for the development of communities of hope in which people can transform circumstances and provide visions of personal and social freedom.[232]

The question that West leaves us with is whether it is intellectually possible to sustain an ethical and religious life without seeking to rise metaphysically above the dynamics of social ocean currents and meanandering sandbars and without trying to dig below them searching for bedrock epistemological foundations. Is it possible for religious groups to recognize that all social and cultural religious practices are humanly constituted practices, even when people are responding ethically and religiously to what is other than the social? Is it possible to stand critically and self-reflectively within a chance-riddled and historically changing social and cultural environment without deifying this all too human world? Is it possible to stand not above or beyond or below this human world but with others as singularly unique persons encountering each other in our unique singularity, singularities that are never only our social masks, as different as those might be from each other? Is it possible to ethically and religiously transcend all craving for perfect representations and ultimate explanations and justifications? Is it possible to let ourselves and others simply be, always and already other than our social treatment of things, and yet resting on no ultimate explanations and remaining without need for any ultimate validations and justifications? In the next chapter, I will attempt to show that it is not unreasonable to do exactly that.

─•─ CHAPTER FIVE POSTMODERNIST INTERPRETATIONS OF FAITHFULNESS TO RELIGIOUS ENCOUNTERS

Is it possible for the world of social rationality to have its other? Is it possible to say "No" to all attempts to treat socially constituted worlds as exhaustive and self-sufficient? Is it possible for us to encounter our worlds' other and to existentially live so as to permit faithfulness to such encounters to permeate our socially constituted lives within our social worlds? Is it possible to use socially constituted language to express such encounters and to call out to other people warning them not to deify finite, social worlds, but rather to make room in their lives for encounters with the nonfinite, the nonworldly, the in-finite? Is it possible to make place in our homes for the changes that faithfulness to such encounters will generate? In this chapter I will attempt to make plausible the hypothesis that not only do all these possibilities obtain but that encounters with the infinite are the inescapable preconditions for all speaking, conceiving, and conceptually constituted experiencing. Religious encounters are the necessary condition for living an existentially workable life.

One of the major tragedies drowning people at the beginning of this twenty-first century is their inability to find religious and ethical air to breathe even while they are being hurled around in vicious currents of religiosity and moralizing. Although billions of people on our planet are deeply involved in religious practices and ethical concerns, the options usually held open to them are thoroughly and often violently self-destructive. So many of the leaders and spokespersons of the world's religions claim that the only way to make room for religious faithfulness is to claim that there is some metaphysical being or power that is other than the beings in our perceptual world. Vicious debates between defenders of metaphysical creation narratives and defenders of astronomical and biological hypotheses rob the great creation stories in the world's religions of their spiritual power to motivate people to not deify socially constituted worlds but to live expecting continuous encounters with the infinite. Ethical concerns about the oppressed and exploited often get swallowed up in efforts to remain faithful to some particular religion's characterization of the infinite, resulting too often in deadly attacks on those who do not endorse such characterizations: Jews and Muslims fighting over the metaphysical status of Jerusalem, pro-choice defenders and antiabortionists warring over the metaphysical status of fetuses, metaphysically grounded religious fundamentalists battling religious nonfundamentalists and secularists over dress codes, dietary regulations, sexual orientation, and the use of state power to enforce mandates supposedly grounded in some metaphysically transcendent authority. Ontotheologies and superstitious appeals to the metaphysically transcendent cause immeasurable pain and suffering even as they deny people the religious and ethical resources they need to attain spiritual maturity.

The reactions to this tragedy by intellectuals too often exacerbate the problem. Intellectuals so often succumb to the self-serving temptation to maintain the supremacy of the intellect over all aspects of human life, to maintain the supremacy and self-sufficiency of social rationality by denying that it has any possible other. Other intellectuals still claim that a metaphysically transcendent world actually exists. Some try to offer arguments supposedly proving or making probable that a metaphysical god exists.[1] Some acknowledge that no such arguments are sound but nevertheless they argue that, since one cannot prove or give good reasons for thinking that such a god does not exist, one can live in the faith that such a god exists.[2] Many intellectuals, convinced that none of the arguments for the actual or even possible existence of such transcendent beings are rationally worth anything, and totally fed up with all the violence being committed in the name of religion, have become faithful secularists seeking to live only in the world of human perceptions and conceptions.[3] Certainly, once one acknowledges the totally social character of all beings and worlds, as has been done in this text, there is no room left for talking about nonsocially constituted beings. This becomes doubly difficult once one senses that all ontotheologies are spiritually antireligious, deifying as they do human attempts to control with their conceptualizations and explanations all human encounters. It is exactly this spiritual indictment of ontotheologies that Kierkegaard, some Buddhists, and some mystics have leveled.

In this chapter, I will attempt to show that the social has its other, that things are not social all the way down, and that religious and ethical encounters with the nonfinite are not just figments of the imagination of people afraid to live in the finite and social. I will examine the rhetoric of Kierkegaard when he confesses that acknowledging the call of the infinite is what alone makes possible the constitution of a human spirit not destroyed by despair. I will examine the writings of Emmanuel Levinas acknowledging the infinite other, ethically and religiously encountered in every interpersonal human encounter, being's other which is the necessary presupposition of all speech about or experience of beings. I then will look at Slavoj Zizek's interpretation of Christianity as a radical alternative to the whole world of social reality and as a revolutionary agape community of people absolutely committed to the one they see as fully human and fully God. I will examine recent Western efforts to appropriate Buddhist and Hindu reflections on human encounters with the nonfinite, in particular Mark Taylor's neo-Buddhist effort to maintain a sense of the sacred after the death of the ontotheological god and Huston Smith's interpretation of mystical encounters as encounters with that which is presupposed by all life with finite beings. I will examine D. Z. Phillip's development of the Wittgensteinian insight that religious language is distinctively unique, sui generis, not to be reduced to psychological, sociological, or metaphysical claims and thus not hopelessly contaminated by ontotheological assumptions. I will try to show that there is great spiritual insight and power in the traditional "proofs" for the existence of an infinite and eternal God, if they are not interpreted as proofs of the existence of some being (x) which has some characteristic F. Finally, I will present interpretations of classical Hindu, Buddhist, Jewish, Christian and Islamic confessions that keep them free from ontotheological constraints. I will do so in order to show how different historical, social, and cultural religious communities have arisen as people have sought to remain faithful to encounters with the infinite. I will do so in order to show why most people, historically and socially constituted as they are, need to remain within specific historical religious communities even as they continuously reconstruct them.

I.   KIERKEGAARD ON FAITHFUL RESPONSE TO THE INVASION OF THE NONRATIONAL INFINITE INTO THE RATIONAL FINITE

Kierkegaard was a Christian who presented an interpretation of what is involved in being a Christian that is radically different from what most Christians and non-Christians think is involved. Being a Christian for Kierkegaard is not a matter of endorsing a set of beliefs or some creed or some set of doctrines.[4] Faithfulness to the infinite and eternal God is not a matter of having beliefs that have the correct relationship (correspondence) to something, some specifiable being that is the object of these beliefs. God is not that kind of externality.[5] God does not exist as such a being about whom we could have correct or incorrect beliefs[6] because God is infinite and eternal.[7]

Again and again Kierkegaard asserts that being a Christian is living with a certain kind of subjective mode of subjectivity and not with any form of objective mode of subjectivity.[8] In chapter 3, we noted that for Kierkegaard everyone has what he calls a mode of subjectivity, a way of conceiving, believing, desiring, thinking, evaluating, hoping, being concerned. Some people have what he calls an objective or objectivistic mode of subjectivity. All of their subjectivity is focused on the conceivable objects their beliefs and desires are about, and on "objective" knowledge of such objects. Other people live with their attention focused on the kind of subjectivity they have, on the kind of life they are living, on the feelings they have toward the life they are living, on the way they are comporting themselves toward conceivable objects and objective knowledge. Kierkegaard calls this a subjective or subjectivistic mode of subjectivitity.

According to Kierkegaard the Christian mode of subjectivity is incompatible with any kind of objectivistic mode of subjectivity in which one could at best have some sort of probabilistic approximation to certainty of truth. Therefore, being a Christian cannot be a matter of having a correct historical point of view or of proving that Christian beliefs are correct. Being a Christian cannot be a matter of merely believing that *The Bible* is correct, that the Church can authoritatively ground certain claims, or that history can demonstrate the truth of Christianity to non-Christians.[9] Kierkegaard does proclaim that Christianity is the Truth, but he claims that it is the living, existential truth of a person's mode of subjectivity that is concerned primarily about whether one's own way of thinking and feeling and living works. For Kierkegaard, being a Christian is being in the truth, having a workable subjectivistic mode of subjectivity. Christianity is the living Truth that can end all the myriad forms of human despair.

It is extremely important not to interpret Kierkegaard as proclaiming that either religion in general or Christianity in particular is reducible to merely psychological phenomena, personal attitudes, and feelings about things in the world. Talking about psychological states and the intentional objects of feelings and attitudes is still talking in an objectivistic mode of subjectivity. Christianity focuses on the Christian's infinitely passionate commitment to the pursuit of eternal happiness. This is not a mere psychological state but is a matter of standing in a God-relationship to the infinite and eternal.

This means that Kierkegaard is not presenting merely a negative theology in which all talk about God is interpreted as merely reminders that people should not absolutize or deify anything finite, anything socially constituted. Kierkegaard certainly is proclaiming that we should not worship such false gods, but he also is claiming that in a certain subjectivistic mode of subjectivity the infinite and eternal can be encountered even though they are never anything merely finite. Encountering the infinite is a matter of being called by the infinite.

Answering this call is a matter of giving up control and letting oneself die to the socially constituted world of objectivistic life and letting oneself be reborn with a nondespairing workable subjectivistic form of subjectivity. The call of the infinite is always something other than the mere presence of a psychological state of a socially constituted self. The "God-relationship" is a relationship and not an objectivistic psychological state of a person.

Christianity, Kierkegaard charges, proclaims that people should be infinitely concerned about themselves,[10] and that such a concern will be fulfilled only when they are passionately committed to seeking eternal happiness. He says that eternal happiness is the highest good of the infinite.[11] It is the self-constituting *telos* (goal) that exists for an individual only when that individual yields it absolute devotion.[12] Eternal happiness is an absolute good, not one definable by social criteria of worth. It is definable only in terms of its acquisition, by venturing everything absolutely, including oneself.[13] Weighing alternatives, specifiable and comparable within the world of social rationality, is not venturing everything absolutely. The entire world of social rationality, with all its objects, events, norms, and ideals must be ventured, and this means venturing one's own socially constituted selfhood. When eternal happiness is one's *telos,* then one will be willing to renounce for the sake of such happiness all finite satisfactions of one's finite, socially constituted self in a world of socially constituted objects.[14] Eternal happiness is not something to be gained in time but always remains a timeless (eternal) goal continuously aimed at throughout the entire time of the religious person's life.[15] Eternity, for finite people in time, can only be the future, a goal aimed at without reservation.[16] It is the expectation of eternal happiness that is the reward for seeking this happiness, a happiness which is radically different from all forms of worldly satisfaction or gain.[17] Although one must be willing to risk everything finite in order to seek such eternal happiness, such willingness to risk gives one no reason to think that one thereby deserves such happiness.[18] The existential effect of seeking such an eternal happiness is not earthly satisfaction but suffering, the suffering that comes by realizing that one's entire finite life in the world has consisted in failing to be faithful to the quest for eternal happiness.[19]

Genuine religious discourse, Kierkegaard claims, speaks of nothing other that the absolute good of infinite, eternal happiness.[20] To speak of the infinite is to proclaim that people are not just finite and not just relatable to the finite. It is to proclaim that the finite, the world of socially constituted objects and subjects, is not exhaustive of that to which people can be existentially related. People can strive for eternal happiness by risking everything finite. People can realize that the absolute good of the finite world's other is eternal happiness. People can realize that they need not live merely worldly lives but that they can live by renouncing the world in their pursuit of eternal happiness, in their pursuit of the reward of seeking eternal happiness rather than worldly satisfaction. Absolute devotion to eternal happiness produces a relationship to the infinite and eternal that consists of worshiping the infinite and eternal God.[21]

God is not an existing being but instead is the infinite (not-finite) and eternal (not-temporally changing or enduring) to which one stands when one stands in the God-relationship, when one is absolutely committed to the pursuit of eternal happiness. The use of the word "God" cannot be compared to the use of any other word, even as the meaning of this word cannot be explained in terms of anything describable, anything existing in the world of objects and subjects. It can only be explained by exploring more fully the religious person's talk about eternal happiness, the nonfinite, and the nontemporal.[22] In commitment to eternal happiness, in worship of God, one thus suffers a dying away from attachment to anything finite[23] and a recognition that one, as a socially constituted finite person, is nothing before God and can do nothing by oneself except respond to the invitation to forsake the finite for the sake of the pursuit of an eternal happiness defined by that pursuit. The suffering unavoidably involved in forsaking the world is not inconsistent with calling the absolute goal of the infinite an infinite happiness because the suffering involved in worshiping God is always accompanied by a strengthening consolation received while worshiping God,[24] by a humble cheerfulness before God.[25]

The suffering involved in worshiping the infinite and eternal God is radically different from the suffering experienced by all people living merely in the finite world. Religious suffering is joined to an ability to be glad in the midst of suffering.[26] It certainly does not consist in any form of self-flagellation because such self-torture is still an effort to do something and thus fails to recognize that the finite self must give up itself if it is to pursue eternal happiness. Surrendering to the call to renounce one's finite self and the world in which one lives as a finite self, in order to pursue eternal happiness, in order to worship God, is an act one can perform. It is an act that frees oneself from everything finite, an act in which the actor is rendered infinite (other than finite), an act in which the finite and the infinite are momentarily united in a transcendence of merely finite existence.[27] Absolutely committed to the pursuit of eternal happiness and worship of God, people are enabled to proclaim that they, as finite persons rendered infinite and singularly unique by their act of self-renunciation and absolute commitment to the pursuit of eternal happiness, are loved by God, are allowed to be in their finiteness, infiniteness, and singularity. They are enabled to proclaim that God is always right, and that, even when it seems to them, as finite persons with their sufferings in the finite world, that God does not love them, still they will love God and remain steadfast in their pursuit of eternal happiness.[28]

Refusing to act as merely a socially constituted person in a socially constituted world, as one pursues with unrestricted commitment eternal happiness, is the most powerful and free act a person can perform because it will free one from merely living in the finite world and because it will produce a radical reconstitution of oneself and the way one sees and lives in the world. Although religious people still live their socially and psychologically constituted lives, with all their inescapable inner conflicts and abysses, they no longer find their lives in the merely finite but they live as strangers in the world of the finite.[29] Their entire lives are transformed as their pursuit of eternal happiness forces everything in their lives to be refocused.[30] All of nature gets reinterpreted; it is now seen as God's creation and God is seen everywhere in it.[31] It is not an easy thing, Kierkegaard writes, to remain faithful to the pursuit of eternal happiness while dealing with all the everyday activities of finite life.[32] He uses the example of a person taking a walk in a deer park in order to show that outwardly a religious person will look like anyone else but inwardly the religious person's commitment to the pursuit of eternal happiness will make everything different.[33] He insists that outwardly religious people will and must remain unexceptional even though inwardly they have been transformed.[34] They do not seek to be seen by others as religious.[35] They do not seek to call attention to themselves by showing others how they humble themselves before God.[36] In the secrecy of their commitment to the pursuit of eternal happiness they pray to God in secret.

By worldly standards, Kierkegaard admits, it is absurd to attempt to find eternal happiness by committing oneself to the pursuit of eternal happiness, the absolute good of the infinite. It is doubly absurd, he claims, to pursue eternal happiness by committing oneself to Jesus Christ, seen as the one in whom the infinite has become finite. It is vital in interpreting Kierkegaard not to confuse his Christology with some sort of Jesusology. The Christian's faithfulness to the Christ does not rest on some objective historical beliefs about the historical Jesus. Seeking eternal happiness as a Christian is living in a Christian subjectivistic mode of subjectivity and not in any objectivistic mode of subjectivity, even one in which one believes that one can prove correct certain beliefs about Jesus.[37] Even if historians were to disprove all the claims about the historical Jesus, Kierkegaard claims that this would not show that Christ has not existed.[38] Kierkegaard insists that Christians in the nineteenth century can encounter Jesus Christ in exactly the same way that Christians, like Paul who never met Jesus, encountered him in the first century.

In the first century and in every century since then, it is faithful Christians who see Jesus as the Christ, as the Messiah, as the Savior, who has broken loose from the whole finite world of social rationality, who has been so totally committed to God's will and the pursuit of eternal happiness that one sees God when one sees him, who has been resurrected to a new life radically free from any socially constituted worldly life and who presents to all Christians dedicated to him the same kind of death to the world and resurrection to a new kind of life. Just as the infinite God lives in the lives of people because they are committed absolutely to the pursuit of eternal happiness, so Jesus Christ lives in the lives of Christians because they are committed absolutely to him as God incarnate and thus committed to his agape way of life. Jesus exists as the Christ, the union in history of the finite and the infinite, because Christians have encountered Jesus as the Christ. Jesus Christ lives in history, present to be encountered by anyone living in the Christian subjectivistic mode of subjectivity, because the community of faithful Christians, the church, exists as his living body, proclaiming his humanity and divinity and that he calls people to die to the world, to seek eternal happiness, and to be resurrected into a new way of life of love and compassion.

Christianity does not need any ontotheology and the Christian subjectivistic mode of subjectivity is made impossible when the pursuit of ontotheological concerns replaces the pursuit of eternal happiness. Christianity can be Christianity, Kierkegaard claims, only when it is freed from all pagan, superstitious beliefs about some superhuman being or power or force being objectively related (by causality, for example) to beings in the world.[39] Talking about creation, divine caring, and resurrection is for the Christian a matter of talking about a Christian subjectivistic mode of subjectivity or it is a matter of making confessional proclamations from within such a mode of subjectivity. The resurrected life begins here and now as people remain absolutely committed to the pursuit of eternal happiness.

II. LEVINAS ON THE PRIORITY OF ETHICAL FACE-TO-FACE INTERPERSONAL ENCOUNTERS TO SOCIAL PRACTICES

Some of the most creative appropriators of Kierkegaard's insights have been the Jewish thinkers Martin Buber,[40] Franz Rosenzweig[41] and Emmanuel Levinas.[42] Derrida predicts that for centuries the readers of Levinas will be seeking to think about what he has written and what other texts, by his intellectual and spiritual children, he will have parented.[43] Levinas himself acknowledges that his writings were given life by his readings of the texts of Kierkegaard, Buber, and Rosenzweig.[44] The early 1920s saw a host of European philosophical/religious thinkers attempting to rethink philosophy and religion in the light of Kierkegaard's texts. Heidegger, coming out of a Christian theological background, was working on *Being and Time,* which would be published in 1927. Reflecting on the place of Judaism in an increasingly secular world, and using Kierkegaard's texts to consider radically new possibilities, Rosenzweig published *The Star of Redemption* in 1921. Buber published *I and Thou* in 1922.

In many ways the projects of these Jewish thinkers are similar to Heidegger's study of Dasein and the worlds into which people are thrown. They present, however, alternative analyses of human life. Although Levinas admits that *Being and Time* is one of the finest books written in Western philosophy,[45] he builds upon the work of Rosenzweig and Buber to show how much is left out if we stay only with Heidegger's beings present-on-hand, ready-to-hand and Dasein, even the Dasein preparing itself to think in a way that new social and cultural worlds might be constituted through it. Rosenzweig, Buber, and Levinas point out that what especially is absent in Heidegger's analysis is any appreciation of the interpersonal, ethical encounters that place Dasein under moral obligation to care for all human beings, encounters that are presupposed by all beings and Dasein itself.

In Rosenzweig, Levinas finds a voice like Kierkegaard's that rejects all forms of metaphysics that present an interpretation of people which locates them as merely functional units in some larger totality or as merely an instantiation of a species or set of descriptive classifications.[46] Each person is irreducibly singular in some way that is other than being an instance of a kind, no matter how complex that kind might be. Levinas builds on Rosenzweig's recognition that all people must die individually for themselves. Levinas finds here a crucial insight lacking in Heidegger's analysis of human life. Heidegger sees death as the possibility of the end of all possibilities, a possibility that people must heroically face and seize as they plot out the course of their future. Levinas sees death as the impossibility of any future possibilities, something we cannot conceive or seize, something that violently seizes us and forces us to be radically passive.[47] The difference between the positions of Heidegger and Levinas may sound like verbal quibbling, but it is much more than that. Heidegger calls for us to individually and heroically remain in control by seizing death by the throat and projecting it as the frame for all of our other projects. Levinas calls for us to reject such a will to power mentality and to live instead recognizing that there is so much we cannot and should not try to control, among which we find death and other people.

Levinas also draws upon Rosenzweig's characterizations of creation, revelation, and redemption. Seeing nature and history as creation is seeing them in such a conjunction with God (the timeless infinite) that neither is separable from the other. God, according to Rosenzweig, is revealed to us when we encounter the nonfiniteness of our singularity and the infinite other of every finite being, when we hear the loving call of the infinite by loving all people and all creation.[48] Responsibly answering this call is, according to Rosenzweig, participating in the redemption of the world. Redemption begins with creation and revelation, with the infinite other that makes nature and history and encounter possible, and it continues through communities bound together by the knowledge that they are loved and by their shared practices of loving each other and everyone else in need. For Rosenzweig this redemption requires the Jewish community and its memory of revelation and the Christian community in its efforts to evangelically redeem the world.[49]

It is Buber's *I and Thou* that most directly develops Kierkegaard's distinction between objectivistic and subjectivistic modes of subjectivity. Buber points out that people take on different identities and live in radically different ways when they are in what he calls "I-It" relationships from what they are in when they are in "I-Thou" relationships.[50] Being in either set of relationships is being in a mode of subjectivity. In the "I-It" mode of life, everything is seen as an object falling under some concept. This would include Heidegger's objects "present-on-hand" and his tools and materials "ready-to-hand." It is Kierkegaard's objectivistic mode of life. "I-Thou" relationships, however, are encounters with people in their singularity, something that is different from experiencing people as being an individual instance of a kind. The person who encounters thous stands in a relationship to these people that is different from perceiving people as instances of a biological or social sort, and this relationship makes them be something other than a subject of thinking or perceiving or an agent using tools.[51] Like Rosenzweig, Buber considers this relationship to be one of love which is a matter of responsibility,[52] of being more concerned to maintain the relationship than anything else. Being merely a conceiving subject or a tool-user never gets to what makes people radically different from classifiable objects or usable tools.[53]

Whenever we encounter another person as a "thou," we are encountering that person without paying attention to the person's physical characteristics or social status. We are encountering the nonfiniteness of the person, and this demands ethical and religious respect.[54] The same thing happens when we encounter, rather than merely experience, nonhuman aspects of our environment. Seeing trees as mere "its," just like seeing people as mere bodies or human resources, is a mode of living in which, through social constitution of them as objects or subjects, their non-finite dimension is subtracted. Living in a subjectivistic mode of life in which people are encountered as "thous" is living in a mode of life in which trees can be seen as sacred creations of God. If we see trees only as "its," then we will be living in an objectivistic mode of life that will lead tragically to seeing ourselves as mere "its" or resources.[55] Experiencing objects and using tools and materials need not have this tragic result. It will, however, if such experiencing and using is treated as the totality of human life. This is what one must watchfully avoid. We have no choice but to live as constituted subjects in worlds of constituted objects, tools and materials,[56] but we need not absolutize this world. People must learn to live in socialized worlds while also refusing to be merely of those worlds, forgetting the infinite which is the presupposition of every constituted finite.

The infinite itself, God, can never be a constituted object to be experienced; it can only be encountered, but only as the infinite other of every finite being.[57] Likewise, only by responding to the call of the infinite to us, by lovingly respecting others, does God's will get carried out in human lives.[58] The infinite and eternal cannot be constituted and postulated as a supernatural being. For Buber, religion needs encounters with the infinite that is other than the constituted subjects and objects in the world of social rationality, but this infinite other is other than any being, including any ontotheological supreme being. Levinas also insists that God is not a being among beings, a supernatural being, the supreme or ultimate being, the being of beings, or the explanatory ground of beings. The God who comes to mind for Levinas is other than all beings and other than all forms of ontotheology.[59] The idea of the infinite God, Levinas writes, signifies the nonfinite that is the presupposition of everything finite.

Levinas presents a description and interpretation of human life, what he calls a phenomenology, without Husserl's reduction of our attention from the lived world to a Platonic world of forms or essences.[60] Heidegger gives a phenomenological interpretation of the lived world that accents people's toolish use of tools and poets waiting for new worlds of being to be constituted through them. Levinas's phenomenology presents descriptions and interpretations which show that there is so much of human life that is other than the lives of constituted subjects experiencing objects, manipulating tools, heroically facing death, or waiting for new and surprising social and cultural worlds to begin. It is the ethical and interpersonal encounters of people with people, Levinas claims, that is missing in Heidegger's phenomenology. It is these encounters that are the necessary preconditions of all intentionality and all laboring with tools.[61] Showing the primacy of the ethical is the objective of Levinas's work.[62] Like Husserl's phenomenology, Levinas's version is aimed at waking us up to what has been lost sight of in so much of modern, objectivistic life, only with Levinas what is lost sight of is social rationality's other.[63] Often Levinas uses the term "metaphysical," not in an effort to refer to what ontotheologies attempted to refer, but rather to indicate what is other than what social rationality covers, to indicate the nonfinite that is an inescapable aspect of human life.[64]

Although we constantly are experiencing objects and using tools, there are occasions, Levinas claims, when we recognize that there is a dimension of living that is more primitive than this conceptual and practical activity. There is the matter of merely being confronted with an environment from which we can't escape, an environment that is not treated as some this or that but which is just some murmuring, such as the silence we hear when lying in bed in a pitch dark room.[65] Close to the condition of insomnia, in which we can't escape wakefulness even though we are trying not to think of anything or experience anything or do anything, we find here an indication of the inescapability of confrontation with something other than particular beings and tools.[66] This confrontation with unconceptualized and uncontrollable otherness often fills us with the horror felt by children alone in their silent, dark bedrooms. Although not yet ethical, this dimension of life does instruct us not to absolutize the worlds of objects and tools.

Thankfully, besides this horrible encounter with brute otherness, there is another way of living that is other than living with constituted objects and tools. This other way fills us with joy. Levinas points out that we live from the elements: drinking cool water, breathing fresh air, eating food, walking and running, feeling the wind in one's face, absorbing the aroma of pine trees, losing oneself in sunrises, sunsets, and starlit nights. This way of living fills us with joy. The elements we live from are not objects of constitution and representation, but objects of enjoyment.[67] For Levinas as for Lacan and Zizek, enjoyment is "Real," other than what is within the domain of social rationality. This is the life of enjoyment that the Zen Buddhist offers as a life option to those who would extinguish the cravings that are part of our socially and personally constituted selves.

Levinas claims that it is this world of enjoyment, which people live in and which is primordially prior to all representations and laboring with tools, that Heidigger ignores. Food for Dasein always remains an implement to be used (to sustain life) and not something that simply is enjoyably eaten.[68] A sensory way of enjoying oneself, Levinas claims, always surrounds our socially constituted conceptions, perceptions, beliefs, desires, and theories. To enjoyably live from the elements is to be an individual person who is neither merely a biological or sociological being. [69] The world I enjoyably live in is prior to the world I constitute in order to stave off the dangers that arise and threaten this joyful living. This primordial priority is not a temporal priority but rather an aspect of living that both prevents reducing people to instances of biological species or social types and that is necessary for conceptual classifications and tools to exist.

Enjoyably living from the elements is presupposed by all conceiving and laboring, and it is expressed in the myths of an original paradise. Humans, Levinas writes, do not find themselves in a meaningless and absurd world, but in a world of sensory delights. Here life is the love of life.[70] People fall into despair over life only because they have tasted the original joyfulness of life. Despair is a parasitic failure to continue enjoying life.[71] Suicide is tragic because it does not bring a resolution to the problems that come with birth and because it cannot humiliate the value of living.[72] All other values connect back to the primordial joyfulness of living; this is the basic insight of hedonism.[73]

Even the call to be morally responsible and just to other people is a call to help remove the barriers that prevent other people from enjoying life. Prior to our intentional efforts to make our lives joyful and to prevent them from becoming miserable is that enjoyable living from the elements that simply comes to us as a gift of living. Only thankfulness can be an appropriate response, a thankfulness expressed by living life joyfully.

For Levinas, living life joyfully, before it is challenged by the call to responsibility that comes through face-to-face encounters with other people, is always an individual thing and carries with it the isolation of solitude.[74] One is primarily immersed and at home with oneself in one's enjoyable living. One is not thinking of oneself as one among many but one is living in one's enjoyment which always maintains that kind of secrecy needed to maintain the particularity of enjoyment. It is precisely this at-home-ness with oneself that gets challenged when one encounters another person face-to-face and one is called to justify one's very existence to that person, called to justify taking up a place in the world possibly occupied by the other person, called to justify enjoying living without being concerned about the joys or suffering of others.[75]

Living joyfully encounters another challenge independent of the ethical challenge. Joyful life can be betrayed by the very other that generates it. The enjoyments of life are the enjoyments of a lived body caught up in the intersection of many threatening forces that can make us slaves to hunger, thirst, and illness.[76] Here the chanciness and insecurities of life enter the picture. Because we are not in control of original joy and because there is no future guarantee that what we need for enjoyable living will be available, we try to take control of things by learning how to avoid disasters, by laboring, by conceptually classifying things and forming general beliefs about the behavior of things, and by constituting and skillfully using tools.[77] That threats to joyful living move us out of merely enjoying living does not indicate that enjoyment is not the measuring stick of life's value. The joys of life provide the motivation for dealing with the threats. We even often find joy in laboring and thinking. That joyful life can be threatened is an indication of the uncontrollable, absolutely surprising, and ungraspable otherness of the future that grasps us, with suffering and death being the supreme examples of such threatening otherness. In physical pain and suffering we encounter what we cannot actively control, just as in death we encounter the impossibility of any further possibilities, any future projects, something we cannot even imagine as a possibility,[78] but which nevertheless we cannot escape.[79]

In order to provide as much help as possible in meeting these threats, people possess a another way of living that is other than living as a conceiving subject or a user of tools. People dwell in a habitation, Levinas writes, in the gentle intimacy of a home. This gentle intimacy is needed in order to suspend immediate enjoyment as one in a practical way takes possession of things and as one labors continuously to postpone death, suffering, and the blocking of enjoyment. Within the home something exterior to enjoyably living from the elements is introduced into human life and it comes as a gentle and warm other. This way of living at home with others is a practical and nonethical way of living. Through labor we take possession of things in a way that does not yet have any of the trappings of legal property ownership. This way of laboring is a practical matter not based on any conceptualization of what is grasped. The others with whom we habitat in the home are not yet encountered face-to-face in an ethical relationship that challenges us to justify our possessions or our presence in the home. Our cohabitators also maintain their individuality as enjoyers of the elements and as laborers in the intimacy of home life. Just as living enjoyably with the elements finds expression in myths of paradise, so living in a gentle, warm, and welcoming home gets expressed in myths of utopia.[80] Both the enjoyable world and the supportive home can only be welcomed thankfully for we do not create them. This is the thankfulness that is present in all of the world's religions.

It is important not to infer from Levinas's phenomenological description of these various modes of living that one occurs temporally prior to the other or that one could exist independent of the other.

Levinas is beginning with our whole way of living and then analytically peeling off ways of living that are different from living as a conceiving, perceiving, theorizing subject or as Heidegger's Dasein carrying out socially constituted projects. Enjoyably living from the elements and dwelling in the warm hospitality of the home cannot be reduced to conceptual living and tool-using. These ways of living are different from living under social norms but they also are presupposed by all such socially rational life. The world of social rationality with its finite subjects and objects is enveloped by and permeated by its other, by that which is radically other than being.

The most important example for Levinas of our encounter with the other is to be found in our face-to-face encounters with other people. Encountering the face of another is radically different from perceiving the physical characteristics of people or seeing them as occupants of social roles. Encountering people face-to-face is always an ethical encounter that places under judgment our enjoyments and our home possessions. It is an event that anchors all our measurements of the injustice of social practices. It is out of our ethical encounters with the faces of other people that the idea of God comes to mind and the spiritual appropriateness of religious worship and prayer are determined. In order to understand Levinas, therefore, it is crucial to understand what he means when he writes about ethically encountering another person face to face.

It seems obvious that Levinas is using the term "face of a person" in a technical way. Normally when we talk about meeting with someone face-to-face rather than just communicating with them by letter or phone, we can describe what the person's face looks like. Levinas, however, tells us that we cannot do a phenomenological description of the face because access to the face is straightaway ethical and not cognitive. Ethically encountering the face of another person is encountering the person as a nondescribable other who transcends all of that person's finite characteristics. Ethically encountering a person face-to-face is having that face call us to be responsible for the other person. It cries out, "Do not murder me."[81]

To understand what Levinas means by "face," we need to note that he says that when we encounter another person, the singularity of that person is something other than all of that person's physical characteristics, social roles, or socially constituted subjectivity. To encounter people in their singularity is to encounter them naked, stripped of all their socially constituted forms. People are not unique because they possess a set of characteristics that are different from every other actual person's set. Even if my set of characteristics were uniquely different from all persons, past, present, or future, some other person could have them. I am different from all other people, Levinas claims, because I am singularly unique, unique by virtue of my capacity to be encountered in my singularity and unique because in encountering others face-to-face, I am placed under a unique obligation that can be transferred to no other person.[82] I am not identical with what I look like or with my various locations in social and cultural worlds, or with my broken and fractured subjectivity, or with my memories or fantasies. My identity is tied to my unique responsibilities incurred by my specific encounters with other people face-to-face and to my nonfinite, infinite singularity that lays responsibilities on others when they encounter me.

Encountering a person face-to-face is, in and of itself, therefore, encountering them ethically. It is encountering them destitute in their singular nakedness, devoid of all material or social resources for defending themselves. It is hearing them cry out to us, "Thou shalt not kill."[83] In encountering the nonfinite otherness of their singularity we can do only one of two things, annihilate them or hear their cry. One ethically encounters another person in such nakedness, hearing this cry, as one recognizes that one is under responsibility to this person, not because of what we have done to each other in an economy of exchange, not even because of this person's perceptible needs, but simply because this person is there to be encountered face-to-face. Simply because of their unique singularity, other to their place in nature and social structures, people have an a priori right to be, an irrevocable and inalienable right conferred by no one.[84] Because this is not a contractual responsibility or one based on a perception of a specific need, it is an open-ended, infinite responsibility, whatever the needs are that might turn up.

Because every person we encounter face to face is an embodied person facing specific threats of loss of enjoyment, violation of home, suffering, death, and denial of respect for that person's unique singularity, our responsibility is to the person encountered whoever that person is, whether it be orphan, widow, or stranger. Also, that many people perceive or meet other people without ethically encountering them in their singularity does not mean that they do not have the same open-ended responsibility to them. The destitute singularity of those we meet does not disappear because we do not ethically encounter them face-to-face. Their cry "Thou shalt not kill," remains in force even when we turn a deaf ear to the cry. Furthermore, because every face we encounter is the face of an embodied person who has responsibilities to other people whom that person meets, our responsibility for them becomes a responsibility for their responsibilities. It is because the people we encounter have responsibilities to third parties, it is necessary to move from personal ethical encounters to general principles of justice and socially constituted laws preventing injustice.

Every time we meet another person we are meeting someone who should be ethically encountered face-to-face. Their unique singularity needs to be respected. According to Levinas, these interpersonal meetings of people with people, of people who can be ethically encountered in that infinite singular uniqueness that cannot be spelled out in any description, are the presuppositions of all conceiving, representing, describing, theorizing. The ethical permeates language itself because whatever gets said presupposes that some person is saying it and thus that all listeners or readers are responsible to ethically respect that speaker.[85] Language includes not just what is said and the rules governing word use, but it includes the saying of what is said and thus the ethical relationships of people linguistically relating to other people.[86] The whole social world, with all of its social, intersubjective practices and constituted objects, and the whole psychological aspect of people's lives (filled as they are with socialized subjectivity, drives, individual fantasies, and desires), presupposes the ethical world of interpersonal encounters.[87] Reductionists' efforts to treat people amorally are both unethical and a pragmatic guarantee of their incorrectness.

Levinas's analysis of the ethical aspect permeating all human life stands in sharp contrast to the analyses of being human presented by Heidegger and Buber. As we have noted, Heidegger focuses on the power and freedom of people to heroically carry out projects informed by their understanding of the social and historical character of themselves, the objects and the tools they use, and on the ability of people to find freedom from this world of social rationality only by taking control in preparing themselves to be possessed and used as poets creating new social and cultural practices. Levinas charges that, for Heidegger, other people are present only as coconstitutors of social practices. Totally missing from Heidegger's analysis are interpersonal ethical encounters calling people to responsibility and justice. Heidegger had no ethical resources available to protest against Nazi poets seeking to create their revolutionary new social order.[88]

Buber, as interpreted by Levinas, is very close to interpreting human life correctly, but he too does not yet see the radical primacy of the ethical encounter with the face of another. It is Buber's accent on the primacy of I-Thou relationships that Levinas finds inadequate. First, Levinas appropriates much from Rosenzweig's criticism that Buber's interpretation is not complex enough because it fails to attend to the gifts necessary for being what we are, gifts necessary for our very creation. For Levinas, enjoyable living upon the elements and habitating in a home are such gifts, and we need to thankfully accept them as loving gifts of creation. Buber's talk about encountering the whole world as a thou fails to recognize the radical difference between the nonethical enjoyable living from the elements and the ethical encounter of people face-to-face. Rosenzweig also claims that Buber fails to deal with the ethical relations we must have with people with whom we do not have I-Thou relationships, if we are to be related to them in a just fashion. These are the social practices that are not interpersonal even though they presuppose the interpersonal. For Levinas, as we have seen, these requirements of justice are introduced as we recognize that the people we encounter face-to-face are also people encountering other people face-to-face, and those other third parties are people to whom I have to answer. "Thous" must become "we's" if justice is to be served. To deal with third parties we need to introduce universal principles of justice institutionalized in social, moral, legal, and political practices and used to judge unjust practices.[89] Thus, in Rosenzweig's language, Buber does not do justice to creation and redemption.

Even at the interpersonal level, Levinas thinks that Buber's I-Thou analysis is not ethical enough. For Buber the Thou that I meet is a person who is saying Thou to me. I-Thou relationships are symmetrical dialogical relationships between people treating each other as equals; they are relationships of friendship that come and go and need to be reestablished again and again. We seem to be able to observe I-Thou relationships from an ethically uninvolved third person point of view. When encountering the face of another, however, the relationship is not one of spiritual, angelic friendship between equals. It is an asymmetrical, ethical encounter of inequality. The face commands from the highest of moral heights and I am an infinitely obligated ethical hostage to that command, a command to be met not with conversation but by not annihilating the other and by clothing the naked and feeding the hungry.[90] The ethical problem with dialogue, Levinas claims, is that if it is introduced to end violence, then we need dialogue to bring people into dialogue.[91] Not dialogical listening but the cry "Thou shalt not kill" is the first ethical word to be heard.

The difference between Buber and Levinas over I-Thou and I-Face relationships makes its appearance again in their interpretation of the relation of people to God. Here, too, there is so much that Buber writes about God with which Levinas can find kinship.

Buber also rejects ontotheological gods. God, Buber says, is neither a being immanent in the world nor outside the world and yet God is wholly other and wholly present. God can neither be experienced nor thought, but people can do justice to their relation to God only by actualizing God in the World.[92] For Buber, however, God is a Thou who, although he never can be encountered as an it, is the Thou we encounter when we actualize God in the world by seeing the whole world not as a collection of "its" but as a Thou. Talking about "seeing-as" is not really adequate for talking about I-Thou encounters. We don't first see "its" and then see them as "Thous." When we encounter people in I-Thou relationships, we do not see them as collections of cells; we encounter them as "thous." So when we encounter God in an I-Thou relationship, we do not see a world of sticks and stones, atoms and galaxies as an eternal "thou," but we encounter God as that within which we live and move and have our being.[93]

Levinas, however, does not find the divine in a Thou to be encountered in dialogue. He does not interpret devotion and prayer as a matter of having a dialogue with an eternal Thou. He does not interpret our encounter with God to be a matter of actualizing God in a way of seeing. For Levinas the coming to mind of God is always linked to our ethical encounters with people in their infinite singularity, to hearing their cries not to be annihilated. For Levinas, God is personal in that he brings about interpersonal ethical relationships between people. Religious feelings like the fear of God is not a matter of fearing what a supernatural being might do to us, but rather it is a matter of fearing for my neighbor. Devoting oneself to God, loving God, is loving one's neighbor and devoting oneself to meeting one's responsibilities to one's neighbor. Praying to God is expressing thanks for creation, confessing one's failure to meet one's responsibilities, listening to the call to be responsible to one's neighbor and all strangers, and seeking to understand what concretely those responsibilities are, that God's will might be done rather than one's own nonmoral will.[94] It is in welcoming the ethical call of the face, Levinas tells us, that we find the first prayers and religious liturgies and services, that we find that the idea of God comes to mind.[95] People in different places and times have developed different social practices for dealing with their ethical responsibilities, practices that include different kinds of religious liturgies, different ways of praying and meditating, different ways of disciplining themselves to encounter people ethically and devote themselves to loving God, different ways of nurturing new generations to live ethically and religiously. Nevertheless, Levinas writes, there is something common in all great spiritualities.[96]

The idea of God comes to mind in an ethical setting, but being religious is not just a matter of being ethical. Ethically encountering the face involves having created in us a desire unlike any desire that can be satisfied. It is out of this desire that the idea of God comes to mind. For Levinas, God is the desirable infinite of this desire. This desire is not one of the desires making up our subjectivity that we can try to satisfy by eating a meal or going to a movie. The "object" of this desire is the ethical desirability of meeting our primordial responsibilities to the face of another. This makes us hostages to that which remains inescapably other to us and our socially constituted world. It is the desire to meet our unlimited responsibilities to the singularity of the person encountered, a singularity that cannot be bound under any concept but which in its ethical height is transcendently infinite. Nourishing this desire for God as the desirable ethical ultimate, which is the ultimate religious imperative definitive of being religious, is always a matter of augmenting this desire into an ever more demanding demand.[97] We desire to ever more deeply desire to meet our responsibilities.

In this desire, the infinite is located within the religious person's subjectivity as a sense of the holy, demolishing all illusions of subjectivity's autonomy or self-sufficiency, revealing the person's creaturely finiteness and the person's call to ethical responsibility. To live from this desire is to place under judgment all the desires of the old ways of living without this desire. It is to desire what is absurd in terms of desires that are subjectively centered lacks. It is the desire to be an ethical hostage to what is radically other than oneself and one's socially constituted world. This desire for what is ultimately desirable, God, is not a desire for a divine servant who meets my lacks. Rather, it is a desire for a God who turns me away from any ontotheological god and turns me toward others to whom I have an infinite responsibility. To love God is to love one's neighbor, the orphan, the widow, and the stranger. This is a god who is other than all being and all encounterable others, who is so transcendent as to be ontotheologically absent and thus able to be the desirable of this unique ethical and religious desire.

Religion for Levinas is not a matter of beliefs about or experiences of some extraordinary being or even the being of beings, and religious discourse is not originally dialogue. Religious discourse is in the beginning crying out "Here I am" in response to the face's call for responsibility and as an embodiment of the desire for the ultimately desirable, a desire manifesting itself in concrete service to other people.[98] This is what lies behind Levinas's claim that the idea of God has no meaning outside of the search for god.[99] God is not visible, not thematizable, not a term in a relation. God is an infinite to which I am destined by my ethically encountering the singularity of other people and thus desiring the supremely desirable.[100] Just as a person's responsibilities do not disappear when the person irresponsibly lives among people rather than ethically encountering them, so God as the supremely desirable does not disappear when someone does not desire God. The ethical and religious are the inescapable other radiating through all of human life.

Interpersonal ethical encounters with other people, involving as they do assuming the responsibilities that are part of recognizing the radical otherness of people in their singularity, tie our unique identity as ethical respondents to the uniqueness of the people we encounter in their unique and nonfinite identity. Our status as ethical hostages to those we encounter ethically, as hostages who desire to ever increase their desire to be responsibly just to all people, takes on a special significance when we are dealing with the ethical relations holding between parents and their children. It is because of this significance that Levinas can claim that death can both be the end of a person's life, since it is the impossibility of any further possibilities, and that death cannot destroy the infinite that gives us our identity. Biologically producing offspring is neither sufficient nor necessary for being the parent of a child, in Levinas's sense of the word. Neither is possessing all the socially constituted duties and privileges definitive of the social role of parent, around which so much of Confucian ethics circulates.[101]

My child is not mine in the way that my car is mine. In one sense my child is other than me and thus someone I can encounter ethically. In another sense the child that I parent is me continuing to live. Ethically I am one striving to live responsibly for the other, for the other of the other, for the responsibilities of the other. My very identity is tied to this ethical project that places me under infinite responsibilities. In one sense my life of living responsibilities dies when it becomes impossible for me to live responsibly any longer. In another sense, when my parenting is ethical parenting, which for Levinas is what parenting is all about, then I am nurturing my child to ethically encounter other people, to live justly with all people, and to desire the ultimately desirable. My child is mine because I have ethically nurtured this child and, given that my ethical identity is determined by the uniqueness of my responsibilities, I am my child as my child in filiality gives new life to my self-defining ethical possibilities, in the sense that these responsibilities now live on in my child.[102]

Just as Rosenzweig had claimed that people love when they have been loved, so Levinas is claiming that people ethically encounter other people face-to-face when they have been trained to encounter people ethically. The most important ethical responsibility that people have is to nurture other people to encounter people ethically and to establish just social practices, including nurturing practices, so that nurturing will continue on throughout historical time. Such nurturing is parenting, and through such nurturing a world wide family of siblings is created. One's very identity lives on in those one nurtures and so on to the next and the next and the next generation.

The history of people is an ethical history and it is other than the history of beings and the being of beings. Since ethical nurturing is part of a project of living ethically and justly with other people, whose singularity and radical otherness must be respected, parents are their children even while their children remain radically other in their own singularity. Living as uniquely singular persons and living as parents, children, and siblings are not mutually exclusive alternatives. The interpersonal world in which we live is radically other than the intersubjective world of social rationality, even though the former radiates through the latter and is the precondition of such intersubjectivity. The ethical and the religious are prior and higher than anything presumed to be nonethical and nonreligious. Injustices in the world of social practices live on in the new generations trained to participate in them. Resistance to injustice lives on in one's spiritual children as they are nurtured to live ethically and responsibly. In the first case we find the presence of bad karma and original sin and in the latter case we find good karma and divine grace. In both cases we exist not as individual substances but as historical beings whose very identities are tied to the past and the future.

III. ZIZEK ON REVOLUTIONARY CHRISTIANITY

Slavoj Zizek is a master at appropriating themes from apparently dissonant writers and then creatively weaving them into an insightful mosaic. By dialogically engaging Kierkegaard, Hegel, Marx, Lenin, and Lacan, Zizek constructs an interpretation of Pauline Christianity as being doubly revolutionary. His interpretation of Christianity radicalizes Kierkegaard's revolutionary rejection of all the traditional objectivistic treatments of Christianity. He presents an existentialist turn on Hegel's dialectical claim that the infinite God becomes fully actualized in finite human history. His Lacanian and Leninist take on Paul's history-shattering-act-of-faithfulness to Jesus Christ gives rise to an interpretation of the origin of Christianity as an act that radically revolutionizes human history. Finally, Zizek interprets Christian faithfulness to Jesus Christ as consisting of a life of universal "agape," love for all people in their singular uniqueness, precarious vulnerability, and agency.

Agape love for Zizek is a love that requires active participation in a quasi-Marxist revolutionary struggle against all oppression and domination, especially that present in the current globalization of neocapitalism and forms of multicultural liberalism. It is a love that allows, without horror or envy, others to remain different in their embodiments of pleasure and *jouissance*. (*Jouissance* is a word used to refer to that kind of enjoyment that Lacan labels "Real" and which Levinas sees as the ultimate base of things we value.) Agape love is a love that cherishes the existence of different sorts of people as agents expressing, preserving, and celebrating their differences. Unlike some forms of liberalism, it does not see suffering people merely as victims arousing our sympathies or as victims to be tolerated while still keeping them as distant others lest they contaminate one's own distinctive way of life.

Zizek presents a Kierkegaardian (Bultmannian)[103] subjectivistic interpretation of St. Paul's proclamations about flesh and spirit, about death, resurrection, and eternal life in Christ. Flesh and spirit, he claims, are not matters of biology but of two ways to live life, two existential attitudes.[104] The life of the flesh is the life of law (social prohibitions) and sin (behaving in accordance with the desire to defy these prohibitions, desire generated by the prohibitions themselves).[105] The way of life of the spirit is a matter of transcending law and sin by opening oneself to living within an eternal life of love in which everything is permitted.[106] The movement from the life of the flesh to the spiritual life of the Christian originates in a decision by the Christian to be absolutely faithful to what the Christian sees as the death and resurrection of Jesus Christ. The decision to die to one world in order to live in another is the decision to be unconditionally faithful to the God-Man, Jesus Christ. Christ's death signifies that the "not finite" in man is inseparable from his finiteness, that the eternal truth that all people can attain eternal life is present in all people and available for any person to grasp.[107] Christ's resurrection signifies that each person can rise after dying to the world of the flesh in order to live a true life filled with agape love.[108] The decision to become a faithful follower of Jesus Christ, Zizek claims, is thoroughly dogmatic, based on no reasons and beyond the possibility of refutation.[109] The crucifixion and resurrection of Jesus Christ are events only for Christians who encounter them as traumatic, world-shattering events. They are events only as the decisions of Christians kill off their old lives and they are raised up as new people with new lives.[110]

All religion and experience of the sacred, according to Zizek, is a matter of putting under question the adequacy and unified completeness of any socially constituted world (the world of the symbolic, Lacan's "reality") and entering into a lived world other than the social world of rules and daily routines.[111] Lacan's "Real" traumatically forces itself upon someone as the inadequacy of the social order becomes all too apparent. The door is opened to the possibility of a radically free religious act of marginalizing the whole social order and initiating a new line of historical development. This, Zizek explains, is the kind of actual freedom to revolutionize the background preconditions of a way of life that Lenin talked about (as opposed to the liberal's formal freedom to function in an established social order).[112]

Only in Judaism and Christianity, Zizek claims, do radical and revolutionary changes in history occur because only in them do we find new communities founded on faithfulness to what is perceived as a world-shattering invasion of the eternal into history.[113] Jews divorced themselves from the socially constituted natural and social order of the day and, while living by their new set of laws, faithfully waited for the messiah, the full presence of the infinite in the finite.[114] Their prohibition of the impossible, making images of the infinite and eternal God, was a protection against the anthropomorphism present in their own talk about the God they worshiped.[115] Christians created a second historical revolution by their constitution of a community of newly born people faithful to what they perceived as the messiah, the savior, who has come. They understood themselves to have transcended worldly and Jewish law and all need to fear anthropomorphism because in Jesus Christ they believed they saw that people not only live as images of God but that they are themselves inescapably infinite and eternal.[116] For Christians, God is personal because they can encounter God when they encounter the sacred infiniteness in people, when God is encountered through seeing the singularly unique pain in a person's face,[117] or in seeing a kindly smile or helpful gesture in an otherwise drab and indifferent world.[118] This, of course, resonates with Levinas's claim that the infinite is encountered when one faithfully responds to the infinite present in face-to-face encounters with people. That God is fully present in the historical Jesus Christ means for Zizek, as for Hegel, that God becomes fully actual as a living God only in the spiritually resurrected lives of Christians.[119] On this point, however, Zizek's Hegel comes with a twist of Kierkegaard. Like Kierkegaard, Zizek claims that it is history-shattering decisions and not the logic of a master narrative that produces these radical historical changes. Since God becomes a living God only in the faithful subjectivity of living people, the absolute, Zizek reminds us, remains fragile and needs to be handled as carefully as a butterfly.[120] There are no guarantees of any kind in history, and thus there is no guarantee that the Christian community always will faithfully reproduce itself.

The Christian life, according to Zizek, is one of agape love that is directed universally to all people. After dying to the whole world of social roles and rules, where people are seen only as men, women, Jews, Greeks, fathers, mothers, Christians see people in that singular uniqueness that makes them different. Here again Zizek echos Levinas.[121] Agape love is universalistic and Christians are called to care equally about all the orphans, widows, and strangers in the world and to resist all forms of oppression and domination, personal and structural. Agape love calls for radical political activity and revolutionary economic, social, and cultural change. Furthermore, out of agape love, the Christian hates it when people are treated by themselves or others as nothing but social role occupants. This hatred, however, disappears as Christians see these role-players as people whose personal significance infinitely transcends their position in a finite social order.[122] This agape love recognizes the terrifying and threatening gaps, ruptures, and conflicts that are present in the lives of all people, including Christians, who always remain very vulnerable.[123] Agape love allows people to recognize and live with inevitably incomplete and fractured psychic and social lives. Agape love also walks hand in hand with eros with its natural and spontaneous kindnesses, pleasures, and indescribable *jouissance*.[124]

As Zizek interprets it, Christianity faces a very unique threat of distortion. First, the dogmatic, nonrational character of Christian faithfulness to the Christ event, and to the "authentic fundamentalism" of the Christian agape way of life which is involved in that faithfulness, can too easily be distorted into a "perverted fundamentalism."[125] Perverted fundamentalists not only see themselves as different from those outside their Christian community, but they are filled with horror and envy over the pleasures of those other than themselves.[126] Not recognizing that the Christian subjectivisitic mode of subjectivity can only be threatened by the Christian's own lack of faithfulness, "perverted fundamentalists" see outsiders not as children of God to whom agape love should be shown but as less than human captives of Evil, Satan, whose freedom must be controlled by all forms of available power (social ostracism, cultural marginalization, economic exclusion, state coercion). Authentic fundamentalists remain faithful within their community, but they neither envy nor are struck with horror by the way others socially organize their *jouissance*. They recognize that the kind of political and social revolution that agape love demands is a spiritual revolution in the mode of subjectivity of believers and not a revolution creating a tyrannical theocracy in which non-Christians end up being dominated and oppressed.

If it is possible for there to be multiple communities of authentic religious fundamentalists, as I shall argue in section 4 of this chapter, then agape love calls for letting, without envy or fear, other communities live in their otherness. It calls for prizing different religious communities. It calls for entering into a dialogue with these communities, which opens up both communities to the possibility of revolutionary change in their dogmatic fundamentals. Given the different radical historical acts that led to the formation of these different religious communities, and given the long historical developments of these different communities of faithful religious people, there need be no fear that a bland, religious homogenization will take place. Trusting the power of such dialogue, however, would be a matter of trusting that history is not yet finished, that radical historical acts can still occur, that the infinite still is active in invading human history, that spiritual development is not yet ended.

IV.   A POSTMODERNIST INTERPRETATION OF BUDDHIST AND MYSTIC TRADITIONS

Analyzing the strengths and weaknesses of two recent interpretations of people encountering social rationality's other in a religious way can enrich our understanding of the varied religious possibilities that remain open even after the death of the ontotheological god. Mark Taylor[127] attempts to show how a fusion of the Kyoto School of Buddhist philosophy[128] with deconstruction, Kierkegaardian existentialism, and a theoretical understanding of the microbiotics of information theory can take us religiously past the deconstruction of ontotheology and the weaknesses of modernism, a journey illustrated in a great deal of postmodern art and literature. Huston Smith[129] presents an interpretation of the world's religions as attempts by people to deal with their encounters with the Other of social rationality, as variations on encounters with the mystic's God, who can never be a describable being and thus is other than all beings, but who is nevertheless necessary for the existence of all beings. Very much can be appropriated from the writings of these two persons even when rejecting some of their objections to certain themes in postmodernism.

A.   MARK TAYLOR ON SACRED ALTERITY AND A DIVINE
       MILIEU

Like Zizek, Taylor is a master appropriator of a diversity of recent
cultural perspectives and projects, Western and Japanese, theological,
philosophical, literary, artistic, and scientific. Like his daughter
Kirsten,[130] he constructs mosaics that are intellectually and existentially
insightful and challenging. With rhetorical power he deconstructs the
many faces of ontotheology while also posting analytical and artistic
reminders that killing off the ontotheological god still leaves present
a radical, nonconceptual otherness, an irreducible, irremovable sacred
no-thingness that scars all beings and thoughts and that indicts all
efforts to absolutize socially constituted subjects and objects. He
frames these postings with an interpretation of socially constituted
subjects and objects that pairs Buddhism's accent on the codependent
origination of all beings with modern scientific investigations of the
global but nontotalizable information systems that are seen as the
basis of all human social, psychological, biological, and microneu-
rological activity. While striving to reduce differences to sameness,
Taylor, like the Hegel he so greatly admires, finds only tension and
not opposition between science's objectivistic mode of subjectivity
and religion's subjectivistic mode of subjectivity, modes that are only
modes of a single commonality which, although being global, is still
radically different from Hegel's eternal, closed, totalizing system.

   Given the fashionableness in so much of recent literature to write
about racial, ethnic, sexual, colonial, and postcolonial otherness, alterity,
Taylor invents the word "altarity" in order to talk about an otherness
to anything describable so as to accent the radical difference between
this latter otherness and the former examples, an invention that is
comparable to Derrida's invention of the word "differance." Trying to
interpret what Taylor has written about the sacred character of alterity
and the divine milieu in which we live is difficult and dangerous
because Taylor is deliberately trying not to present an account of
things that can be turned into a totalizing system that can be justified

or refuted. In spite of this effort, however, it does seem possible to organize what he writes so as to present an interpretation that does not do inexcusable violence to his texts. The prosaic interpretations offered here, of course, cannot possibly have the rhetorical effect of Taylor's very poetic and artistic writing, especially his play of signifiers (altarity, altar, alter, alternate, alternative, alternation, alterity).[131]

I will begin by looking at his deconstruction of ontotheology and his deconstructive a/theological alternative to both theological ontotheology and antitheological atheism. Then I will look at his examination of postmodern art's religious attempt to point to radical altarity. I will analyze his argument that an alternative must be found to social universalism and to neofoundational efforts to counter the antifoundationalism of those who postulate that there is no other to the social. I then will examine the alternative he constructs drawing upon recent informational interpretations in biology and Buddhist writings about dependent origination. Finally, I will offer some critical responses to Taylor's concerns about postmodernism and to his appropriation of Buddhism.

Taylor interprets classical theism as always being ontotheological, with God as the unified supreme being who creates all other beings and who directs the course of nature, with people as unified individuals who are given freedom by God, with history being a single line of change caused by the interaction of God and his created people, and with the whole story of nature and history being understandable and explainable in a single theoretical book.[132] Rather than simply deny the correctness of "classical theism" as humanistic atheism does, Taylor seeks to deconstruct the binary oppositions that bind both theism and atheism (God/world, eternity/time, infinite/finite, etc.). Atheism is theism's offspring trying to kill off the father and take his place, and it fails to recognize that the death of god implies also the death of the self that atheism prizes.[133] A religious alternative to both theism and atheism is needed, and Taylor offers deconstructive a/theology.

Before analyzing Taylor's third, middle way alternative, it is important to note that Kierkegaard, Levinas, Zizek, and, as we shall see, Wittgenstein and D. Z. Phillips deny that theistic language, as used either in worship or in theological reflection on encounters with the infinite, has to be interpreted ontotheologically. If they are correct, as I think they are, then Taylor's deconstruction of ontotheology can be appropriated without abandoning theism. I suggest that it is Taylor's similar characterization of philosophy as always (mostly) being ontotheological,[134] thus preventing him from drawing upon the pragmatic tradition, that leads him unnecessarily to indict quests for truth[135] and postmodernism's claim that all beings are socially constituted.[136] I will suggest that a more pragmatic reading of Buddhism would have enabled him to appreciate better the Buddha's noble silence on objectivistic, global interpretations and the Buddha's recommendation not to crave objectivistic opinions, even nontotalizing Hegelian ones.

In his first a/theological effort to rise to a level above the theism/atheism opposition, Taylor draws upon Thomas Altizer's radical Death of God Christology,[137] in which the divine is seen as thoroughly incarnational.[138] Taylor posts Altizer's position alongside Buddhism's doctrine of codependent origination. In this Buddhist interpretive schema, determinate beings are replaced by an everlasting flow,[139] a divine milieu in which all events are interrelated and originate in codependence.[140] If we understand that we live in this divine milieu, which has no beginning, no end, no governing law of change, then we can gracefully wander carnivalistically without security, letting becoming be valued at every moment, aimlessly drifting like the free floating of childhood.[141] God, as a supreme being other to a world of substantial beings, is seen as dead. Incarnate divinity is proclaimed as other to any totalizable world of independent substances, as an other of process and interdependency that is treated as a divine milieu in order to protect against atheism's treatment of people and things as self-sufficient substances. Taylor quotes with admiration[142] Mikhail Bakhtin's claim that unrestrained, carnivalistic laughter and joy free us "from dogmatism, from the intolerant and petrified; it liberates us from fanaticism and pedantry, from fear and intimidation, from didacticism, naiveté and illusion, from the single meaning, single level, from sentimentality."[143]

Taylor came to see, however, that it is not as easy to get rid of God as he had thought when he wrote *Erring*.[144] Confessing that he cannot believe in the ontotheological god, he admits that he cannot avoid believing in the sacred, which for him is a de-negation of God that allows god to be radically other than everything that is not god. This radical otherness, however, is different from Karl Barth's interpretation of God as wholly other, as transcendent and totally independent from the world of the finite.[145] The infinite, Taylor proclaims, remains inescapably related to the finite even if the infinite is not of our socially constituted world. Taylor's infinite is different from the infinite in Hegel's synthesis of both the infinite and the finite in the lawfully developing world of social rationality. It also is different from Kierkegaard's infinite, which is open to human encounter when we either choose a mode of subjectivity defined by loyalty to the pursuit of eternal happiness or we choose a mode of subjectivity that leaves us living despairingly in some world of the finite.[146] Taylor now recognizes that Altizer's God, who dies that the divine might become incarnate, is Barth's wholly other God, thus making the incarnate divine so immanent in the finite world that radical altarity is impossible.[147] In order not to absolutize or deify the finite, and in order not to erase the sacred altarity present in the absence of the dead God of ontotheology and the absence of all of atheism's independent substances and law totalizing processes, Taylor turns to Derrida's writings about differance and trace to help his reader appreciate the interrelatedness and nonsubstantiality of every person, thing, word, belief, and desire, the chanciness of all occurrences and conditions, the absence of origins, innocent or demonic, and the absence of eschatological completions.[148]

The milieu in which we live, with its sacred altarity, is divine because everything presupposes it and because nothing else dare be worshiped as divine. Sacred altarity is the indescribable other that makes the describable possible; it is the radically different void that makes possible the relatively determinate differences between all the interdependent and thus limited and finite foci in the world in which we find ourselves, a world of change and chance without beginning or end. The carnivalistic joy that Taylor highlights in the deconstructive a/theology of *Erring* is strikingly similar to the Real of enjoyment that Lacan and Zizek find as the indescribable Other to our whole symbolic world.[149] Although Taylor provides some extremely careful analysis of Levinas's writings about radical alterity beyond a world of determinate beings, especially the alterity present in face-to-face encounters and in the saying of what is said,[150] he does not turn to Levinas's phenomenological pointing to enjoyment, living on the elements, living at home, death, and fecundity to direct us to altarity. Instead, he focuses his accent on the void and to the poets and artists who create works pointing out this void.

In addition to Derrida, the writer whom Taylor draws most heavily upon to point at the infinite absence, so menacing and so attractive, haunting all writing, is Maurice Blanchot.[151] It is in post-modernist art, however, that Taylor locates his most impressive examples of the altarity that tears apart ontotheological culture. Already in modernist art, Taylor points out, religion had become for many displaced by art.[152] In romantic paintings such as William Turner's *Glacier and Source of the Averyon* and Albert Hierstadt's *Among the Sierra Nevada Mountains in California*, efforts were made to indicate the sublime character of the perceptible world that concepts and Newtonian mechanics could not represent. Van Gogh had been a theology student who found personal redemption by painting his utopian vision of what things should be like and Gauguin saw artists as uninhibited divine creators who seek pure perceptions free of corrupted European life. Taylor finds in Eduard Munch's four paintings *(The Scream, Despair, Anxiety,* and *The Dead Mother and her Child),* lived personally by him in reverse order of their painting, a Kierkegaardian understanding of the significance of encountering death in a leveled'down world in which no one listens to one's screams of anxiety and despair.[153]

The history of modern art can be interpreted as a series of ever more radical efforts to break free from a Newtonian, Kantian world of perceptible beings with inescapable spatial and temporal forms and to paint instead what is other than such a world of beings.[154] Monet frees sensory impressions from depth perception of space; Cezanne transforms the actual forms of corrupt urban life into harmonious, pure, rural works of art; Picasso uses pre-Roman, Spanish, and African forms to go beyond the still too conventional forms of Cezanne; Matisse paints emotions of perceivers rather than perceived objects; cubism superimposes mentally generated geometric forms to challenge all perceptual forms; Kadinski challenges all form regardless of how it is generated; dadaism sees everything as nonsensical as its name derived from babytalk; Salvador Dali seeks to escape the requirements of conscious perception and turns to dreams where time can stand still; Jackson Pollack finds even Dali still too tied to Kantian requirements of form; performance art makes art objects disappear when the performance is over; and conceptual art produces no perceptual artworks at all. In seeking to express what is different from the world of beings with all of its corruptions, modern art is doing what religion classically was doing.

Taylor charges that modern art reached a dead end because its abstraction from everyday life robbed it of all relevance, its accent on the autonomy of a work of art failed to recognize the inescapable interconnection of things, its utopian dreams turned into the terrifying nightmares of world wars, concentration camps, and gulags, and its commercialized ritual repetitions robbed it of its critical power.[155] Postmodern art, however, Taylor claims, gives expression to the sacred altarity and divine milieu of a/theological religious interpretations. He presents rich and inspiring analyses of many forms of postmodern art. Four projects in particular give expression to his a/theological perspective.

Anne and Patrick Poirer in their sculptures *Thunderstruck Landscape, Death of Mimas,* and *Death of Encceladus,* illustrate that there are no presents that artists can present because the very identity of all present moments are tied to ancient pasts that are both nonoriginal and indispensable for all the differences that we perceive.[156] Arata Isozaki, in his work *The Future City*, illustrates the absence of all centers and boundaries in our post-Hiroshima lives where the past cannot be erased and utopian expectations are indecent, where lives are lived on the edge of life-threatening cliffs, in the midst of ruins, with bottomless fissures running through reconstruction projects.[157] Isozaki and his collaborator Madaline Gins in their artistic construction *Bridge of Reversible Destiny*, illustrate how hope can live on without modernist utopian expectations. They take seriously Heidegger's charge that poets are artistic world creators. They construct a labyrinth of unilluminated and crooked pathways through spheres, cubes, cylinders, pyramids, circles, squares, through rooms within rooms and rooms above rooms divided sometimes and lined sometimes with black mesh. Through this labyrinth perceivers can walk, and during this walk they can get radically disoriented and possibly reconstituted as new worlds filled with gaps and fissures are constituted for them.[158]

Daniel Libeskind's architectural design *Berlin, City Edge*, subverts the Berlin Wall by deconstructing the ideological binary opposition of East and West Berlin through foldings and refoldings of the wall that is raised above a public street and through the decentering interpenetration of interior and exterior walls.[159] Even more expressive of the postmodernism move beyond modernism is Libeskind's *Extension to the Berlin Museum with the Jewish Museum*. In this extension everything is a supplement to everything else (the Jewish museum can be entered only through the old museum). In it, outsides determine insides (the design of the museum is a function of a Star of David plotted on the map of Berlin with its six points commemorating three of Berlin's Jewish and three of its non-Jewish cultural heroes). At the core of the museum is a void structuring the whole museum and mirrored in the Holocaust Tower outside (inside, beside) the museum, around which stretches a plaza that is a memory book on which is engraved the names of the Berliners deported and killed in the concentration camps.[160]

As praiseworthy as Taylor finds postmodernist art, there are aspects of postmodernism that he finds unsatisfactory. First, most surprisingly, he opposes postmodernism's antifoundationalism and its rejection of transcendent norms or universal principles, because he believes that postmodernism's interpretation of such norms and principles as being socially constituted entails a relativism that leads to nihilism and "the ceaseless exercise of competing wills to power."[161] As I have already tried to show, however, norms and principles need to be linguistically formulated and thus they are a part of a symbolic order that inescapably is socially specific and historically variable. Everything Taylor has written about deconstruction reinforces this claim, and his analysis of postmodern art shows that what is radically other than the symbolic order is not linguistically formulatable. In the last two chapters I have attempted to show that transcendent norms and principles are not needed in order to carry out social criticism. Universal normative claims, such as Foucault's principle of minimizing nonconsentuality, can be made and used in moral deliberations without these principles being transcendental, asocial, or ahistorical. Examining the pragmatics of such deliberations shows this. Tsun-tzu, with his accent on the creative use of tradition, pointed this out centuries ago in China. Levinas has shown that the transcendent that enables radical social criticism is not a norm or a principle, but the singularity of people who are encountered face-to-face. Life does not begin in the symbolic order and then transcend it to get critical norms and principles, but rather life is ethical from the beginning and the saying of the said never permits the said to be some morally neutral social set of practices. Taylor has said as much in his study of Levinas[162] and in his analysis of Derrida's appropriation of Levinas.[163]

Taylor's concern that focusing on singularities, differences, and otherness leads to a failure to recognize and appreciate commonality among people[164] seems to forget Levinas's point that the universality that is crucial for ethics is the universality of people whose singular identities are ethical and thus protected from being reduced to their social or biological identities, although meeting one's obligations to such singular people requires caring for them in their many describable differences. Furthermore, to alleviate Taylor's concern about community we can turn to Levinas's analysis of what is involved in parenting ethical children to accept the responsibilities that go with face-to-face encounters. Ethical families and communities are created and recreated generation after generation. We also can turn to Zizek's charge that Christian ecounters with the Christ are possible only because of the Christian community's confession and proclamation of their memory of the truth event that creates their community.

Taylor, again surprisingly, turns to an objectivistic interpretation of the whole world of social rationality (language, cybernetics, information theory, disease, genes, neurological processes) to get past the problems he sees in poststructuralism.[165] If the problem is epistemological or ethical relativism, however, then giving a general interpretation of how things are does not seem to supply what is needed. That interpretation, as fascinating as it is, is also socially and historically located and in that sense part of our mode of subjectivity, using only one among many possible vocabularies, descriptions, and explanatory schema. If information theory is to say something relevant about ethical concerns, then an ethical vocabulary will have to be built into it. This is not currently present in neurophysiological interpretations. Also, if Levinas is correct, then that ethical vocabulary will have to be tied back to ethical encounters that transcend all worlds of socially constituted beings, including Taylor's world of information interdependencies.

Taylor's concern about postmodernism's claim that all beings are socially constituted gets generated only because he still tries to use in these contexts the words "nature" and "reality" to refer to something that is not socially constituted. He tells us that we must consider "the possibility that social constructions of reality relate to something other than themselves"[166] and we must not dogmatically assert that nature is culturally relative.[167] Taylor is forgetting about the pragmatics that govern the use of these words. There is no nonsocially constituted language in which to talk about some indeterminate stuff that gets socially constituted in one way here and another way there. There are only the vocabularies people use and the claims they make about the things they use this vocabulary to talk about. This is why Rorty tells us that we are better off dropping talk about worlds other than socially constituted worlds. All of Taylor's reminders about the death of the metaphysical god and the closure of the book are sufficient to remind us that one can try to make claims about the relativity of interpretations only if one presumes the possibility of an "objective," "nonrelative" picture of things as they really are. Kant, Kierkegaard, Nietzsche, Davidson, Derrida, and Taylor himself taught us that such a presumption is incoherent.

The general interpretation that Taylor offers is one very different from the systematic interpretations offered by the Hegelians or structuralists. Although he recommends interpreting everything as a system of interrelated information systems, thus undercutting the oppositions between brains and minds or physical processes and cultural activities, he acknowledges that such an interpretive system would be "incomplete nets and open-ended webs, which are riddled by operations that are irreducible, incalculable and hence undecidable"[168] because of quantum and Godel like preventions. Such a system would avoid the charge of dangerous totalizations leveled by antistructuralists against structuralists. With its deconstruction of independent beings and its systemwide gaps and unrepresentable boundaries, Taylor offers here an interpretation of the milieu in which we find ourselves with all the radical Altarity that cannot be driven out, a milieu that can be seen as divine and an Altarity that can be seen as sacred when we live with this way of interpreting things.

It is because of the religious potential of this deconstructive interpretation that Taylor finds in Buddhism's accents on process, universal interrelatedness, no souls or substances, and dependent origination, many suggestive resonances.[169] He reads in a theoretical rather than practical way Nishida's discussion of the self possessing itself through a self-negation.[170] He does the same with Nishitani's discussion of the Buddhist's great doubt about the existence of self-contained and enduring selves or material substances, of sunyata which is realized when false selves constituted through craving are negated, of everything being interrelated and codependent on everything else.[171]

Taylor's theoretical interpretation, however, ignores the Buddha's exhortation to maintain a noble silence on theoretical claims made about how things are. Part of the Buddha's motivation for doing so is his understanding that cravings for theoretical opinions can sidetrack people from their primary spiritual task, which is practical. Taylor wants to find a middle way between the totalities of structuralism and what he sees as the absence of global claims in poststructuralism, but the Buddha talked about a middle way between Jain asceticism and Charvaka hedonistic self-indulgence. Buddhist philosophers again and again succumbed to the temptation to theoretically speculate about what things are like, but Buddhist sages like Nagarjuna called them back to their practical, spiritual task.[172] Nagarjuna's advice is similar to Kierkegaard's advice not to fall into an objectivistic mode of subjectivity but to find an effective subjective mode of subjectivity that focuses on one's spiritual condition.

Buddhism's "Four Noble Truths" are all practical (diagnostic and therapeutic) and not theoretical. These truths are:

> (1) Life as we usually live it is filled with suffering, not primarily physical suffering, which does not destroy a person when it has meaning, but the suffering and anguish of feeling fear, regrets, guilt, embarrassment, shame, humiliation, inferiority, of being unwanted, worthless, lonely, totally dependent, no control of one's body, and useless. It is this second kind of suffering that drives people to slow or quick suicide.

> (2) The cause of this suffering is all the cravings produced by *Tanha*, a sense of self and self-esteem tied to comparative evaluations of oneself relative to others. We crave what we think we need in order to be superior to others (smarter, prettier, stronger, more successful, more creative, more independent), to avoid being inferior to others, to be popular and well thought

of by others, to possess self-esteem. Suffering is dependent on these cravings, and these cravings are dependent upon this secondary self we build for ourselves. Suffering is also dependent on the social practices constitutive of our vocabularies, taken-for-granteds, norms, explanatory and justificatory principles, ideologies, and microphysics of power. As Zizek/Lacan point out, we cravingly desire to satisfy the desires of others, the norms and ideals of our social world, something we never can do successfully. These cravings not only make their possessor miserable but they motivate people to cause incalculable suffering in others.

(3) This suffering can be ended because just as we make our lives and the lives of others miserable, so we can put to death this secondary self and its cravings.

(4) The eightfold path is the practical, spiritual therapy we have to follow in order to extinguish *Tanha* and suffering. Diagnose the problem of suffering correctly, don't increase *Tanha* by deceptive or harmful speech or action, put forth the therapeutic effort needed to undue years of work building up *Tanha*, and live joyfully through the moments of life filled with delights of living with the elements that were incomprehensive in the life of *Tanha*, live with compassionate thoughts and actions no longer prevented by the cravings of *Tanha*. Extinguishing *Tanha* means no longer trying to maintain total control over the past or the future, the mountains or the bamboo, ourselves or other people or animals, or the chanciness present in all of living.

The Buddhist analysis of dependent origination is offered in the classical Samyutta Nikaya, Visuddhi Magga, and Digha-Nikaya, Mahanidana sutta as part of the diagnosis of the causes of suffering that have to be removed if *Tanha* is to die off and suffering is to be ended so that the delights of living and compassion may be freed.[173] Suffering is dependent on craving attachments that are dependent on our ways of conceiving and perceiving the world and ourselves, that are dependent on our ignorance of the four noble truths.

Taylor's global but nontotalizing interpretation of human life is fascinating and it may be as he thinks it is, moving in the right direction, but it still is only an intellectual feat of interpretation and that does not by itself provide the diagnosis needed of the human condition. Besides, intellectual feats are never by themselves therapeutically sufficient. Because it is so fascinating, one must be careful that it is not a spiritual distraction. As part of a project of spiritual diagnosis, Taylor's interpretation would have been even more effective if he had retained the postmodernist claim that all conception, perception, belief and desire are social all the way down. The first step in the Buddhist story about the dependent origination of suffering is karma, the law of moral causality, which Nishitani interprets as a law of social history determining the Heideggerian world or milieu into which people are thrown, influencing thereby the social character of people's *Tanha* or secondary self.[174] What we currently are is inescapably tied to the social practices we have inherited, with all the misunderstanding and injustice they generate and with all the saving remnants usually marginalized in them. We are tied to the social and cultural legacy that lives on after us molding the worlds into which future generations are thrown. We inherit good and bad karma and we live on in the good and bad karma we leave for others to inherit.

Buddhism as a living religion does seem to have the potential for being one of those fundamentalistic religious communities that Zizek talks about. In the Buddhist encounter with the no-thingness, which is presupposed both by secondary selves and the things they crave, in the extinguishing of *Tanha*, which liberates people and their environments so that both can simply be allowed to be in their "suchness," we find a religious encounter with the nonfinite that is other to the whole world of social rationality. Unfortunately, Buddhism, in its twenty-five-hundred-year history, has seen appear within it not only many varied interpretations of the Buddhist texts and many spiritual therapies but also many superstitious practices and ontotheological claims. Again and again spiritual giants within the Buddhist tradition have had to take up Nagarjuna's project of deconstructing these claims and extinguishing these superstitions. Although Buddhists now find it very helpful in strengthening their own traditions to engage in dialogue with Christians, they still find their religious traditions to be spiritually efficacious. Some Christians are finding the same thing resulting from their dialogues with Buddhists. Neither need nor should be expected to shed their historical skins, although, as Gadamer points out, surprising and world-changing things might happen to both if dialogue continues. Taylor's dialogue with Buddhism seems to be capable of doing just that.

B.   HUSTON SMITH ON THE GOD OF MYSTICISM AS THE NECESSARY CONDITION FOR EVERYTHING FINITE

Through the million and a half copies of his book *The World's Religions,* Huston Smith has communicated the idea that there are a multitude of different ways that people with different historical and social backgrounds can construct religious practices in response to their encounters with the other of social rationality. He has also demonstrated the hegemonic power that scientism has accumulated in our contemporary world, being so entrenched in higher education, the media, and the law that many people now take it without question that only a scientific method grounded in controlled experiments can produce human knowledge and that only reductively interpreting life, sentient experience, and social rationality in terms of evolving material neurological conditions is objectively acceptable.[175] In spite of the power of scientism, Smith offers an interpretation of human life that he thinks does justice to the many and varied religious practices that continue in spite of the power of scientism, an interpretation that he claims is in harmony with the traditional religious interpretations and practices that existed before the rise of scientism during the past three centuries.

What needs to be examined here, in order to appropriate the many spiritually rich things Smith has to say about religious people's encounters with social rationality's other, is his argument that such encounters, and the religious practices and the modes of subjectivity tied to them, should be interpreted in terms of an ontotheological metaphysics that postulates a pure, infinitely powerful and intelligent "consciousness" that is identical with light itself, which is the source of emanations or creation of all finite things, and which directs all changes in the world of the finite toward a supremely good end, thereby guaranteeing ultimate meaningful explanations and value for everything. As interpreted in the previous sections, Kierkegaard, Levinas, Zizek, and Taylor find no need to make such a postulation in their interpretations of religious encounters and practices. Why does Smith think that his metaphysical postulations are not unreasonable?

By a metaphysics Smith says that he means a worldview, a big picture, something he claims no one can avoid because all beliefs, including scientism, are framed by such a worldview.[176] The world, he says, comes to us as an inkblot that is susceptible to different interpretations.[177] He admits that disputes among worldviews are unresolvable because what one counts as justifying claims are framed by the worldview with which one is working and the best one can offer as a worldview is one's perspective on things.[178] Still, Smith thinks that one can point out shortcomings in the scientistic worldview. I would suggest, however, that most of the shortcomings he points out in a scientism that reduces all knowledge about human beings to theoretical knowledge of brain phenomena that can be simulated in computers can be endorsed without making the metaphysical postulations Smith also makes.

As Heidegger and Dreyfus point out, you cannot reduce human know-how to the theoretical data you can feed into a computer.[179] Theoretical knowledge is derivative from the practical know-how or coping skills that constitute the more primary worlds into which people are thrown. With practice being primary to theory, there is no need to postulate some kind of intuitive intelligence to explain their presence, as Smith does.[180] Only if coping skills were an anomaly in some more primitive way of living would they need any explanation at all. Also, as Merleau-Ponty and Wittgenstein point out,[181] when you make the perception of people primary over the perception of neurophysiological brain phenomena, then there is again no need either to deny the existence of sensory states, as some scientistic reductionists do, or to declare that sensory experiences along with our acts of thinking are invisible, as Smith does.[182] We can see people in pain, viewing sunsets, listening to sad music, and we can hear or read what they are thinking. People sometimes can hide their feelings and thoughts from others, but most people are not very good in carrying out such attempts to pretend, pretenses that always are parasitic on our normal expression of our feelings and thoughts. Only if one assumes that one only can have sensory perceptions of nonliving, nonsentient, nonthinking materials does one end up with a dualism of perceptible material beings and their behavior, on the one hand, and "inner" or "invisible" perceptual experiences and thoughts on the other.

Similarly, scientism tries to restrict all knowledge to what can be learned by restricting oneself to science's methodological focus only on countable beings subject to controlled experiments, thereby excluding all claims about the moral significance of people or the norms to be used in criticizing individual actions and social practices.[183] As Levinas has pointed out, however, by giving primacy to ethics over theories of being and, as I have tried to demonstrate by examining the pragmatics governing the terms "true" and "justified," that kind of scientism can be rejected without postulating metaphysically transcendent tiers of being. Scientism may be a worldview that frames its particular claims, but this does not demonstrate that everything has a worldview functioning at the periphery. Kierkegaard and Heidegger claim that at the periphery of all human experience and thought are practical concerns and ways of coping. Levinas claims that the presupposed frame consists of ethical encounters with people who are other than any beings that might be described in a worldview and of ways of living with the elements that are other than experiences governed by the norms of social rationality.

Smith again seems correct in charging that a scientistic, objectivistic description of beings and things happening to them is devoid of any effort to show the significance of these beings, events, and processes.[184]

Since significance always is a function of the relationship of some item to someone who cares about it, one has to focus on such caring to focus on significance, something scientism does not do. This is one of Kierkegaard's criticisms of all objectivistic modes of subjectivity. Smith often appears to be writing out of a Kierkegaardian religious, subjective mode of subjectivity, focusing his attention on the existential efficacy of the various modes of subjectivity of contemporary people.[185] Whereas Kierkegaard attempts to show the inadequacies of aesthetic, moral, and religious subjective modes of subjectivity as well as objectivistic modes of subjectivity, Smith accents the Hindu analysis of the inadequacies of building lives focused primarily on the pursuit of sensual pleasure, worldly power or success, or a morality of fulfilling the Code of Manu's social role requirements.[186] Kierkegaard proclaims that only faithfulness to encounters with the infinite can allow people to escape despair, and Smith endorses the Hindu claim that people can find satisfaction only if they attain *moksha*—liberation from being merely a socially constituted being or a psychologically isolated person, liberation from frustrating limitations on knowing how to live well, and from limitations on joyful, blissful life.[187]

Kierkegaard, Levinas, Zizek, and Taylor all make valuable contemporary contributions to our understanding of what such a liberated life would be like. They do so without claiming that it is necessary to make Smith's metaphysical postulations. Smith's insistence that religious, subjective modes of subjectivity can sustain themselves only if tied to an objectivistic mode of subjectivity, focused on a worldview containing theoretical postulations of transcendent tiers of being, divorces Smith from Kierkegaardian existentialism. Smith's form of objectivistic subjectivity is subject to all of Kierkegaard's criticisms as well as those that follow from Nargarjuna's interpretation of the Buddha's noble silence. In the second century A.D., Nagarjuna warned early Buddhists not to get entangled in metaphysical speculations about time and causality. By trying to satisfy people's cravings and longing for big pictures,[188] Smith, the metaphysical theorist, speculating about unprovable tiers of transcendent being, is in danger of undercutting the efforts of Smith, the follower of Hindu and Abrahamic religious traditions, to strengthen religious efforts to get people to focus on the hard practical, spiritual work needed to change their modes of subjectivity.

Smith is seeking to get people to intellectually assert that (1) there is a transcendent, omniscient, omnipotent point of pure light/consciousness/intelligibility by whom everything was created or from whom everything emanated, (2) that this godhead guarantees that everything has its place in its perfect master plan,[189] and (3) that natural evolution and human history are being directed by it toward a utopian goal.[190] Smith's project is open to the charge that it is seeking to satisfy cravings and longings that increase *Tanha* and human suffering rather than reduce them. Even though people might say, as Smith charges we should, that the pure consciousness of the infinite godhead is beyond their ability to conceive, still they would know that it is they who possess this worldview of the ineffable. This theoretical possession can remain theirs even if they do not maintain faithfulness to the infinite. It could be such a prized possession that they could lose interest in doing the hard spiritual disciplining needed to be religious. This worldview still remains as a Promethean threat that Kierkegaard and the Buddha would critique. Intellectual endorsement of even this world view, with its claims that we are finite units of consciousness in an infinite sea of pure consciousness,[191] does not guarantee that we will have the living knowledge and commitment that faithfulness and the four noble truths require. Smith's world picture could be one taken only from the grandstand above life and would not necessarily produce a religious life on the playing field. It is still an ontotheology, one that Kierkegaard, Levinas, and Zizek find unnecessary and counterproductive for religious life on the playing field.

In what ways is this world picture both dangerous and unnecessary? It is dangerous for all the reasons Kierkegaard found Hegel's worldview dangerous. It leaves no room for the unique, nonfinite singularity of people, which is the locus of all intrinsic value and ethical norms. Smith's big picture, with universal "meaning" guaranteed because everything is in the place assigned to it by an infinite intelligence which determines from an eternal location the course of all temporal changes, reduces people to be nothing but functional units in the grand scheme of things. The dangerousness of this position is clearly shown by Smith's unfortunate use of aesthetic models to explain away evil, which he claims ultimately drops out of the picture. The evil of human suffering and violation supposedly becomes only a shade in a beautiful picture or a tone in heavenly music. Even the Holocaust becomes comparable to the unfortunate dropping of a scoop of ice cream from its cone.[192] People, with their priceless, infinite, unique singularity, are not allowed to exist in their radical ethical otherness but are swallowed up in an eternal and infinite consciousness as drops are swallowed up in the ocean. Smith's criticism of scientism's failure to leave room for human freedom can be leveled at Smith's own world picture aimed at making everything meaningful by giving it an explanation in terms of the transcendent godhead. If the evil that people create doesn't finally count in the big picture of things, then people are not really free, even as their singularity is not allowed to be. Given our inability to know the supposed mind of this ineffable godhead, this opens the dangerous door for the horrible misuse of people by people who think (mistakenly, of course) that they know what the master plan is and how people are to be used to carry it out.

Furthermore, Smith's effort to tie religion to ontotheology, in an effort to comfort people who have suffered the undesirable effects of natural disasters or evil human actions, will only further undermine religion because it permits the reintroduction of the argument from evil against the existence of God. If God and the Godhead are all-good, all-knowing, and all-controlling, then there should be no evil. Smith's reassuring word that evil is not really and ultimately "real" will not be persuasive to those who are suffering or being violated. The indictment that Dostoyevsky puts in Ivan Karamazov's mouth applies to Smith's ontotheology as well as to all the metaphysical theories of a Leibniz or Hegel: "...I absolutely renounce all higher harmony. It is not worth one little tear of even one tormented child

...if the suffering of children goes to make up the sum of suffering needed to buy truth, then I assert beforehand that the whole of truth is not worth such a price."[193]

What makes Smith's metaphysical postulations so unfortunate is that they are so unnecessary. The religions of the world do not need theologies tied to explanatory metaphysical systems. Phenomena are not meaningless because they are not given metaphysical explanations. Our natural environment, immediate and distant, can remain meaningful and significant even if it is not alive and sentient. As Levinas reminds us, living with the elements, breathing fresh air and seeing sunrises, can fill our lives with joy. Taylor reminds us of the joys of carnivalistic life that remain when ontotheologies are deconstructed. The Buddhists remind us that extinguishing *Tanha* involves moving from seeing constituted beings, such as mountains, to not seeing them that way, to letting the environment one encounters be in its infinitely rich suchness, encounters that fill our lives with sensory ecstasy. Even Smith admits that his ultimate aspiration is to lose himself in the enjoyment of a sunset,[194] something that does not require making theoretical postulations about transcendent realms of being. The infinite Tao, which transcends humanly constituted beings, does not require any other realm of being in order for us to see all finite beings as being constituted beings with an infinite otherness, to see nature as always manifesting that infinite Tao, that infinite way of things, that infinite otherness. Likewise, when the Japanese followers of Shinto, *kami no michi,* the way of the *kami,* see the *kami* in all constituted beings, they are seeing in a certain religious way and not seeing beings called *kami.* They see and therefore treat everything as sacred and not as mere materials available for human use. There is no need to say that they see transcendent spiritual beings in the mountains and trees of Japan or that they see transcendent gods or a godhead of pure light and consciousness. Faithful Buddhists, Taoists and followers of the way of the *kami* see nature religiously and do not need metaphysical explanations for them to find what they see as significant and meaningful.

As was pointed out in chapter 2, the pragmatics governing the use of the term "explanation'"show that explanations are in order only when phenomena become problematic, when anomalies appear, and explanations are successful when the conflicting beliefs producing the anomaly are reconciled. Smith himself seems to be working with such a notion of explaining when he points out problems in dealing with phenomena in biology and psychology that he thinks can be made unproblematic only by postulating transcendent realms of consciousness. It is by examining what he thinks are inadequacies in current scientific or scientistic treatment of these problems, and not by an examination of whether religious practices need metaphysical speculations, that Smith attempts to offer justifying reasons for his world picture. Are these phenomena problematic, however, and does his metaphysical theory solve the problem?

Smith finds nothing unproblematic in the Darwinian description of the fossil record,[195] but he charges that using the principle of natural selection to explain the surprising presence of such a record is inadequate in two ways. First, Smith claims that it provides no explanation at all because this principle is merely an expression of the uninformative tautology that the species that leaves the most offspring leaves the most offspring.[196] The principle, however, does seem to be more than a mere tautology because it states that in a competitive reproductive setting, some animals with certain charac-teristics that their competitors do not possess are more successful in reproducing offspring because of those characteristics than their competitors are. Second, Smith claims that the principle of natural selection, with its requirement that long stretches of time are needed to produce evolutionary changes in species, cannot account for that part of the fossil record which indicates that major groups of animals appeared together within a very limited time frame and that all the fossil remains of these animals are of fully formed animals and show no evidence of any common ancestry.[197]

Even if evolutionary biologists were to accept this interpretation of the fossil record, that does not show that the only or best way to explain this record is by postulating a transcendent consciousness that created these animals. Not only is this metaphysical hypothesis in principle unverifiable, unfalsifiable, and incapable of being integrated into any holistic theoretical framework now operating in any of the sciences, but it seems impossible to specify the pragmatics that would govern the use of the term "creative" here to designate some kind of causal relation between finite beings or temporal processes and an infinite, eternal godhead. How can pure light and pure consciousness "break itself up" into distinguishable photons and atoms? This is the same problem that many Kantians faced when they used one concept of causality to specify a relation between phenomenal events and another idea of causality to specify a relation between things-in-themselves and empirical beings and events. Furthermore, how can the nontemporal be causally related to the temporal without itself become involved in time? This is the problem that forced Charles Hartshorne in his process metaphysics to postulate that God must be both eternal and in time. The same problem faces any effort to say that the eternal can know temporal events without itself undergoing any changes.[198] Quite apart from the issue of the coherence of Smith's supposed metaphysical solution to the problems in evolutionary biology, there remains the epistemological difficulty present in Smith's attempt to argue from the ignorance that the fossil record leaves us with to knowledge about a postulated cause of this record.

Smith also thinks that life and sentience remain problematic unless one postulates an eternal consciousness from which everything emanates. How, he asks, can mere organizations of physical and chemical phenomena by alive or sentient unless these phenomena themselves are manifestations of life and sentience?[199] It is difficult to specify, however, what Smith finds problematic here. The defining characteristics of life all seem to be compatible with the characteristics of physical and chemical phenomena. Scientists are now close to producing living cells through laboratory experiments with nonliving physical and chemical materials. That sentience appears on the scene when certain physical and chemical materials and structures are present also seems unproblematic. Why can't wholes have properties and capacities that their parts do not have? What really seems to turn life and sentience into a problem for Smith is his belief that most of the universe would be insignificant if panpsychism were not correct, if life, sentience, thinking, and choosing were occurring only in a few tiny places in this immense universe of galaxies.[200] This belief, however, is based on unnecessary assumptions. Even if sentience were present only with animals on earth, this would not make our lives meaningless and insignificant to us. Why should any people measure the significance of their lives by their physical size relative to the size of the galaxies? Only if people are still under the influence of the ontotheological notion that they are and ought to be the center of the universe, and that the whole universe is significant because it exists for them, will the discovery that they are tiny mortals on the third rock from a medium-sized sun surrounded by billions of suns threaten their ability to find their lives meaningful. The Kierkegaardian accent on faith calls for efforts to dissolve the craving for big pictures rather than for efforts to paint a better picture.

There is one other line of reasoning Smith offers to show the insufficiency of contemporary efforts to avoid metaphysical theorizing. All postmodernist efforts to deconstruct metaphysics and to interpret all human experience and thought as socially constituted and historically variable are interpreted by Smith as relativistic rejections of objectivisim, as subjectivisms and historicisms that are cases of social solipsism. He rejects pragmatism's analysis of our vocabulary of "true" and "real," claiming that a correspondence theory of truth is both natural and required.[201] Smith's objections to pragmatism are objections to the theory of truth that interprets truth as that which works. In chapter 2, however, I have attempted to show that pragmatism offers no theory of truth, none being needed, and that it only shows the incoherence of correspondence theories of truth and analyzes the pragmatics governing our use of the words "true" and "real."

Smith's attempt to support metaphysical theorizing about a transcendent, eternal level of being by charging that postmodernism and pragmatism are relativistic denials of objectivity is located on a slippery slope leading to social solipsism and nihilism. His effort fails, however, because it begs the question. Derrida and Rorty reject all talk about truth being relative to the beliefs or vocabulary of a particular community. Smith's talk about relative truth and perspectives on a cosmic inkblot are tied to his correspondence theory of truth, which is an internal component of his metaphysical theory about transcendent realms of being that could be referred to in a nonrelativistic way by viewing them from everywhere, through every socially constituted language. Saying that alternative vocabularies exist and that signifieds are always tied to floating signifiers is not endorsing relativism or solipsism, but it is only saying that people live, experience, and think in socially constituted worlds, that different people live in different worlds, and that people and their worlds are subject to historical change. Smith must assume that he can talk about another nonsocially constituted worlds behind the plurality of social and historical worlds in which people live in order to charge the postmodernists and pragmatists with relativism or social solipsism. He can't use this charge to assign to postmodernists and pragmatists a worldview, one which is the main competitor to his realistic, metaphysical theory and whose insufficiency as a world theory increases the reasonableness of Smith's own theory. That is begging the question. Post-structuralists and Pragmatists, however, are not guilty of the same epistemological sin of begging the case when they point out that all of Smith's vocabulary and claims, including his godhead talk, are governed by social norms and presuppose a social form of life. One can encounter the infinite that transcends the world of social rationality, as Kierkegaard and Levinas point out, but one can't say that it is a being or tiered levels of being. In his claim that admitting that one cannot conceive of something does not prove that it does not exist,[202] Smith seems to forget that the word "it" is a pronoun that is a stand-in for some noun. One cannot try to use the word "it" to refer to something unless it is possible to replace it with some noun or noun phrase, unless it is possible to describe it or conceive it.

Perhaps what motivates Smith's postulation of the godhead is not his belief that only this postulation can make up for what he thinks are the inadequate explanations that are possible without his metaphysical worldview. That project may simply be his intellectual effort to account for the texts written by Hindus about the mystical experiences that occur when raja yoga is used to attain spiritual enlightenment.[203] Smith provides a wonderful description of the kind of self-disciplining that is necessary to reach the final stage of raja yoga.[204] One must concentrate one's attention so as to remove a whole host of preventive conditions. Be at peace with one's social environment so that no envy, resentment, hate, or anger can distract. Eliminate all kinesthetic sensations by cleansing one's body to preventing itchings, by ending all cravings for cigarettes, drugs, and alcohol, by sitting in the lotus position, by slow and controlled breathing. Eliminate all the sensations that come with seeing, hearing, tasting, smelling, and touching by so focusing one's attention that one is no longer conscious of them. Stop all remembering, worrying, daydreaming, wondering, and thinking. Finally, without passing out, stop all trying to discipline oneself and stop distinguishing oneself from the unbounded, undifferentiated, "white light" of "pure consciousness."

Enough people, with little or no reason to pretend, who followed this discipline to its completion, reported having such experiences that there is little reason to doubt that yoga can be carried out. What is open to doubt is any given interpretation, including Smith's, of the cognitive significance of these stages of eliminating sensations, thoughts, and differentiations. It may be surprising to many people that such a process of elimination can be carried out without losing consciousness but, given that some have carried it out, it should not really be surprising that the final "mystical experience" occurs. This is just what one would expect to occur once all sensing and thinking is ended. This experience could be given a nonreligious, psychological interpretation. It, of course, has provided some people with powerful motivation for moving toward a certain sort of religious life. It certainly shows that much of our perceptual knowledge of the world is due to social rationality and personal cravings, and yet there is more to us than that. It shows that there is more to human life than living merely as a socially constituted being among beings. By dropping off our habitual, perceptual, conceptual, and noncompassionate subjectivity, it increases our ability to see beyond the social masks other people wear and to relate to them compassionately in their singularity. Again, however, this religious significance seems to be quite able to stand on its own without being attached to an interpretation which claims that in this mystical experience one has been united with a universal pure light/pure consciousness of which all beings are creations or emanations. Instead of Smith's attempt to preserve the significance of the world's religions by interpreting them as variations of a neo-Platonic metaphysical worldview, perhaps it is better to follow Levinas's effort to show that the Abrahamic religions are better off if they are not contaminated with Western ontotheologies. As I read the Buddhist texts and Nargarjuna, they are saying the same thing about efforts by Indian and Chinese thinkers to metaphysically interpret Hindu, Buddhist, and Taoist religious practices. Smith tells us something very important when he claims that all of the world's religious traditions have mystics in their communities. If by the mystical we mean encounters with social rationality's other, then this seems to be correct. However, Smith cannot use this global phenomena as a justifying reason supporting his metaphysical postulations. There are good reasons to think that these encounters are always culturally coded even if what is encountered is other than any socially constituted being. Mystical experiences, disciplinary practices producing mystical experiences, and reports of mystical experiences all seem to be internally related to each other and they vary from one religious tradition to the other.[205] As Levinas points out, encountering social rationality's other is part and parcel of our way of living in the world, even when we deny it. The infinite other is presupposed by everything finite but it is not a supernatural being transcendentally existing independent of human life, although this inescapable infinitude applies also to everything we want to say existed prior to human existence. Buddhism accents this when it point out that the infinite permeates everything finite. Smith is correct when he points out that Mahayana Buddhism introduced worship of a personal god, but this sort of introduction can be interpreted in the same way that Zizek claims that the Christian community constituted Jesus as the Christ, the Son of God. The Mahayana Buddhist community constituted Gautama, the Buddha, the awakened one, as the heavenly Buddha, even as other awakened followers of Gautama were constituted as bodhisattvas on whom worship might be focused, with such worship being a means to spiritual liberation even as bhakti yoga is in Hinduism. Smith's encyclopedic knowledge of the world's religions and his spiritual sensitivity to their practices cannot be praised sufficiently. All of these religions, however, are culturally specific and, although they all presuppose encountering the infinite, none of them need to be contaminated with ontotheological metaphysics. Just as the Buddha advises us to let all things simply be and not to try to control them with our concepts and theories, so we would be well advised to simply let the world's religions be. Worship and spiritual discipline are at the heart of these religions, and not metaphysical theorizing, as tempting as it is to try to satisfy that craving.

V. A POSTMODERN FUSION OF PRAGMATIC RATIONALITY AND EXISTENTIAL RELIGION: A WITTGENSTEINIAN INTERPRETATION OF EVERYDAY RELIGIOUS DISCOURSE

There is an old Zen saying. First, see the mountains. Then, don't see the mountains. Then, see the mountains again. First, there is the way we all too often see the mountains through a conceptual lens constituted to serve very limited human interests. We see mountains of raw materials; we see barriers to be cut through for a new highway; we see great places to build profitable ski runs; we see tourist attractions for city dwellers. Some might see material substances with eternal essences. Then, some people recognize that the things they are seeing this way are only socially constituted objects serving their interests as socially constituted subjects. No longer can they see them as just piles of raw materials. There is something more in front of them even though they are unable to say what that more is. Finally, some people find a way to view the mountains again without forcing them to serve social and personal purposes and without assigning to them some metaphysical status; they find a way to just let the mountains be in their nonsocially constituted suchness; they find a way to simply, enjoyably, visually encounter them. As Levinas points out, this last way of encountering mountains really is our primordial way of living. Socially constituting what we encounter as mountainous materials or barriers is secondary to joyously living with them, even though the secondary often becomes primary and veils us from what can be so enjoyably encountered if just allowed to be.

For many contemporary people, much of their lives consist of seeing objects and people, including themselves, in objectivistic, scientistic, positivistic, and/or ontotheological ways. One of the reasons they do so is that so many institutionally sanctioned theoretical interpretations of human life fail to see the social constitution of major portions of our way of living: our concepts, perceptions, words, beliefs, desires, values, norms, explanations, justifications, sense of self-identity, and self-worth. In the first four chapters in this text I have attempted to break the hold of such interpretations and perceptions. I have attempted to present an interpretation of the human way of life which shows that an immense amount of human life is social and intersubjective through and through. Having made that effort, so far in this chapter I have tried to show that, in spite of the vital role that social constitution plays in human life, one must not absolutize the social. There is that which is other than socialized subjects and objects. There is the interpersonal ethical and religious other to the social, which is the inescapable presupposition of the social. Now the question must be asked: Is that the end of the story? Can I now close the book on my interpretation of the human form of life? Is it enough to point out that there is social subjectivity, sometimes reduced to an objectivistic form of subjectivity, and then there is the interpersonal other to the social?

Were I to end the story here I would be closing a book, but I would end up with a dualism of the social and its other which in the end would prove to be incoherent. What is needed now is to show that neither the social nor its other exist independent of each other. We need to show what is involved in seeing the mountains in their suchness, or, more important, to see people in their suchness. We need to add some reminders of the need to understand that normally and for the most part the interpersonal is folded back into the intersubjective, the infinite frames and fractures the finite. Taylor's postmodern artists are trying to show this in many different ways. Folding the infinite back into the finite is itself a misleading way of talking. Primordially, the human form of life is interpersonal, with social subjectivity being nothing but a reduced form of the interpersonal even when it claims to be autonomous and self-sufficient, even as objectivism is a form of subjectivity even when it claims to be autonomous and self-sufficient.

Seeing and encountering people in their suchness is just encountering people when one is not treating them as merely instances of a social type or as merely physical objects present on hand. The human form of life is primarily and for the most part ethically interpersonal, which sometimes, often unfortunately, is treated as merely an intersubjective social life, and sometimes, usually even more unfortunately, as relations between mere physical objects. The interpersonal is more than the socially constituted which in turn is more than the merely physical, but this more, which is other than what is less, is the more in which the less is inescapably embedded. From time immemorial the more of interpersonal living has never existed without the less of socially constituted living. Some forms of human life, however, seem to have existed without any objectivistic mode of subjectivity. It is in the modern world that objectivisim has been imperialistically trying to colonize interpersonal and intersubjective ways of living. Although it can never divorce itself from its intersubjective and interpersonal presuppositions, the very notion that a merely objectivistic mode of life is possible and desirable poses a major threat to contemporary human life.

Deconstructionist opponents of ontotheology warn about getting trapped into forming binary oppositions: Scientistic/nonreductionistically human, secular/sacred, sayable/showable, conceptual/nonconceptual. As we have just seen, this warning also applies when talking about the other to social rationality. Social rationality and its other are not two separate realms that need to be glued together. Saying that the objectivistic presupposes the intersubjective, and the intersubjective presupposes the interpersonal, is not saying that the interpersonal is a Hegelian third synthesizing the objectivisitic and the intersubjective. Likewise, saying that social rationality and its other are not to be treated as binary opposites is not saying that there is a Hegelian third that synthesizes together social rationality and its other. It is simply reminding us that human life is to be allowed to rest in its suchness, filled with elements we enjoyably encounter and live from, filled with ethical encounters with people in their singularity and suffering, filled with people seeking to meet their responsibilities by socially constituting worlds of social rationality, which include historically and socially specific vocabularies, subjects, objects, tools, economic and political orders, moralities, and religions. No one remains totally free of socialization into one or more social moralities. Billions of people have been empowered through nurturing to participate in religious practices and to strive to be more or less faithful to religious desires and commitments. Although living ethically, morally, and religiously are just ordinary human forms of living that need to be allowed to be in their suchness, not reductively eliminated or burdened with ontotheological baggage, still in our contemporary world there is a need to remind ourselves of this need to allow the religious and the ethical to simply be. Thus the rhetorical motivation for constructing this interpretation.

It is Wittgenstein and his appropriators who are saying that the human form of life, in its suchness, is the precondition for all human conceiving, thinking, judging, desiring, feeling, and doing. This primordial form of life is inescapably ethical and often religious. Neither the ethical nor the religious can be reduced to anything else and neither needs to justify itself by appealing to merely social or merely physical perceptions. Ethical and religious ways of living and speaking can be investigated and described but they cannot be reduced to or translated into something less than what they are. Many times people can become confused about ethics and religion because of the effects of the practices and interpretations that attempt to reduce ethical and religious life to something less than what they are. These reductive efforts can cause problems in people's ability to understand the human way of living, but these are problems that need to be dissolved rather than solved, dissolved by showing the confusions on which they are based. When these problems are dissolved, then human life can be allowed to be just what it is: joyful, painful, ethical, and religious.

The other to social rationality and its other is our ordinary life of ethical encounters, religious desires and aspirations, social moralities, and political economies constituted to meet perceived ethical responsibilities, and socially constituted religious practices whose point is to enable people to remain faithful to their desire for the most desirable. Against relativists, it is important to point out that there is a global otherness to social rationality. Against absolutizers of a certain form of morality or religion, it is important to show that there are differences in social and cultural political, economic, moral, and religious practices, and that, although they can be judged in terms of their faithfulness to ethical encounters and religious desires for the ultimately desirable, these different political/economic orders, moralities, and religions sometimes simply need to be allowed to be in their suchness because they are only historically constituted different ways of being ethically and religiously faithful. Living ethically is living with a human form of life and living religiously is for many people not different from seeing colors; neither can be reduced to anything else and neither needs ontotheological justifications. As Kierkegaard pointed out, in the lives of people neither the finite nor the infinite can be separated from each other.

Letting the human form of life just be also requires rejecting the notion that all of human language and life is so overwhelmed by ontotheological contamination that seeking to resist such contamination is hopeless. This notion that ontotheology has succeeded in totally occupying the human form of life is still a humanistic fantasy about the power of the human intellect, supposing as it does that humans are powerful enough to use their metaphysical speculations to take total control over the human form of life. Ontotheologies have successfully colonized far too much of the human form of life, but their defenders are not omnipotent or omniscient. Deviations from a sound understanding of how to live in the human form of life always presuppose the soundness from which they are deviating. This is what Wittgenstein means when he says that in all discussions it is the human form of life that simply has to be allowed to be. This form of life is always ethical and often religious.

When I claim that we should let the world's different religions simply be, there are several things I am trying to say and several possible interpretations I want to avoid. First, I want to endorse the criticisms that Wittgenstein and some of his followers have made of objectivistic efforts to explain away religious practices and attitudes by reducing them to behavior that can be given a sociological explanation or by reducing them to feelings and attitudes that can be given a psychological explanation, with these explanations never dealing with ethical encounters with the infinite or with religious desires to be faithful to the most desirable. Wittgenstein rejected James Frazer's effort to explain away "primitive" religions by interpreting their religious practices and utterances as the mistaken, stupid, primitive efforts to give scientific explanations or to exercise control over natural phenomena.[206] Appeals to the rain king, Wittgenstein writes, are not primitive efforts to control the rain but are thanksgiving ceremonies made at the beginning of the rainy season.[207] The anthropologist E. E. Evans Pritchard has carefully examined a whole host of psychological and sociological efforts to reductively eliminate any distinctiveness to religious practices and has argued that none of them provide interpretations adequate to the practices being studied.[208] The philosopher D. Z. Phillips, trying to remain as faithful as possible to Wittgenstein's project, has drawn upon a Wittgensteinian analysis of religious life to reinforce Evans-Pritchard's research and critique.[209]

Just as religion cannot be explained away, so Wittgenstein argues that it cannot be justified and it does not need any justification.[210] Thinking that a justification could be offered is repellent to a religious person because such an effort makes three unacceptable assumptions. First, it assumes that religious faithfulness is a matter of endorsing some doctrine.[211] Second, it assumes that one can reason from within social rationality to a warranted faithfulness to rationality's other.[212] Third, it assumes that religious life is not all right just as it is and that it needs some external justification.[213] As Levinas has pointed out, and Wittgenstein asserts again, religious faith is a matter of passion and action and not an ontotheological belief.[214] It is a religious passion fused out of thankfulness for the joyousness of life, out of hearing a revelatory call to unlimited responsibility, out of a sense of guilt for having failed to adequately meet the demands of this call, out of a commitment to try one's best to meet these demands in one's present physical life and in one's continuing life in the lives of those who are one's ethical and spiritual children. One cannot argue people into encountering people ethically or into having a religious desire for the most desirable. All ethical and religious life finds its origin back in the ethical encounter. No prima facie case can be built for indicting ethically encountering other people and thus the ethical and the religious do not need to justify themselves. Therefore, let the religions of the world be in their suchness, free of reductionist explanations and inappropriate attempts to justify.

Second, by urging people to just let the world's religions be, I am endorsing what Wittgenstein once said, "All religions are wonderful, even those of the most primitive tribes. The way in which people express their religious beliefs differ enormously."[215] This is what Levinas, Zizek, and Smith have said also. A religious person needs to be passionately committed to one religious form of life, but different people with different social inheritances and environments will find that ethical and religious faithfulness is best expressed in different religious traditions. Although some people may be motivated by their desire to remain faithful to the infinite, to move from the religious tradition in which they were nurtured to another religious tradition, there is no need to try to eliminate religious diversity by seeking one common universal form of religious life. There is a great need to let other religious traditions be and not to try to use gross or subtle forms of coercion to get people to jump from one tradition to another. In our contemporary world, letting religion be also means recognizing that new religious traditions must be allowed to be formed because many people are finding that they cannot live faithful to their religious desire within the institutional apparatuses present in any of the long-standing religious traditions. As Taylor points out, religious faithfulness for some may find their yoga in the world of postmodern art infused with efforts to meet their ethical obligations. Wittgenstein confessed that he would have to live without the consolation of any established church[216] because, although he saw all problems from a religious point of view, he was not religious,[217] even though he often engaged in prayer and is reported to have had deep religious feelings about being safe in the world, fearing the last judgment, and desiring that his philosophical work be God's will.[218]

There are two ways of interpreting the sentence "Let the World's Religions Be" that I believe need to be resisted. First, calling certain practices "religious" does not make them religious, does not place them beyond the bar of critical appraisal. One can always raise the question whether the practices so labeled are faithful efforts to meet the responsibilities incurred in ethical encounters with people and whether they are efforts motivated by a desire for the supremely desirable. Religious practices do not live in pure isolation from other practices. Most of the world's religions unfortunately have had ontotheological claims and theories introduced when followers have talked about their religious practices. Many voices claiming ontotheological authoritative legitimacy have denied the social and historical character of all claims and practices and have attempted to rule out religious traditions other than their own. Vulgar fundamentalisms not only have not allowed other religions to simply be different expressions of religious faithfulness, but they have attempted to use ontotheological claims to legitimize the coercive exclusion or destruction of competing traditions, even to legitimize the use of violence and murder to carry out this destruction. Ontotheological claims cloaked as religious beliefs have also been used in an attempt to justify the use of the police power of the state to compel all others to obey prohibitions and requirements that can only be given an ontotheological justification. Restrictions are placed on ways of attaining genital pleasure. Abortions are prohibited. Genital mutilation is sanctioned. Ontotheological creationism is forced into the public school biology curricula. In liberal societies in which protections for religious freedom have become a part of the legal practices, it is important to recognize that labeling something religious does not immunize it against ethical and religious criticism. Granting religious freedom, letting religions be, requires the exclusion of ontotheological justifications for state mandates. For the world's religions to be respected it is necessary to reject charges of sacrilege when these can be defended only on the basis of ontotheological claims. Liberal tolerance must degenerate neither into the unjust branding of religious convictions as irrational nor into any surrender of the ability to critique efforts to use the blanket of religious liberty to cover ethically and religiously unjust behavior.[219]

Finally, proclaiming that the world's religions should be allowed to be is not excluding the possibility of religious dialogue between participants in these different religions. Religions are not timeless, impenetrable fortresses in which practitioners are imprisoned and isolated. The world's religions are historically changing, socially constituted efforts to meet one's ethical responsibilities and pursue one's religious desires and aspirations. Religious practices always have been undergoing change through dialogue within them between participants in their different divisions and sects and through dialogue with faithful followers in other traditions. The various religious language games used in the world's religions are not isolated and insulated from other religious and non-religious language games. This linguistic and social commerce requires, on the one hand, vigilance that religious faithfulness is not compromised and, on the other hand, a courageous, creative, poetic openness to social and cultural changes that, as Heidegger and Gadamer point out, cannot be predicted or controlled. New revelations are always possible. Through spiritual crossfertilization, spiritual growth can occur and religious faithfulness can be deepened and widened.[220]

Levinas's interpretation of ethical encounters and religious desires, in dialogue with Kierkegaard's and Zizek's interpretation of the religious and historical constitution of Jesus as the Christ, makes it possible to interpret the major religions of the world in a way that allows each of them to remain in their distinctiveness without reduction, need for justification, or ontotheology. Levinas provides such an interpretation of Jewish forms of faithfulness and Kierkegaard and Zizek do so for Christianity. Levinas's interpretation of the Jewish God, of whom no graven images are to be made, provides the framework for what Islam proclaims about the God, Allah. That Islam is a historical religious tradition, which calls for participation in practices of worship of Allah without constituting any divine incarnations, need not be interpreted, once unfortunate ontotheological trappings historically attached to it are removed, as ruling out practices in other religious traditions that call for religious faithfulness to such incarnations.

As I have already tried to point out, classical Buddhism's four noble truths, with its accent on extinguishing that painful form of living that prevents us from enjoyably letting mountains be mountains and from compassionately caring for other living things, yield to Levinas's interpretation of the human form of life. Likewise, Kierkegaard's and Zizek's account of Christianity's constitution of a divine incarnation can be used to give an account of Mahayana Buddhism's constitution of divine bodhisattvas. Levinas's interpretation of the infinite can help explain what is involved in the Hindu proclamations that *jiva*, human subjectivity formed by absolutizing the pursuit of pleasure, power, or the fulfillment of social role requirements, can never be a satisfactory way of living because the identity of people lies in themselves as Atman, something radically different from *jiva*, something infinite, something that is identical with Brahman, the infinite other to the whole world of constituted objects and subjects that too often is mistakenly taken as exhaustive and self-sufficient. Zizek's position again can help us understand the Hindu bhakti way of gaining liberation by worshiping some constituted god. That Hinduism offers other yoga, other ways of gaining liberation, only further illustrates that Judaism, Islam, classical Buddhism, and Taoism can be allowed to be what they are, ways of being ethically and religiously faithful without worshiping constituted incarnations of the infinite. Jhana yoga is presented as an option for people who can come to a way of living responsibly and faithfully by meditation on the infinite, the necessary presupposition of the finite. Dharma yoga is an option for those who seek to remain faithful to the infinite by committing themselves to obey the call of the infinite to meet their infinite responsibilities. Raja yoga is an option for all those seeking mystical experiences specific to their traditions that can break the hold of tendencies to absolutize the finite. Taoism in many ways seems to be a perfect illustration of Levinas's position. The way for humans to live, says Taoism, is to cease trying to consciously run things and instead to let oneself and one's environment be what they are, encounterable incarnations of the transcendent tao that cannot be conceptualized, a finite world that is always more than finite in that in its finiteness it presupposes the infinite that permeates every aspect of its finiteness.

Many of the classical arguments for the existence of God can be interpereted as expressions of one's religious life once their ontotheological colorings are removed. The ontological argument can be taken as saying that only a fool, and no religious person, would try to assert what is both pragmatically self-refuting and a rejection of the supremely desirable, that the the finite does not have its infinite other. The cosmological argument can be interpreted as saying that the finite as finite can exist only because of the infinite. The design argument can be taken as saying that joyful living, thanks-inspiring nature, comforting dwelling, ethical encountering, social rationality, and social and ethical immortality can exist only because the infinite penetrates all aspects of the finite. The moral argument can be seen as pointing out that all of morality depends upon the infinite other that people encounter when they encounter the face of another. As so interpreted, all of these "arguments" are located within this interpretation of the human form of life and would have rhetorical significance only to those who have ethical encounters and religious desires. They are not trying to do the impossible, to argue from positions that have reductively eliminated the interpersonal to the conclusion that this reduced position has an infinite Other.

Even as the world's religions must be allowed to be in their suchness, so the world's moralities need to be allowed to be in their differences when they remain faithful efforts to meet the responsibilities that our ethical encounters mandate. In different parts of the world and at different times in their histories, different kinds of moral practices have developed, and in many cases people are socialized to utilize several of these moralities at the same time, sometimes finding them reinforcing each other and sometimes experiencing what seem to be irresolvable incompatibilities. In the world today, sometimes the accent is on training people to have certain virtues (courage, truthfulness, compassion) needed to fulfill the obligations definitive of certain social roles; sometimes the accent is on getting people to endorse and use certain rules, commandments, and principles in making their choices; sometimes it is focused on developing in people the skills needed for making fair-minded and compassionate practical choices and actions without trying to apply a rule; sometimes the accent is on training people to emulate moral heros; sometimes the accent is on training people to apply moral precedents and create new ways of responsibly acting when precedents can't resolve a moral dilemma; sometimes the accent is on nurturing people to respect the singular uniqueness of people and discover strategies and tactics for compassionately meeting the responsibilities that follow from such encounters, such as the responsibility to minimize nonconsentuality and the injustices of domination and oppression. Given that different social practices around the globe have produced different forms of subjectivity, different self-identities and senses of self-esteem, different kinds of humiliation, suffering, and senses of failure, it should not be surprising that different moralities have been socially constituted.

Allowing the world's moralities to simply be in their suchness means not trying to reductively eliminate them by trying to interpret them as mere expressions of emotional tastes, as merely personal or socially sanctioned commands, as mere calculations of prudentially or socially beneficial consequences. Morally living with other people is not a way of living that can be reduced to any other way of living. Letting the world's moralities simply be also means not treating moralities as though they need to be justified by some global, ontotheologically sanctioned, or rationally necessary principle. It is faithfulness to the global character of ethical encounters with the other of social rationality that determines whether and how a specific social morality is to be criticized as being inadequate. Such faithfulness, however, can take the form of many different moralities which, although subject to criticism for a failure to be faithful to ethical encounters, otherwise should be allowed simply to be in their suchness, not reductively eliminated and not subjected to a demand for justification in terms of an asocial and ahistorical, rational principle.

Every human way of living and every form of social rationality presupposes ethical encounters that influence greatly the way people feel and act, the way they see other people, the way they make choices, indict actions, excuse actions, and justify actions. We can see wives, children, teachers, students, orphans, and widows, and to do so means being aware of the obligations definitive of our respective social roles. We can see people acting cowardly and courageously, cruelly and kindly, out of vengeance and forgivingly, oppressively and self-sacrificially. Seeing, thinking, choosing, and acting morally are as much a part of our human form of life, as enjoying a drink of fresh water or seeing colors. This is what Wittgenstein and his close followers have been trying to show.

Arthur Murphy has claimed that the very selfhood of all people is tied to their practice as moral agents of meeting their moral obligations.[221] All people, he claims, are trained in historically specific moral communities to use practical moral reasons in their actions, deliberations, and justifications.[222] Moral forms of life simply exist, and it is in terms of them that all moral justifications must be made. Moral obligations are obligations holding between people in a specific moral form of life, and moral communities are social groups of people who are training their members to act for moral reasons and resolve disagreements about moral obligations through the use of such moral reasons.[223] Moral communities have a moral way of proceeding when problems arise because of conflicting options in the application of moral reasons.[224] There are different sets of moral reasons that different moral communities train their members to use; there is moral diversity and not unjustified moral pluralism.[225] Different moral communities are morally constituted in different ways because different social roles get constituted, different items in life get prized, different commitments get made. What makes them all moral communities in spite of their moral differences is their operational commitment to finding a way of living together that meets people's ethical obligations to respect the status of each other as ethical persons and moral agents, a way of living that always keeps open the moral game of people making moral indictments of problematic parts of their moral inheritance, and that calls on people in different moralities to find moral ways of living together on the same planet. Sometimes such crosscultural moral resolutions will consist of creating new moral reasons covering people in both moral communities, and often it will consist of people in each community resolving to mind their own moral business.[226]

Murphy's pragmatic and Wittgensteinian accent on seeing the moral form of life as a way of life using moral reasons that are historically constituted through social practice and training, and which often requires imaginative application and reconstruction, is remarkably similar to Hsun-tzu's 4th Century B.C. interpretation of Confucian ethics.[227] For Hsun-tzu, moral reasoning is comparable to reasoning in common law. The point of moral reasoning is to create a moral community in which people with different interests can live in harmony. When a moral problem arises, try to resolve it by appealing to past handlings of similar cases that have become a part of one's moral tradition. When conflicting traditions seem applicable and no traditional reason exists for resolving such a conflict among competing reasons, then creatively innovate a new rationale that preserves as much of the tradition as possible and that allows the whole process of moral reasoning and problem-solving to continue. As opposed to the usual practice in Western common law cases, the participants in this Confucian moral discussion are not trying to win the case for their clients but are striving to respect each other and to find an acceptable resolution of the problem, one by which the people involved in the specific case that raised the problem can live and one by which all future people living under the traditions strengthened or modified by the decision can live in harmony. Moral reasoning always deals with specific concrete cases, not abstract hypothetical cases, always proceeds against a background of moral precedents and moral training in seeking harmonious social living, and always remains open for future reconstruction when morally required.

Three aspects of the Wittgensteinian position help reinforce the claim being made here that moral forms of life are to be allowed to be in their suchness. First, followers of Wittgenstein keeping pointing out that moral claims are not and need not be justified in terms of some ontotheological claim or some general timeless principle. Sabina Lovibond points out that all moral reasoning takes place within a social and historical form of life.[228] James Edwards points out that Wittgenstein rejects the whole idea that philosophy provides ultimate justifications for moral claims, suggesting instead that attempts to escape contingent forms of life in order to see things from a god's-eye point of view are symptoms of a diseased understanding.[229] D. Z. Phillips makes the same claims about our moral form of life that he did for religious forms of life: they are not reducible to something else and they are not in need of ontotheological explanations or justifications.[230]

Second, Wittgensteinians affirm that there are a multiplicity of not unjustified moral traditions that can creatively enter into dialogue with each other. Lovibond talks of moral pluralism, diversity, and heterogeneity, and the need to exercise moral imagination in dealing with crosscultural moral disagreements.[231] Phillips points out that there is an irreducible heterogeneity of morals and that the moral character of human forms of life varies enormously in different cultures, societies, and even among subcultural groups and individuals.[232]

Third, Wittgensteinians seek to free morality and all other aspects of the human form of life from various unsound ways of understanding things and thus to permit people to morally and religiously encounter other people and their entire environment. Lovibond reminds us of Wittgenstein's comment that our primary relationship to other people is not one of forming beliefs about them but one of encountering them with attitudes appropriate to the embodied souls that they are.[233] Edwards adds that the attitude toward other people that the sound understanding possesses is one of loving attention to the singularity and specificity of people and that the attitude toward the whole world we encounter is one of wonder that it is and a sense of the infinitely deep mystery of everything in it, a mysterious otherness that no amount of conceptualization, perception, and theorizing can exhaust.[234]

We ethically encounter each other. We live in the enjoyment of living. We live together as co-inhabitors in homes. We are socially constituted. We participate in common social practices. We share common know-how. We are fractured subjectively even as our common social practices are fractured. We draw upon a common cultural storehouse in constructing personal fantasies to give us the semblance of a unified subjective identity. We have unique personal identities because of the unique responsibilities our ethical encounters place us under. We are bound together intersubjectively and we are bound together interpersonally. We are finite and infinite. We, as social subjects and agents, are always singularly unique persons with a unique set of responsibilities from which we cannot escape even when we refuse to live responsibly. As singularly unique persons we desire the supremely desirable. We are bound together in socially constituted moralities and religious forms of life thoroughly penetrated by ethical encounters and religious desires. We live in a holistic form of life in which neither the singular, the interpersonal, the social, nor the psychologically particular can live without the other three. We live in a form of life that is always thoroughly finite and thoroughly infinite.

Who are we? We have to give different answers to that question. We sometimes are everyone since we all ethically encounter other people and since we have moral responsibilities to each other. We sometimes are everyone who speaks the same language. We sometimes are everyone who shares the same form of social rationality. We sometimes are everyone who shares the same religious tradition. We sometimes are everyone in the same family as ethical parents, children, and siblings. We sometimes are those who share the same misunderstandings and confusions. We always can say "we" with many different groups of people with whom we always share commonness and difference. We right now can say that we are a writer and reader relating to each other.

The infinite other that we encounter and that penetrates all sameness and identity in the world of social rationality prevents any interpretation, including this one, from saying the last word, from closing the book on the matter. Fractures, fizzures, tears, abysses, mysteries will always remain when we stop talking and writing. To leave human life be in its suchness is to be willing to stop writing when one thinks one has said something to help some people avoid some forms of misunderstanding. Interpretations are only rhetorical devices aimed at removing specific instances of misunderstanding so that people have that "know-how" that is called understanding, knowing how to go on. There is no doubt that there are many ways of misunderstanding things that were not addressed by the interpretations offered here. It is very probable that the interpretations offered here also contain misunderstanding, although, of course, if I knew what they were I would have written something else. It is also very probable that people who read this text will misunderstand things that are written here. Some such possible misunderstandings have been anticipated and attempts have been made to respond to them. It is impossible to anticipate all of them. Besides, as was stated in the beginning, no writer can control how a text will be interpreted by other people living in other worlds at other times. In addition, human beings have a remarkably creative ability both to misunderstand themselves and their world and to misunderstand what others have written. Anyone who does not want to be misunderstood should never start writing. It is impossible to totally liberate anyone from confusion and misunderstanding. The best one can do is to take Foucault's and Dewey's advice and be a resistance fighter dealing with specific problems existing at a specific time in a specific intellectual setting of people trying to remove hindrances to understanding things so they can go on with the enjoyable and challenging business of living.

⊷ NOTES

CHAPTER ONE

1. For an excellent analysis and criticism of scientism, see Huston Smith, *Why Religion Matters* (San Francisco: Harper, 2001), chapter 4.

2. The insight that dialogical understanding can add to the meaning of a text is the contribution of Hans-Georg Gadamer. See his *Truth and Method*, trans. Garrett Bardan and John Cumming (New York: Continuum, 1975) and *Philosophical Hermeneutics*, trans. and ed. D. Laing (Berkeley: University of California Press, 1977).

3. Stressing the singular uniqueness of people, and standing in opposition to totalitarianism in all its forms, have been two of the primary motives driving Levinas's philosophical efforts. See Emmanuel Levinas, *Otherwise than Being or Beyond Essence*, trans. Alphonso Lingis (The Hague-Boston: Nijhoff, 1981) and *Totality and Infinity*, trans. Alphonso Lingis (Pittsburgh: Duquesne University Press, 1969).

4. The set of texts written by Derrida is immense and ever growing. For an excellent selection of his writings and a bibliography current until 1991, see *A Derrida Reader: Between the Lines* (New York: Columbia University Press, 1991).

5. For an extremely creative use of the material similarity between words, see Mark Taylor, *Erring: A Postmodern A/theology* (Chicago: University of Chicago Press, 1984), *Altarity* (Chicago: University of Chicago Press, 1987); *Tears* (Albany: SUNY Press, 1990); *Nots* (Chicago: University Of Chicago Press, 1993).

6. For an insightful comparison of the projects of Wittgenstein and Derrida, see Henry Staten, *Wittgenstein and Derrida* (Lincoln: University of Nebraska Press, 1986).

7. See John L. Austin, *Sense and Sensibility* (Oxford: Clarendon, 1962), 68-77; "Truth," *Philosophical Papers*, 85-101.

8. This double negative interpretation of the pragmatics of 'true' differs from the notion of truth as a double negative which Donald Davidson rejects in "True to Facts" in *Truth and Interpretation* (Oxford: Clarendon, 1984), 38. He identifies this notion with a redundancy theory of truth such as Strawson advocated in "Truth," "A Problem of Truth," and "Truth: A Reconstruction of Austin's Views" in *Logico-Linguistic Papers* (London: Methuen, 1971), 190-249. I, however, am siding with Austin when he insists that the statement "Elvis is dead" is about Elvis whereas the statement "It is true that Elvis is dead" is about the statement or supposal that Elvis is dead. Also, the interpretation of the use of "true" presented here differs from the one defended by Alasdair MacIntyre in *Whose Justice? Which Rationality?* (Notre Dame: University of Notre Dame Press, 1988), 356-357, 81. While congenial to his advocacy of the primacy of falsity over truth and the interpretation of falsity as a lack of correspondence between what someone earlier had judged and what is now being perceived, classified, and understood, my interpretation excludes his Peircian notion of "truth as such." The perfect adequacy of mind to things as they are absolutely, as God sees them, must

supposedly be the final goal of all inquiry.

9. See W. V. O. Quine, "Two Dogmas of Empiricism" in *From a Logical Point of View* (New York: Harper and Row, 1953), 20-46..

10. I once tried to use a speech act interpretation of all possible statements to reestablish a Kantian realm of synthetic a priori undeniables. See my "Transcendental Logic: An Essay on Critical Metaphysics," *Man and World* (1969): 38-64; "On Being Morally Justified," *The Journal of Value Inquiry*" 111 no. 1 (Spring 1969): 1-18. For a decisive critique of the position I defended there, see Mottke Gram, "Do Transcendental Arguments Have a Future?" in *Zur Zukunft Der Transzendental Philosophie* (Gottinger: Vandenhoeck and Ruprect, 1978), 39-42. As we shall see, the claims that I am now making about interpretive undeniables are similar to Habermas's claims about a historical a priori. The differences will become apparent as I side with Gadamer's critique of Habermas's ahistorical ideals, Foucault's critique of Habermas's effort to maximize consensus rather than minimize nonconsensuality, and Levinas's and Benhabid's criticism of Habermas's appeal when doing social criticism to a generalized other rather than a specific other.

11. Ludwig Wittgenstein stressed seeing understanding as a kind of skillful know-how. See his *Philosophical Investigations*, trans. G. E. M. Anscombe (New York: Macmillan, 1953), and *On Certainty*, ed. G. E. M. Anscombe and G. H. von Wright, trans. Dennis Paul and G. E. M. Anscombe (Oxford: Basil Blackwell, 1969).

12. It is the German philosopher Martin Heidegger who showed that most objects are what they are to us because of the way we make toolish use of them. See his *Being and Time*, trans. Joan Stambaugh (Albany, NY: SUNY Press, 1996). Also, see Hubert Dreyfus's interpretation of Heidegger's interpretation of understanding in his *Being-in-the-World: A Study of Heidegger's Being and Time Part I* (Cambridge, MA: MIT Press, 1991), 184-214.

13. It is the religious/philosophical thinker,Emmanuel Levinas who locates precon-ceptual enjoyment as a necessary precondition for all conceptualizing. See his *Totality and Infinity,* 109-151. Levinas's interpretation of enjoyment provides good reasons for listening again to the texts of Henry Thoreau and Ralph Waldo Emerson on experiencing nature.

14. If one listens in a certain way, one can hear in this understanding of indeterminateness the Taoist reminders that the Tao of which one can speak is not the transcendent Tao and that he who speaks [only about conceivable things] does not know [understand] while he who knows [understands the transcendent Tao] does not speak [of such transcendence as if it were a conceivable object].

15. This is the great insight of those Buddhists who see everything resting on absolute nothingness and who find in the nonconceptual experience and understanding of such nothingness the answer to the human problem of suffering caused by trying to live only as a socially constituted being. See Masao Abe, *Zen and Western Thought* (Honolulu: The University of Hawaii Press, 1985).

16. For an extended argument against the reduction of religious language games to some other metaphysical, scientific. or superstitious mode of speech, see D. Z, Phillips, *Wittgenstein*

and Religion (New York: St. Martin's, 1993), *Religion without Explanation* (London: Basil Blackwell, 1976), *Faith and Philosophical Enquiry* (New York: Schocken, 1971).

17. For further developments of this kind of criticism of contemporary professional philosophy in the English-speaking world, see John Dewey, "The Need for a Recovery of Philosophy" and "Philosophy's Search for the Immutable" in *The Philosophy of John Dewey*, ed. John J. McDermott (New York: G. P. Putnam's Sons, 1975), 58-97, 371-387; Richard Rorty, "Professionalized Philosophy and Transcendentalist Culture," *Consequences of Pragmatism* (Minneapolis: University of Minnesota Press, 1982), 60-71, and "Philosophy as Science, as Metaphor, and as Politics," *Essays on Heidegger and Others* (Cambridge: Cambridge University Press, 1991) 9-26; Cornell West, *The American Evasion of Philosophy: A Genealogy of Pragmatism* (Madison: University of Wisconsin Press, 1989; Richard Shusterman, *Pragmatist Aesthetics: Living Beauty, Rethinking Art* (Oxford: Basil Blackwell, 1992), 3-33, 236-261.

18. For Asian influence on Heidegeer, see Paul Shih-yi Hsiao, "Heidegger and our Translation of the Tao Te Ching" in *Heidegger and Asian Thought*, ed. Graham Parkes (Honolulu: University of Hawaii Press, 1987), 93-104; and Otto Poggeler, "Destruction and Moment" in *Reading Heidegger from the Start: Essays in His Earliest Thought*, ed. Theodore Kisiel and John van Buren (Albany: SUNY Press, 1994), 139.

19. See David Kalipahana, *Nagarjuna's Karika: The Philosophy of the Middle Way* (Albany: SUNY Press, 1986), 81-91.

CHAPTER TWO

1. See *Auguste Comte and Positivism: The Essential Writings, ed.*, Gertrud Lenzer (New York: Harper and Row, 1975). Comte argues that knowledge consists only of logic and mathematics on the one hand and science on the other, with science telling us only how things are and not trying to find underlying metaphysical explanations.

2. See Ernest Mach, "The Economy of Science," in *Readings in Philosophy of Science, ed.* Philip P. Wiener. (New York: Charles Scribner's Sons, 1953), 447. He claims that science gives answers to the only "why" questions that are meaningful when it turns the unfamiliar, the unexpected anomaly, which occasions the "why" question, into the familiar and expected.

3. For an excellent anthology of the classic writings of the logical positivists, see *Logical Positivism, ed.*, A.J. Ayer (Glencoe, IL: Free Press, 1959).

4. See Michel de Montaigne, "The Apology for Raimond Sebond," in *The Philosophy of the]6th and 17th Centuries.*, Richard H. Popkin, ed. (New York: Free Press, 1966), 69-81.

5. It is excusable that Descartes did not anticipate Hegel but it is less excusable that Chomsky thinks that we have only two choices to account for the existence of ideas or language, either his interpretation of Cartesian innate ideas as the structures of our brains mirroring the structure of language or B. F. Skinner's atomistic, individualist attempt to give a behavioristic account of the origin of language.

6. This theme will be developed in my discussion in chapter 5 of Emmanuel Levinas's claim that the sensory lies in a realm of enjoyment that is other than realms of cognition or conceptualization. I will also leave until then my discussion of Levinas's analysis of the role that the idea of a positive infinite plays in Descartes' account of the origin of our ideas and knowledge.

7. One of the major projects of some contemporary American philosophers who reject the social character of all rationality is grounded on the supposition that it is possible for us to talk about possibilities and possible worlds without having the social and historical nature of our talk in any way place contingent conditions on the existence of such possibilities. For presentations and discussions of this position, see Saul A. Kripke, *Naming and Necessity* (Cambridge: Harvard University Press, 1972), 15-22. For a critique of Kripke's position that accents the pragmatics of modal language, see Leonard Linsky, *Oblique Contexts* (Chicago: University Of Chicago Press, 1989), 118-148. A pragmatic criticism of such attempts to transcend human possibilities to a realm of asocial, ahistorical possibilities will be given below when Pragmatism's challenge is presented. See also my "The Impossibility of Hartshorne's God," *The Philosophical Forum*, vol. VII, nos. 3-4.

8. For a full presentation and attempted defense of a variation of Spinoza's ontological argument see James Ross, *Philosophical Theology* (New York: Bobbs-Merrill, 1969), 86-139.

9. See Alfred North Whitehead, *Process and Reality* (New York: Macmillan, 1929) 46-50, 521–23.

10. See Charles Hartshorne, *The Divine Relativity* (New Haven: Yale University Press, 1948), and *The Logic of Perfection* (LaSalle, IL: Open Court, 1962), 28-117.

11. Immanuel Kant, *Critique of Pure Reason*, trans. Norman Kemp Smith (New York: St. Martin's, 1965), A201, A783.

12. Ibid, A218-A235.

13. Ibid, A6-A10.

14. For a fuller discussion of this interpretation of Kant's synthetic a priori judgments, see my "Transcendental Logic," 38-64. This is not a position I any longer defend. Only a contingent, corrigible interpretation of language and the making of claims could establish what conditions are necessary for the making of claims. These conditions, I now hold, are pragmatic, contextual, and historically variable.

15. Kant, *Critique of Pure Reason*, Bxx-Bxxvii, A236-A260.

16. For an excellent analysis of Kant's arguments from the purported form of all practical reasoning to the universal and undeniable categorical requirement of morality, see T. E. Hill Jr., *Dignity and Practical Reason in Kant's Moral Theory* (Ithaca: Cornell University Press, 1992), chapters 6 and 7. See also my "On Being Morally Justified," 1-18.

17. Kant, *Critique of Pure Reason*, B276-B279.

18. Ibid, Bxi-Bxii, Al 94-A201.

19. For an interpretation of the impact on Kant of the Romanticists Herder and Lessing, see John MacMurray, *The Self as Agent* (London: Faber and Faber, 1956) 39-61.

20. Kant, *Critique of Pure Reason*, Avii-Axii.

21. Hegel, "Introduction," *The Phenomenology of Spirit*, trans. A. V. Miller (Oxford: Oxford University Press, 1977), 47.

22. See Walter Kaufmann, *Hegel: Reinterpretation, Texts, and Commentary* (Garden City, NJ: Doubleday, 1965), 193ff.

23. Remnants of this Hegelian idea of complete understanding remain in Peirce's ideas of reality and truth. The real, for Peirce, is that which the "ideal" scientific community understands it to be; asserting that a claim is true is asserting that it is a claim the ideal scientific community would make. Peirce, however, is a universal corrigiblist and, unlike Hegel, does not think that humans actually acquire this complete understanding. See Charles Sanders Peirce, "How to Make Our Ideas Clear," in *Philosophical Writings of Peirce*, ed., Justus Buehler (New York: Dover, 1955), 38.

24. Alfred North Whitehead, in his process philosophy, attempts to include time in his metaphysical system by making events, interrelated by sensory prehensions, rather than Aristotle's independent substances (sensible particulars), the basic elements in his system. Time, however, gets swallowed up as Whitehead tries to meet the demands of the metaphysical principle of sufficient reason. Events and processes are as they are because of their conceptual prehension of Platonic eternal objects and because of the eternal aesthetic principle God operates under in controlling event and process formation. See his *Process and Reality*. Charles Hartshorne attempts to add to the Whiteheadian metaphysical system Peirce's accent on the place of chance in the world, but this runs into conflict with the metaphysical use of the principle of sufficient reason which demands that all contingent actualities receive an explanation. Hartshorne only claims that there must be a reason why the metaphysically inexplicable details of concrete events are possibilities falling within necessary lawful boundaries that order such chance occurrences. See *Divine Relativity*, 137ff. If details are interpreted as being metaphysically inexplicable, however, then it is difficult to maintain that physical laws need metaphysical explanations. Hartshorne tries to meet this difficulty with his defense of an ontological argument for the necessary existence of God, but this begs the question, for it presupposes asocial and ahistorical notions of possibility and necessity.

25. See Moritz Schlick, "Meaning and Verification," in *Readings in Philosophical Analysis*, ed. Herbert Feigl and Wilfred Sellars (New York: Appleton-Century-Croft, 1949), 19-49, and Rudolph Carnap, *The Logical Syntax of Language* (Patterson, NJ: Littlefield, Adams, 1959), 277-281.

26. See Thomas Kuhn, *The Structure of Scientific Revolutions* (Chicago: University of Chicago Press, 1962).

27. Soren Kierkegaard's critique of Hegel's metaphysical system is best found in the

texts written under the pseudonym Johannes Climacus (John the Climber), *Philosophical Fragments,* trans. David Swenson and Howard V. Hong (Princeton, NJ: Princeton University Press, 1936), and *Concluding Unscientific Postscript,* trans. David Swenson and Walter Lowrie (Princeton, NJ: Princeton University Press, 1944). Nietzsche's critique can be found in his *Human, All Too Human,* trans. Marion Faber and Stephen Lehmann (Lincoln, NE: University of Nebraska Press, 1984); *The Gay Science,* trans. Walter Kaufmann (New York: Vintage, 1974); "Thus Spoke Zarathustra," trans. Walter Kaufmann, in *The Portable Nietzsche* (New York: Penguin, 1959) 115-439; *Twilight of the Idols,* trans. Walter Kaufmann, in *The Portable Nietzsche,* 465-563.

28. Numerous recent philosophers have pointed out that Hegel himself seems to have recognized that he cannot complete his system, his effort to totalize human understanding of everything. Mark Taylor, in *Altarity,* has analyzed how Heidegger, Merleau-Ponty, Lacan, Bataille, Kristeva, Levinas, Blanchot and Derrida have all focused on the manner that Hegel's system presupposes that which cannot be contained in his system. For example, Maurice Blanchot, in "The Absence of the Book," *The Gaze of Orpheus,* trans. L. Davis (Barrytown, NY: Station Hill Press, 1981), 145ff, points out that Hegel himself at the end of his *Encyclopedia,* which supposedly expresses the whole system, admits that it is not complete because it cannot explain how the world of everyday life can come to embody the understanding of the philosophers who have to remain an isolated priesthood protecting the truth from the many present forms of worldly misunderstanding. Jacques Derrida, in *Dissemination,* trans. B. Johnson (Chicago: University of Chicago Press, 1980), 11,17, points out that Hegel recognized that the *Encyclopedia,* which couldn't be ended, really couldn't be begun; it needed a preface, *Phenomenology of Spirit,* to explain how it is to be read.

29. Kierkegaard, *Philosophical Fragments,* 15.

30. In Chapter V we will examine Levinas' interpretation of Plato's accent on the need of people to be related to the Good to be cognitively capable of having adequate conceptions of the forms or an understanding of their relations to each other and thus an understanding of why everything must be as it is.

31. Kierkegaard, *Concluding Unscientific Postscript,* II 5.

32. Ibid, 178.

33. Ibid, 181.

34. Ibid, 181.

35. Ibid, 112-113.

36. Ibid, 115.

37. Ibid, 178.

38. Ibid, 306.

39. This is the driving thrust of the later Wittgenstein's interpretation of all grammars of language games and the forms of life they presuppose. See *Philosophical Investigations,* 4

90, 241, 371, 373.

40. In chapter 5, I investigate the rich implications of Levinas's claim that the act of saying something cannot be swallowed up in the content of what is said because the act of saying is ethical and other than the socially constituted character of the said.

41. For extended defenses of the interpretation of the background of all claims as being unrepresentable, see Hubert L. Dreyfus, *Being-in-the-World,* 45-59, 115-127; and "Holism and Hermeneutics," *Review of Metaphysics* 34 (September 1980), 3-23.

42. Nietzsche, *Thus Spoke Zarathustra,* 1.5. 43.

43. Ibid, III,4.

44. Nietzsche, *Twilight of the Idols,* 493.

45. Nietzsche, *The Gay Science,* # 59.

46. Ibid, # 168

47. Ibid, # 276.

48. Ibid, # 341.

49. Ibid, # 125.

50. Nietzsche, *Thus Spoke Zarathustra,* 214, 225.

51. The one major exception is Pierre Duhem, if he can be called a positivist, who continued to accent a Hegelian form of theoretical holism. See his *Physics: Its Object and Its Structure,* trans. Phillip Weiner (Princeton: Princeton University Press, 1954).

52. Johann Hamann (173 0-1788), a fellow resident in Kant's home city of Konigsberg and one of the founders of the Romantic Movement, had also argued for the priority of believing over doubting by using Hume's skeptical results to indict rationalistic and empiricist efforts to end the universal doubting begun by Descartes. See his *Socratic Memorabilia,* trans. James C. O'Flaherty(Baltimore: Johns Hopkins University Press, 1967). Unfortunately, Hamann's writings challenging epistemology also constituted a challenge to the rising professionalizing of philosophy in European universities and thus never developed the following among philosophers that epistemology and the other accents in Romanticism did. The Scottish commonsense realists also responded to Hume's skepticism with a defense of the primacy of believing over doubting. See Thomas Reid, *An Inquiry Into the Human Mind,* ed. Timothy Duggan (Chicago: University of Chicago Press, 1970) and William Hamilton, "On the Philosophy of the Unconditioned," *Edinburgh Review,* vol. 1 (1829): 194-221. It was their realism that G. E. Moore revised in his defense of our common sense beliefs (such as I can see the hand in front of my face) against the supposed superiority of philosophical arguments for skepticism. See his "Defense of Common Sense" and "Certainty" in *Philosophical Papers* (New York: Collier, 1959) 32-59. 223-246. Moore greatly weakened the effect of his effort by not recognizing that he really was rejecting the whole epistemological project by rejecting its beginning point. His continued concern with getting clear about "sense data reports that

could provide final justification for perceptual claims made it seem that he was just producing one more product for the epistemology industry.

53. Charles Sanders Peirce, "The Fixation of Belief '"in *Philosophical Writings of Peirce*, 5-22.

54. John Dewey, "Some Stages of Logical Thought" in *Essays in Experimental Logic* (New York: Dover, 1916), 183-219; "Social Inquiry" in *The Philosophy of John Dewey*, 397-420.

55. Wittgenstein, *On Certainty* # 122, #110. Wittgenstein is hesitant to let his project be called a pragmatism, probably because in his circle of British philosophical friends pragmatism was interpreted as one more epistemological theory. He writes, "So I am trying to say something that sounds like pragmatism. Here I am being thwarted by a kind of *Weltanschauung*" (#422). Similarities between Wittgenstein's project of rejecting the search for epistemological foundations and Thomas Reid's earlier effort to do this is brought out in Rom Harre and Daniel N. Robinson, "What Makes Language Possible? Ethological Foundationalism in Reid and Wittgenstein," *Review of Metaphysics*, 50, no. 3 (March 1997), 483-498.

56. Wittgenstein, *On Certainty*, #232.

57. Ibid, 354.

58. The name "Descartes" is here being used to designate what became the traditional interpretation of Descartes' philosophy by those establishing and maintaining the epistemological project. There is good reason to suppose that Descartes actually was engaged in a quite different project. See Martin Heidegger's interpretation of Descartes' involvement in what Heidegger calls the "mathematization" of things begun by Galileo and climaxing in Newton's "Law of Inertia," in "Modern Science, Metaphysics, and Mathematics," in *Martin Heidegger: Basic Writings*, ed. David Farrell Krell (London: Routledge & Kegan Paul, 1978) 274-282.

59. Wittgenstein, *On Certainty*, #550.

60. My interpretation of understanding and interpretation is heavily indebted to Richard Shusterman's investigation in his *Pragmatist Aesthetics*, especially chapters 4 and 5, "Pragmatism and Interpretation" and "Beneath Interpretation." My disagreements with Shusterman will be noted in later chapters.

61. See Steven Mailloux, "Interpretation" in *Critical Terms for Literary Study*, 2d ed., ed. Frank Lentricchia and Thomas McLaughlin (Chicago: University of Chicago Press, 1995), 121, 134.

62. William James, "What Pragmatism Means," Lecture 2 in *Pragmatism: A New Name for Some Old Ways of Thinking* (New York: Longmans, Green, 1907), 49.

63. John Dewey, "What Pragmatism Means," in *Essays in Experimental Logic*, 305, 325-328.

64. For a further defense of the claim that a correspondence theory of truth has no

explanatory worth, see Richard Rorty, "Pragmatism, Davidson and Truth" in *Objectivity, Relativism and Truth* (Cambridge: Cambridge University Press, 1991), 126-150. Rorty claims that "is true" only has an endorsing use, a cautionary use reminding us that current justifications may turn out inadequate in the future, and a disquotational use to say metalinguistic things like "S" is true if S. I shall try to say a little more about the pragmatics of "is true" in order to expand on Rorty's first two uses.

65. For example, see Alan White, *Truth* (Garden, City, NY: Anchor, 1970), 125–27.

66. This accounts for the belief implication in all truth claims that G. E. Moore was so concerned to demonstrate. See his contribution to *The Philosophy of Bertrand Russell*, ed. P. A. Schilpp (Evanston, IL: Open Court, 1944), 204.

67. The position I am defending here is close to the position defended by Alasdair MacIntyre, who also prioritizes falsity and interprets truth as a double negative. He writes, "It is this lack of correspondence, between what the mind (earlier) judged and reality as now perceived, classified and understood, which is ascribed when these earlier judgments and beliefs are *called false.*" *Whose Justice? Which Rationality?* (356). Unfortunately, from my point of view, MacIntyre then abandons a pragmatic approach to truth by insisting that we must add talk about how the mind judges falsely when it fails to represent objects as they "manifest" themselves to the mind and when he postulates "truth as such" as the necessary final goal of inquiry, with such truth being God's vision of things, from which "it will be possible to deduce every relevant truth concerning the subject matter of the enquiry" (81).

68. This provides a resolution to Aristotle's famous "sea battle argument." See Aristotle, "On Interpretation," in *The Basic Works of Aristotle*, ed. Richard McKeon (New York: Random House, 1941), Section 9, 45–48. Only by buying into a correspondence theory of truth and the notion that one has explained something by saying that the conditions of things "makes" our beliefs true does Aristotle get caught in the need to deny future contingencies, since what has not occurred and might not occur can't provide what is necessary to make a present prediction of the future true.

69. See Peter Strawson, "Truth," in *Logico-Linguistic Papers*, 204–6. Donald Davidson rejects such double negative, redundance theories of truth by pointing out that "is true" is not only used to reaffirm with emphasis what we had already said but it also is used to endorse what others have claimed: "The Pythagorean theorem is true." See his "True to Facts" in *Inquiries into Truth and Interpretation* (Oxford: Oxford University Press, 1984), 38.

70. John Austin, "Unfair to Facts" in *Philosophical Papers*, 102–22.

71. This is what the early Wittgenstein did in *Tractatus Logico-Philosophicus* (New York: Humanities, 1961) when he wrote that logical, mathematical, causal, ethical, aesthetic, and religious utterances "say" nothing true or false, because they cannot be truth functionally analyzed into simple pictures of relations between objects.

72. Wittgenstein, *Philosophical Investigations*, #7, 23.

73. Frege's semantic theory of signs is presented in a series of three papers published in 1891 and 1892: "Sense and Reference," "Concept and Object," and "Function and Concept."

These appear in English in *Translations from the Philosophical Writings of Gottlob Frege*, ed. P. Geatch and M. Black (Oxford: Basil Blackwell, 1960).

74. Frege here is endorsing the claim by Bernard Bolzano that asocial, ahistorical propositions must be postulated to account for the sameness of what is said at different times, by different people, using different words, even different languages. See Bolzano's *Theory of Science*, ed. and trans. Rolf George (Berkeley: University of California Press, 1972).

75. In order to preserve a truth value for sayings in which apparently designating expressions lack reference, Bertrand Russell claimed that it is necessary to interpret all propositions in such a way that all supposedly designating signs be analyzed into predicative expressions. See his classic 1903 essay "On Denoting" in *Logic and Knowledge* (London: George Allen and Unwin, 1956), 39–56. Using the symbolism of his mathematical logic, all propositions are taken to have the same reference, all the objects in the domain of discourse to which the symbolism is applied. Every proposition then says either that all these objects [(x)] have certain properties or that at least one of them [(Ex)] has the property. The sentence "The present king of France is bald" is analyzed into its set of truth conditions and found to be false. It is interpreted as the false conjunctive proposition that all things are such that if there exists something which is a present king of France, then it is bald, and there does exist such a king of France. Russell further claims that the meanings of predicative expressions are Platonic universals that have ontological status independent of shifting and variable historical languages. See his *The Problems of Philosophy* (Oxford: Oxford University Press, 1912), 91–100.

76. For a discussion of the pragmatic considerations that need to be introduced in order to specify identity criteria for the contents of beliefs, see Edgar Pace, "Propositional Identity," in *Philosophical Review* (January 1970).

77. Frege criticized the confusion he saw among mathematicians when they talked about functions due to their failure to distinguish marks on a piece of paper [±] from functions themselves. See his "Functions and Concepts" in *Translations from the Philosophical Writings of Gottlob Frege, 21–41*.

78. Speech act theorists, such as John Searle, acknowledge the need to introduce a consideration of the pragmatics of people doing things with words, but he focuses only on the pragmatics of individual speech acts and not on the social pragmatics of talk about language, the meanings of words and the meaning of what we say, with all the social variability and historically changing character of such talk. Searle still claims one must postulate transcendent propositions, intentions, rule constituted illocutionary speech acts that have necessary and sufficient conditions as well as rigid distinctions between literal and metaphorical, direct and indirect, and serious and pretense speech acts in order to account for linguistic communication. See his "What Is a Speech Act?" *Philosophy in America*, ed. Max Black (New York: George Allen & Unwin, 1965), and *Speech Acts: An Essay in the Philosophy of Language* (Cambridge: Cambridge University Press, 1969). Social pragmatics begin to creep into his interpretation of speech acts in his later works when he introduces considerations about the background conditions to speech acts. See his *Intentionality* (Cambridge: Cambridge University Press, 1983), 141–59.

79. This rejection of any absolutizing of an analytic-synthetic distinction is, of course, the heart of the claim of the pragmatist, W. V. O. Quine. See his "Two Dogmas of Empiricism," in *From a Logical Point of View.*

80. The inability of an act of speaking or thinking to only be about itself is a key feature of intentionality. Recognizing this inability is the key to dissolving the so-called "semantical paradoxes." For extended discussions of these issues, see J. L. Austin, "Truth" in *Philosophical Papers* and Max Black, "Frege on Functions" in *Problems in Analysis.*

81. Frege, *The Foundations of Arithmetic,* trans. J. L. Austin (New York: Harper and Bros., 1950), 5–23.

82. In 1870, F. Klein proved that the axioms of Lobachevsky's hyperbolic geometry, which denied Euclid's parallel line postulate, were consistent if Euclid's axioms and postulate were consistent. In 1844 the Irish mathematician William Rowand Hamilton developed a consistent algebra that denied the commutation law for multiplication. See William Kneale and Martha Kneale, *The Development of Logic* (Oxford: Oxford University Press, 1962), 383, 399, 401.

83. Frege, "Begriffsschrift: A Formalized Language of Pure Thought Modeled upon the Language of Arithmetic," in *Translations from the Philosophical Writings of Gottlob Frege,* 3.

84. Husserl borrowed the idea of intentionality from Franz Brentano, who had retrieved it from medieval scholastic forms of Aristotelianism. See Brentano, *Psychology from an Empirical Standpoint,* ed. Linda McAlister, trans. Antos C. Rancurello, D. B. Terrell, Linda McAlister (New York: Humanities Press, 1973).

85. For a defense of the idea of implicit rules governing word usage, see Max Black, "The Analysis of Rules," in *Models and Metaphors* (Ithaca: Cornell University Press, 1962), 95–129. For a refutation of such de jure theories of word meanings, see L. Jonathan Cohen, *Diversity of Meaning* (New York: Herder & Herder, 1963), chapters 11—IV. For a refutation of this whole program of truth functional semantics, see Gordon Baker and P. M. S. Hacker, *Language, Sense and Nonsense* (Oxford: Blackwell, 1984), chapters 4–6.

86. Ferdinand de Saussure, *Course in General Linguistics,* trans. Wade Baskin (New York: McGraw Hill, 1966).

87. Noam Chomsky, *Syntactic Structures* (The Hague: Mouton, 1957); *Aspects of the Theory of Syntax* (Cambridge: MIT Press, 1965); and *Language and Mind* (New York: Harcourt Brace Jovanovich, 1968).

88. The language word/utterance word distinction is not the same as the traditional type/token distinction. If I make a carbon copy of what I have written, I double the number of word tokens produced but I do not double the number of words uttered or the number of language words used.

89. Saussure's linguistic theory has served as the springboard for a large variety of theories in other fields that accent timeless structures or objective meanings. For example, Claude Levi-Strauss charges that we can explain why myths throughout the world are so

similar, even though it seems that anything can happen in a myth, only by noticing [1] that certain relationships between the mythemes in a myth have the same relationship to each other as certain relationships between other mythemes in the myth; (overemphasis on blood relations; giving precedence to kinship relations over state relations) is to underrating blood relations (people kill kinsmen) as earthy monsters being killed for man to be born (the denial that man is born of the earth) is to names with meanings such as "difficult in walking straight" or "standing upright" (the affirmation that man is born from the earth), and [2] that these functional relationships between relationships appear in the myths of people from many different social and cultural worlds. See Levi-Strauss's "The Structural Study of Myth" in *Structural Anthropology* (New York: Basic Books, 1963). For criticisms of Levi-Strauss's structural anthropology, see John Carlos Rowe, "Structure," in *Critical Terms in Literary Theory,* ed. Frank Lentricchia and Thomas McLaughlin (Chicago: University of Chicago Press, 1995), 23–38; and E. E. Evans-Prichard, *Theories of Primitive Religion* (Oxford: Clarendon, 1965), Chapters 111, IV.

90. B. F. Skinner, *Verbal Behavior* (New York: Appleton-Century-Crofts, 1957).

91. W. V. O. Quine, *Word and Object* (Cambridge: MIT Press, 1960).

92. For a rejection of the claim that time constraints on children's learning of language require the postulation of innate syntactical knowledge, see Hilary Putnam, "The Innate Hypothesis and Explanatory Models in Linguistics," *Mind, Language and Reality* (Cambridge: Cambridge University Press, 1975), 107–16.

93. See Stanley Fish, "Rhetoric," in *Critical Terms for Literary Study* (203–22) for an insightful characterization of the manner in which "serious" traditional philosophers have dismissed rhetorical interpreters as irresponsible manipulators of reality and partisan biased panderers to the lowest passions of the promiscuous crowd, and rhetorical interpreters have branded such philosophers as simply dishonest, class serving, and self-deceiving practitioners of a style of seriousness whose rhetorical interpretation of language and thought as innocently transparent is preventing them from including the recognition of the social materiality of language.

94. Ludwig Wittgenstein, *Tractatus Logico-Philosophicus,* trans, D. F. Pears and B. F. McGuiness (London: Routledge and Kegan Paul, 1961).

95. Bertrand Russell, "The Philosophy of Logical Atomism," *Logic and Knowledge,* 175–282. Russell claims that complex propositions had to be so analyzed into truth functional compounds of simple propositions presentable in the language of his symbolic logic that contained only predicate expressions and bound variables, with the predicate expressions naming universals and the variables ranging over uncharacterized particulars which could be referred to only with the demonstrative pronoun "this" when encountered. Rather than working with Russell's two kinds of objects, the objects that Wittgenstein in the *Tractatus* offers as the necessary meanings of the logically proper names in a proposition seem to be both particulars (contingently related) and universals (logically and therefore necessarily related) at the same time. See Max Black, *The Companion to the Tractatus* (Ithaca: Cornell University Press, 1964), 57–65. That it is impossible for something to be both at least should

suggest to interpreters of the *Tractatus* that something is going on in this text other than presenting a variation on Russell's theory.

96. See Eric Stenius, *Wittgenstein's Tractatus* (Ithaca: Cornell University Press, 1960), 5. *The Tractatus begins* with a theme (sentence I), followed by variations on it (sentences 1. I–1. 21). Then a second theme is struck (sentence 2), followed by variations on it and its relations to 1. These are numbered 2.01–2.063. Sentences 2.1–2.19 really are building up to 3. From here on, 3.0, 4.0, 5.0, and 6.0 sentences are variations on 3, 4, 5, and 6 respectfully, and 3.1, 4.1, 5.1, and 6.1 are introductions to 4, 5, 6, and 7 ("What we cannot speak about we pass over in silence"). This last sentence is the final crescendo of the entire work. Most interpreters never even consider the possibility that the musical form of the *Tractatus* plays a crucial rhetorical function in the working of the text as a whole. Most interpreters likewise take Wittgenstein's footnote, giving his apparent instructions for interpreting his number system, instructions he does not follow once he reaches sentence 2, as simply due to his carelessness or his failure to understand his own numbering system. An alternative interpretation could take this footnote as a warning not to read this text as a deductive system, but to attend to its musical form and what this can show about efforts to restrict what people can "say" to truth functional compounds of simple pictures (logically proper names being related to logically proper names).

97. See George Henrik von Wright, "Biographical Sketch," in Norman Malcolm, *Ludwig Wittgenstein: A Memoir* (Oxford: Oxford University Press, 1958), 11; Ray Monk, *Ludwig Wittgenstein: The Duty of Genius* (New York: Free Press, 1990), 182–83.

98. In a letter to Moritz Schlick on August 8, 1932, Wittgenstein wrote, "...and I cannot imagine that Carnap should have so completely misunderstood the last sentences of the *Tractatus*—and hence the fundamental idea of the whole book," in *Ludwig Wittgenstein, Sein Leben in Bildern und Texten,* ed. M. Nedo and M Ranchetti (Frankfurt am Main: SuhrkamPress, 1983), 255. See also Monk, *Ludwig Wittgenstein: The Duty of Genius,* 241–44, and Allan Janick and Stephen Toulmin, *Wittgenstein's Vienna* (New York: Simon & Shuster, 1973), 215–22, 257–62.

99. See James Conant, "Throwing Away the Top of the Ladder," *Yale Review* 79, no. 3; Peter Winch, "Discussion of Malcolm's Essay," in Norman Malcolm, *Wittgenstein: A Religious Point of View* (Ithaca: Cornell University Press, 1994), 99.

100. Wittgenstein, *Tractatus,* 3, 5.

101. Wittgenstein, *Philosophical Investigations.*

102. Ibid, 126, 128.

103. Ibid, 255. This, of course, sounds just like Nietzsche. In what follows I will attempt to show that the similarity is not just superficial.

104. Ibid, #309.

105. Wittgenstein, *Tractatus,* 5.

106. For excellent accounts of Wittgenstein's actions at this time in his life, see Janick and Toulmin, *Wittgenstein's Vienna*, 204–5; Monk, *Ludwig Wittgenstein: The Duty of Genius*, 169–73.

107. Wittgenstein, *Tractatus*, 6.54.

108. Ibid.

109. For an excellent presentation of this sort of interpretation of Wittgenstein's project, see O. K. Bousma, "The Blue Book," in *Ludwig Wittgenstein: The Man and His Philosophy*, ed. K. T. Fann (New York: Dell, 1967), 148–70.

110. Wittgenstein, *Philosophical Investigations*, #12.

111. Ibid, #13, 15.

112. These six linguistic acts are the ones systematically presented in John Searle's *Speech Acts* and *Expression and Meaning* (Cambridge: Cambridge University Press, 1979). He complicates his account of speech acts by adding the speech acts of using words to deceive people into thinking we are performing these acts, to pretend we are performing them, to perform them indirectly, or by using words in nonliteral ways. Derrida has attempted to show that Searle's theoretical treatment of speech acts still is located in a metaphysical fly bottle. See Jacques Derrida, "Signature, Event, Context" in *Margins of Philosophy*, trans. Alan Bass (Chicago: University of Chicago Press, 1982), and "Limited Inc." in *Limited Inc.*, ed. Gerald Graff (Evanston, IL: Northwestern University Press, 1988).

113. These are but some of the examples given by Mikhail M. Bakhtin in his denial that language can be turned into a syntactical or semantic system. There is, he claims, a heteroglossia to language. See his *The Dialogic Imagination*, ed. Michael Holquist, trans. Caryl Emerson and Michael Holquist (Austin: University of Texas Press, 1981).

114. Wittgenstein, *Philosophical Investigations*, #23.

115. Wittgenstein charges that this is what Frazer did in his anthropological interpretation of religion. See *Remarks on Frazer's Golden Bough*, ed. Rush Rhees, trans. A. C. Miles (Atlantic Highlands, NJ: Humanities Press, 1979). For a full development of a Wittgensteinian attack on reductionist approaches to religious language, see D. Z. Phillips, *Religion without Explanation;* 1976); "Knowing Where to Stop," in *Belief, Change and Forms of Life* (Atlantic Highlands, NJ: Humanities Press, 1986), 17–41; "Primitive Reactions and the Reactions of Primitives," in *Wittgenstein and Religion*, 103–22.

116. See Max Black, "Explanations of Meaning," *Models and Metaphors*, 17–24.

117. Wittgenstein, *Philosophical Investigations*, #560.

118. For an excellent development of a Wittgensteinian interpretation of understanding, see Richard Shusterman, *Pragmatist Aesthetics*, chapters 4 and 5.

119. Wittgenstein, *Philosophical Investigations*, #67.

120. Ibid, #66–76.

121. Ibid, #125.

122. Ibid, #139ff, 527.

123. Ibid, #155, 202, 206, 321–23.

124. Ibid, #244–46, 350, 384, 403–8.

125. Ibid, 22.

126. Ibid, #178, 422, 391–93.

127. Rudolf Carnap, "The Overcoming of Metaphysics through Logical Analysis of Language," in *Heidegger and Modern Philosophy*, ed. Michael Murray (New Haven: Yale University Press, 1978), 23–34.

128. For an excellent interpretation of Heidegger's interpretation of understanding, see Hubert L. Dreyfus, *Being-in-the- World*, chapter 11.

129. Ibid, chapter 4.

130. See Heidegger, "Modern Science, Metaphysics, and Mathematics," in *Martin Heidegger: Basic Writings*, 247–82.

131. Martin Heidegger, *Being and Time*, 19.

132. Martin Heidegger, "The Onto-Theo-Logical Nature of Metaphysics," in *Essays in Metaphysics: Identity and Difference*, trans. Kurt F. Leidecker (New York: Philosophical Library, 1960), 52–67.

133. Martin Heidegger, "Letter on Humanism," in *Basic Writings*, 208–19. See also my "The Origin of the Debate over Ontotheology in the Texts of Heidegger and Derrida," in *Religion, Ontotheology and Deconstruction*, ed. Henry Ruf (New York: Paragon House, 1989), 3–42.

134. Martin Heidegger, "The Origin of the Work of Art," in *Basic Writings*, 149–87.

135. That interpretations based on an open listening to a text can add to the meaning of the text is the primary message in Gadamer's explication of "ontological hermeneutics." See Hans-Georg Gadamer, *Philosophical Hermeneutics*.

136. The occurrence of ruptures in history is a crucial claim made by Foucault in his project of "interpretive analytics." See Michel Foucault, "Nietzsche, Genealogy, History," in *Foucault Reader*, ed. Paul Rabinow, trans. Donald F. Bouchard and Sherry Simon (New York: Pantheon, 1984), 80–97.

137. Heidegger charges that ordinary humanisms are not humanistic enough or they would understand that it is the destiny and freedom of Being which is the necessary condition of the human situation and of human freedom. See "Letter on Humanism," *Basic Writings*, 199–210.

138. For a fuller discussion of the difference between socially constituted people and

robots, see Dreyfus, *Being-in-the-World,* 68–69.

139. Donald Davidson argues against the idea that we could encounter alternative conceptual systems, so different we could not understand people functioning with one of these system, by pointing out that if this were so then we would not even be able to understand that we were encountering other people or an alternative conceptual system. See his "On the Very Idea of a Conceptual System," *Truth and Interpretation,* 183–98. Davidson does not, however, use his rejection of the possibility of such an alternative conceptual system to argue for ahistorical and asocial meanings, claiming that philosophers would be better off not talking about meanings at all.

140. For a fuller interpretation of the natural correlations that form the prelinguistic, background frame of human social rationality, see Harre and Robinson, "What Makes Language Possible?" and Gordon P. Baker and Peter M. S. Hacker, *Wittgenstein: Rules, Grammar and Necessity* (Oxford: Blackwell, 1985), 8–24.

141. Harre and Robinson, "What Makes Language Possible?," 494.

142. Wittgenstein, *Philosophical Investigations,* #206.

143. Gadamer, *Truth and Method,* 239–45, 211–14.

144. Ibid, 245–53.

145. Gadamer rejects Wilhelm Dilthey's contention that the historian or sociologist must strive to represent the actor's interpretation of her or his action. The actor or author is in no privileged position to interpret the whole social, cultural, and historical background of the action. For Dilthey's position, see *Selected Writings,* trans. and ed. H. P. Rickman (Cambridge: Cambridge University Press, 1976). For Gadamer's critique, see *Truth and Method,* 192–214.

146. Friderick Schliermacher gave priority to a writer's contemporaries who would be most able to reconstruct the author's construction of the text. See his *Hermeneutics: The Handwritten Manuscripts of F. D. Schliermacher,* ed. Heinz Kimmerle, trans. James Duke and Jack Frostman (Missoula, MT: Scholars Press, 1977). For Gadamer's criticisms, see *Truth and Method,* 168–73.

147. Gadamer, *Truth and Method,* 338–41, 345–51. For an excellent interpretation of Gadamer's interpretation of cross-cultural understanding, see David Cousins Hoy, "Gadamer's Hermeneutical Pluralism" in Hoy and Thomas McCarthy, *Critical Theory* (Cambridge: Blackwell, 1994), 188–200.

148. Jacques Derrida, *Of Grammatology,* trans. Gayatri Chakravorty Spivak (Baltimore: Johns Hopkins University Press, 1974), 27–30, 74–75.

149. Derrida, "Plato's Pharmacy," in *Dissemination,* 61–171.

150. Derrida, "That Dangerous Supplement," in *Of Grammatology,* Part 11.

151. Derrida, *Glass,* trans. J. P. Leavey and R. A. Rand (Lincoln: University of Nebraska

Press, 1986); "The Pit and the Pyramid: Introduction to Hegel's Semiology," *Margins of Philosophy*, 69–108.

152. Derrida, *Speech and Phenomena and Other Essays on Husserl's Theory of Signs*, trans. David B. Allison (Evanston: Northwestern University Press, 1973); *Edmund Husserl's Origins of Geometry: An Introduction*, trans. John P. Leavey (Stony Brook, NY: Nicolas Hayes, 1978).

153. Derrida, "Linguistics and Grammatology," *Of Grammatology*, 30–65; *Positions*, trans. Alan Bass (Chicago: University of Chicago Press, 1981), 18–36.

154. Derrida writes, "Now, 'everyday language' is not innocent or neutral. It is the language of Western metaphysics, and it carries with it not only a considerable number of presuppositions of all types, but also presuppositions inseparable from metaphysics, which, although little attended to, are knotted into a system." *Positions*, 19.

155. At times Derrida himself acknowledges that metaphysical contamination is only a danger and not a totalizing effect. "But I have never believed that there were metaphysical concepts in and of themselves. No concept is by itself, and consequently in and of itself, metaphysical, outside all textual work in which it is inscribed." *Positions*, 57. On this issue, see Staten, *Wittgenstein and Derrida*, 20, 107.

156. Derrida, *Positions*, 23.

157. For Derrida's use and criticism of Austin, see "Signature, Event Context," *Margins of Philosophy*, 321–27.

158. Derrida's endorsement of a Heideggerian practical holism is at the heart of his deconstructive reading of John Searle's writings about speaker intentions in his speech act theory. See Derrida, *Limited Inc.*, 29–110.

159. Ibid, 19–20.

160. Ibid, 21.

161. Ibid, 22.

162. Derrida, "Structure, Sign, and Play in the Discourse of the Human Sciences," in *Writing and Difference*, trans. Alan Bass (Chicago: University of Chicago Press, 1978), 285–86.

163. See Mark Taylor, *Tears*.

164. Derrida, *Of Grammatology*, 30–73; "Writing and Telecommunication" in *Margins of Philosophy*, 314–18; "Grafts, a Return to Overcasting" in *Dissemination*, 355–58.

165. Derrida, "Difference," in *Speech and Phenomena*, 129–60.

166. Derrida, "Structure, Sign, and Play in the Discourse of the Human Sciences," in *Writing and Difference*, 283.

167. Michel Foucault, "The Discourse on Language," in *The Archeology of Knowledge & The Discourse of Language*, trans. A. M. Sheridan Smith (New York: Harper & Row, 1972), 215–37; "What is an Author?" in *The Foucault Reader*, 101–20.

168. Foucault, "The Discourse on Language" in *Archeology of Knowledge*, 216.

169. Foucault, "What Is an Author?" in *The Foucault Reader*, 113–14.

170. Foucault, "The Discourse on Language" in *Archeology of Knowledge*, 227.

171. Ibid, 225.

172. Hegel's "theodicy...does not acquit God of the charge of cruelty and injustice, it merely calls our attention to extenuating circumstances. There is some reason in the madness of history, and the suffering is not wholly pointless... At times, [people] may well have been driven largely by ambition and other passions; but they also produced results they did not intend and, however far this may have been from their consciousness, they contributed in the long run to the development of freedom in the modern world." Walter Kaufmann, *Hegel: Reinterpretation, Texts and Commentary*, 263. Dewey, Rorty, and Bernstein all retain some of this Hegelian optimism, Dewey being most hopeful and Bernstein most sympathetic to European characterizations of the "dark" side of the social and cultural practices of the North Atlantic people.

173. See especially Rorty, *Contingency, Irony, and Solidarity*, (Cambridge: Cambridge University Press, 1989), Part 1: "Contingency"; and "Representation, Social Practice, and Truth" in *Objectivity, Relativism, and Truth*, 151–61.

174. For Rorty's sustained criticism of the postulation of subjects and representations by the creators and sustainers of the epistemological project, see Rorty, *Philosophy and the Mirror of Nature* (Princeton: Princeton University Press, 1979), parts 1 and 2.

175. Rorty sometimes has characterized his general interpretation of people as a materialism that does without talk about the mind as an independent substance, or about purely mental events, and thus without talk about any mind-body identity; see his *Philosophy and the Mirror of Nature*, 114–25. He also has labeled his position "Nonreductive physicalism"; see his *Objectivity, Relativism, and Truth*, 113–25.

176. On Rorty's views on the lack of any metaphysical self in people, see *Contingency, Irony, and Solidarity*, 33–43; *Objectivity, Relativism, and Truth*, 199.

177. See Rorty, "The World Well Lost," in *Consequences of Pragmatism;* "Pragmatism, Davidson and Truth" in *Objectivity, Relativism, and Truth*, 126, 149.

178. Rorty, "Inquiry as Recontextualization," in *Objectivity, Relativism, and Truth*, 97.

179. Rorty, *Objectivity, Relativism, and Truth*, 5–8.

180. See Rorty, "The Contingency of Language" in *Contingency, Irony, and Solidarity*, 5–7; "Texts and Lumps" in *Objectivity, Relativism, and Truth*, 79–84; "Pragmatism, Davidson and truth" in *Objectivity, Relativism, and Truth*, 126–129.

181. Richard Bernstein, *Philosophical Profiles* (Philadelphia: University of Pennsylvania Press, 1986), 90.

182. Ibid, 195.

183. Richard Bernstein, *Praxis and Action* (Philadelphia: University of Pennsylvania Press, 1971).

184. Ibid, 224.

185. Ibid, 306.

186. Bernstein, *The Restructuring of Social and Political Theory* (Philadelphia: University of Pennsylvania Press, 1978), 145.

187. Bernstein, *The New Constellation: The Ethical-Political Horizons of Modernity/Postmodernity* (Cambridge: MIT Press, 1992), 328.

188. Bernstein, *The Restructuring of Social and Political Theory*, 229–30.

189. Ibid, 32.

190. Bernstein, *Beyond Objectivism and Relativism: Science, Hermeneutics, and Praxis* (Philadelphia: University of Pennsylvania Press, 1983), 24–25.

191. Bernstein, *The New Constellation*, 307.

192. Ibid, 312.

193. Ibid, 318–19.

194. Bernstein, *Beyond Objectivism and Relativism*, 25.

195. Bernstein, *Philosophical Profiles*, 114, 195; *Beyond Objectivism and Relativism*, 223–31.

196. Bernstein, "Foucault: Critique as a Philosophical *Ethos*" in *The New Constellation*, 142–71.

197. Bernstein, *The New Constellation*, 312–13.

198. Bernstein, *Beyond Objectivism and Relativism*, 195. See also *The Restructuring of Social and Political Theory*, 219–25.

199. Rorty, *Contingency, Irony, and Solidarity*, 84–85.

200. Ibid, 60.

201. Ibid, 68.

202. Ibid, xv.

203. Rorty, *Essays on Heidegger and Others*, 81.

204. Rorty, *Objectivity, Relativism, and Truth*, 177.

205. Rorty, *Contingency, irony, and solidarity*, 198.

206. Ibid, 63.

207. *Rorty & Pragmatism: The Philosopher Responds To His Critics.*, ed. Herman K. Saatkamp, Jr. (Nashville: Vanderbilt University Press, 1995), 201–3.

208. Rorty, *Essays on Heidegger and Others*, 24.

209. Ibid, 67.

210. Ibid, 78.

211. Rorty, *Contingency, Irony, and Solidarity*, 91.

212. Ibid, 170, 175.

213. Bernstein, *Praxis and Action*, 82–83.

214. Bernstein, *The New Constellation*, 203.

215. Ibid, 163.

216. Ibid, 162, 165.

217. Ibid, 245.

218. Ibid, 287.

219. Ibid, 286.

220. Ibid, 264, 274.

221. Ibid, 288.

222. Rorty, *Essays on Heidegger and Others*, 36.

223. Ibid, 17.

224. Ibid, 27.

225. Rorty, *Contingency, Irony and Solidarity*, 77–78.

226. Bernstein in *The New Constellation* (1993), page 4, reaffirms what he wrote in *Praxis and Action* in 1971, that social *praxis* has been the basic concern of his pragmatic philosophizing even as he has seen it as central to Dewey's philosophical project.

227. Rorty, *Essays on Heidegger and Others*, 61–62.

228. *Ibid*, 51, 64, 71.

229. Bernstein, *Philosophical Profiles*, 220.

230. Bernstein, *The New Constellation*, 136.

231. Ibid, 278.

232. Ibid, 74-75.

233. Ibid, 71.

CHAPTER THREE

1. My interpretation of the common goal sought by many of the West's social and cultural critics is, of course, merely a generalization of the goal Michel Foucault sets for himself in his critical project. See his "Politics and Ethics: An Interview," in *Foucault Reader*, 373–80.

2. I am appropriating the term "appropriate' from Heidegger's use of it to characterize the way we should relate ourselves to traditional ways of understanding things, recognizing how we are a product of having been socialized into a world of traditions but understanding that we can destructure and reconstruct such traditions so as to give space for possibilities closed off as the tradition solidified. See Heidegger, *Being and Time*, n2/18. Heidegger's notion of appropriating traditions is the forerunner of Gadamer's notion of entering into dialogue with texts and traditions, listening to them, speaking back to them, and having one's prejudgments modified by the dialogue.

3. See John van Buren, "Martin Heidegger, Martin Luther" in *Reading Heidegger from the Start: Essays in His Earliest Thought*, ed. Theodore Kisiel and John van Buren (Albany: SUNY, 1994), 159–74.

4. Thomas Hobbes, *Leviathan: Parts I and II* (Indianapolis: Liberal Arts, 1958), 139–43.

5. See John Locke, *Second Treatise of Government*, ed. C. B. Macpherson (Indianapolis: Hackett, 1980), 8–18.

6. Ibid, 19–30.

7. That one can separate the enlightenment project, of resisting domination through critical interpretation of the human situation, from the the metaphysical humanism and scientism of the modern world is the theme of Michel Foucault's essay, "What is Enlightenment?" found in *Foucault Reader*, 32–50.

8. A number of interpreters of the early thinking of Heidegger have pointed out how dependent upon Kierkegaard is his thinking about the need for a destruction or overcoming of the philosophical (metaphysical) tradition through an appropriation of that tradition that gives life in the present to options rejected in the development of that tradition. See Jeffrey Andrew Barash, "Heidegger's Ontological 'Destruction' of Western Intellectual Traditions"; Robert Bernasconi, "Repetition and Tradition: Heidegger's Destructuring of the Distinction between Essence and Existence in *Basic Problems of Phenomenology*; Otto Poggler, "Destruction and Moment" in *Reading Heidegger from the Start: Essays in His Earliest Writing*, 111–22, 123–36, 137–58.

9. Soren Kierkegaard, *The Present Age*, trans. Alexander Dru (New York: Harper, 1962), 48–69.

10. For further resonances of this theme in a Buddhist chord, see Masao Abe, "The Idea of Purity in Mahayana Buddhism" and "Emptiness is Suchness," in *Zen and Western Thought*, 216–30.

11. Soren Kierkegaard, *Concluding Unscientific Postscript*, 116.

12. For his critical interpretations of the aesthetic and moral forms of life see, Soren Kierkegaard, *Either/Or*, trans. David Swenson and Lillian Marvin Swenson (Princeton, NJ: Princeton University Press, 1944, 1959). It is vital to recognize that prior to choosing either an aesthetic or moral or one of the religious forms of life there is the much more critical choice either to take responsibility for one's way of living or to merely continue as socialization and chance dictate.

13. Soren Kierkegaard, *The Sickness Unto Death*, trans. Alastair Hannay (New York: Penguin, 1989), 59–72.

14. Ibid, 44–51.

15. Ibid, 80–98.

16. Ibid, 98–99.

17. Ibid, 105.

18 . For a complimentary development of this theme, see Soren Kierkegaard, *Repetition*, trans. Walter Lowrie (Princeton, NJ: Princeton University Press, 1941, 1969). In this work, Kierkegaard's persona, Constantine Constatius, points out that one can gain the constancy needed for repetition of aesthetically agreeable experiences only by carefully ordering one's life. Furthermore, the more competent one becomes in one's aesthetic tastes and abilities, the less content one becomes because one knows one will never be entirely and absolutely content in every way and becoming tolerably content is not worth the trouble. It is better to be entirely discontent; that at least is interesting. The aesthete, in flight from leveled-down, conformist boredom, demands that things be interesting.

19. Kierkegaard, *Either/Or*, 23–24, 33.

20. Ibid, 81–82.

21. Ibid, 87.

22. Ibid, 86–94.

23. The moral life as characterized by Kierkegaard bears striking similarities to the call in the Confucian ethic for all persons to rectify their names, to fulfill the requirements that define the social roles they occupy [father, wife, older brother, friend, emperor].

24. Kierkegaard, *Either/Or*, vol. 2, 256–57, 328–29.

25. Ibid, 258–61.

26. Ibid, 352.

27. Ibid, 72–74.

28. The interpretation that I am offering here has been heavily influenced by my reading and appropriation of the following two texts: Gilles Deleuze, *Nietzsche and Philosophy*, trans. Hugh Tomlinson (New York: Columbia University Press, 1983), and Alexander Nehamas, *Nietzsche: Life as Literature* (Cambridge: Harvard University Press, 1985).

29. Friedrich Nietzsche, *The Gay Science*, 253.

30. Nietzsche, *Beyond Good and Evil*, trans. Walter Kaufmann (New York: Vintage, 1966), 30–31.

31. For a decisive refutation of the thesis that Nietzsche's theory of universal hermeneutics is self-refuting, see Nehamas, *Nietzsche: Life as Literature*, 64–73.

32. Nietzsche, *The Gay Science*, 35.

33. Nietzsche, *Human, All Too Human*, 13.

34. Nietzsche, *Beyond Good and Evil*, 97.

35. Nietzsche, *Twilight of the Idols*, 465–66.

36. Nietzsche, *Beyond Good and Evil*, 65, 209; *On the Genealogy of Morals*, trans. Walter Kaufmann (New York: Vintage, 1969), 84–85, 114.

37. Nietzsche, *Thus Spoke Zarathustra*, 168.

38. Nietzsche, *The Gay Science*, 36.

39. Nietzsche, *On the Genealogy of Morals*, 68.

40. Nietzsche, *Human, All Too Human*, 77.

41. Ibid, 249.

42. In *Beyond Good and Evil*, 48, Nietzsche proposes that we explain all "instinctive" life as developments and ramifications of a will to power. See also *Thus Spoke Zarathustra*, 225–26, and *On the Genealogy of Morals*, 45–46.

43. Nietzsche calls for people to recover a way of living in which one is light, flying and dancing and singing, living in a garden of delight. See *The Gay Science,* 347, and *Thus Spoke Zarathustra,* 231, 238.

44. Nietzsche charges that the slaves to fear, revenge, and resentment use morality, religion, and philosophy in an effort to enslave those able to enjoy life with their eyes wide open to its misfortunes. For example, see *On the Genealogy of Morals,* 36–39, and *The Gay Science,* 314–15.

45. Nietzsche claims that metaphysics attempts to control chance with its claims about unity and permanence and it attempts to rationalize away suffering with its theoretical

postulation of an ultimately real and rational world as opposed to this apparent world with its misfortunes. (*Beyond Good and Evil*, 13–17, and *Twilight of the Idols*, 482–84). He also charges that it is suffering and an incapacity to remove or justify it plus a weariness with ordinary life that lead to postulations of metaphysical gods and afterlives (*Thus Spoke Zarathustra*, 30–31).

46. As Nietzsche interprets his world, the massive herd of slaves to fear and resentment use religion, morality, and philosophy to get those few who are able to celebrate life as it is found into people who internalize the slave's cultural practices and thus into people supporting the interests of the slaves. See *Genealogy of Morals*, 36–43.

47. Nietzsche claims that some people have the power to be free spirits caring for themselves both by personally endorsing what they are and by overcoming what their social and cultural training has made them be. See *Human, All Too Human*, 7–11, 139–40.

48. Nietzsche writes that people, presuming that size is important in measuring the significance of human life, make everything about human life small as they come to see that the earth has become small. See *Thus Spoke Zarathustra*, 17.

49. Nietzsche, *Human, All Too Human*, 77; *Beyond Good and Evil*, 16–17; *Twilight of the Idols*, 482–83.

50. See Nietzsche, *Beyond Good and Evil*, 116–17

51. See Nietzsche, *Human, All Too Human*, 37.

52. Ibid, 5, 139.

53. Nietzsche, *Beyond Good and Evil*, 75; *The Gay Science*, 256.

54. Nietzsche's death of God rhetoric appears in many different contexts in his writing. See *Human, All Too Human* [78], *The Gay Science* [181], *Thus Spoke Zarathustra* [12, 90, 182], *On the Genealogy of Morals* [92].

55. Nietzsche, *Thus Spoke Zarathustra*, 133, 204.

56. Nietzsche, *Beyond Good and Evil*, 207–9, 218; *On the Genealogy of Morals*, 42–43.

57. In *Twilight of the Idols*, 501, Nietzsche did write that there are no moral facts, but this does not require us to ignore his comments about multiple moralities. Nietzsche rejects in general the metaphysical claim that there obtain what are called facts by defenders of correspondence theories of truth. He therefore rejects any talk about moral facts. In an interpretation of the pragmatics of using expressions such as "is true" and "is a fact," one can claim, as was pointed out in the last chapter, that these are used to reject rejections of one's claims. Talking about moral facts, about what ought to be done, is even more problematic than talking about how true descriptive claims correspond to facts (how things are), as discussions of the naturalistic fallacy point out. Besides, in different social and cultural worlds, different prohibitions and requirements might exist, all of which might satisfy the criteria for being moral when the word "moral" is used to describe second order social norms and principles used in critiquing first order social norms. Finally, Nietzsche probably did think

that none of the moralities existing in the world at his time gave priority to the principle of maximizing human freedom because these moralities were being used to increase conformity and sameness in a given society and not to protect the freedom of dissidents and free spirits to be different.

58. See Nietzsche, *Beyond Good and Evil*, 98. In *Human, All Too Human*, 7, he writes that free spirits might create different kinds of good lives, all of which are permitted by free spirits.

59. Nietzsche, *On the Genealogy of Morals*, 20.

60. Nietzsche, *Beyond Good and Evil*, 115.

61. See Nietzsche's "First Essay" in *On the Genealogy of Morals* [24–56], *Beyond Good and Evil* [205], *Twilight of the Idols* [489–90].

62. Nietzsche, *On the Genealogy of Morals*, 37.

63. In *The Gay Science*, 117, Nietzsche recommends finding values that could not even be measured by the scales now used in existing slave moralities, and at 131 he expresses his support for exceptional people who determine for themselves what will be for them a good life but who never strive to force their way of life on others. Maximization of freedom or minimization of nonconsentuality become the ruling norm in the morality of good and bad.

64. In *Human, All Too Human*, 146, Nietzsche claims that the Renaissance had almost made the proper diagnosis and recommended the correct medicine when it fought for the unshackling of the individual, liberation of thought, disdain for authority, and the prioritizing of education over lineage.

65. Nietzsche, *Ecco Homo*, trans. Walter Kaufmann (New York: Vintage, 1967), 232–33.

66. Nietzsche, *Thus Spoke Zarathustra*, 209–10.

67. Nietzsche, *The Gay Science*, 250.

68. Nietzsche writes in *Human, All Too Human* [89] that there is not enough love and kindness in the world, but he also warns that being kind does not mean pitying those who are suffering because by presuming that one can understand the idiosyncratic character of their suffering one refuses to respect their individuality and uniqueness. Don't pity their suffering, but attempt to increase their freedom, if this is possible. See *The Gay Science*, 269–71.

69. Nietzsche in *The Gay Science* [242] warns that free spirits pay for that freedom by becoming more sensitive than ever to suffering. Of course, they nevertheless remain life-affirmers.

70. Nietzsche on many occasions imagines the general outlines of the joyful life of the free spirit. See: *Human, All Too Human*, 37; *The Gay Science*, 346–47; *Thus Spoke Zarathustra*, 74–79.

71. Nietzsche, *The Gay Science*, 86.

72. In *Human, All Too Human*, Nietzsche recommends being interested in and finding joy in all forms of nonnihilistic life [136–37] and of living in the "gentle sunshine of continued spiritual joyfulness" [175].

73. Nietzsche, *The Gay Science*, 164, 255.

74. Nietzsche, *Twilight of the Idols*, 562–63.

75. Nietzsche, *Human, All Too Human*, 149.

76. Nietzsche, *The Gay Science*, 156.

77. Nietzsche in *The Gay Science* points out that one must work to be free, that it is not given to one [156], that one must give style to one's life by fitting all the conflicting pieces in one's life into a plan governed by a law of one's own [232], that one must develop habits and then develop the lifelong habit of maintaining habits only for a brief time [236–37].

78. Nietzsche, *Beyond Good and Evil*, 100.

79. Nietzsche, *Twilight of the Idols*, 486, 545, 542, 546, 554.

80. Nietzsche, *Human, All Too Human*, 169.

81. Nietzsche repeatedly makes rhetorical use of the trope of eternal return. See *The Gay Science* [273–74], *Thus Spoke Zarathustra* [157, 318], *Beyond Good and Evil* [68]. Sometimes he is urging people to celebrate life in all its forms by unendingly taking up the dice of life and throwing them again and again, regardless of whether craps or seven and elevens turn up. Sometimes he is writing about becoming such artistic masters of one's beautiful life that one would jump at the chance of living it again and again.

82. Nietzsche, *Human, All Too Human*, 66.

83. Ibid, 89–90.

84. Nietzsche proclaims in *The Gay Science* [180–81] that killing off the holiest and mightiest that our social world has owned can wipe away the horizon that produces orientation through absolutes, but it does not drink up the sea or erase the awesome other to socially constituted finiteness.

85. Nietzsche, *The Antichrist*, trans. Walter Kaufmann, in *The Portable Nietzsche*, 594–95.

86. Ibid, 562.

87. Ibid, 586–87.

88. Ibid, 606–9, 612–13.

89. Kierkegaard, *Concluding Unscientific Postscript*, 425–48.

90. See Rudolf Bernet, "Phenomenological Reduction and the Double Life of the Subject," in *Reading Heidegger from the Start: Essays in His Earliest Thought*, 245–67.

91. See Franco Volpi, *"Being and Time*: A 'Translation' of the *Nicomachean Ethics*," in *Reading Heidegger from the Start: Essays in His Earliest Thought*, 195–211.

92. Michel Foucault, "The Return of Morality," in *Politics, Philosophy, Culture*, trans. Thomas Levic and Isabelle Lorenz (New York: Routledge, 1988), 250–51.

93. "Interpretive Analytics" is the name given to Foucault's Nietzschean project of interpreting subjectivity forming social practices in terms of power relationships by Hubert L. Dryfus and Paul Rabinow in their book *Michael Foucault: Beyond Structuralism and Hermeneutics* (Chicago: University Of Chicago Press, 1982).

94. See Istvan M. Feher, "Phenomenology, Hermeneutics and Lebensphilosophie," in *Reading Heidegger from the Start*, 76. For an excellent narrative of the biographical development of Heidegger's life as a thinker and person, see Rudiger Safranski, *Martin Heidegger: Between Good and Evil*, trans. Ewald Osers (Cambridge: Harvard University Press, 1998).

95. See Karl Barth, *The Epistle To the Romans*, trans. Edwyn C. Hoskyns (New York: Oxford University Press, 1968).

96. See Rudolf Bultmann, *Primitive Christianity in Its Contemporary Setting*, trans. R. H. Fuller (New York: Meridian, 1957).

97. See Hans-Georg Gadamer, "The Marburg Theology," in *Heidegger's Ways*, trans. John W. Stanley (Albany: SUNY Press, 1994), 29–43; see also Jeffrey Andrew Barash, "Heidegger's Ontological Destruction," and John van Buren, "Martin Heidegger, Martin Luther," in *Reading Heidegger from the Start*, 112–15, 160.

98. Safranski presents an excellent narrative and analysis of the widespread dissatisfaction that culture critics like the dadaists Robert Musil, Nikolay Berdyayev, and Ernest Junger felt in Europe after World War I. See his *Martin Heidegger: Between Good and Evil*, 99, 161, 203, 226.

99. Heidegger, *Being and Time*, 351.

100. Heidegger, "Letter on Humanism," in *Basic Writings*, 197.

101. See Franco Volpi, *"Being and Time: A 'Translation' of the *Nicomachean Ethic*,"* 200–204.

102. Heidegger points out that no matter how far along we are in universalizing the technological ethos, still at its very core there is that which resists its totalization. See his "The Turning" in *The Question Concerning Technology and Other Essays*, trans. William Lovitt (New York: Harper, 1977), 36–49.

103. Heidegger, "Letter on Humanism," in *Basic Writings*, 217–19, 232.

104. Heidegger, "The Question Concerning Technology," in *Basic Writings*, 306.

105. Heidegger, "The Origin of a Work of Art," in *Basic Writings*, 181.

106. Heidegger, "Letter on Humanism," in *Basic Writings*, 223.

107. Heidegger, "Recollections in Metaphysics," in *The End of Philosophy*, trans. Joan Stambaugh (New York: Harper & Row, 1973), 78.

108. Heidegger, *Being and Time*, 297–304.

109. Ibid, 333–35.

110. Heidegger, *Being and Time*, 204; "Letter on Humanism," in *Basic Writings*, 212.

111. Heidegger, *Being and Time*, 33.

112. Heidegger, "Letter on Humanism," in *Basic Writings*, 196.

113. Heidegger, "The Origin of a Work of Art," in *Basic Writings*, 177. The contrast between nature and culture had been circulating in intellectual circles since the rise of Romanticism in the eighteenth century, but Heidegger radicalizes the notion of nature by drawing upon mystics such as Meister Eckhart to accent possibilities not yet encountered even by nature lovers. He also draws upon his earlier study of Duns Scotus and the category of *haecceitas,* singularity, this-here-now, which no set of general descriptive terms could ever exhaustively capture.

114. Heidegger, "What Is Metaphysics?" in *Basic Writings*, 112, 106.

115. Heidegger, *Being and Time*, 19–20.

116. Heidegger, *What Is Called Thinking*, trans. Fred D. Wieck and J. Glenn Gray (New York: Harper & Row, 1968), 231.

117. Ibid, 96–97.

118. Heidegger, "The Question Concerning Technology," in *Basic Writings*, 304.

119. Heidegger, "Memorial Address," in *Discourse on Thinking*, trans. John M. Anderson and E. Hans Freund (New York: Harper & Row, 1959), 57.

120. Heidegger, "Letter on Humanism," in *Basic Writings*, 221.

121. Heidegger, "Dwelling, Building, Thinking," in *Basic Writings*, 324.

122. Heidegger, in "Memorial Address" *(Discourse on Thinking)*, 57, charges that if we let calculative reasoning become accepted and practiced as the only way of thinking, then we will face a danger greater than the threat of atomic war, and that is the danger of denying and throwing away our own special nature.

123. Heidegger, *Being and Time*, 352.

124. Ibid, 186, 243–46.

125. Heidegger, "What Is Metaphysics?" in *Basic Writings*, 102–10. "The Word of Nietzsche: 'God is Dead'," in *The Question Concerning Technology and Other Essays*, 104–7; "The Onto-Theo-Logical Nature of Metaphysics," in *Essays in Metaphysics: Identity and Difference,* trans. Kurt F. Leidecker (New York: Philosophical Library, 1960), 48, 64–66.

126. Heidegger's interpretation of the growing power in the West of a technological mode of subjectivity is found in his "The Question Concerning Technology" in *The Question Concerning Technology and Other Essays*, 3–35. See also Hubert L. Dreyfus's interpretation of Heidegger on technology in "On the Ordering of Things: Being and Power in Heidegger and Foucault," in *Michael Foucault: Philosopher* (New York: Routledge, 1992), 80–94.

127. Heidegger, "The Origin of a Work of Art," in *Basic Writings*, 187.

128. Heidegger, "Building, Dwelling, Thinking," in *Basic Writings*, 328, 336.

129. Heidegger, "Only a God Can Save Us: *Der Spiegel's* Interview with Martin Heidegger," trans. M. P. Alter and J. D. Caputo, *Philosophy Today* 20, no. 4 (winter 1976): 267–84.

130. Heidegger, "What Is Metaphysics?" in *Basic Writings*, 112.

131. Ibid, 101.

132. Ibid, 105, 110–11.

133. "Our thinking today is charged with the task to think what the Greeks have thought in an even more Greek Manner." Martin Heidegger, "A Dialogue on Language," in *On The Way to Language*, trans. Peter D. Hertz (New York: Harper & Row, 1971), 39.

134. Heidegger, "What Is Metaphysics?" in *Basic Writings*, 105.

135. In order to understand how Heidegger views tradition as both a barrier and a doorway to enlightenment and freedom, see Robert Bernasconi, "Repetition and Tradition," in *Reading Heidegger from the Start, 133–36*.

136. For a narrative of the correlation between Heidegger's early 1930s lectures on Plato's allegory of the cave and his involvement in National Socialism, see Safranski, *Martin Heidegger: Between Good and Evil*, chapter 13.

137. For a most insightful interpretation of the involvement of Martin Heidegger the philosopher in the Nazi movement, see Safranski, *Martin Heidegger: Between Good and Evil*, chapters 13 and 15.

138. That the significance of the failure of the Nazi experiment in social/cultural revolution was not appreciated even as late as the 1960s is evidenced by the massive support by French intellectuals of Mao's Cultural Revolution in China, another effort to achieve utopian ends by disastrously counterproductive means.

139. Heidegger in "Overcoming Metaphysics" in *The End of Philosophy* [110] declares that no mere action can overcome the influence of the fallenness of the modern world and thus produce revolutionary change.

140. Heidegger, "The Origin of a Work of Art," in *Basic Writings*, 187; "Conversation on a Country Path about Thinking," in *Discourse on Thinking*, 62.

141. Heidegger, "Letter on Humanism," in *Basic Writings*, 218.

142. Ibid, 221.

143. Heidegger, "Memorial Address," in *Discourse on Thinking*, 46–47.

144. Heidegger, "The Origin of the Work of Art" in *Basic Writings*, 183.

145. In an otherwise sympathetic interpretation of Heidegger's call to release ourselves trustingly into the unpredictable freedom of social/cultural history, John Caputo expresses concern about giving up all ability to ethically judge the radically new things that might appear. See his *The Mystical Element in Heidegger's Thought* (Athens, OH: Ohio University Press, 1984), 247–54. Heidegger, however, charges that only when dreams of self-control are dropped and we live so as to let social/cultural radical freedom occur can one trust the rules and laws that come from people. "Letter of Humanism" in *Basic Writings*, 238. As Nietzsche points out, it is only the illusion that we can control chance and contingency that leads us to think that things will be better if we through our efforts to control things delimit radical historical freedom rather than if we just let social and culture history develop free of such efforts to control. Trusting and celebrating life with all its contingencies will result in more freedom for people than will any social engineering projects that conflict with such trust and celebration.

146. For a criticism of Heidegger's omission of any consideration of people as suffering patients, see John Caputo, "*Sorge* and *Kardia*: The Hermeneutics of Factical Life and the Categories of the Heart," in *Reading Heidegger from the Start*, 334–43; *De-mythologizing Heidegger* (Bloomington: Indiana University Press, 1993).

147. For an excellent critique of the nature/culture, body/mind, paternity/maternity warring opposition, see Kelly Oliver, *Family Values: Subjects between Nature and Culture* (New York: Routledge, 1997).

148. Michel Foucault, "Politics and Ethics: An Interview," in *Foucault Reader*, 379.

149. Foucault presents a sketch of his "ethics" in "On the Genealogy of Ethics: An Overview of Work in Progress," in *Foucault Reader*, 352–55. For more extended discussions, see Foucault's "The Ethic of Care for the Self as a Practice of Freedom," in *The Final Foucault*, ed. James Bernauer and David Rasmussen (Cambridge: MIT Press, 1988), 1–20; "Technologies of the Self," in *Technologies of the Self*, ed. Luther H. Martin, Huck Gutman, and Patrick H. Hutton (Amherst: University of Massachusetts Press, 1988), 16–49.

150. For a Foucaultian critique of efforts to treat justice in terms of a distribution paradigm, see Iris Marion Young, *Justice and the Politics of Difference* (Princeton: Princeton University Press, 1989), chapter 1.

151. Michel Foucault, "The Concern for Truth," in *Politics, Philosophy, Culture*, 259.

152. Foucault acknowledges his debt to Nietzsche and to his Nietzschean reading of Heidegger in "The Return to Morality," in *Politics, Philosophy, Culture*, 250–51.

153. The following works by Zizek will be referred to in this section: *The Sublime Object of Ideology* (London: Verso, 1989); *Tarrying with the Negative* (Durham, NC: Duke

University Press, 1993); "The Specter of Ideology," in *Mapping Ideology*, ed. Slavoj Zizek (London: Verso, 1994), 1–33; *Looking Awry: An Introduction To Jacques Lacan through Popular Culture* (Cambridge: MIT Press, 1997); *The Abyss of Freedom/Ages of the World* (Ann Arbor: University of Michigan Press, 1997); *The Ticklish Subject: The Absent Center of Political Ontology*, (London: Verso, 1999); *The Zizek Reader*, ed. Elizabeth Wright and Edmond Wright (Oxford: Blackwell, 1999).

154. Zizek, *Tarrying with the Negative,* 169, 221-227.

155. Ibid, 190.

156. Zizek, *The Sublime Object of Ideology*, 5.

157. Zizek, *Looking Awry,* 87; *The Abyss of Freedom,* 43.

158. For a brief but useful synopsis of Zizek's analysis of the relationships holding between desires and personal and social fantasies, see Elizabeth Wright, *Psychoanalytic Criticism: A Reappraisal,* 2d ed. (New York: Routledge, 1998), 166–69.

159. Zizek, *Looking Awry,* 4–6, *Tarrying with the Negative,* 120–21.

160. Zizek, *Tarrying with the Negative;* 132, *The Ticklish Subject,* 109.

161. Zizek, *Looking Awry,* 13.

162. Zizek, *The Sublime Object of Ideology,* 24.

163. Ibid, 4–6, 8.

164. Zizek, *The Abyss of Freedom,* 63–64.

165. Zizek, *The Sublime Object of Ideology,* 169.

166. Zizek, *Tarrying with the Negative,* 36.

167. Ibid, 15–16.

168. Zizek, *The Sublime Object of Ideology,* 121–24, 173.

169. Zizek, *Looking Awry,* 29.

170. Zizek, *Tarrying with the Negative,* 116.

171. Zizek, *The Sublime Object of Ideology,* 162–65.

172. Zizek, *Looking Awry,* 40.

173. Ibid, 15.

174. Zizek, *The Sublime Object of Ideology,* 103–10.

175. Ibid, 40–43, 34–36.

176. Ibid, 45–46; *Looking Awry,* 16–17.

177. Zizek, *Looking Awry*, 18–20.

178. Zizek, *The Sublime Object of Ideology*, x–xiii, 130, 174; *The Zizek Reader*, 87–101.

179. Zizek, *Looking Awry*, 44.

180. Zizek, *The Sublime Object of Ideology*, 124–28.

181. Ibid, 95, 106.

182. Zizek, *Tarrying with the Negative*, 87.

183. Zizek, *The Sublime Object of Ideology*, 48–49, *Tarrying with the Negative*, 210–12.

184. Zizek, *Tarrying with the Negative*, 201–2.

185. Ibid, 205–6.

186. Zizek, *The Sublime Object of Ideology*, 72.

187. Ibid, 180–81.

188. Zizek, *Looking Awry*, 18–20, 98; *The Sublime Object of Ideology*, 53.

189. Zizek, *Looking Awry*, 23; *The Sublime Object of Ideology*, 53, 84, 170.

190. Zizek, *Tarrying with the Negative*, 209, *The Ticklish Subject*, 211, 347–59.

191. Zizek, *Tarrying with the Negative*, 87–89, 94.

192. Zizek, *The Abyss of Freedom*, 25.

193. Ibid, 71–72.

194. Zizek, *Looking Awry*, 75.

195. Zizek, *The Sublime Object of Ideology*, 195.

196. Zizek, *Looking Awry*, 155–57. In opposing invasions of a person's fantasy space, Zizek is endorsing Rorty's call to avoid as much as possible humiliating other people, but he rejects Rorty's analysis of this humiliation (as breaking down a person's symbolic and imaginary identifications) and Rorty's call to separate a public realm of formal and neutral law from a private realm of private fantasy-making. For Zizek, Rorty's analysis blinds us to the role that unsymbolizable enjoyment plays in motivating the construction of personal fantasies and the fact that even formal law is not neutral but gains its motive power from the enjoyment that it seeks to curtail. See Zizek, *Looking Awry*, 158–59.

197. Zizek, *Tarrying With the Negative*, 237.

198. Zizek, *The Ticklish Subject*, 109.

199. Ibid, 199, 223, 235.

200. Zizek, *The Zizek Reader*, ix–x.

201. Zizek, *Tarrying with the Negative*, 169, 221–27; *Looking Awry*, 28.

202. Zizek, *The Ticklish Subject*, 147–51, 274.

203. Ibid, 144, 380–82.

204. Zizek, *The Abyss of Freedom*, 50.

205. Zizek, *The Ticklish Subject*, 392.

CHAPTER FOUR

1. See Rorty, *Achieving Our Country* (Cambridge: Harvard University Press, 1998), 79–80; "The End of Leninism, Havel, and Social Hope," in *Truth and Progress: Philosophical Papers Vol. 3* (Cambridge: Cambridge University Press, 1998), 228–43; "Philosophy and the Future," in *Rorty & Pragmatism* (Nashville: Vanderbilt University Press, 1995), 201–2; "De Man and the American Cultural Left," in *Essays on Heidegger and Others: Philosophical Papers Vol. 2* (Cambridge: Cambridge University Press, 1991), 129–39; "Orwell on Cruelty," in *Contingency, Irony, and Solidarity* (Cambridge: Cambridge University Press, 1989), 169–88.

2. Peter Singer, *Marx* (Oxford: Oxford University Press, 1980), 73.

3. One can read, as an advocacy of positive freedom, Jeremy Bentham's call in the late eighteenth century for the utilization of the principle of utility in determining what legislation should be passed. Parliaments should not just leave people alone but should act to lessen human suffering and increase possibilities for human enjoyment. The British Fabians certainly read Marx this way.

4. Karl Marx, *Economic and Philosophical Manuscripts of 1844*, trans. Martin Milligan (New York: International Publishers, 1964), 137, 138, 141.

5. Marx, "Theses on Feuerbach," in *Marx/Engels: Feuerbach. Opposition of the Materialist and Idealist Outlooks* (Moscow: Progress Publishers, 1976), 97.

6. Marx, *The German Ideology* (New York: International Publishers, 1947), 70.

7. Marx, *The 18th Brumaire of Louis Bonaparte* (New York: International Publishers, 1990), 15.

8. For an excellent historical analysis of the social and cultural environment that made Marx's critical interpretation possible, see Alvin W. Gouldner, *Against Fragmentation: The Origins of Marxism and the Sociology of Intellectuals* (New York: Oxford University Press, 1985), sections 1 and 2.

9. Karl Marx, "For a Ruthless Criticism of Everything Existing," in *The Marx-Engels Reader*, ed. Robert Tucker (New York: W. W. Norton, 1978), 13–15.

10. Marx, *Economic & Philosophical Manuscripts of 1844*, 146.

11. Marx, *Capital,* vol. 3 (Moscow: Progress Publishers, 1959), 818–20.

12. Marx, *The German Ideology*, 53.

13. For excellent analyses of Marx's ideas about human freedom, see Cornell West, *The Ethical Dimensions of Marxist Thought* (New York: Monthly Review Press, 1991), chapter 2; R. G. Peffer, *Marxism, Morality, and Social Justice* (Princeton: Princeton University Press, 1990), chapters 3 and 10; Richard Schmitt, *Introduction To Marx and Engels* (Boulder, CO: Westview Press, 1987), 11–12, 156–59, 200–3; George Brenkert, *Marx's Ethics of Freedom* (Boston: Routledge and Allenheld, 1982).

14. Marx, "The Jewish Question," in *Karl Marx: Early Writings*, trans. and ed. T. B. Bottomore (New York: McGraw-Hill, 1963), 13.

15. Marx, *The German Ideology*, 117.

16. Marx, "The Jewish Question," in *Karl Marx: Early Writings,* 15.

17. Marx, "Critique of the Gotha Program," in *The Marx-Engels Reader*, 540.

18. Marx, *The German Ideology*, 53.

19. Marx, "Critique of the Gotha Program," in *The Marx-Engels Reader,* 528–29.

20. Ibid, 533.

21. Marx, *Economic and Philosophical Manuscripts of 1844*, 107–10.

22. *Marx, Economic and Philosophical Manuscripts of 1844*, 110–15

23. Marx, *Capital*. See especially volume 1, chapter 10, "The Working Day," and volume 3, chapter 5, "Economy in the Employment of Constant Capital."

24. For masterful analyses and critiques of neocapitalism's commodification of everyday life and its success in selling simulations, see Jean Baudrillard, *Jean Baudrillard: Selected Writings*, ed. Mark Poster (Stanford: Stanford University Press, 1988). For excellent interpretations and criticisms (including neo-Marxist criticisms) of Baudrillard's work, see Douglas Kellner, *Baudrillard: A Critical Reader*, ed. Douglas Kellner (Oxford: Blackwell, 1994).

25. As examples of feminists who appropriate a Marxist form of criticism, see the essays by Juliet Mitchell, Heidi Hartmann, Barbara Ehrenrich, and Ann Ferguson in *An Anthology of Western Marxism: From Lukacs and Gramsci to Socialist-Feminism*, ed. Roger S. Gottlieb (New York: Oxford University Press, 1989), part 5. For an African-American feminist appropriation, see bell hooks, *Outlaw Culture: Resisting Representations* (New York: Routledge, 1994), chapter 13, "Spending Culture: Marketing the Black Underclass," and chapter 15, "Seeing and Making Culture: Representing the Poor," and *Feminist Theory: From Margin to Center* (Boston: South End, 1984), chapter 3, "The Significance of the Feminist Movement," and chapter 7, "Rethinking the Nature of Work." As other examples of African-American critics who appropriate Marx, see the essays by John H. McClendon, Cornell West, Lucius Outlaw, and Angela Y. Davis in *Philosophy Born of Struggle*, ed. Leonard Harris (Dubuque: Kendall/Hunt, 1983); Lucius T. Outlaw Jr., *On Race and Philosophy* (New York: Routledge,

1996), chapter 2 "Philosophy, African-Americans, and the Unfinished American Revolution," and chapter 7, "Life-Worlds, Modernity, and Philosophical Praxis." Perhaps the leading African-American critic who is creatively appropriating Marx is Cornell West; see his *Ethical Dimensions of Marxist Thought; Prophesy Deliverance! An Afro-American Revolutionary Christianity* (Philadelphia: Westminster, 1982); *Prophetic Reflections: Notes on Race and Power in America* (Monroe, ME: Common Courage, 1993); *Keeping Faith: Philosophy and Race in America* (New York: Routledge, 1993).

26. Karl Korsch, *Marxism and Philosophy,* trans. F. Halliday (New York: Monthly Review Press, 1970).

27. For the crucial selections of the writings of members of the Frankfurt school such as Horkheimer, Adorno, and Marcuse, see Andrew Arato and Eike Gebhardt, *The Essential Frankfurt School Reader* (New York: Continuum, 1982). For a masterful study of this school, see David Held, *Introduction To Critical Theory: Horkheimer To Habermas* (Berkeley: University of California Press, 1980).

28. Georg Lukacs, *History and Class Consciousness,* trans. R. Livingston (Cambridge: MIT Press, 1971). For an extensive study of the relationship between the ideas of Lukacs and those of the early Marx, see Andrew Feinberg, *Lukacs, Marx, and the Sources of Critical Theory* (New York: Oxford University Press, 1986).

29. Theodore Veblen, *The Theory of the Leisure Class* (Boston: Houghton Mifflin, 1973). For an excellent study of Veblen's relationship to Marxism, see Donald Stabile, *Prophets of Order* (Boston: South End, 1984), chapters 7 and 8.

30. Antonio Gramsci, *Selections from the Prison Notebooks,* ed. and trans. Quinton Hoare and Geoffrey Nowell Smith (New York: International Publishers, 1971). For a marvelous study of Gramsci's ideas and practices, see Anne Showstack Sasoon, *Gramsci's Politics* (London: Hutchinson, 1987).

31. An excellent collection of the key writings setting forth the interdependency of economic and other social practices is found in Roger S. Gottlieb, *An Anthology of Western Marxism: From Lukacs and Gramsci To Socialist-Feminism* (New York: Oxford Univeristy Press, 1989).

32. For Trotsky's prophecy at the 1903 Russian Socialist Congress, see Robert Vincent Daniel, *A Documentary History of Communism* (New York: Vintage, 1960), vol. 1, 31.

33. For a useful translation of key Bakunin writings, see Michael Bakunin, *The Political Philosophy of Bakunin,* ed. G. P. Maximoff (Glencoe, IL: Free Press, 1953).

34. Rosa Luxemburg, "Organizational Questions of the Russian Social Democracy" in *Selected Political Writings* (New York: Monthly Review Press, 1971), 191.

35. Karl Korsch, "The Present State of the Problem of *Marxism and Philosophy*: An Anti-Critique," in *Marxism and Philosophy.*

36. For many of Horkheimer's critical essays, see Max Horkheimer, *Critical Theory:*

Selected Essays, trans. Matthew J. O'Donnell et al. (New York: Herder & Herder, 1972). See also Arato & Gebhardt, *The Essential Frankfurt School Reader*.

37. See Theodore Adorno, *Negative Dialectics* (New York: Seabury, 1973), and his essays in *The Essential Frankfurt School Reader*.

38. Horkheimer and Adorno, *Dialectic of the Enlightenment*, trans. John Cumming (New York: Continuum, 1987).

39. The aim of Horkheimer and Adorno to enlighten Western readers of the historical character and consequences of its Enlightenment movement, in order to enhance their freedom, implies that they would not have had to oppose the valuable points made by Amartya Sen in his essay, "East and West: The Reach of Reason," *New York Review of Books*, July 20, 2000, 33–38, in which he points out that voices in Asia (such as Muslim emperor Akbar of India in 1592) argued for religious and class tolerance by requiring people to offer justifying reasons for discriminating among people, thus appealing to reason to enlighten and liberate them.

40. See Walter Benjamin, *Illuminations*, ed. Hannah Arendt, trans. Harry Zohn (New York: Schocken Books, 1968). See also Benjamin's essays in Gary Smith, ed., *Benjamin: Philosophy, History, Aesthetics* (Chicago: University of Chicago Press, 1989).

41. Jurgen Habermas, *The Philosophical Discourse of Modernity*, trans. Frederick G. Lawrence (Cambridge: MIT Press, 1987), 304. For the best study in English of Habermas's entire comprehensive theory, see Thomas McCarthy, *The Critical Theory of Jurgen Habermas* (Cambridge: MIT Press, 1981).

42. Habermas, *Knowledge and Human Interests*, trans. Jeremy J. Shapiro (Boston: Beacon Press, 1971), 97.

43. Habermas, *On the Logic of the Social Sciences*, trans. Sherry Weber Nicholson and Jerry A. Stark (Cambridge: MIT Press, 1984), 125.

44. Habermas, *The Philosophical Discourse of Modernity*, 321.

45. Habermas, *Moral Consciousness and Communicative Action*, trans. Christian Lenhardt and Sherry Weber Nicholson (Cambridge: MIT Press, 1991), 98–103.

46. Habermas, *Knowledge and Human Interests*, 91, 178, 191; *Communication and the Evolution of Society*, trans. Thomas McCarthy (Boston: Beacon Press, 1979), 32–33.

47. Habermas, *Knowledge and Human Interests*, 178, 191, 309.

48. Ibid, 191, 310.

49. Ibid, 196.

50. Habermas, *Communication and the Evolution of Society*, 122, 139, 147–48.

51. Ibid, 100–105; *Legitimation Crisis*, trans. Thomas McCarthy (Boston: Beacon Press, 1975), 12.

52. Habermas's most eloquent American interpreter, Thomas McCarthy, stresses the contingent and fallible character of Habermas's comprehensive account of things. See David Cousins Hoy and Thomas McCarthy, *Critical Theory*, 219.

53. Habermas, *Knowledge and Human Interests*, 198; *Theory and Practice*, trans. John Viertel (Boston: Beacon Press, 1973), 254. For an excellent discussion of Habermas's notion of autonomy, see Hoy and McCarthy, *Critical Theory*, 44–47.

54. See Jean-Francois Lyotard, "The Sign of History," in *The Different Phrases in Dispute,* trans. Van Den Abbeele (Minneapolis: University of Minnesota Press, 1988), 151–81; "Missive on Universal History," in *The Postmodern Explained*, trans. Don Barry, Bernadette Maher, Julian Pefanis, Virginia Spate, and Morgan Thomas (Minneapolis: University of Minnesota Press, 1993), 23–38; "Universal History and Cultural Differences," in *The Lyotard Reader*, ed. Andrew Benjamin (Oxford: Basil Blackwell, 1989), 314–23.

55. Habermas, "What is Universal Pragmatics?" in *Communication and the Evolution of Society*, 1–68.

56. Habermas, *Moral Consciousness and Communicative Action*, 210.

57. Habermas, *On the Logic of the Social Sciences*, 136.

58. For Wittgensteinian defenses of the nonreducibility of religious language games, see E. E. Evans-Pritchard, *Theories of Primitive Religion* (Oxford: Clarendon, 1965); D. Z. Phillips, *Religion without Explanation*.

59. Habermas, *Communication and the Evolution of Society*, 32–33. Habermas's classification schema is significantly different from the one used by John Searle in his effort to systematize our understanding of speech acts. Searle refers to assertive, directive, commisive, and expressive communicative acts and effective and verdictive linguistic acts of establishing social roles and institutionally established "facts." Searle also appropriates Dreyfus's claim that speech acts are performed against a background of skills that cannot be fully represented, thus pragmatically contextualizing all general theorizing about speech acts. See John Searle, *Speech Acts;* "A Taxonomy of Illocutionary Acts," in *Expression and Meaning*, 1–29; "The Background," in *Intentionality*, 141–59.

60. Habermas, *The Philosophical Discourse of Modernity*, 298.

61. Habermas, *Moral Consciousness and Communicative Action*, 103; *Communication and the Evolution of Society*, 3–4.

62. Ibid, 88–89, 95.

63. Habermas, *Theory and Practice*, 17; *Communication and the Evolution of Society*, 1; *On the Logic of the Social Sciences*, 145.

64. Habermas, *Communication and the Evolution of Society*, 57.

65. Habermas, *Theory and Practice*, 18; *Communication and the Evolution of Society*, 56–57; *Moral Consciousness and Communicative Action*, 58.

66. Habermas, *Between Facts and Norms*, trans. William Rehg (Cambridge: MIT Press, 1996), 11–13, 19.

67. Ibid, 13–15.

68. Habermas, *Communication and the Evolution of Society*, 29–33.

69. Ibid, 63–65.

70. Habermas, *Moral Consciousness and Communicative Action*, 63.

71. Ibid, 96–101, 133–34.

72. See Hubert Dreyfus's defense of ontological pluralism in his *Being-in-the-World*, 260–65.

73. John Rawls argues that, in the case of basic moral disagreements, only pragmatic, working solutions are needed with each side remaining free to use its own morality to justify the agreement to itself. See his *Political Liberalism* (New York: Columbia Unverisity Press, 1993), 136–58.

74. Habermas, *The Inclusion of the Other: Studies in Political Theory*, ed. Ciaran Cronin and Pablo De Greiff (Cambridge: MIT Press, 1999), 96–97.

75. Anthony S. Cua in his interpretation of the Confucian ethic argues that creative imagination is needed in settling moral disputes when hermeneutical explication of existing precedents is not sufficient. See his *Ethical Argumentation: A Study in Hsun Tzu's Moral Epistemology* (Honolulu: University of Hawaii Press, 1985), 93, 99, 101. A similar argument for respecting moral differences and the need for moral creativity is found in various Wittgensteinian accounts of morality. See Arthur Murphy, *The Theory of Practical Reason* (La Salle, IL: Open Court, 1964), 344–52; Sabina Lovibond, *Realism and Imagination in Ethics* (Minneapolis: University of Minnesota Press, 1983), 194–205; D. Z. Phillips, *Interventions in Ethics* (Albany: SUNY Press, 1992), 82–85.

76. Lorenzo C. Simpson, a very sympathetic appropriator of Habermas's project, suggests that Habermas's search for foundations in the necessary presuppositions of actual language communities be replaced by a project that views humanity as an unfinished project that gets completed only through crosscultural conversations free of domination that aim at producing in some future time a Gadamer-type fusion of conflictual differences. Simpson still, however, views fusion as a removal of differences rather than a humble respect for differences that are allowed to simply be different. See his *Technology: Time and the Conversation of Modernity* (New York: Routledge, 1995), 104, 122–32, 163–64, 173–74.

77. Habermas, *Moral Consciousness and Communicative Action*, 67.

78. Ibid, 104.

79. Ibid, 79, 64–65.

80. Ibid, 104–8.

81. Ibid, 90.

82. Ibid, 58.

83. Ibid.

84. Habermas, *Between Facts and Norms*, 4.

85. For a forceful feminist development of Habermas's analysis of the difficulties in our current economic and political systems and public and private spheres of life, see Nancy Fraser, *Unruly Practices: Power, Discourse and Gender in Contemporary Social Theory* (Minneapolis: University of Minnesota Press, 1989), especially chapter 6, "What's Critical about Critical Theory? The Case of Habermas and Gender," 113–43.

86. Habermas, *Between Facts and Norms*, 296; *The Inclusion of the Other*, 246–49.

87. Habermas, *Legitimation Crisis*, 75.

88. Habermas, *Between Facts and Norms*, 360–61.

89. Habermas, *Legitimation Crisis*, 36–37.

90. Habermas, *Between Facts and Norms*, 386.

91. Habermas, *Legitimation Crisis*, 37.

92. Habermas, *Theory and Practice*, 254–55.

93. Habermas, *Between Facts and Norms*, 386.

94. Ibid, 448.

95. Habermas, *The New Conservatism*, ed. And trans. Sherry Weber Nicholson (Cambridge: MIT Press, 1989), 56–57.

96. Ibid, 60–62.

97. Foucault, *Politics, Philosophy, Culture*, 26.

98. The difference between seeking to maximize consensus and to minimize non-consentuality is remarkably similar to the difference between the Christian's "Golden Rule" enjoining people to do unto others what you want others to do to you and the Confucian "Silver Rules," which call for people not to force on others what they do not want others to force on them. We may not want done to us what others are willing to do to themselves. If we use our desire to be free of coercion, however, as the measure of our treatment of others, then we will be seeking to maximize freedom in all cases.

99. Foucault, "The Subject and Power," in Hubert L. Dreyfus and Paul Rabinow, *Michel Foucault: Beyond Structuralism and Hermeneutics, with an Afterword by and Interview with Michel Foucault* (Chicago: University of Chicago Press, 1983), 216.

100. Foucault, *Discipline and Punish*, trans. Alan Sheridan (New York: Vintage, 1979), 26–31, 136–141; "Governmentality," in *The Foucault Effect*, ed. Graham Burchell, Colin Gordon, Peter Miller (Chicago: University of Chicago Press, 1991) 87-104.

101. Foucault, *Power/Knowledge: Selected Interviews and Other Writings, 1972–1977*, ed. Colin Gordon, trans. Colin Gordon, Leo Marshall, John Mepham, Kate Soper (New York: Pantheon, 1971, 1980), 97; *The History of Sexuality I: An Introduction*, trans. Robert Hurley (New York: Pantheon, 1978), 95.

102. Foucault, *Power/Knowledge*, 122.

103. Foucault, *Power, Truth, Strategy*, ed. Meaghan Morris and Paul Patton (Sydney: Feral Press, 1979), 59–62.

104. Foucault, *Power/Knowledge*, 119.

105. Foucault, "The Subject and Power," in Dreyfus and Rainbow, *Michael Foucault,* 219–22.

106. Foucault, *The Final Foucault*, 3, 9, 12; *Politics, Philosophy, Culture*, 123.

107. Kierkegaard, *The Sickness Unto Death*, 65–72.

108. Foucault, *Power/Knowledge*, 89–91; *Politics, Philosophy, Culture*, 250–51.

109. Foucault, *The Final Foucault*, 15; *Politics, Philosophy, Culture*, 51, 267.

110. Foucault, *Power/Knowledge* 93, 94; *Politics, Philosophy, Culture*, 267.

111. Foucault, *Discipline and Punish*, 27.

112. For a summation of his project, see Foucault, "The Subject and Power," in Dreyfus and Rainbow, *Michael Foucault,* 208; *The Final Foucault,* 16–17. The main archaeological and genealogical works written by Foucault are: *Madness and Civilization: A History of Insanity in the Age of Reason* (New York: Vintage, 1965); *The Order of Things: An Archaeology of the Human Sciences* (New York: Vintage, 1970); *The Archaeology of Knowledge and The Discourse on Language*; *The Birth of the Clinic: An Archaeology of Medical Perception*, trans. A. M. Sheridan Smith (New York: Vintage, 1973); and *Discipline & Punish: The Birth of the Prison.* For an excellent analysis of Foucault's analysis of discursive archives as a way of resisting social and cultural domination, see Ian Hacking, "The Archaeology of Foucault," in David Cousins Hoy, *Foucault: A Critical Reader* (New York: Basil Blackwell, 1986), 27–40.

113. Foucault, *Discipline and Punish*, 26, 27, 170–94; *Politics, Philosophy, Culture*, 30, 39, 50, 256.

114. Foucault, *Politics, Philosophy, Culture*, 106.

115. Foucault, *Discipline and Punish*, 128–29; *Technologies of the Self*, 160–61.

116. Foucault, *Power/Knowledge*, 95.

117. Foucault, *Politics, Philosophy, Culture*, 154–55.

118. Foucault, "Polemics, Politics and Problemizations," in *Foucault Reader*, 381–83.

119. Foucault, "On the Genealogy of Ethics," in *Foucault Reader*, 231.

120. Foucault, "What Is an Author?" in *Foucault Reader*, 114–15; *Power/Knowledge*, 52–53.

121. Foucault, "Intellectuals and Power," in *Language, Counter-memory, Practice*, ed. Donald F. Bouchard, trans. Donald F. Bouchard and Sherry Simon (Ithaca: Cornell University Press, 1977), 213–16.

122. Foucault, "Politics and Ethics: An Interview," in *Foucault Reader*, 375; *Discipline and Punish*, 296, 301, 303–4.

123. Foucault, *The History of Sexuality, Vol. 1: An Introduction*, 141.

124. Foucault, "Truth and Power," in *Foucault Reader*, 59–61.

125. Foucault, "What Is the Enlightenment?" in *Foucault Reader*, 50.

126. Foucault, preface to Gilles Deleuze and Felix Guattari, *Anti-Oedipus: Capitalism and Schizophrenia,* trans. Robert Hurley, Mark Seem, and Helen R. Lane (Minneapolis: University of Minnesota Press, 1983), xii–xiv; *Final Foucault*, 2.

127. Foucault, "What Is Enlightenment?" in *Foucault Reader*, 32–56.

128. For excellent biographies of Foucault's life as a freedom fighter, see Didier Eribon, *Michel Foucault*, trans. Betsy Wing (Cambridge: Harvard University Press, 1991), and David Macey, *The Lives of Michel Foucault: A Biography* (New York: Vintage, 1995).

129. Alvin Gouldner, *The Dialectic of Ideology and Technology: The Origins, Grammar, and Future of Ideology* (New York: Oxford University Press, 1976).

130. Gouldner, *The Future of Intellectuals and the Rise of the New Class* (New York: Seabury, 1979).

131. Gouldner, *Against Fragmentation.*

132. Gouldner, *The Dialectic of Ideology and Technology*, 210–27.

133. Gouldner, *The Future of Intellectuals and the Rise of the New Class, 1–7.*

134. Gouldner, *The Dialectic of Ideology and Technology*, 91–102, 195–207.

135. Gouldner, *The Dialectic of Ideology and Technology*, 229–49; *The Future of Intellectuals and the Rise of the New Class, 48–53.*

136. Gouldner, *The Future of Intellectuals and the Rise of the New Class*, 53–57. For an insider's analysis of the place of intellectuals in Eastern European socialist states, see George Konrad and Ivan Szelenyi, *The Intellectuals on the Road To Class Power* (New York: Harcourt Brace Jovanovich, 1979).

137. Galbraith, *The New Industrial State* (Boston: Houghton Mifflin, 1967).

138. See "After the Revolution: Marx Debates Bakunin," in Karl Marx, *The Marx-Engels Reader*, 542–48.

139. Talcott Parsons, *Essays in Sociological Theory* (Glencoe, IL: Free Press, 1954), chapter 18.

140. Noam Chomsky, "Intellectuals and the State," in *American Power and the New Mandarins* (New York: New Press, 1969, 2002).

141. Gouldner, *Against Fragmentation*, 284–94.

142. See Paul Bove, *Intellectuals in Power: A Genealogy of Critical Humanism* (New York: Columbia University Press, 1986), and *In the Wake of Theory* (Hanover, NH: Wesleyan University Press, 1992).

143. For his most famous study, see Edward W. Said, *Orientalism* (New York: Vintage, 1978). See also *The Edward Said Reader*, ed. Moustafa Bayoumi and Andrew Rubin (New York: Vintage Books, 2000).

144. Iris Marion Young, *Justice and the Politics of Difference*, and *Intersecting Voices: Dilemmas of Gender, Political Philosophy, and Policy* (Princeton: Princeton University Press, 1997). Young provides, in *Intersecting Voices*, note 43, 176–77, a very useful list of other feminist writers who have appropriated Foucault's work.

145. Young, *Justice and the Politics of Difference*, 102–7.

146. Ibid, 25–33.

147. Ibid, 111–16.

148. Ibid, 42–48.

149. Ibid, 37–38.

150. In *Intersecting Voices*, Young points out how current practices for treating pregnant drug addicts produce dominated women who are marked as deviant, excluding them from the class of upstanding women, without doing anything to prevent the birth of harmed babies, (81) and how current practices defining the family unjustly focus on regulating sexuality, unnecessarily tying sexuality (which should not be the business of the state) to domestic partnerships, and thus excluding from the privileged category of "family" many prizeworthy unions that could be contractually regulated (109–13).

151. Young, *Justice and the Politics of Difference*, 39–65.

152. Ibid, 122–55.

153. For a more recent comprehensive summary of evidence demonstrating the ineffectiveness and unfairness of "merit" exams for employment and college entrance, see Susan Sturm and Lani Guinier, "The Future of Affirmative Action: Promoting Diversity in Education and Employment Requires Us to Rethink Testing and 'Meritocracy' in *Boston Review* 25, no. 6 (December 2000/January 2001): 4–10.

154. Young, *Justice and the Politics of Difference*, 96–115, 200–213.

155. See Young, *Inclusion and Democracy*, (New York: Oxford University Press, 2000).

156. bell hooks, *Outlaw Culture: Resisting Representations*, 232.

157. Just running through the titles of bell hooks's major writings at this time gives one a good idea of the range of her concerns. *Ain't I a Woman: Black Women and Feminism* (Boston: South End, 1981); *Feminist Theory: From Margin To Center; Talking Back: Thinking Feminist, Thinking Black* (Boston: South End, 1989); *Yearning: Race, Gender, and Cultural Politics* (Boston: South End, 1990); *Breaking Bread: Insurgent Black Intellectual Life* (with Cornell West) (Boston: South End, 1991); *Black Looks: Race and Representation* (Boston: South End, 1992); *Sisters of Yam: Black Women and Self-Recovery* (Boston: South End, 1993); *Teaching to Transgress: Education as the Practice of Freedom* (New York: Routledge, 1994); *Art on My Mind: Visual Politics* (New York: New Press, 1995); *Reel To Reel: Race, Sex, and Class in the Movies* (New York: Routledge, 1996); *Wounds of Passion: A Writing Life* (New York: Henry Holt, 1997); *Remembered Rapture: The Writer at Work* (New York: Henry Holt, 1999); *Where We Stand: Class Matters* (New York: Routledge, 2000); *Feminism Is for Everybody: Passionate Politics* (Boston: South End, 2000); and *Outlaw Culture*.

158. hooks, *Art on My Mind*, 73.

159. hooks, *Feminist Theory*, 60–61; *Ain't I a Woman*, 119–58; *Talking Back*, 25; *Outlaw Culture*, 165–72.

160. hooks, *Ain't I a Woman*, 24–51.

161. hooks, *Feminist Theory*, 43–45.

162. hooks, *Outlaw Culture*, 53.

163. hooks, *Feminist Theory*, 37.

164. Ibid, 95–105.

165. hooks, *Outlaw Culture*, 5.

166. Ibid, 173–82.

167. Ibid, 150–52.

168. hooks, *Feminist Theory*, 159–63.

169. hooks, *Outlaw Culture*, 207–8.

170. hooks, *Feminist Theory*, 152.

171. Ibid, 64–65.

172. hooks. *Black Looks*, 9–20; *Outlaw Culture*, 243–50.

173. Lucius T. Outlaw Jr., *On Race and Philosophy*, 40–41.

174. Ibid, 53.

175. Ibid, 145.

176. Ibid, 151.

177. Ibid, 112–13.

178. Ibid, 100–101.

179. Ibid, 177.

180. Ibid, 145.

181. Ibid, 189, 197.

182. Michael Eric Dyson at the time of this writing has written four major texts: *Reflecting Black: African-American Cultural Criticism* (Minneapolis: University of Minnesota Press, 1993); *Making Malcolm: The Myth and Meaning of Malcolm X* (New York: Oxford University Press, 1996); *Between God and Gangsta Rap: Bearing Witness to Black Culture* (New York: Oxford University Press, 1996); *Race Rules: Navigating the Color Line* (New York: Vintage, 1996).

183. Dyson, *Between God and Gangsta Ra*Press, 133.

184. Dyson, *Race Rules*, 33–36.

185. Ibid, 217, 220, 233, 157.

186. Dyson, *Between God and Gangsta Ra*Press, 122–24, 101–3.

187. Dyson, *Reflecting Black*, 136–37, 151.

188. Dyson, *Race Rules*, 148.

189. Dyson, *Reflecting Black*, 48.

190. Ibid, 93.

192. Dyson, *Between God and Gangsta Ra*Press, 177.

193. Dyson, *Race Rules*, 112; *Reflecting Black*, 36.

194. Dyson, *Between God and Gangsta Ra*Press, 151–56, 161–71.

195. Dyson, *Race Rules, 152.*

196. Ibid, 135–40.

197. Ibid, 140–45.

198. Dyson, *Reflecting Black*, 305–6.

199. Cornell West, *The American Evasion of Philosophy*, 9–41.

200. Ibid, 201–9.

201. See West, *Prophetic Fragments: Illuminations of the Crisis in American Religion and Culture* (Grand Rapids, MI: William B. Eerdmans, 1988), 122, where he calls for Christian prophetic freedom fighters to draw upon the insights of Marxism, anarchism, Weberism, Garveyism, feminism, womanism, antihomophobism, ecologism, liberalism, and even some parts of conservatism.

202. Ibid, 261–62, 269.

203. Ibid, 270.

204. Ibid, 267.

205. Ibid, 170.

206. West, *The American Evasion of Philosophy*, 69–111.

207. West, *Keeping Faith*, 129–40.

208. West, *Prophetic Fragments*, 74–77.

209. Ibid, 80.

210. West, *The Ethical Dimensions of Marxist Thought*, xxiii.

211. West, *Prophesy Deliverance!* 101, 111–27.

212. West, *Prophetic Fragments*, 130–35.

213. West, *The Ethical Dimensions of Marxist Thought*, xxvii.

214. West, *Prophetic Fragments*, 118.

215. Ibid, 116.

216. Ibid, 114.

217. West, *Prophesy Deliverance!* 48–50, 55.

218. West, *The American Evasion of Philosophy*, 236.

219. West, *Keeping Faith*, 79–82, 99.

220. West, *The American Evasion of Philosophy*, 229; *Prophecy Deliverance!* 120; *Prophetic Fragments*, 38, 113, 128, 164; *Prophetic Reflections*, 225.

221. West, *The American Evasion of Philosophy*, 224.

222. Ibid, 225.

223. West, *Prophetic Reflections*, 84.

224. West, *The American Evasion of Philosophy*, 226.

225. West, *Prophetic Reflections*, 225; *Prophetic Fragments*, 128.

226. West, *Prophetic Fragments*, 112–13.

227. West, *Prophetic Reflections*, 108.

228. West, *The American Evasion of Philosophy*, 233.

229. West, *Prophetic Fragments*, 93.

230. West, *Prophecy Deliverance*, 105–6.

231. West, *Prophetic Fragments*, 35–36, 68, 155–56.

232. Ibid, 38.

CHAPTER FIVE

1. See Richard Swinburne, *Faith and Reason* (Oxford: Clarendon, 1987).

2. See Alvin Plantinga, *God and Other Minds* (Ithaca, NY: Cornell University Press, 1967).

3. See Michael Martin, *Atheism: A Philosophical Justification* (Philadelphia: Temple University Press, 1990), and Theodore M. Drange, *Non-Belief and Evil: Two Arguments for the Non-Existence of God,* (Amherst, NY: Prometheus, 1998).

4. Kierkegaard, *Concluding Unscientific Postscript*, 291.

5. Ibid, 145.

6. Ibid, 25.

7. Ibid, 296.

8. Ibid, 116, 178, 201, 251.

9. Ibid, 25–47.

10. Ibid, 116.

11. Ibid, 360.

12. Ibid, 355.

13. Ibid, 382.

14. Ibid, 350.

15. Ibid, 355.

16. Ibid, 271.

17. Ibid, 360.

18. Ibid, 362.

19. Ibid, 360.

20. Ibid, 383.

21. Ibid, 369.

22. Ibid, 197.

23. Ibid, 413.

24. Ibid, 437.

25. Ibid, 440.

26. Ibid, 392.

27. Ibidt, 176.

28. Ibid, 239.

29. Ibid, 367.

30. Ibid, 348, 386.

31. Ibid, 218, 220–21.

32. Ibid, 365.

33. Ibid, 417, 422ff.

34. Ibid, 364.

35. Ibid, 450.

36. Ibid, 456.

37. Ibid, 29–30.

38. Ibid, 31–33.

39. Ibid, 45, 61.

40. In my comments about Martin Buber, I will focus only on his text *I and Thou*, trans. Walter Kaufmann (New York: Charles Scribner's Sons, 1970).

41. See Franz Rosenzweig, *Star of Redemption*, trans. William W. Hallo (New York: Holt, Rinehart & Winston, 1971; Boston: Beacon, 1972; Notre Dame, IN: University of Notre Dame Press, 1985).

42. In presenting my interpretation of Levinas's position, reference will be made to the following texts by him: *Existence and Existents*, trans. Alphonso Lingis (The Hague: Martinus

Nijhoff, 1978); *Totality and Infinity; Otherwise than Being or Beyond Essence; Ethics and Infinity,* trans. Richard A. Cohen (Pittsburgh: Duquesne University Press, 1985); *The Levinas Reader,* ed. Sean Hand (Oxford: Basil Blackwell, 1989); *Outside the Subject,* trans. Michael B. Smith (Stanford, CA: Stanford University Press, 1994); *Proper Names,* trans. Michael B. Smith (Stanford, CA: Stanford University Press, 1996); *Of God Who Comes To Mind,* trans. Bettina Bergo (Stanford, CA: Stanford University Press, 1998); *Alterity and Transcendence,* trans. Michael B. Smith (New York: Columbia University Press, 1999).

43. Jacques Derrida, *Adieu To Emmanuel Levinas,* trans. Pascale-Anne Brault and Michael Naas (Stanford, CA: Stanford University Press, 1999), 3.

44. Levinas again and again expresses his debt to Kierkegaard, Buber, and Rosenzweig. For his interpretation of Kierkegaard, see *Proper Names,* 66–79; *Of God Who Comes To Mind,* 109. For his comments about Buber, see *Proper Names,* 17–35; *Of God Who Comes To Mind,* 137–51; *Outside the Subject,* 4–48; and *Alterity and Transcendence,* 93–103. For his appropriation of Rosenzweig, see *Outside the Subject,* 49–66; *Totality and Infinity,* 28; *Ethics and Infinity,* 75–76.

45. Levinas, *Ethics and Infinity,* 37.

46. Levinas, *Outside the Subject,* 55–59. For an excellent interpretation of the relationship between the thinking of Rosenzweig and Levinas, see Richard A. Cohen, *Elevations: The Height of the Good in Rosenzweig and Levinas* (Chicago: University of Chicago Press, 1994).

47. Levinas, *Totality and Infinity,* 234–36.

48. Rosenzweig, *Star of Redemption,* book 2, part 2.

49. Levinas, *Outside the Subject,* 56–59.

50. Buber, *I and Thou,* 53.

51. Ibid, 62–64.

52. Ibid, 66.

53. Ibid, 54–56.

54. Ibid, 57.

55. Ibid, 80–82, 104–7.

56. Ibid, 68.

57. Ibid, 160, 127.

58. Ibid, 163.

59. Levinas, *Of God Who Comes to Mind,* 63.

60. Ibid, 87.

61. Levinas, *Alterity and Transcendence*, 19.

62. Levinas, *Totality and Infinity*, 79.

63. Levinas, *Of God Who Comes To Mind*, 18–31.

64. Levinas, *Totality and Infinity*, 24–30.

65. Levinas, "There Is: Existence without Existents," in *The Levinas Reader*, 29–36.

66. Levinas, *Ethics and Infinity*, 47–52; *Alterity and Transcendence*, 99.

67. Levinas, *Totality and Infinity*, 110.

68. Ibid, 130–34.

69. Ibid, 120.

70. Ibid, 112.

71. Ibid, 115.

72. Ibid, 146.

73. Ibid, 134.

74. Ibid, 117–19.

75. Levinas, *Ethics and Infinity*, 121.

76. Levinas, *Totality and Infinity*, 164.

77. Ibid, 142, 144.

78. Trying to imagine what it is like to be dead by imagining that one is watching one's funeral is not really imagining one's own death. One is still there watching. Refusing to acknowledge death as the impossibility of any further possibilities may well be a significant factor leading people to believe that death is not really death but only a change in one's way of life. Levinas refuses this refusal of death and presents instead an account of how we can live past death without postulating immortal beings.

79. Levinas, "Time and the Other," in *The Levinas Reader*, 38–44.

80. Levinas, *Totality and Infinity*, 150–65.

81. Levinas, *Ethics and Infinity*, 85–87; *Alterity and Transcendence*, 104–5.

82. Levinas, *Totality and Infinity*, 194–201.

83. Levinas, *Ethics and Infinity*, 87.

84. Levinas, *Outside the Subject*, 116–17.

85. Levinas, *Of God Who Comes To Mind*, 74–75.

86. Levinas has repeatedly tried to show that in spite of Western philosophy's long-standing love affair with ontotheology, there have been philosophers who have gone beyond ontotheology to indicate that beyond the world of beings and subjects knowing beings there is an infinite which being and all talk and knowledge of beings presupposes. Although their talk about the infinite usually was colored by their ontotheological interests, still they are pointing to an infinite other than being. For Plato it was the Good which was the source of all being and knowledge. For Descartes it was the idea of the infinite necessary for affirming the existence of finite beings. See *Totality and Infinity*, 48–50, 103, 211; *Ethics and Infinity*, 91–92; *Alterity and Transcendence*, 4, 54–55, 63, 65–67.

87. Levinas, *Ethics and Infinity*, 95.

88. Levinas, *Totality and Infinity*, 45–48. For an excellent presentation of Levinas's critical appraisal of Heidegger's position, see Adriaan Peperzak's "Text and Commentary (on Levinas') Philosophy and the Idea of the Infinite," *To the Other: An Introduction To the Philosophy of Emmanuel Levinas* (West Lafayette, IN: Purdue University Press, 1993), 88–119.

89. Levinas, *Outside the Subject*, 45, 116–25; *Alterity & Transcendence*, 101–3; *Totality and Infinity*, 213.

90. Levinas, *Proper Names*, 32–33; *Outside the Subject*, 42–44; *Of God Who Comes To Mind*, 150–51.

91. Levinas, *Of God Who Comes To Mind*, 142.

92. Buber, *I and Thou*, 127, 163.

93. Ibid, 123, 143, 148.

94. Levinas, *Outside the Subject*, 47; *Of God Who Comes To Mind*, 120..

95. Levinas, *Of God Who Comes To Mind*, 151.

96. Ibid, 93.

97. Ibid, 66–67.

98. Ibid, 75.

99. Ibid, 95.

100. Ibid, 166.

101. Levinas, *Totality and Infinity*, 277.

102. Ibid, 279–80.

103. Rudolf Bultmann, *Primitive Christianity in Its Contemporary Setting*.

104. Slavoj Zizek, *The Ticklish Subject*, 146.

105. Ibid, 148.

106. Ibid, 150.

107. Ibid, 146.

108. Ibid, 147.

109. Ibid, 144.

110. Ibid, 141.

111. Slavoj Zizek, *On Belief* (London: Routledge, 2001), 110.

112. Ibid, 113–26.

113. Ibid, 111. Muslims and Buddhists certainly would challenge Zizek's claim that only the foundings of the Jewish and Christian communities were authentic historical acts revolutionizing history. The former are members of a religious community founded in faithfulness to a renewal of Jewish-type opposition to anthropomorphizing God and to a post-Christian, Arab-oriented alternative to Jewish religious law. The latter are members of a religious community founded in faithfulness to a disciplined pursuit of eternal happiness (nirvana) in which, in a subjectivistic mode of subjectivity, the infinite and eternal are experienced as present in a sensory and interpersonal world allowed to be free of cravings generated by counterproductive, socially constituted selves and ideals of self-worth.

114. Zizek, *On Belief,* 126–27.

115. Ibid, 128. See also his *The Fragile Absolute* (London: Verso, 2000), 104.

116. Zizek, *On Belief,* 126, 131.

117. Zizek, *The Fragile Absolute,* 104.

118. Zizek, *On Belief,* 98. Zizek's point here resembles in many ways what John Caputo has to say when he talks about what one loves when one loves God, who is love. See his *On Religion* (London: Routledge, 2001).

119. Zizek, *The Fragile Absolute,* 107.

120. Ibid, 128.

121. Ibid, 120–21.

122. Ibid, 126.

123. Ibid, 146–47.

124. Ibid, 100.

125. Ibid, 68–69.

126. Zizek, *On Belief,* 68–69.

127. The following works by Mark Taylor will be examined in this section: *Erring:*

A Postmodern A/theology (Chicago: University of Chicago Press, 1984); *Alterity* (Chicago: University of Chicago Press, 1987); *Tears* (Albany: SUNY Press, 1990); *Nots* (Chicago: University of Chicago Press, 1993); *Hidings* (Chicago: University of Chicago Press, 1997); *About Religion: Economics of Faith in Virtual Culture* (Chicago: University of Chicago Press, 1999).

128. The major texts that give expression to the Kyoto school's position are: Kitaro Nishida, *Intelligibility and the Philosophy of Nothingness: Three Philosophical Essays* (Tokyo: Maruzen, 1958); Keiji Nishitani, *Religion and Nothingness,* trans. Jan Van Bragt, (Berkeley: University of California Press, 1982); Masao Abe, *Zen and Western Thought.*

129. The following works by Huston Smith will be examined in this section: *The World's Religions* (New York: HarperCollins, 1991); *Forgotten Truth: The Primordial Tradition* (New York: Harper & Row, 1976); *Beyond the Post-Modern Mind* (New York: Crossroad, 1982); *Why Religion Matters* (New York: HarperCollins, 2001).

130. Mark Taylor, *Nots,* 167–70, 211.

131. Mark Taylor, *Altarity,* xxviii–xxix.

132. Taylor, *Erring,* 7. Taylor sometimes says only that "most" (not "all") Western theology and philosophy is ontotheological (*Erring,* 10), making room for Kierkegaard, Nietzsche, Derrida, and Anselm. For his analysis of Anselm's ontological proof of God, see *Nots,* 21–27.

133. Ibid, 20.

134. Ibid, 9.

135. Ibid, 176. In *Nots,* 59, Taylor claims that since God is seen as truth, then the death of God entails the death of truth.

136. Taylor, *Nots,* 220–21; *Hidings,* 271–72; *About Religion,* 2–3.

137. See Thomas Altizer, *The Gospel of Christian Atheism* (Philadelphia: Westminster, 1971).

138. Taylor, *Erring,* 103–4.

139. Ibid, 169.

140. Ibid, 111–18.

141. Ibid, 150–60.

142. Ibid, 164.

143. Mikhail Bakhtin, *Rabelais and His World,* trans. H. Iwilsky (Cambridge: MIT Press, 1968), 11–12.

144. Taylor, *About Religion,* 29–30.

145. See Karl Barth, *Epistle To the Romans*, 242.

146. Taylor, *Tears*, 75; *About Religion*, 39.

147. Ibid, 76.

148. Taylor, *Erring*, 116–18; *Nots*, 54; *About Religion*, 40.

149. Taylor presents a very insightful analysis of Lacan's claims about *jouissance* as the feminine Real, the radical Other to our paternalistic dominated symbolic world, in *Altarity*, 83–113.

150. Taylor, *Altarity*, 185–216.

151. For examples of Taylor's appropriation of Blanchot, see his *Altarity*, 229–53; *Tears*, 1; *Nots*, 1, 10.

152. Taylor, *Tears*, 2.

153. Ibid, 174–78.

154. Taylor praises Clement Greenberg's analysis of modern art as an effort to get beyond Kant's categories of the understanding and to find some Other comparable to Kant's sublime. *About Religion*, 180–83.

155. Taylor, *About Religion*, 183; *Tears*, 6; *Nots*, 100, 166.

156. Taylor, *Tears*, 5–12.

157. Ibid, 41–43.

158. Taylor, *Nots*, 96–121.

159. Ibid, 134–38.

160. Ibid, 138–62.

161. Taylor, *About Religion*, 81.

162. Taylor, *Altarity*, 185–216.

163. Taylor, *About Religion*, 75–94.

164. Ibid, 2-3; *Hidings*, 271–72.

165. Taylor, *Nots*, 216–55; *Hidings*, 318–29; *About Religion*, 83–115.

166. Taylor, *Nots*, 220.

167. Taylor, *About Religion*, 80.

168. Ibid, 114. See also *Hidings*, 272, and *Nots* 238–39.

169. Taylor, *Erring*, 118, 141.

170. Taylor, *About Religion*, 211.

171. Taylor, *Nots*, 62–69.

172. For an excellent pragmatic interpretation of Nagarjuna's project, see David J. Kalipahana, *Nagarjuna's Karika*.

173. To study translations of the texts of the Samyutta Nikaya, Visuddhi Magga, and Digha-Nikaya, Mahanidana sutta on the topic of dependent origination, see *a Sourcebook in Asian Philosophy*, ed. John M. Koller and Patricia Koller (New York: Macmillan, 1991) 235-238.

174. Keiji Nishitani, *Religion and Nothingness*, 244–50.

175. See Huston Smith, *Forgotten Truth* 6, 9; *Why Religion Matters*, 64–70, 79–134.

176. Huston, Smith, *Forgotten Truth*, 97; *Why Religion Matters*, 12.

177. Huston Smith, *Why Religion Matters*, 205

178. Huston Smith, *Beyond the Post-Modern Mind*, 23; *Why Religion Matters*, 232; Smith's metaphysical interpretation is most thoroughly presented in *Forgotten Truth*, chapter 3 "The Levels of Reality," and chapter 4, "The Levels of Selfhood."

179. See Hubert L. Dreyfus, *Being-in-the-World*, 85–99.

180. Huston Smith, *Why Religion Matters*, 258.

181. Maurice Merleau-Ponty, *Phenomenology of Perception*, trans. Colin Smith (London: Routledge & Kegan Paul, 1962), 355; Ludwig Wittgenstein, *Philosophical Investigations*, vol. 1, 244–318; vol.2, iv–v.

182. Huston Smith, *Why Religion Matters*, 50, 199.

183. Huston Smith repeatedly makes the charge that scientism cannot account for values or norms. See *Forgotten Truth*, 114–16, 67; *Beyond the Post-Modern Mind*, 111; *Why Religion Matters*, 197.

184. Huston Smith, *Beyond the Post-Modern Mind*, 3, 112; *Why Religion Matters*, 37, 198.

185. Huston Smith, *Why Religion Matters*, 28. Smith, however, fails to see how close he is to Kierkegaard because he unfortunately interprets Kierkegaard's claim that subjectivity is truth as implying that Kierkegaard is some kind of epistemological subjectivist who cannot claim, when challenged, that his assertions are correct. See *Forgotten Truth*, 7.

186. Huston Smith, *The World's Religions*, 13–20.

187. Ibid, 20–26.

188. Huston Smith, *Why Religion Matters*, 26, 28.

189. Huston Smith, *The Post-Modern Mind*, 45.

190. Huston Smith, *Why Religion Matters*, 31.

191. Huston Smith, *Forgotten Truth*, 48–51.

192. Huston Smith, *Why Religion Matters*, 251–53.

193. Fyodor Dostoyevsky, *The Brothers Karamazov*, trans. Richard Pevear and Laarissa Volokhonsky (New York: Vintage, 1991), 245.

194. Huston Smith, *Why Religion Matters*, 270.

195. Huston Smith, *Forgotten Truth*, 128; *Beyond the Post-Modern Mind*, 170; *Why Religion Matters*, 162–63.

196. Huston Smith, *Beyond the Post-Modern Mind*, 170.

197. Huston Smith, *Why Religion Matters*, 181.

198. Smith acknowledges in *Why Religion Matters*, 74, that he developed his metaphysics out of his earlier involvement with the naturalistic theism of Henry Nelson Wieman [*Religious Experience and Scientific Method* (New York: Macmillan, 1926)] and the process philosophy of his former teacher, Charles Hartshorne [*The Divine Relativity*]. The metaphysical craving apparently was there from his earliest years in college. Smith may be correct in his charge that Hartshorne's dipolar God is unacceptable because the infinite must be other than the limited and temporally changing, but this does not show that the infinite must be an infinite consciousness. Levinas's infinite is also not finite or temporal.

199. Huston Smith, *Beyond the Post-Modern Mind*, 165; *Why Religion Matters*, 183.

200. Huston Smith, *Why Religion Matters*, 24.

201. Huston Smith, "The View From Nowhere," in Henry L. Ruf, ed., *Religion, Ontotheology, and Deconstruction*, (New York: Paragon House, 1989), 58–60; *Beyond the Post-Modern Mind*, 3–9, 149; *Why Religion Matters*, 15, 20–21, 43–45.

202. Huston Smith, *Forgotten Truth*, 58.

203. See Smith's characterization of mysticism in *Forgotten Truth*, 110–17.

204. Huston Smith, *The World's Religions*, 41–50.

205. After examining the many claims about mystical experiences in the world's different religious traditions, Steven T. Katz has argued that such experiences are quite varied and specific to the religious traditions of which they are a part. See his "Language, Epistemology and Mysticism," in S. Katz, ed., *Mysticism and Philosophical Analysis* (New York: Oxford University Press, 1978), 22–74; and "The Conservative Character of Mysticism," in S. Katz, ed., *Mysticism and Religious Traditions* (New York: Oxford University Press, 1983), 3–60.

206. Ludwig Wittgenstein, *Remarks on Frazer's Golden Bough*.

207. Ibid, 2, 12.

208. E. E. Evans-Pritchard, *Theories of Primitive Religion.*

209. D. Z. Phillips, "Primitive Reactions and the Reactions of Primitives: The 1983 Maret Lectures," in his *Wittgenstein and Religion,* 103–22; "Knowing Where to Stop," in *Belief, Change, and Forms of Life,* 34–41.

210. M. O. C. Drury reports that Wittgenstein said to him that he never could be a part of any religious tradition requiring one to believe that one can prove God's existence and that if he thought God was an infinitely powerful being it would be his duty to defy him. See "Conversations with Wittgenstein," in ed. Rush Rhees, *Recollections of Wittgenstein,* (Oxford: Oxford University Press, 107–8.

211. Wittgenstein, *Culture and Value,* trans. Peter Winch (Chicago: University of Chicago Press, 1980), 53.

212. Ibid, 32. Rush Rhees gives a Wittgensteinian analysis and critique of natural theology, the traditional philosophical effort to argue from claims about nature to the claim that God exists, in his *Without Answers* (London: Routledge & Kegan Paul, 1969), 110–14.

213. Wittgenstein, *Lectures and Conversations of Aesthetics, Psychology, and Religious Belief,* ed. Cyril Barrett (Berkeley: University of California Press, 1967), 56–57. A major thrust in much of D. Z. Phillips's writing on religion is his attempt to show that religion needs no explanation or justification. See his *Faith and Philosophical Enquiry* (New York: Schocken, 1971); *Religion without Explanation; Wittgenstein and Religion,* chapters 2–6.

214. Drury, "Conversations with Wittgenstein" in Rhees, *Recollections of Wittgenstein,* 114.

215. Ibid, 102.

216. Ibid, 114.

217. Drury, "Some Notes on Conversations," in Rhees, *Recollections of Wittgenstein,* 79.

218. For a characterization of Wittgenstein's religious life, see Norman Malcolm, "A Religious Man?" in his *Wittgenstein: A Religious Point of View,* 7–23.

219 . I have tried to present a defense of a radicalized form of liberalism in Henry L. Ruf, "Radicalizing Liberalism and Modernity," *Philosophy, Religion, and the Question of Intolerance,* ed. Mehdi Amin Razavi and David Ambuel (Albany, NY: SUNY Press, 1997), 170–85.

220. For a beginning glimpse of what crosscultural moral and religious dialogue might look like, see Ruf, "Moral Problems and Religious Mysteries: A Cross-Cultural Perspective," in *Dialogue & Alliance* 1, no. 3, (fall 1987): 77–92.

221. Arthur Edward Murphy, *Theory of Practical Reason,* 135–38.

222. Ibid, 10, 157, 191–95.

223. Ibid, 208–20.

224. Ibid, 243–44.

225. Ibid, 336–38.

226. Ibid, 366–69, 374–80, 407, 413–19.

227. Hsun-tzu, *Basic Writings*, trans. Burton Watson (New York: Columbia University Press, 1963). For an excellent interpretation of Hsun-tzu's moral philosophy, see A. S. Cua, *Ethical Argumentation*.

228. Sabina Lovibond, *Realism and Imagination in Ethics,* 93, 122–23, 140, 156.

229. James C. Edwards, *Ethics without Philosophy: Wittgenstein and the Moral Life* (Tampa: University of Florida Press, 1982), 112–13, 221.

230. D. Z. Phillips, *Interventions in Ethics* 86–87, 103.

231. Lovibond, *Realism and Imagination in Ethics*, 79–80, 127–28, 182–85.

232. Phillips, *Intrerventions in Ethics*, 105, 63.

233. Lovibond, *Realism and Imagination,* 175.

234. Edwards, *Ethics without Philosophy,* 233–34, 238, 240–41, 247.

━━ BIBLIOGRAPHY

Abe, Masao. *Zen and Western Thought* (Honolulu: University of Hawaii Press, 1985).

Adams, Hazard. *Critical Theory since Plato* (New York: Harcourt Brace Jovanovich, 1971).

Adorno, Theodore. *Negative Dialectics* (New York: Seabury, 1973).

Altizer, Thomas. *The Gospel of Christian Atheism* (Philadelphia: Westminster, 1971).

Arato, Andrew, and Eike Gebhardt. *The Essential Frankfurt School Reader* (New York: Continuum, 1982).

Aristotle. *The Basic Works of Aristotle,* ed. Richard McKeon (New York: Random House, 1941).

Austin, J. L. *Philosophical Papers* (Oxford: Clarendon, 1961).

————. *Sense and Sensibility* (Oxford: Clarendon, 1962).

Ayer, A. J. ed, *Logical Positivism* (Glencoe, IL: Free Press, 1959).

Baker, Gordon, and P. M. S. Hacker. *Language, Sense and Nonsense* (Oxford: Blackwell, 1984).

————. *Wittgenstein: Rules, Grammar and Necessity* (Oxford: Blackwell, 1985)

Bakhtin, Mikhail. *The Dialogic Imagination*, ed. Michael Holquist, trans. Caryl Emerson and Michael Holquist (Austin: University of Texas Press, 1981).

————. *Rabelais and His World*, trans. H. Iwilsky (Cambridge: MIT Press, 1968).

Bakunin, Michael. *The Political Philosophy of Bakunin*, ed. G. P. Maximoff (Glencoe, IL: Free Press, 1953).

Barth, Karl. *The Epistle To the Romans*, trans. Edwyn C. Hoskyns (New York: Oxford University Press, 1968).

Baudrillard, Jean. *Jean Baudrillard: Selected Writings,* ed. Mark Poster (Stanford: Stanford University Press, 1988).

Benjamin, Walter. *Illuminations*, ed. Hannah Arendt, trans. Harry Zohn (New York: Schocken Books, 1968).

Bernstein, Richard. *Philosophical Profiles* (Philadelphia: University of Pennsylvania Press, 1971).

————. *Praxis and Action* (Philadelphia: University of Pennsylvania Press, 1971).

————. *The Restructuring of Social and Political Theory* (Philadelphia: University of Pennsylvania Press, 1978).

————. *Beyond Objectivism and Relativism: Science, Hermeneutics and Praxis* (Philadelphia: University of Pennsylvania Press, 1983).

————. *The New Constellation: The Ethical-Political Horizons of Modernity/Postmodernity* (Cambridge: MIT Press, 1992).

Black, Max. *Problems in Analysis* (New York: Greenwood, 1971).

————. *Models and Metaphors* (Ithaca: Cornell University Press, 1962).

————., ed. *Philosophy in America* (New York: George Allen & Unwin, 1965).

————. *The Companion To the Tractatus* (Ithaca: Cornell University Press, 1964).

Blanchot, Maurice. *The Gaze of Orpheus*, trans. L. Davis (Barrytown, NY: Station Hill Press, 1981).

Bolzano, Bernard. *Theory of Science*, ed. and trans. Rolf George (Berkeley: University of California Press, 1972).

Bousma, O. K. "The Blue Book," in *Ludwig Wittgenstein: The Man and His Philosophy*, ed. K. T. Fann (New York: Dell, 1967).

Bove, Paul. *Intellectuals in Power: A Genealogy of Critical Humanism* (New York: Columbia University Press, 1986).

Brenkert, George. *Marx's Ethics of Freedom* (Boston: Routledge and Allenheld, 1982).

Brentano, Franz. *Psychology from an Empirical Standpoint*, ed. Linda McAlister, trans. Antos C. Rancurello, D. B. Terrell, and Linda McAlister (New York: Humanities Press, 1973).

Buber, Martin. *I and Thou*, trans. Walter Kaufmann (New York: Charles Scribner's Sons, 1970).

Bultmann, Rudolf. *Primitive Christianity in Its Contemporary Setting*, trans. R. H. Fuller (New York: Meridian, 1957).

Caputo, John. *The Mystical Element in Heidegger's Thought* (Athens: Ohio University Press, 1984).

————. *De-Mythjologizing Heidegger* (Bloomington: Indiana University Press, 1993).

Carnap, Rudolph. *The Logical Syntax of Language* (Paterson, NJ: Littlefield, Adams, 1959).

Chomsky, Noam. *Syntactic Structures* (The Hague: Mouton, 1957).

———. *Aspects of the Theory of Syntax* (Cambridge: MIT Press, 1965).

———. *Language and Mind* (New York: Harcourt Brace Jovanovich, 1968).

———. *American Power and the New Mandarins* (New York: New Press, 1969, 2002).

Cohen, L. Jonathan. *Diversity of Meaning* (New York: Herder & Herder, 1963).

Cohen, Richard. *Elevations: The Height of the Good in Rosenzweig and Levinas* (Chicago: University of Chicago Press, 1994).

Conant, James. "Throwing Way the Top of the Ladder," in *Yale Review* 79, no. 3.

Cua, Anthony. *Ethical Argumentation: A Study in Hsun Tzu's Moral Epistemology* (Honolulu: University of Hawaii Press, 1985).

Daniel, Robert Vincent. *A Documentary History of Communism*, vol. 1 (New York: Vintage, 1960).

Davidson, David, *Truth and Interpretation* (Oxford: Clarendon Press, 1984).

———. *Inquiries into Truth and Interpretation* (Oxford: Oxford University Press, 1984).

Deleuze, Gilles. *Nietzsche and Philosophy*, trans. Hugh Tomlinson (New York: Columbia University Press, 1983).

———and Felix Guattari. *Anti-Oedipus: Capitalism and Schizophrenia*. trans. Robert Hurley, Mark Seem, and Helen R. Lane (Minneapolis: University of Minnesota Press, 1983).

De Man, Paul. *Allegories of Reading: Figural Language in Rousseau, Nietzsche, Riulke, and Proust* (New Haven: Yale University Press, 1979).

Derrida, Jacques. *Speech and Phenomena and Other Essays on Husserl's Theory of Signs*, trans. David Allison (Evanston: Northwestern University Press, 1973).

———. *Of Grammatology*, trans. Gayatri Chakravorty Spivak (Baltimore: Johns Hopkins University Press, 1974).

———. *Writing and Difference*, trans. Alan Bass (Chicago: University of Chicago Press, 1978).

———. *Edmund Husserl's Origins of Geometry: An Introduction*, trans. John P. Leavey (Stony Brook, NY: Nicolas Hayes, 1978).

———. *Dissemination*, trans. B. Johnson (Chicago: University of Chicago Press, 1980).

———. *Positions*, trans. Alan Bass (Chicago: University of Chicago Press, 1981).

————. *Margins of Philosophy*, trans. Alan Bass (Chicago: University of Chicago Press, 1982).

————. *Glass*, trans. J. P. Leavey and R. A. Rand (Lincoln: University of Nebraska Press, 1986).

————. *Limited Inc.*, ed. Gerald Graff (Evanston, IL: Northwestern University Press, 1988).

————. *A Derrida Reader*, ed. Peggy Kamuf (New York: Columbia University Press, 1991)

————. *Adieu to Emmanuel Levinas*, trans. Pascale-Anne Brault and Michael Naas (Stanford: Stanford University Press, 1999).

Dewey, John. *Essays in Experimental Logic* (New York: Dover, 1916).

————. *The Philosophy of John Dewey*, ed. John McDermott (New York: G. P. Putnam's Sons, 1975).

Dilthey, Wilhelm. *Selected Writings*, trans. and ed. H. P. Rickman (Cambridge: Cambridge University Press, 1976).

Dostoyevsky, Fyodor. *The Brothers Karamazov*, trans. Richard Pevear and Laarissa Volokhonsky (New York: Vintage, 1991).

Drange, Theodore. *Non-Belief and Evil: Two Arguments for the Non-Existence of God* (Amherst, NY: Prometheus, 1998).

Dreyfus, Hubert. *Being-in-the-World: A Study of Heidegger's Being and Time Part I* (Cambridge, MA: MIT Press, 1991).

————. "Holism and Hermeneutics," in *Review of Metaphysics* 34 (September 1980), 3–23.

———— and Paul Rabinow, *Michel Foucault: Beyond Structuralism and Hermeneutics* (Chicago: University of Chicago Press, 1983).

————. "On the Ordering of Things: Being and Power in Heidegger and Foucault," in *Michel Foucault: Philosopher* (New York: Routledge, 1992), 80–94.

Duhem, Pierre. *Physics: Its Object and Its Structure*, trans. Phillip Weiner (Princeton: Princeton University Press, 1954).

Dyson, Michael Eric. *Reflecting Black: African-American Cultural Criticism* (Minneapolis: University of Minnesota Press, 1993).

————. *Making Malcolm: The Myth and Meaning of Malcolm X* (New York: Oxford University Press, 1996).

————. *Between God and Gangsta Rap: Bearing Witness To Black Culture* (New York: Oxford University Press, 1996).

———. *Race Rules: Navigating the Color Line* (New York: Vintage, 1996).

Edwards, James. *Ethics without Philosophy: Wittgenstein and the Moral Life* (Tampa: University Press of Florida, 1982).

Eribon, Didier. *Michel Foucault*, trans. Betsy Wing (Cambridge: Harvard University Press, 1991).

Evans-Pritchard, E. E. *Theories of Primitive Religion* (Oxford: Clarendon, 1965).

Feinberg, Andrew. *Lukacs, Marx, and the Sources of Critical Theory* (New York: Oxford University Press, 1986).

Foucault, Michel. *Madness and Civilization: A History of Insanity in the Age of Reason*, trans. Richard Howard (New York: Vintage, 1965).

———. *The Order of Things: An Archaeology of the Human Sciences* (New York: Vintage, 1970).

———. *Power/Knowledge: Selected Interviews and Other Writings, 1972–1977*, ed. Colin Gordon, trans. Colin Gordon, Leo Marshall, John Mepham, and Kate Soper (New York: Pantheon, 1971, 1980).

———. *The Archaeology of Knowledge and The Discourse on Language*, trans. A. M. Sheridan Smith (New York: Harper & Row, 1972).

———. *The Birth of the Clinic: An Archaeology of Medical Perception*, trans. A. M. Sheridan Smith (New York: Vintage, 1973).

———. *Language, Counter-memory, Practice*, ed. Donald F. Bouchard, trans. Donald F. Bouchard and Sherry Simon (Ithaca: Cornell University Press, 1977).

———. *The History of Sexuality, vol. 1: An Introduction*, trans. Robert Hurley (New York: Pantheon, 1978).

———. *Discipline and Punish*, trans. Alan Sheridan (New York: Vintage, 1979).

———. *Power, Truth, Strategy*, ed. Meaghan Morris and Paul Patton (Sydney: Feral Press, 1979).

———. *Foucault Reader*, ed. Paul Rabinow, trans. Donald F. Bouchard and Sherry Simon (New York: Pantheon, 1984).

———. *Politics, Philosophy, Culture*, trans. Thomas Levic and Isabelle Lorenz (New York: Routledge, 1988).

———. *The Final Foucault*, ed. James Bernauer and David Rasmussen (Cambridge: MIT Press, 1988).

———. *Technologies of the Self*, ed. Luther Martin, Huck Gutman, and Patrick H. Hutton (Amherst: University of Massachusetts Press, 1988).

———. *The Foucault Effect*, ed. Graham burchell, Colin Gordon, and Peter Miller (Chicago: University of Chicago Press, 1991).

———. *The Essential Works of Foucault, vol. 1, Ethics, Subjectivity, and Truth*, ed. Paul Rabinow, trans. Robert Hurley et al. (New York: New Press, 1997).

———. *The Essential Works of Foucault, vol. 2, Aesthetics, Method and Epistemology*, ed. James D. Fabion, trans. Robert Hurley et al. (New York: New Press, 1998).

———. *The Essential Works of Foucault, vol. 3, Power*, ed. James D. Fabion, trans. Robert Hurley et al. (New York: New Press, 2000).

Fraser, Nancy. *Unruly Practices: Power, Discourse and Gender in Contemporary Social Theory* (Minneapolis: University of Minnesota Press, 1989).

Frege, Gottlob. *The Foundations of Arithmetic,* trans. J. L. Austin (New York: Harper, 1950).

———. *Translations from the Philosophical Writings of Gottlob Frege*, ed. Peter Geatch and Max Black (Oxford: Basil Blackwell, 1960).

Gadamer, Hans-Georg. *Truth and Method*, trans. Garrett Bardan and John Cumming (New York: Continuum, 1975).

———. *Philosophical Hermeneutics*, trans. and ed. D. Laing (Berkeley: University of California Press, 1977).

———. *Heidegger's Ways*, trans. John W. Stanley (Albany: SUNY Press, 1994).

Galbraith, John Kenneth. *The New Industrial State* (Boston: Houghton Mifflin, 1967).

Gottlieb, Roger S. *An Anthology of Western Marxism: From Lukacs and Gramsci To Socialist-Feminism* (New York: Oxford University Press, 1989).

Gouldner, Alvin W. *The Dialectic of Ideology and Technology: The Origins, Grammar, and Future of Ideology* (New York: Oxford University Press, 1976).

———. *The Future of Intellectuals and the Rise of the New Class* (New York: Seabury, 1979).

———. *Against Fragmentation: The Origins of Marxism and the Sociology of Intellectuals* (New York: Oxford University Press, 1985).

Gram, Mottke. "Do Transcendental Arguments Have a Future?" in *Zur Zukunft Der Transzendental Philosophie* (Gottinger: Vandenhoeck & Ruprect, 1978) 39–42.

Gramsci, Antonio. *Selections from the Prison Notebooks,* ed. and trans. Quinton Hoare and Geoffrey Nowell Smith (New York: International Publishers, 1971).

Habermas, Jurgen. *Knowledge and Human Interests,* trans. Jeremy J. Shapiro (Boston: Beacon Press, 1971).

———. *Theory and Practice,* trans. John Viertel (Boston: Beacon Press, 1973).

———. *Legitimation Crisis,* trans. Thomas McCarthy (Boston: Beacon Press, 1975).

———. *Communication and the Evolution of Society,* trans. Thomas McCarthy (Boston: Beacon Press, 1979).

———. *On the Logic of the Social Sciences,* trans. Sherry Weber Nicholson and Jerry A. Stark (Cambridge: MIT Press, 1984).

———. *The Philosophical Discourse of Modernity,* trans. Frederick G. Lawrence (Cambridge: MIT Press, 1987).

———. *The New Conservatism,* ed. and trans. Sherry Weber Nicholson (Cambridge: MIT Press, 1989).

———. *Moral Consciousness and Communicative Action,* trans. Christian Lenhardt and Sherry Weber Nicholson (Cambridge: MIT Press, 1991).

———. *Between Facts and Norms,* trans. William Rehg (Cambridge: MIT Press, 1996).

———. *The Inclusion of the Other: Studies in Political Theory,* ed. Ciaran Cronin and Pablo De Greiff (Cambridge: MIT Press, 1999).

Hamann, Johann, *Socratic Memorabilia,* trans. James C. O'Flaherty (Baltimore: Johns Hopkins University Press, 1967).

Hamilton, William. "On the Philosophy of the Unconditioned," *Edinburgh Review.* 1 (1829): 194–221.

Harre, Rom, and Daniel N. Robinson. "What Makes Language Possible? Ethological Foundationalism in Reid and Wittgenstein," *Review of Metaphysics* 50, no. 3 (March 1997): 483–98.

Harris, Leonard, ed. *Philosophy Born of Struggle* (Dubuque: Kendall/Hunt, 1983).

Hartshorne, Charles. *The Divine Relativity* (New Haven: Yale University Press, 1948).

———. *The Logic of Perfection* (LaSalle, IL: Open Court, 1962).

Hegel, Frederick. *The Phenomenology of Spirit,* trans. A. V. Miller (Oxford: Oxford University Press, 1977).

Heidegger, Martin. *Being and Time,* trans. Joan Stambaugh (Albany, NY: SUNY Press, 1996).

————. *Discourse on Thinking*, trans. John M. Anderson and E. Hans Freund (New York: Harper & Row, 1959).

————. *Essays in Metaphysics: Identity and Difference*, trans. Kurt F. Leidecker (New York: Philosophical Library, 1960).

————. *What Is Called Thinking*, trans. Fred D. Wieck and J. Glenn Gray (New York: Harper & Row, 1968).

————. *Essays in Metaphysics: Identity and Difference*, trans. Kurt F. Leidecker (New York: Philosophical Library, 1960).

————. *On The Way to Language*, trans. Peter D. Hertz (New York: Harper & Row, 1971).

————. *The End of Philosophy*, trans. Joan Stambaugh (New York: Harper & Row, 1973).

————. "Only a God Can Save Us: *Der Spiegel's* Interview with Martin Heidegger," trans. M. P. Alter and J. D. Caputo, *Philosophy Today* 20, no. 4 (winter 1976): 267–84.

————. *The Question Concerning Technology and Other Essays*, trans. William Lovitt (New York: Harper, 1977).

————. *Martin Heidegger: Basic Writings*, ed. David Farrell Krell (London: Routledge & Kegan Paul, 1978).

Held, David. *Introduction To Critical Theory: Horkheimer To Habermas* (Berkeley: University of California Press, 1980).

Hill, Thomas E. Jr. *Dignity and Practical Reason in Kant's Moral Theory* (Ithaca: Cornell University Press, 1992).

Hobbes, Thomas. *Leviathan: Parts I and II* (Indianapolis: Liberal Arts, 1958).

hooks, bell. *Ain't I a Woman: Black Women and Feminism* (Boston: South End, 1981).

————. *Feminist Theory: From Margin To Center* (Boston: South End, 1984).

————. *Talking Back: Thinking Feminist, Thinking Black* (Boston: South End, 1989).

————. *Yearning: Race, Gender, and Cultural Politics* (Boston: South End, 1990).

———— with Cornell West. *Breaking Bread: Insurgent Black Intellectual Life* (Boston: South End, 1991).

————. *Sisters of Yam: Black Women and Self-Recovery* (Boston: South End, 1993).

———. *Teaching to Transgress: Education as the Practice of Freedom* (New York: Routledge, 1994).

———. *Art on My Mind: Visual Politics* (New York: New Press, 1995).

———. *Reel To Reel: Race, Sex and Class in the Movies* (New York: Routledge, 1996).

———. *Wounds of Passion: A Writing Life* (New York: Henry Holt, 1997).

———. *Remembered Rapture: The Writer at Work* (New York: Henry Holt, 1999).

———. *Where We Stand: Class Matters* (New York: Routledge, 2000).

———. *Feminism Is for Everybody: Passionate Politics* (Boston: South End, 2000).

———. *Outlaw Culture: Resisting Representations* (New York: Routledge, 1994).

Horkheimer, Max. *Critical Theory: Selected Essays*, trans. Matthew J. O'Donnell (New York: Herder & Herder, 1972).

Horkheimer, Max and Theodore Adorno. *Dialectic of the Enlightenment*, trans. John Cumming (New York: Continuum, 1987).

Hoy, David Cousins, ed. *Foucault: A Critical Reader* (New York: Basil Blackwell, 1986).

———, and Thomas McCarthy. *Critical Theory* (Cambridge: Blackwell, 1994).

Hsun-tzu, *Basic Writings*, trans. Burton Watson (New York: Columbia University Press, 1963).

James, William. *Pragmatism: A New Name for Some Old Ways of Thinking* (New York: Longmans, Green, 1907).

Janick, Allan, and Stephen Toulmin. *Wittgenstein's Vienna* (New York: Simon & Shuster, 1973).

Kalipahana, David. *Nargarjuna's Karika: The Philosophy of the Middle Way* (Albany: SUNY Press, 1986).

Kant, Immanuel. *Critique of Pure Reason,* trans. Norman Kemp Smith (New York: St. Martin's, 1965).

Katz, Stephen, ed. *Mysticism and Philosophical Analysis* (New York: Oxford University Press, 1978).

———, ed. *Mysticism and Religious Traditions* (New York: Oxford University Press, 1983).

Kellner, Douglas. *Baudrillard: A Critical Reader,* ed. Douglas Kellner (Oxford: Blackwell, 1994).

Kierkegaard, Soren. *Philosophical Fragments,* trans. David Swenson and Howard V. Hong (Princeton: Princeton University Press, 1936).

————. *Repetition,* trans. Walter Lowrie (Princeton: Princeton University Press, 1941, 1969).

————. *Concluding Unscientific Postscript,* trans. David Swenson and Walter Lowrie (Princeton: Princeton University Press, 1944).

————. *Either/Or,* trans. David Swenson and Lillian Marvin Swenson (Princeton: Princeton University Press, 1944, 1959).

————. *The Present Age,* trans. Alexander Dru (New York: Harper, 1962).

————. *The Sickness Unto Death,* trans. Alastair Hannay (New York: Penguin, 1989).

Kisiel, Theodore, and John van Buren. *Reading Heidegger from the Start: Essays in His Earliest Thought* (Albany: SUNY Press, 1994).

Kneale, William, and Martha Kneale. *The Development of Logic* (Oxford: Oxford University Press, 1962).

Koller, John, and Patricia Koller. *A Sourcebook in Asian Philosophy* (New York: Macmillan, 1991).

Konrad, George, and Ivan Szelenyi. *The Intellectuals on the Road To Class Power* (New York: Harcourt Brace Jovanovich, 1979).

Korsch, Karl. *Marxism and Philosophy,* trans. F. Halliday (New York: Monthly Review Press, 1970).

Kripke, Saul A. *Naming and Necessity* (Cambridge: Harvard University Press, 1972).

Kuhn, Thomas. *The Structure of Scientific Revolutions* (Chicago: University of Chicago Press, 1962).

Lentriccia, Frank, and Thomas McLaughlin, eds. *Critical Terms in Literary Studies,* 2d ed. (Chicago: University of Chicago Press, 1995).

Lenzer, Gertrud, ed. *Auguste Comte and Positivism: The Essential Writings* (New York: Harper & Row, 1975).

Levinas, Emmanuel. *Totality and Infinity,* trans. Alphonso Lingis (Pittsburgh, PA: Duquesne University Press, 1969).

————. *Existence and Existents,* trans. Alphonso Lingis (The Hague: Martinus Nijhoff, 1978).

————. *Otherwise than Being or Beyond Essence,* trans. Alphonso Lingis (The Hague-Boston: Nijhoff, 1981).

———. *Ethics and Infinity*, trans. Richard A. Cohen (Pittsburgh: Duquesne University Press, 1985).

———. *The Levinas Reader*, ed. Sean Holt (Oxford: Basil Blackwell, 1989).

———. *Outside the Subject*, trans. Michael B. Smith (Stanford: Stanford University Press, 1994).

———. *Proper Names*, trans. Michael B. Smith (Stanford: Stanford University Press, 1996).

———. *Of God Who Comes to Mind*, trans. Bettina Bergo (Stanford: Stanford University Press, 1998).

———. *Alterity and Transcendence*, trans. Michael B. Smith (New York: Columbia University Press, 1999).

Levi-Strauss, Claude. *Structural Anthropology* (New York: Basic Books, 1963).

Linsky, Leonard. *Oblique Contexts* (Chicago: University of Chicago Press, 1989).

Locke, John. *Second Treatise of Government*, ed. C. B. Macpherson (Indianapolis,: Hackett, 1980).

Lovibond, Sabina. *Realism and Imagination in Ethics* (Minneapolis: University of Minnesota Press, 1983).

Lukacs, Georg. *History and Class Consciousness*, trans. R. Livingston (Cambridge: MIT Press, 1971).

Luxemberg, Rosa. *Selected Political Writings* (New York: Monthly Review Press, 1971).

Lyotard, Jean-Fraancois. *The Different Phrases in Dispute*, trans. Van Den Abbeele (Minneapolis: University of Minnesota Press, 1988).

———. *The Lyotard Reader*, ed. Andrew Benjamin (Oxford: Basil Blackwell, 1989).

———. *The Postmodern Explained*, trans. Don Barry, Bernadette Maher, Julian Pefanis, Virginia Spate, and Morgan Thomas (Minneapolis: University of Minnesota Press, 1993).

Macey, David. *The Lives of Michel Foucault: A Biography* (New York: Vintage, 1995).

Mach, Ernest. "The Economy of Science," in *Readings in Philosophy of Science*, ed. Philip P. Wiener (New York: Charles Scribner's Sons, 1953).

MacIntyre, Alasdair. *Whose Justice? Which Rationality?* (Notre Dame, IN: Notre Dame University Press, 1988).

MacMurray, John. *The Self as Agent* (London: Faber and Faber, 1956).

Malcolm, Norman. *Ludwig Wittgenstein: A Memoir* (Oxford: Oxford University Press, 1958).

———. *Wittgenstein: A Religious Point of View* (Ithaca: Cornell University Press, 1994).

Martin, Michael. *Atheism: A Philosophical Justification* (Philadelphia: Temple University Press, 1990).

Marx, Karl. *The German Ideology,* ed. R. Pascal (New York: International Publishers, 1947).

———. *Capital* (Moscow: Progress Publishers, 1959).

———. *Economic and Philosophical Manuscripts of 1844,* trans. Martin Milligan (New York: International Publishers, 1964).

———. *Karl Marx: Early Writings,* trans. and ed. T. B. Bottomore (New York: McGraw-Hill, 1963).

———. *The Marx-Engels Reader,* 2d ed., ed.Robert Tucker (New York: W. W. Norton, 1978).

———. "Theses on Feuerbach," in *Marx/Engels: Feuerbach. Opposition of the Materialist and Idealist Outlooks* (Moscow: Progress Publishers, 1976).

———. *The 18th Brumaire of Louis Bonaparte* (New York: International Publishers, 1990).

McCarthy, Thomas. *The Critical Theory of Jurgen Habermas* (Cambridge: MIT Press, 1981).

———, and David Cousins Hoy. *Critical Theory* (Cambridge: Blackwell, 1994).

Merleau-Ponty, Maurice. *Phenomenology of Perception,* trans. Colin Smith (London: Routledge & Kegan Paul, 1962).

Monk, Ray. *Ludwig Wittgenstein: The Duty of Genius* (New York: Free Press, 1990).

Montaigne, Michel de, "The Apology for Raimond Sebond" in *The Philosophy of the 16th and 17th Centureis,* Richard H, Popkin, ed. (New York: Free, 1966).

Moore, G. E. *Philosophical Papers* (New York: Collier, 1959).

Murphy, Arthur. *The Theory of Practical Reason* (La Salle, IL: Open Court, 1964).

Murray, Michael, ed. *Heidegger and Modern Philosophy* (New Haven: Yale University Press, 1978).

Nehamas, Alexander. *Nietzsche: Life as Literature* (Cambridge: Harvard University Press, 1985).

Nietzsche, Friedrich. *Ecco Homo*, trans. Walter Kaufmann (New York: Vintage, 1967).

———. *On the Genealogy of Morals*, trans. Walter Kaufmann (New York: Vintage, 1969).

———. *The Gay Science*, trans. Walter Kaufmann (New York: Vintage, 1974).

———. *Thus Spoke Zarathustra*, in *The Portable Nietzsche*, ed. and trans.Walter Kaufmann (New York: Penguin, 1959),115–439.

———. *The Antichrist*, in *The Portable Nietzsche*, 568–656.

———. *Beyond Good and Evil*, trans. Walter Kaufmann (New York: Vintage, 1966).

———. *Twilight of the Idols*, in *The Portable Nietzsche,* ed. and trans. Walter Kaufmann (New York: Penguin, 1959), 465–563.

———. *Human, All Too Human*, trans. Marion Faber and Stephen Lehmann (Lincoln: University of Nebraska Press, 1984).

Nishida, Kitaro. *Intelligibility and the Philosophy of Nothingness: Three Philosophical Essays* (Tokyo: Maruzen, 1958).

Nishitani, Keiji. *Religion and Nothingness*, trans. Jan Van Bragt (Berkeley: University of California Press, 1982).

Oliver, Kelly. *Family Values: Subjects between Nature and Culture* (New York: Routledge, 1997).

Outlaw, Lucius T. *On Race and Philosophy* (New York: Routledge, 1996).

Pace, Edgar. "Propositional Identity," in *Philosophical Review* (January 1970), 43–62.

Parkes, Graham. *Heidegger and Asian Thought* (Honolulu: University of Hawaii Press, 1987).

Parsons, Talcott. *Essays in Sociological Theory* (Glencoe, IL: Free, 1954).

Peffer, R. G., *Marxism, Morality, and Social Justice* (Princeton: Princeton University Press, 1990).

Peirce, Charles Sanders. *Philosophical Writings of Peirce*, ed. Justus Buchler (New York: Dover, 1955).

Peperzak, Adriaan. *To the Other* (West Lafayette, IN: Purdue University Press, 1993).

Phillips, D. Z. *Religion Without Explanation* (London: Basil Blackwell, 1976).

―――. *Belief, Change, and Forms of Life* (Atlantic Highlands, NJ: Humanities Press, 1986).

―――. *Interventions in Ethics* (Albany: SUNY Press, 1992).

―――. *Wittgenstein and Religion* (New York: St. Martin's, 1993).

Plantinga, Alvin. *God and Other Minds* (Ithaca, NY: Cornell University Press, 1967).

Putnam, Hilary. *Mind, Language and Reality* (Cambridge: Cambridge University Press, 1975).

Quine, W. V. O. *From a Logical Point of View* (New York: Harper & Row, 1953).

―――. *Word and Object,* (Cambridge: MIT Press, 1960).

Rawls, John. *Political Liberalism* (New York: Columbia University Press, 1993).

Reid, Thomas. *An Inquiry into the Human Mind*, ed. Timothy Duggan (Chicago: University of Chicago Press, 1970).

Rhees, Rush. *Without Answers* (London: Routledge & Kegan Paul, 1969).

―――, ed. *Recollections of Wittgenstein* (Oxford: Oxford University Press, 1984).

Rorty, Richard. *Consequences of Pragmatism* (Minneapolis: University of Minnesota Press, 1982).

―――. *Contingency, Irony, and Solidarity* (Cambridge: Cambridge University Press, 1989).

―――. *Essays on Heidegger and Others* (Cambridge: Cambridge University Press, 1991.

―――. *Objectivity, Relativism and Truth* (Cambridge: Cambridge University Press, 1991.

―――. *Achieving Our Country* (Cambridge: Harvard University Press, 1998).

―――. *Truth and Progress: Philosophical Papers Vol. 3* (Cambridge: Cambridge University Press, 1998).

Rosenzweig, Franz. *Star of Redemption*, trans. William W. Hallo (New York: Holt, Rinehart & Winston, 1971; Boston: Beacon Press, 1972; Notre Dame, IN: University of Notre Dame Press, 1985).

Ross, James F. *Philosophical Theology* (New York: Bobbs-Merrill, 1969).

Ruf, Henry L. "Transcendental Logic: An Essay on Critical Metaphysics," *Man and World* (1969): 38–64.

————. "On Being Morally Justified," *Journal of Value Inquiry* 111, no. 1 (spring 1969): 1–18.

————. "The Impossibility of Hartshorne's God," in *The Philosophical Forum*, 7. nos. 3–4: 345–63.

————. "Moral Problems and Religioius Mysteries: A Cross-Cultural Perspective" in *Dialogue & Alliance*, 1.3 (1987) 77-92.

————. "The Origin of the Debate over Ontotheology in the Texts of Heidegger and Derrida," in *Religion, Ontotheology, and Deconstruction*, ed. Henry L. Ruf (New York: Paragon House, 1989), 3–42.

————. "Radicalizing Liberalism and Modernity," in *Philosophy, Religion, and the Question of Intolerance*, ed. Mehdi Amin Razavi and David Ambuel (Albany, NY: SUNY Press, 1997), 170–85.

Russell, Bertrand. *The Problems of Philosophy* (Oxford: Oxford University Press, 1912).

————. *Logic and Knowledge* (London: George Allen and Unwin, 1956).

Saatkamp, Herman K. Jr., ed. *Rorty and Pragmatism: The Philosopher Responds To His Critics* (Nashville: Vanderbilt University Press, 1995).

Safranski, Rudiger. *Martin Heidegger: Between Good and Evil*, trans. Ewald Osers (Cambridge: Harvard University Press, 1998).

Said, Edward W. *Orientalism* (New York: Vintage, 1978).

————. *The Edward Said Reader*, ed. Moustafa Bayoumi and Andrew Rubin (New York: Vintage, 2000).

Saussure, Ferdinand de. *Course in General Linguistics*, trans. Wade Baskin (New York: McGraw Hill, 1966).

Schilpp, P. A. *The Philosophy of Bertrand Russell* (Evanston, IL.: Open Court, 1944).

Schlick, Moritz, "Meaning and Verification," in *Readings in Philosophical Analysis*, ed. Herbert Feigl and Wilfred Sellars (New York: Appleton-Century-Croft, 1949).

Schliermacher, Friderick,. *Hermeneutics: The Handwritten Manuscripts of F. D. Schliermacher*, ed. Heinz Kimmerle, trans. James Duke and Jack Froistman (Missoula, MT: Scholars Press, 1977).

Schmitt, Richard. *Introduction to Marx and Engels* (Boulder, CO: Westview Press, 1987).

Searle, John. *Speech Acts: An Essay in the Philosophy of Language* (Cambridge: Cambridge University Press, 1969).

———. *Expression and Meaning: Studies in the Theory of Speech Acts* (Cambridge: Cambridge University Press, 1979).

———. *Intentionality: An Essay in Philosophy of Mind* (Cambridge: Cambridge University Press, 1983).

Sen, Amarta. "East and West: The Reach of Reason," in *New York Review of Books*, July 20, 2000, 33–38.

Shusterman, Richard. *Pragmatist Aesthetics: Living Beauty, Rethinking Art* (Oxford: Basil Blackwell, 1992).

Simpson, Lorenzo. *Technology: Time and the Conversation of Modernity* (New York: Routldge, 1995).

Singer, Peter. *Marx* (Oxford: Oxford University Press, 1980).

Skinner, B. F. *Verbal Behavior* (New York: Appleton-Century-Crofts, 1957).

Smith, Gary, ed. *Benjamin: Philosophy, History, Aesthetics* (Chicago: University of Chicago Press, 1989).

Smith, Huston. *The World's Religions* (New York: HarperCollins, 1991).

———. *Forgotten Truth: The Primordial Tradition* (New York: Harper & Row, 1976).

———. *Beyond the Post-Modern Mind* (New York: Crossroad, 1982).

———. *Why Religion Matters* (New York: HarperCollins, 2001).

Stabile, Donald. *Prophets of Order* (Boston: South End, 1984).

Staten, Henry. *Wittgenstein and Derrida* (Lincoln: University of Nebraska Press, 1986).

Strawson, Peter. *Logico-Linguistic Papers* (London: Methuen, 1971).

Swinburne, Richard. *Faith and Reason* (Oxford: Clarendon, 1987).

Taylor, Mark. *Erring: A Postmodern A/theology* (Chicago: University of Chicago Press, 1984).

———. *Altarity* (Chicago: University of Chicago Press, 1987).

———. *Tears* (Albany: SUNY Press, 1990).

———. *Nots* (Chicago: University of Chicago Press, 1993).

———. *Hidings.* (Chicago: University of Chicago Press, 1997).

————. *About Religion: Economics of Faith in Virtual Culture* (Chicago: University of Chicago Press, 1999).

Veblen, Theodore. *The Theory of the Leisure Class* (Boston: Houghton Mifflin, 1973).

West, Cornell. *The American Evasion of Philosophy: A Genealogy of Pragmatism* (Madison: University of Wisconsin Press, 1989).

————. *Prophesy Deliverance! An Afro-American Revolutionary Christianity* (Philadelphia: Westminster, 1982).

————. *Prophetic Fragments: Illuminations of the Crisis in American Religion and Culture* (Grand Rapids, MI: William B. Eerdmans, 1988).

————. *The Ethical Dimensions of Marxist Thought* (New York: Monthly Review Press, 1991).

————. *Prophetic Reflections: Notes on Race and Power in America* (Monroe, ME: Common Courage, 1993).

————. *Keeping Faith: Philosophy and Race in America* (New York: Routledge, 1993).

White, Alan. *Truth* (Garden City, NY: Anchor, 1970).

Whitehead, Alfred North. *Process and Reality* (New York: Macmillan, 1929).

Wieman, Henry Nelson. *Religious Experience and Scientific Method* (New York: Macmillan, 1926).

Wittgenstein, Ludwig. *Tractatus Logico-Philosophicus*, trans. D. F. Pears and B. F. McGuinness (New York: Humanities Press, 1961).

————. *Philosophical Investigations*, trans. G. E. M. Anscombe (New York: Macmillan, 1953).

————. *Lectures and Coversations of Aesthetics, Psychology, and Religious Belief*, ed. Cyril Barrett (Berkeley: University of California Press, 1967).

————. *On Certainty*, ed. G. E. M. Anscombe and G. H. von Wright, trans. Dennis Paul and G. E. M. Anscombe (Oxford: Basil Blackwell, 1969).

————. *Culture and Value*, trans. Peter Winch (Chicago: University of Chicago Press, 1980)

————. *Ludwig Wittgenstein: Sein Leben in Bildern und Texten*, ed. M. Nedo and M. Ranchetti (Frankfurt am Main: Suhrkamp, 1983).

————. *Remarks on Frazer's Golden Bough*, ed. Rush Rhees, trans. A. C. Miles (Atlantic Highlands, NJ: Humanities Press, 1979).

Wright, Elizabeth. *Psychoanalytic Criticism: A Reappraisal*, 2d ed. (New York: Routledge, 1998).

Young, Iris Marion. *Justice and the Politics of Difference* (Princeton: Princeton University Press, 1989).

———. *Intersecting Voices: Dilemmas of Gender, Political Philosophy, and Policy* (Princeton: Princeton University Press, 1997).

———. *Inclusion and Democracy* (New York: Oxford University Press, 2000).

Zizek, Slavoj. *The Sublime Object of Ideology* (London: Verso, 1989).

———. *Tarrying with the Negative* (Durham, NC: Duke University Press, 1993).

———. "The Specter of Ideology," in *Mapping Ideology*, ed. Slavoj Zizek (London: Verso, 1994), 1–33.

———. *Looking Awry: An Introduction to Jacques Lacan through Popular Culture* (Cambridge: MIT Press, 1997).

———. *The Abyss of Freedom/Ages of the World* (Ann Arbor: University of Michigan Press, 1997).

———. *The Ticklish Subject: The Absent Center of Political Ontology* (London: Verso, 1999).

———. *The Zizek Reader*, ed. Elizabeth Wright and Edmond Wright (Oxford: Blackwell, 1999).

———. *The Fragile Absolute* (London: Verso, 2000).

———. *On Belief* (London: Routledge, 2001).

╼╌ GLOSSARY

Absolute Idealism: The name given to Hegelianism and metaphysical systems like it. Such systems endorse the Principle of Sufficient Reason and find in universal, unchanging ideas or the historical development of our intellectual life the ultimate reason why everything is as it is and not otherwise.

Ahistorical: Not subject to historical change; eternal or everlasting.

Analytic Judgment: A judgment (statement, proposition) whose truth or falsity is determined by something internal to the judgment (its meaning). Examples: Tautologies (Either the cat is all black or it is not all black) and contradictions (The cat is all black and it is not all black).

Analytic Philosophy: A movement that took philosophy's job to be that of analyzing the meanings of the things we say or think and the words and ideas with which we do our speaking and thinking, taking such meanings to be free of cultural differences and historical change.

Apollonian: A word made famous by Friedrich Nietzsche (1844–1900) when he used it to designate the kind of creating one does when one uses old ideas, patterns, reasons, or rules to create new combinations. Apollonians see this as the only kind of creating that is possible. Apollo was the ancient Greek God of Reason.

A priori: Initially a kind of knowledge. A judgment, statement, or proposition is declared to be a priori when its truth or falsity can be known without having to justify the judgment by any appeal to evidence gained by sensory observation or personal experience. Since the truth of analytic judgments is determined solely by conditions internal to the judgment, they are usually taken to be a priori.

Aristotelianism: An epistemological and metaphysical theory claimed to be derived from the texts authored by the ancient Greek philosopher Aristotle (384–321 B.C.). This theory claims that all knowledge claims about the world of observable objects must include in their justification [1] sensory impressions passively received from the objects being observed, and [2] an explanation of why these objects are as they appear to be, an explanation so ultimate that it makes no sense to ask any longer why things are like that, an explanation that refers to the necessary, unchanging character of a necessarily existing being, which is the ultimate cause of all beings and change.

Asocial: Not subject to social and cultural variations; universal.

Cartesianism: A theory attributed to the French philosopher René Descartes (1596–1650) primarily epistemological in nature, which claims that all knowledge rests on individual self-knowledge because the only way to gain knowledge is to doubt every possible belief until one finds beliefs that are impossible to doubt, ones such as "I am now doubting (thinking)" and "I exist."

Coherence: A characteristic of a set of claims in which none of the claims in the set contradict any of the other claims in the set.

Constituted: To say that objects or subjects are socially constituted objects or subjects is to say that such objects and subjects can be talked and thought about, experienced, or dealt with only in terms of the way we have have been socially trained to talk and think about them, experience or deal with them, and the way we have modified these social practices. The very identities that objects and subjects have to us is determined by social practices of living with them in a certain way. Just as Great Britain has a specific identity because of the social practices making up its unwritten constitution, so apples and people have social identities for us because of the social practices making up the way of life in which such apples and people are located.

Contingent: Not necessary. Could be different. Could have been different. A claim or belief is a contingent one if it is not necessarily true or necessarily false.

Correspondence Theory of Truth: A theory that says that a claim, judgment, statement, belief, or proposition is true if and only if it pictures or corresponds to the way things are in the world, if and only if the object(s) being referred to to in the claim has (have) the characteristics being attributed to it (them) in the claim.

Cosmological Argument: An argument or proof purportedly proving that change and contingency can be explained only by postulating a necessarily existing being (a supreme being, a god) that is necessary for all change and contingency.

Cultural Imperialism: A form of domination in which one group exercises asymmetrical power over another group for its own benefit by silencing or marginalizing the second group's ability to express effectively its values and meanings, thereby giving a dominant position to the first group's values and meanings.

Culture of Critical Rationality: The tendency and practice common among intellectuals during the past century and a half to critically examine with a skeptical eye controversial claims about how things are or how they ought to be, demanding that such claims must be supported with reasons open to public scrutiny.

Deconstruction: The phenomena of certain claims (those about universal and unchanging meanings or explanatory or justificatory principles) being in conflict with the unavoidable, socially variable, and historically changeable conditions that make all claims possible. Also, the practice of showing that certain claims in certain texts are in conflict with the conditions necessary for these claims and texts to be possible.

Dialogue: Listening and speaking with another, against a background of prejudgments, prejudices, and presuppositions while opening up one's prejudices to radical change as one respectfully listens to what is being said against a background of different prejudgments and one respectfully answers back.

Disciplinary Practices: A term the French thinker Michel Foucault (1926–1984) uses to designate social practices disciplining people to behave, think, feel, and live in ways tending usually to produce socially docile and useful people and to designate self-disciplining practices aimed at removing personal obstacles to one's own desired goals.

Eidetic Reduction: A method advocated by the phenomenologist Edmund Husserl (1859–1938) which reduces the focus of one's attention when examining one's own experiences in order to isolate an idea or meaning present in the experience. The word "eidetic" comes from the ancient Greek word *eidos* which means "idea."

Empiricism: A theory of knowledge founded in the modern age by the British thinkers John Locke (1632–1704), George Berkeley (1685–1753), and David Hume (1711–76), which claims that beliefs constitute knowledge only if they can be justified in terms of the sensory perceptions of individuals.

Epistemology: Theory of knowledge. The term is derived from the ancient Greek words *epistemos* meaning "knowledge" and *logos* meaning "theory" or "principle."

Eternal Happiness: According to the thinker Soren Kierkegaard (1813–55), the condition achieved when a person is striving without reservation to achieve this condition, a striving that consists in not craving without reservation anything finite and conceivable but rather in living with a life-defining, continuous recognition of the infinite other to the finite and conceivable.

Existentialism: A movement in philosophy, literature, and religion that accents our need to go beyond being social conformists and to be actively involved in creating our own individual nature, and which describes the despair and anxiety we will experience if we do it poorly.

Gram: A term that the French thinker Jacques Derrida uses as a substitute for the word "concept" in order to direct attention to the material character of language (words as written marks, sounds, socially variable and historically changing tools) and thus avoid overlooking that thought is dependent on language and itself has a similar material character.

Hegelianism: A metaphysical explanatory theory supposedly derived from the texts written by the German philosopher Georg Wilhelm Hegel (1770–1831), that attempts to explain everything in terms of the historical development of people's understanding of themselves and the worlds in which they live.

Hegemony: A historical situation in which one nation or group exercises political, economic, or cultural domination over another nation or group.

Humanism: A theory or way of life that treats human beings as the ultimate basis of value and knowledge.

Incommensurate: The characteristic of different sets of vocabularies, beliefs, or theories being incapable of comparison; they cannot be added together or reduced to each other or contradict each other.

Incorrigible: Beliefs that cannot be in error.

Intentionality: The characteristic of experiences (thoughts, beliefs, memories, emotions) being about something that might or might not exist.

Kantianism: A set of ideas and theories of knowledge, moral obligations, and aesthetic worth attributed to the German philosopher Immanuel Kant (1724–1804), claiming that knowledge is limited to either the form or content of the empirical world, that certain general forms of behavior are undeniably obligatory, and that the aesthetically sublime transcends human concepts and knowledge.

Logocentric: The characteristic that theories or ways of living possess when they presume that there is one ultimate principle or final word at the center of all explanations or understanding of things.

Logos: The ancient Greek word meaning "ultimate explanatory principle of things" or "the final word."

Marginalization: Forcing the beliefs, values, and practices of a social group out of the mainstream of a society's cultural life so that it is denigrated or ignored and not taken seriously.

Meaning of Being: What it means for something to simply be, not to be this or that or like this or like that, but simply to be at all.

Metaphysics: The word is derived from the ancient Greek words *meta* and *physis*. It is the name given to a book attributed to the philosopher Aristotle in which he attempts to explain all change in terms of an ultimate cause that supposedly exists necessarily and is necessary for everything else. The word now usually is used to designate attempts to give ultimate explanations for all beings and events.

Modernism: The word designates different but related periods in historical narratives given by philosophers or historians of literature or art. In philosophy it usually is used to designate the period after the seventeenth-century scientific revolution in physics, often called the Enlightenment, when asocial and ahistorical standards of meaning and justification are accented, and up to the postmodern period when the social character of rationality is accented.

Mode of Subjectivity: The way of conceiving things, the beliefs, the desires, and emotions (conscious and unconscious), the moods, the dispositions, the habits, and the tendencies that make up a way of living for a single person or a social group of people.

Negative Rights: The right to be left alone by the government or other individuals or groups. The American Bill of Rights is a list of negative legal rights that stipulates what the government is constitutionally prohibited from doing.

Nihilism: The belief that nothing has significance or value, that everything is worth the same thing—nothing.

Noble Silence: The Buddhist injunction not to seek for ultimate, metaphysical descriptions or explanations of things, an injunction based on the conviction that the craving for such beliefs will lead to suffering and distract one from the practical task of ending all cravings producing suffering.

Objectivistic Mode of Subjectivity: A way of life focused on the world of objects of one's beliefs, desires, feelings, etc., and on supposedly asocial and ahistorical knowledge of such objects (rather than focusing on what one is because of one's way of relating to the objects of one's beliefs, desires, and emotions).

Ontotheology: The word is derived from three Greek words: *ontos,* meaning "being," *theos* meaning "divine," and *logos* meaning "theory." It is now used to designate metaphysical theories that attempt to explain everything in terms of a necessarily existent supreme being that is the ultimate cause of everything and the final source for the value of everything.

Perspectivalism: A theory of knowledge which claims that all perception of things and beliefs about things provide only a perspective on things, how they appear when viewed from a particular point of view, and thus one cannot know what things are like independent of the limitations of such a perspective.

Phallocentrism: A characteristic of a way of taking things, a way of living, in which dominating masculine interests, as constituted in a certain social and cultural world, play a central role in determining what men and women generally believe, desire, feel, and do in that world.

Phenomenological Method: A method devised by the German mathematician and philosopher Edmund Husserl (1859–1938) for describing the meanings present in human experiences. The method calls for one to focus one's attention only on the experience (and not on what it is of) and only on the supposedly unchanging meaning of the experience.

Platonism: The set of ideas and theories traditionally attributed to the ancient Greek philosopher Plato (428–347 B.C.), which claim that the meaning of ideas are asocial and ahistorical, that our only possible knowledge is knowledge of such ideas, and that states need to be governed by wise people who have such knowledge of the ideas of human nature and of what makes people and states just.

Positive Rights: The moral and/or legal right to goods, services, opportunities, and power. Going beyond negative rights that obligate people and governments to just leave people alone, positive rights obligate others to act so as to provide that to which they have a positive right.

Positivism: The theory that says that only those beliefs that are relevantly similar to beliefs in logic, mathematics, and science (physics) can be counted as knowledge. It was first enunciated by the French philosopher Auguste Comte (1798–1857) who rejected metaphysical efforts to give final answers to Why? questions by claiming that science tells us only how things are. It was given new life in the 1920s by logical positivists in Vienna, Berlin, and Warsaw who claimed that, beyond logic and math, claims to knowledge must be empirically verifiable, something the merely emotive expressions in ethics and religion could not do.

Postmodernism: Theories and ways of understanding things that deny that there are any asocial or ahistorical meanings, standards, norms, values, or ideals, claiming instead that rationality is social through and through.

Pragmatics: The study of the relation of language to the users of language, the relation of the words and sentences to the people producing them in speech and writing, the relation of words, sentences, speeches, books, and discourses to the social practices making them possible.

Pragmatically Indexed: The characteristic of a word or phrase that requires knowing who is using the word, when it is being used, and in what context it is being used in order to know how it is being used and what is being said when it is used. Pronouns (I, you, she, we, etc.) and tensed verbs have this characteristic. Some pragmatists claim that this is also true of the words "justify," "explain," "free," "real," "true," and "know."

Pragmatism: Originated in the United States by Charles Sanders Peirce (1839–1914), William James (1842–1910), and John Dewey (1859–1952), this philosophical orientation rejected the main projects of traditional epistemologists and metaphysicians (finding "ultimate" justifications for beliefs and "ultimate" explanations for events) by focusing on how knowledge claims and explanations actually work, claiming that justifications are needed only when there are reasons to doubt, explanations are needed only when events are unexpected anomalies given the general beliefs in the community, and truth claims are just more claims about beliefs.

Presuppositions: The conditions necessary for a particular claim to exist and thus to be able to labeled as true or false.

Pretext: The conditions (presuppositions) necessary for a text to exist.

Principle of Sufficient Reason: The principle which says that there is a reason why everything (beings, characteristics of beings, events, processes, and sometimes even possibilities) is as it is and not otherwise. The principle is used by thinkers seeking to give ultimate, metaphysical explanations of things.

Proposition: The words is a technical philosophical word used to designate the supposed asocial and ahistorical meaning of what someone says or thinks, when what is said or thought can be claimed to be true or false.

Rationalism: The philosophical movement founded by René Descartes, Benedict Spinoza (1632–77) and Gottfried Leibniz (1644–1716) that used the principle of sufficient reason to claim that all knowledge had to consist of mathematical or quasi-mathematical proofs, sensory observations being unreliable.

Rationality: As used in this book, this word designates all of people's conceiving, thinking, believing, judging, evaluating, carried out in accordance with social norms.

Reductive: An attribute of a theory or discourse that can be restated without loss of meaning or purpose in the vocabulary and claims made in some other theory or discourse. Some thinkers claim that all psychological talk about sensory states, beliefs, and desires can be restated in a discourse that uses only neurophysiological talk about brain states.

Redundancy Theory of Truth: A theory endorsed by some philosophers in which it is claimed that saying that a statement is true is just a matter of restating the original claim, only now with more emphasis.

Reference: The objects, events, or characteristics one is talking when making claims or asking questions. Some thinkers contrast it with the meaning of the words used in saying these things.

Relativism: The theory that says the truth of a belief or claim is relative to the person making the claim or relative to the social group endorsing the claim.

Rhetorical: The intended or actual effect of a speech act or text on the listener or reader that would meet those interests of speakers or authors that go beyond producing mere intellectual understanding of what is said; persuading, making angry, creating sympathy or envy or fear, producing hegemonic control.

Romanticism: The eighteenth- and nineteenth-century intellectual and artistic movement that challenged modernist modelings of human knowledge based on physics (rationalists accenting its mathematical side and empiricists accenting its observational side) and claimed that such models could not deal adequately with the treatment of the uniqueness of individual people or the organic wholeness of nature and culture.

Scientism: The intellectual, cultural, and social movement that treats the knowledge gained in the observational and experimental sciences as the only kind of knowledge that people can gain.

Semantics: The study of the relation of language to that which language is used to talk or write about and the study of the meanings linguistic units have in order for such relations to be possible.

Signified: A term given its primary contemporary use by the linguist Ferdinand de Saussure (1857–1913) to designate the meaning aspect of every sign (as opposed to its material aspect—the sign as signifier). It is not be confused with something outside the sign, objects being referred to and characteristics being described when using the sign.

Signifier: The material aspect of a sign; the written or spoken word.

Socially Constituted: A term used to point out that for people the very identity of beings, characteristics, concepts, norms, ideals, and themselves is a product of the social practices by means of which they were trained and in which they participate.

Subjectivistic Mode of Subjectivity: A human way of life (conceiving, thinking, prizing, feeling, acting) in which attention by individual persons is passionately focused on the nature of that way of life and whether it is a workable way of life for them.

Syntactics: The linguistic study of the correct relation of words to words (grammar) and things said with words to other things said with words (logic).

Synthetic Judgment: A judgment (thought, claim, statement) that is either true or false and whose truth is determined by something external to that judgment, and thus whose truth is neither logically necessary nor logically impossible. (Examples: "I have six children." "By 2003 no person had yet set foot on Mars.")

Transcendental Arguments: Arguments that prove that certain general synthetic claims are undeniably true by showing that the conditions that would make them false are excluded by the conditions necessary for the very existence of these claims

Transcendental Reductions: Thought experiments in Husserl's phenomenological method in which supposedly one can reduce one's attention to the eternal meanings assumed to be present in an experience by bracketing out the personal and social idiosyncratic meanings that the experience has to the individual experiencing it.

Truth Is Subjectivity: The claim made by Kierkegaard which says that people can gain the truth by which they can live only if they focus their attention on the quality of their subjective mode of life, only if they find a subjectivistic mode of subjectivity that works. Kierkegaard believed that a Christian subjectivistic mode of subjectivity did work because in it the Christian remains refuses to deify the finite and remains faithful to that person's encounter with the infinite no matter how absurd this appears to be to those despairingly lost in objectivistic modes of subjectivity.

Will To Power: A term made famous by Friedrich Nietzsche that he uses to designate what he takes to be one of the most important causes of human life as he found it in his age, and that is the attempt by people individually and socially to exercise power and control over other people, enjoying the effort to control even more than what additionally is gained through control.

Will To Truth: A term introduced by Nietzsche and appropriated by Michel Foucault, used to designate the manner in which the will to power often becomes an effort to control what will be institutionally established as true, uncontestable claims in a society because of the tremendous power gained over people's minds when such control is gained.

━ INDEX

DATE DUE

#47-0108 Peel Off Pressure Sensitive